Compulsive Gambling

Theory, Research, and Practice

Edited by

Howard J. Shaffer

Sharon A. Stein

Blase Gambino
Center for Addiction Studies
Harvard Medical School and
The Cambridge Hospital

Thomas N. Cummings
Massachusetts Council on Compulsive Gambling

Foreword by
Robert L. Custer, M.D.

Lexington Books
D.C. Heath and Company/Lexington, Massachusetts/Toronto

Library of Congress Cataloging-in-Publication Data

Compulsive gambling: theory, research, and practice / edited by
 Howard J. Shaffer . . . [et al.].
  p. cm.
  Includes index.
  ISBN 0-669-20715-2 (alk. paper)
  1. Compulsive gambling.   I. Shaffer, Howard, 1948–
RC569.5.G35C66 1989   89-8114
616.85′227—dc20   CIP

Published simultaneously in Canada
Printed in the United States of America
International Standard Book Number: 0-669-20715-2
Library of Congress Catalog Card Number: 89-8114

The paper used in this publication meets the minimum requirements of
American National Standard for Information Sciences—Permanence of
Paper for Printed Library Materials, ANSI Z39.48-1984. ∞™

Year and number of this printing:

89 90 91 92 10 9 8 7 6 5 4 3 2 1

For their pioneering efforts and lifetime devotion to the understanding of compulsive gambling, this book is dedicated to Dr. Robert Custer and Monsignor Joseph Dunne.

Contents

Foreword

Robert L. Custer, M.D.

> Perhaps passing through so many sensations [while gambling], my soul was not more satisfied, but only irritated by them, and craved still more sensations—and stronger and stronger ones till utterly exhausted.
>
> —Fyodor Dostoevsky, *The Gambler*, 1866

The foregoing excerpt is a vivid description of the forces that drive the pathological gambler. The novelist was able to give an intimate and terrifying description of an individual who, because of his disorder, has lost control of his own destiny.

Some will think this is a book about adventurers, rogues, or of madmen. It is none of these. What it reveals is the euphoria and anguish of the pathological gambler. . . .who, what, where, when, and why they are.

The metamorphosis from recreational gambler into pathological gambler is subtle. It can be compared to a man in a canoe who is floating gently beyond the periphery of a whirlpool and then drifts leisurely into the outer whirls. At this stage, the water seems calm and safe. But there has been a change: the man no longer controls the canoe's direction. The canoe picks up speed, slowly at first, then with frightening rapidity, and the man is carried to his doom.

Gambling is an extremely complicated behavior with polarized attitudes that has recently been weighed toward the permissive. There have been clear public desires for the expansion of legal gambling, but also outcries of angry protest. No one knew exactly what he was fighting for—tradition, faith, fashion, morals, desires, fantasies, or financial gain. Within this context, the pathological gambler was obscured or simply treated with apathy, insignificance, or nonexistence.

This book represents a landmark, a fulfillment of a dream of the early therapists, in that it takes us out of the mist into scientific light. The experts brought together to express their observations from knowledge and experience bring an enormous number of opportunities to launch further studies into this incredibly complex disorder.

This book represents an early but solid direction into scientific progress. The Harvard Medical School, Center for Addiction Studies, and the Massachusetts Council on Compulsive Gambling are to be praised for this effort to bring together diverse scientific experts and present us with new insights into human behavior.

This a new and fascinating chapter in our social and scientific development and a splendid memento in American history.

Acknowledgments

This volume is the product of a great deal of hard work on the part of many people. To begin, we want to take this opportunity to thank Dr. Myron Belfer and the department of psychiatry at The Cambridge Hospital for providing the atmosphere of scientific curiosity and adventure that encouraged us to explore new areas. This support helped us develop the first national "think tank" on compulsive gambling. This arena tolerated, nourished, and facilitated the development of this book.

This book also received support from the Massachusetts Department of Public Health. In particular, we want to thank the efforts of Thomas Salmon, David Mulligan, and Paul Tierney. They are public health pioneers and innovators. Each was willing to visualize, develop, and implement a coordinated system of health services for understanding and treating compulsive gamblers. The field of addictive behaviors is indebted to them for their willingness to take a chance.

We want to thank Dorothy Corbeil, Michael Furstenberg, Ovid Neal, Melissa Robbins, Richard Rogers, and Kathy Scanlan for their help with a variety of administrative and organizational tasks. These people helped us organize and correspond with the many participants who contributed directly to this project.

We want to extend our special thanks to every contributor to this book. They worked long and hard to complete their work in a timely way. We appreciate their efforts.

We offer special thanks to our families, especially Linda Shaffer, Jeff Coniaris, Norine Robbins, and Nancy Cummings, as well as to our colleagues, who made the space in their lives that afforded us the time to undertake this venture. We recognize their gift of time as the most precious contribution of all.

We extend our most sincere thanks to the compulsive gamblers who have opened their hearts and minds and permitted us to better understand their pain. We hope this text will help diminish the suffering of gamblers caught by their compulsions.

Our thanks would be incomplete if we did not acknowledge the remarkable efforts of Dr. Robert Custer and Monsignor Joseph Dunne. Their tireless work on behalf of compulsive gamblers is responsible for, and the moving force behind, this work. They are the pioneers of today. They have opened a new field that promises to unlock many of the mysteries of addictive behavior. They were willing to get involved and contribute when others could only despair. As a result, gambling treatment specialists have been able to restore the fabric of hopes and dreams to many thousands of families. We want to express our most sincere thanks on behalf of those gamblers who struggle against their impulses.

Introduction

During June third and fourth of 1988, a renowned group of experts met at Harvard University. This meeting was the first national "think tank" to deal with the spectrum of issues that surround compulsive gambling. This book is an extension of the process that began in Cambridge.

Although gambling behavior is many thousands of years old, the study of this phenomenon is of recent origin. Even more recent is the study of the harmful and potentially harmful effects of excessive gambling on the individual, their family, and society at large. Like many other behaviors, gambling can provide pleasure; when abused, however, it can cause pain.

We are at the very beginning of understanding the myriad ways in which people are affected by gambling-related problems. We are just learning how many people are affected, either directly or indirectly, by gambling turned harmful. We are learning how to detect these people and reach them to offer help. Only nine states, at present, have formal programs that treat those who are caught up in the wash of excessive gambling aftereffects.

Further, we know little about the vulnerabilities that expose people to gambling excesses. Attempts to intervene with excessive gamblers often yield disappointing results. Nevertheless, we are making advances. Prevalence studies are emerging; diagnostic guides are developing; treatment approaches are just beginning to flourish.

Problem and Compulsive Gambling as an Addictive Behavior

Currently, many experts view excessive gambling (that is, both problem and compulsive) as an addiction. As a consequence, the concepts of addiction and addictive behavior influence our understanding of gambling behavior. Gambling only recently entered the fold of addiction. As a result, our understanding of addiction offers us a running start toward explanations of gambling. However, the same concepts that increase our ability to make sense out of gambling restrict our view and blind us to new and creative approaches. For example, current explanations of addictive behaviors rest upon a body of research that primarily examines people who experience drug dependence. The study of compulsive gambling affords an opportunity to examine addiction in the occasional absence of psychoactive drug abuse. The presence of addiction in the individual and the concomitant absence of drug effects is a scintillating combination. Compulsive gambling provides an opportunity to study the struggle against human impulses without the confounding effects of uncontrolled biochemical interference.

Research has just begun to explore the biochemical correlates of pathological gambling (Roy, Adinoff, Roehrich, Lamparski, Custer, et al. 1988). For example, in the Roy et al. study, the data suggest that pathological gamblers may have a functional disturbance of the noradrenergic system. Elsewhere, researchers believe they have found evidence indicating the possibility that compulsive gambling is related to a chemical imbalance. The study of compulsive gambling also provides a unique opportunity to cross-check biochemical addiction research on the alcohol and drug abuser under conditions in which the processes do not reflect the effects of a substance.

Gambling and Society

Gambling in our society affords us an opportunity to observe a natural experiment in social psychology. A complex network of human emotions is acted out as people win and lose through gambling. For example, we live in a era of lotteries. Economic pressures encourage a variety of groups to employ gambling activities to balance the budget. Churches, states, and regions are in the business of gambling. Soon the federal government[1] will be. While these organizations profit from the losses of others, these same losses may affect the losers in ways that rebound to society's detriment. It is also uncertain that winners are always winners. For example, there is some question about how lottery winners experience their gains. Some short-term winners may turn out to be losers when the game finally ends.

---

[1] With the advent of a national lottery, the government will benefit directly from gambling monies.

How This Book Is Organized

Compulsive Gambling: Theory, Research, and Practice attempts to reconcile some important gaps in our knowledge. It is a collection of works designed to weave a tapestry from theory, research, and clinical practice. *Compulsive Gambling* is a collection about what is known and unknown in the gambling field. It is an integration of thoughts generated by the leading figures in this fledgling field.

The ideas about compulsive gambling published here are the result of cyclical interactions between and among those who seek help for the problem of compulsive gambling: treatment providers who minister to that need, researchers who make discoveries about the nature of compulsive gambling, legislators and the criminal justice system that creates, interprets, and enforces policy regarding gambling in general, and theoreticians who attempt to organize and reflect on the information about compulsive gambling gathered by them all.

Compulsive gambling as a field is also informed by sister fields of addictive behavior, such as overeating, alcoholism, and drug addiction. Compulsive gambling as an "addiction" is unique in that it looks like a disorder similar to alcoholism or drug addiction, but does not require ingestion of a chemical substance. Many of the chapters here illuminate the field of addictions in general by making comparison and contrasts between compulsive gambling and other addictions.

Language forces us to use an ordered, linear method, with one sentence following another. The sections of this book, therefore, may give the impression that compulsive gambling started with theory, which led to treatment, policy, and research, as the section headings reflect. In fact, the section placement is best conceived of as one possible rotation of an interactive cycle. This cycle is frozen temporarily so that we can reflect upon it.

Historically, treatment of the compulsive gambler began with isolated individual therapists, usually of psychoanalytic persuasion, dealing with gambling problems as these were revealed by their patients. The movement toward recognition of compulsive gambling as a widespread phenomenon has been slow to take root. As a consequence, Gamblers Anonymous was already at hard work presenting its message to those in need when the pioneering efforts of Robert Custer and his associates created the first professional program of treatment at the Brecksville Veterans Administration Hospital in Ohio. These efforts came about because compulsive gamblers asked for treatment. Again, the adage that necessity is the mother of invention proves true. As a result of the need for treatment, and the attempt to meet it, theory, research, and policy followed.

Theory. The order of the sections and the chapters attempts to be most helpful to the reader new to the field of compulsive gambling. First presented is an overview of theoretical models about the nature of compulsive gambling as well as other addictions. Shaffer's chapter takes a reading of the field of addictions in general, and finds it to be in conceptual chaos. His chapter offers ways in which models of compulsive gambling can make clear the problem of addiction as a behavior, and not a disorder caused only by the ingestion of chemical substance. Jacobs also offers a theoretical framework for addictions in general, looking for a common cause among compulsive behaviors. His theory is that there is a common physiological and psychological stress condition present for any addicted individual. The compulsive, repeated behavior provides temporary relief for that stress condition by creating a dissociative state. Stein focuses on the way compulsive gamblers appear to make choices when gambling. She finds their choice strategy to be developmentally different from the general population regarding gambling. The choice a gambler makes when repeating a behavior that has long-term destructive consequences is based on a short-term pleasure or relief from pain, and no understanding of long-term consequences. Stein goes on to show how this apparent harmful paradox is resolved so that the compulsive gambler can become free of the trap. This demonstrates that excessive behavior need not be a hopeless condition without end.

Treatment. The next section on models of treatment for compulsive gamblers covers a variety of treatment settings and components from self-help to inpatient, as well as controlled gambling, as treatment alternatives. This section opens with Zinberg's comparison between the programs of Alcoholics Anonymous and Gamblers Anonymous as well as other self-help programs. His chapter highlights the differences and similarities between compulsive gambling and other addictive disorders. Rosenthal's chapter gives a detailed overview of patterns and problems in diagnosing the pathological gambler, and provides a look at what can be expected from efforts to come to terms with the always difficult concept of "caseness" (Valliant & Schnurr 1988); that is, what exactly constitutes a clinical case. Rosenthal includes clinical descriptions of many gambling types. He also maps the process by which social gambling can progress from recreational to harmful. Nora's chapter describes the components of inpatient treatment settings for gamblers from the past to the present. Franklin and Thom's chapter highlights family treatment for compulsive gambling by profiling the spouse of an excessive gambler. Finally, Rosecrance's chapter offers a controversial alternative for treatment: the use of active gamblers as peer counselors for problem gamblers.

Public Policy and Gambling. The section on the relationship between public policy and gambling comes out of a long history. Gambling has been a problem for many cultures for many years. The issue of "social responsibility" that emerged in the eighties as a gathering force that will lead us into the nineties is reflected in this section. Policy makers need to be aware of the consequences that occur when gambling is legalized and advertised in a particular city or state.

This section begins with Volberg and Steadman's chapter on the policy implications of prevalence estimates of pathological gambling. One conclusion they reach is that prevalence estimates of pathological gambling in the general population include more women and minorities than are currently seen in treatment. Eadington's chapter describes various public policy alternatives that could help the commercial gaming industry reduce the incidence of pathological gambling. Kaplan's chapter on state lotteries looks at the effect these games have on the general public. He questions whether government can afford, politically or economically, to be a player or ignore those who are injured in the game. Finally, Burglass's chapter on forensic issues gives the history of how compulsive gambling and other addictive behaviors have been understood by the criminal justice system in the United States.

Research. The last section of this book covers the most current research regarding pathological or compulsive gambling behavior. Lesieur's chapter provides a review of the extant research literature. He concludes that there are large gaps in our knowledge of the multiple causes of compulsive gambling at this time. Gambino's chapter offers clinicians a tool for identifying and assessing the strength of variables that may serve as risk factors for relapse as well as successful treatment outcomes. He discusses ways in which the clinician can become more involved in research by using the concepts of relative risk and attributable risk to develop clinical hypotheses for empirical testing. Jacobs' chapter offers new data on the prevalence of teenage gambling, as well as demonstrating the harmful effects of parental compulsive gambling on children. Jacobs draws the necessary connections and parallels with parental alcoholism, providing fresh evidence on the extent to which parental lifestyles operate to make our children vulnerable. This research points to the fact that legalized gambling causes problems for many individuals. Finally, the chapter by Gambino and Cummings provides information from a survey of the directors of all treatment programs of compulsive gambling across the country. This final chapter shows how treatment is effected by the theoretical perceptions of the treatment providers, which brings us full circle to theory.

Conclusion

We hope this book will be useful to a range of individuals, including gamblers and their family members, clinicians, lawyers, legislators and public policy makers, educators, students, and members of the commercial gaming industry. Gambling is a humanly created activity which crosses cultural barriers. Its effects touch many complex social systems from the local courthouse to church basements. The understanding of gambling behavior can illuminate the understanding of human behavior in general.

Howard J. Shaffer
Sharon A. Stein
Blase Gambino
Thomas N. Cummings

Cambridge, Massachusetts

References

Roy, A., Adinoff, B., Roehrich, L., Lamparski, D., Custer, R., Lorenz, V., Barbaccia, M., Guidotti, A., Costa, E., & Linnoila, M. 1988. Pathological gambling: A psychobiological study. *Archives of General Psychiatry, 45,* 369–373.
Valliant, G. E., & Schnurr, P. 1988. What is a case? *Archives of General Psychiatry, 45,* 313–319.

Part I
Theories of Compulsive Gambling

1

Conceptual Crises in the Addictions: The Role of Models in the Field of Compulsive Gambling

Howard J. Shaffer, Ph.D.

Introduction

The study of compulsive gambling is a field in conceptual crisis. The field is in a stage of development that lacks guidelines necessary to focus theory and instruct research. Assertions in the field lack fact status. Diverse explanations of excessive gambling coexist with little opportunity for confrontation and disconfirmation. Without the conceptual support obtained by the resolution of this scientific crisis, all available evidence can seem equally important. Scientific confusion and frustration often can result.

This chapter will review the conceptual crises in the addictions and explore how scientific disciplines move through these crises as a natural stage in their development. In spite of any differences that may exist between gambling and drug addiction,[2] an understanding of the evolution of conceptual approaches to these other addictions can provide insights and a better appreciation of compulsive gambling models. This appreciation is important because these representations contribute to a conceptual foundation that serves the entire field of addictive behaviors. In addition, these models reflect similarities and differences throughout the domain of addictive phenomena.

[1]Portions of this chapter were adapted from Shaffer (1986).

Thanks are extended to Blase Gambino, Sharon Stein, and Michelle Bowdler for their helpful suggestions and comments on earlier drafts of this chapter.

Preparation of this chapter was supported in part by a contract (#2322905893) from the Massachusetts Department of Public Health.

Requests for reprints should be sent to Howard J. Shaffer, Center for Addiction Studies, Department of Psychiatry, Harvard Medical School at The Cambridge Hospital, 1493 Cambridge Street, Cambridge, Massachusetts 02139.

[2]In a later chapter, Zinberg examines some important differences among the addictions in his work on the "Applicability of the Twelve-Step Model to Compulsive Intoxicant Use and Other Compulsive Behaviors."

The fields of alcohol and drug abuse experience a similar crisis (Shaffer 1986) to that in compulsive gambling. By understanding some of the characteristics of the crises that affect the other addictions, gambling workers can more clearly identify some of the issues that (a) confront them currently, and (b) will serve as obstacles in the future. As a result, they will be in a position to improve theory, research, and practice as they relate to compulsive gambling.

Before beginning to review the nature of scientific thought and compulsive gambling, I digress briefly to examine some of the history of gambling. This discussion provides some background to the field and the nature of lay explanation and intervention. Following this review, I will return to an analysis of the scientific models and explanatory systems that exist to explain addictive behaviors. This will lead to a general discussion of scientific crises as well as their consequences.

In the Beginning: Moments in the History of Gambling

The history of gambling behavior is long and interesting. Fleming (1978, 1) noted that, "Human beings bet on everything from backgammon to bullfights . . . . large numbers of people are willing to risk their money on the outcome of some unpredictable event. This has been true since the beginning of civilization." The Babylonian, Etruscans, and ancient Chinese were among the first civilizations to participate in organized gambling (Fleming 1978). The Bible mentions casting lots.

Fleming (1978) reviewed gambling's ancient history. The appearance of dice, several centuries before the birth of Christ, was responsible for the development of more sophisticated forms of gambling. To take people's minds off their hunger during periods of famine, the rulers of Lydia in Asia Minor gave away dice! However, dice were not used at first for gambling. Rather, people used these objects to explain the world. They used dice to provide security and structure where explanations were absent. They used dice as instruments for dream interpretation and predicting the future. Dice rapidly became popular throughout the world. According to the New Testament, Roman soldiers standing guard at Jesus' cross threw dice to win his garments (Fleming 1978).

After some seven centuries without much notoriety, dice playing again emerged during the crusades. As it did, so came a concern for its consequences. During the Third Crusade in 1190, King Richard the Lion-Hearted issued orders that restricted dice playing among his troops. Knights and clergymen were limited to only twenty shillings in losses. Ordinary soldiers were not allowed to play at all (Fleming 1978). These social policies reflect the idea that some people think some people can control their gambling while others cannot. In some ways, this idea is an early lay explanation that there may be certain personal characteristics that predispose people to loss of control and addictive behavior.

Four centuries later, English monarchs were troubled personally by behavior patterns—previously thought to affect only the lower classes—that can accompany dice and gambling. Playing dice with his noblemen, King Henry VIII once lost the Jesus bells that hung from the tower of St. Paul's Cathedral (Fleming 1978). These events provide early evidence that gambling and addiction problems cut across all social strata.

During the early days of America, before Europeans arrived, settlers observed the Iroquois Indians playing with dice carved from peach stones. The Narragansett Indians of Rhode Island played dice games that sometimes involved whole towns or tribes! (Fleming 1978). Although it is difficult to determine, we can assume that most of this gambling was social in nature. Some gambling, however, was compulsive and led to patterns of excessive behavior. Observers questioned how some people controlled their gambling while others turned themselves over "feverishly" to the action.

"Nobody knows when gambling was invented, but it seems more than probable that cheating began at the same time. Loaded dice have been found in the excavations at Pompeii and unscrupulous card players date back to the fourteenth century. On their account most of the early playing cards had plain white backs on which cheaters' marks could easily be detected" (Fleming 1978, 109). If understanding excessive behavior was not enough motivation, the entrance of illegal gambling behavior required better explanations so that governments could develop new social policies to reduce these unacceptable forms of gambling behavior.

Neither understanding nor social policies stopped gambling behavior, however. Wolkowitz, Roy & Doran (1985) report that "In 1980, the estimated yearly gambling 'take' in the United States was 40 to 75 billion dollars and the prevalence of pathologic gambling was estimated at between 3 million and 12 million persons" (p. 311). In 1986, gamblers bet 198.7 billion dollars. The amount of money retained by gambling operators during 1986 was about 22.6 billion dollars (Rosecrance 1988).

About 80 to 90 percent of the American public engage in some form of gambling behavior; only 3 to 5 percent gamble beyond the point at which they would like to stop (e.g., Cotler 1971; Wolkowitz, Roy & Doran 1985). Gambling observers estimate that four times as much money is wagered illegally as legally. The result is a pattern of behavior that, at the very least, can influence the gambler's extended family and, at most, affect society.

The nature of intervention—either social or medical—requires the development of models that provide a context for understanding the behavior. This explanatory system directs and guides attempts to treat and/ or control the behavior in question. In the next section, I examine the role of models in the addictions and how these structures influence the field of gambling.

The Models

It seems clear that from the earliest beginnings, observers tried to explain excessive gambling.[3] These explanations guided the development and implementation of government strategies and social policies intended to limit any negative consequences of gambling. Consequently, these early explanations provide the historical foundation for the development of early treatment programs.

Scientific models of compulsive or excessive gambling are relatively new. Because compulsive gambling is one of the last excesses to be included under the addictive behaviors umbrella, theories of drug and alcohol addiction provide most of the early explanations of this phenomenon. We may readily be able to generalize explanations of alcohol and substance addiction to gambling. If so, we do not have to reinvent the conceptual wheel. If not, explanations of gambling will have to be framed as an excessive behavior unlike the others. We must be ready for either outcome.

"The compulsive gambler is an elusive creature. Like the yeti we all know of his existence, yet his customary habitat is localised and unfamiliar and there is a lack of well-authenticated sightings" (Oldman 1978, 349). Everybody seems to think they know what a compulsive gambler is even though social science provides relatively few guides. The problem is that " 'Everyone' does not know, or rather what is known is highly variable and varies with the relationship of the 'knower'. . ." to what is known about gambling (Oldman 1978, 349).

When competing models for understanding compulsive gambling coexist, each offering a viable explanatory system, a field experiences a crisis of concepts. Systematic research capable of resolving the crisis is delayed because the basic concepts that direct investigative research remain in chaos. To minimize this confusion, it is helpful to examine the extant models of drug and alcohol addiction, the two most studied excessive behaviors.

---

[3]Throughout this chapter, I exchange the terms compulsive, pathological, and excessive to describe immoderate gambling. Certainly theorists have their favorite expressions. However, disagreement among gambling experts as to the relevance of descriptive and explanatory language reflects, in part, the existence of a conceptual crisis.

In spite of differences that may exist, an understanding of the development of conceptual approaches to substance addictions is essential to an appreciation of compulsive gambling models. It provides a conceptual foundation that serves the entire field of addictive behaviors. In addition, a study of these models highlights similarities and differences throughout the domain of addictive phenomena.[4]

For example, many theorists and clinicians consider compulsive gambling as a *pure* addiction. A pure addiction is uncomplicated conceptually by matters of physical dependence and biochemistry. Yet Wray & Dickerson (1981) found that 30 to 50 percent of Gamblers Anonymous members reported withdrawal symptoms when they stopped gambling. The anxiety, agitation, and depression reported by this sample suggests that gambling may have much in common with drug addictions even though physical dependence upon chemicals is not present. Recently, Carlton & Manowitz (1987) and Carlton & Goldstein (1987) reviewed physiological and biological correlates of compulsive gambling behavior. They demonstrated that these factors, similar to alcohol and drug dependence, do indeed need to be considered in any formulation of gambling and its excesses. There are social similarities among gambling and drug addiction as well. For example, Brown (1987) identified the resemblance between the crime patterns of compulsive gamblers and narcotic addicts. Finally, Lesieur, Blume & Zoppa (1986) and Blume & Lesieur (1987) describe many of the similarities among patients who drug and gamble to excess.

Nevertheless, models of compulsive gambling behavior are more pure in the sense that theorists are not confused conceptually by the presence of dependence producing chemistry. Thinking in the gambling field starts with the behavior in question. Thankfully, few people make assumptions about outside substances (such as dice, cards, poker chips) and their inherent dependence-producing capacity.

It is likely—at least in the short term—that the conceptual future of the compulsive gambling field will be shaped in part by the important concepts drawn from the better-known addictions. After all, we now view compulsive gambling—for better or worse—as an addictive behavior. It is

---

[4]There is no single, standard definition of addictive behavior. For our purposes addictive behavior is a pattern that (1) continues in spite of adverse consequences, (2) appears to the actor as if the behavior is out of his or her conscious control, and (3) is precipitated by a feeling that can range from a mild craving to an intense obsession. Addictive behaviors typically serve the addict in the short run at the price of longer-term destructiveness. Physical dependence is not a requisite for addiction. It is often present among substance addicts, but it is not necessary for a behavior to be labeled addictive. Finally, addictive behaviors organize the addict's life. All of life's other activities fit in the gaps that the addictive behavior permits.

very important, then, that we understand—and hopefully learn from—the conceptual problems of the other addictions.

Conceptual History of the Other Addictions

The multiplicity of phenomena collectively known as the addictive behaviors have a long and rich social history. The field spawned by the study of these behaviors is of much more recent vintage. As a result of its youth, the addictions field displays energy, naivete, curiosity, and conflicting explanations of its identity and purpose. Shifts in viewpoint have been identified as responsible for the discovery or, perhaps, even the development of the concept of addiction (Peele 1984, 1985; Levine 1978; Shaffer & Zinberg 1985; Zinberg & Shaffer 1985). In spite of its youth, the addictions as a circumscribed field of endeavor rest upon a foundation of philosophy. The following discussion will apply a philosophy of science perspective to the early history of the substance abuse field and consider some of the implications that result from this type of examination.

Philosophy of Science and the Addictions

Philosophers engage in the ". . . study, or pursuit of wisdom, or of knowledge of things and their causes, whether theoretical or practical" (Oxford English Dictionary 1971, 2155). Philosophers study the principles of human behavior by natural reason. Philosophers of science distinguish themselves by their examination of how science comes to know things. The scientific method serves both as the object of this study and the vehicle that manages the conduct of experimental investigation. As we begin our study of compulsive gambling and its relationship to addiction, we must choose the philosophical route that will serve as our guide. Many approaches to knowing can serve effectively as a map: consider, for example, the differences that might be found among philosophies of theology, health, economics, ethics, or social control. Though each of these courses would yield useful and fascinating approaches to the addictions, I have selected the philosophy of science to direct our examination of the conceptual crises that surround the addictions. I have selected a Kuhnian or "normal science" model to mark the way during our conceptual examination and introduction to the addictions (Shaffer 1986).

Normal Science and Addiction.

Normal Science and Addiction. "Normal science," according to Kuhn (1962), is characterized by a cumulative growth in knowledge that is interrupted by temporary periods of discontinuity and disagreement. These intervals of conflict can exist for a brief or extended period. They yield a new set of rules (that is, a paradigm) for continued scientific inquiry. There are a variety of other models of scientific development (Price 1970) that might alter our interpretations of the existing evidence or how that evidence is applied to the questions under consideration. Viewed from the differing focus of any one of these scientifically based models, our gaze might be altered so that the available data have new or different meaning.

Models of science, perhaps, are inappropriate instruments to focus our gaze. If "science" as a way of knowing is not applicable to the field of compulsive gambling—both as a discipline and a field of practice—we will have made a very important discovery about the principles that explain addictive behavior and compulsive gambling. However, in the absence of scientific methods, we may be unable to articulate meaningfully what these principles are. For the purposes of this chapter, Kuhn's (1962) notion of normal science will serve as our guide.

The Addictions

It is difficult to gain perspective on a field as diverse and complex as the addictions. This field is rooted historically in a variety of disciplines, including medicine, psychology, physiology, sociology, social work, biology, chemistry, politics, and witchcraft, to name only a few. Furthermore, the addictive behaviors seem to defy classification and explanation. The addition of compulsive gambling serves to further muddy the conceptual waters.

The documented history of compulsive gambling is as old as the most ancient civilizations. Governments first attempted to control gambling activities as early as 300 B.C. However, compulsive or pathological gambling has been a diagnostic category only since 1980. It is truly remarkable that for thousands of years mankind observed excessive gambling and only during the past decade compulsive gambling behaviors were accepted as a target of medical/clinical intervention! While some people readily accept that drug abuse and chemical dependence should fall under the aegis of medical authorities, the place of compulsive gambling is less clear (Oldman 1978). One of the premises underlying this chapter is that when something—like medical treatment for addiction—seems so obvious that it goes without question, it probably is not that indisputable.

For example, gambling and drug addiction became objects of medical intervention when early explanations of these phenomena featured disorders of the personality and compulsion (for example, Abraham 1960; Freud 1928; Rado 1926; Rosenthal 1987). Since then, challenges to the question of defective personality can be found in both drug (Gendreau & Gendreau 1970, 1971) and gambling literature (Eadington 1987; Oldman 1978; Rosecrance 1985).

It may seem unusual to question the relationship between health care providers and the addictive behaviors. In the addictions, "turf" issues such as these can be analyzed best against the historical and political landscape. Wallack & Winkleby (1987) encourage just such a systems approach to health promotion and disease prevention. Systems approaches can minimize the turf struggles that exist in the addictions. They urge us, for example, to integrate micro and macro environmental influences into our models of health maintenance. Further, they suggest that we attend to the specific social and physical environments in which the behavior occurs. With the exception of Lesieur (1979, 1984), Oldman (1978), and Rosecrance (1988), workers in the field of gambling do not pay attention to the gambler's gambling environment.

Consider, for example, the contemporary emphasis against drinking and driving and the medical and psychoeducational interventions that promise problem resolution. Rarely can one enter the arena of the drinking and driving debate without the presence of medical authorities. Yet is the drinking and driving problem an issue limited to the gaze of medical researchers, clinicians, and other health care professionals? Perhaps these concerns can be resolved by the automobile industry, transportation experts, or the high-tech industry.

Similarly, the social problems attendant to excessive gambling need not be the sole responsibility of self-help and professional care providers. These concerns should interest the gaming industry, state and national lotteries, and economic and financial institutions. After all, gambling is, in part or in whole, a "money management problem."

Historical Background. Throughout history, society has demonstrated an interest in regulating its member's excessive behaviors. In the substance abuse field, the development of this pursuit mirrors the succession of religious and secular rules, laws, sanctions, and policies that define certain substances as acceptable or unacceptable, either as "food" or "drugs" and certain forms and patterns of ingestion as proper use or abuse. Contemporary society, scientifically informed and religiously pluralistic, continues this tradition of regulating ingestible substances, though now less explicitly in the name of religion as in earlier times and more so in the cause of public health and safety. The ill-specified nature of these latter-day causes and the zeal and fervor with which regulatory activities are pursued has led some observers to characterize our present food and drug laws, their medical and scientific "justifications" notwithstanding, as religious in intent, purpose, and effect. Thus, these food and drug laws can easily be construed as the dietary and liturgical principles of the modern secular religion of science (Burglass & Shaffer 1983).

By studying the models that explain drug and alcohol addiction, the field of compulsive gambling can look squarely at its future. Understanding the conceptual problems that plague the other addictions can guide the development of gambling models so that the field does not repeat its failings and can build upon its strengths. Those who ignore history are doomed to repeat it.

A Succession of Explanatory Models. In this century, as the church yielded the primary responsibility for the promulgation of values and the regulation of individual conduct to the state, the phenomenon of the addictions came to be seen as the social problem of addiction and as such the object of formal inquiry and intervention. Social concern to prevent or stop individuals from using certain substances in certain ways has prompted a multiplicity of theories designed to explain both the cause and treatment of addiction. The earliest of these emphasized personal responsibility; the moral turpitude of the individual was cited as the cause; and addiction, like poverty and ignorance, was understood as the consequence of spiritual weakness.

As society became increasingly urban, a widening segment of the population became exposed to so-called "dangerous drugs" in the cities and some individuals fell under the influence of this "plague." Less personally condemning theories were soon supplied by the fledgling fields of psychology and psychiatry. Moral turpitude gradually yielded to psychological defect as the preferred explanation for an individual's addiction (Abraham 1960; Rado 1926). Addicts came to be seen as patients to be cured by treatment rather than as sinners to be saved by piety. The Great Depression of the 1930s and World War II in the 1940s stimulated society's appreciation of the role of external conditions and forces in shaping individual behavior; consequently, social and environmental theories emerged to explain the social problem of addiction in the 1940s and 1950s (Lindesmith 1947).

The 1960s brought wide prosperity, profound cultural changes, and unprecedented drug use at all levels of society. The attending dissolution of the social value consensus, the perceived inadequacy of the then-current social and psychological models to explain or solve the problem at the individual or social level, and the growing fascination with technology, perhaps explain the appeal of the behavioral theories that appeared in the 1960s. In the 1970s, although recreational drug use became somewhat more culturally acceptable as it became more prevalent, explanations and solutions were still thought necessary for the statistically small but numerically large number of individuals whose drug use was perceived to have disenabling, disruptive social and individual consequences. Theories appeared that further minimized personal responsibility for drug use and abuse by suggesting causes at the involuntary physiological (e.g., Dole &

Nyswander 1965, 1966; Goldstein & Goldstein 1968; Martin 1968) and cultural levels. The analysis of broad cultural/historical (cf. Brecher 1972; Szasz 1974) factors provides considerable insight into why knowledge about the phenomenon of the addictions takes the various forms that it has to date. To understand how this knowledge base develops, one must examine the addictions field and consider the many structures and processes responsible for the generation, dissemination, and use of this data base by researchers and practitioners. Each of these issues will be examined in more detail later in this chapter.

The Addictions: Preparadigms, Paradigms, and Identity

Identity problems in young sciences are not uncommon. Workers in young disciplines regularly stimulate theoretical and clinical controversies. Recently, Shaffer and his associates described the addiction field as in a preparadigm stage of scientific development (Burglass & Shaffer 1983; Gambino & Shaffer 1979; Khantzian & Shaffer 1981; Shaffer, 1982, 1983a, 1983b, 1986; Shaffer & Burglass 1981; Shaffer & Gambino 1979; Shaffer & Gambino 1983; Shaffer & Kauffman 1985). Compulsive gambling—a addiction subfield—also is struggling with the effects of a preparadigm era.

A paradigm according to Kuhn (1962) is essentially the framework, or perspective, that defines the rules and standards of practice for a particular community of workers (such as physicists, psychiatrists, psychologists, and so on). Individuals working in the field of addiction do not share a unitary set of rules or standards for the treatment of compulsive or pathological gambling disorders; in fact, there is controversy as to whether these disorders are multi- or unidimensional. For example, as some clinicians who treat addictive disorders debate the efficacy and morality of gambling versus gambling-free treatment, and whether psychotherapy can proceed or be useful while a patient is engaged in any form of behavior that might be construed as gambling, other clinicians and researchers argue the utility of abstinence or controlled gambling as a treatment outcome. Taber (1987), in his review of the relevant models of compulsive gambling, notes that, "Unsettling as it may seem, it is entirely possible for equally qualified scholars to be correct while holding what may seem to be opposing views" (p. 222).

Similarly, there are many opposing views about the etiology of substance abuse disorders. For example, pharmacologists understand the addictions as a set of pharmacological problems involving such pharmacological categories as drugs, tolerance, or binding sites. Psychologists and psychiatrists are typically willing to read into the phenomenon of addiction those problems of learning, compulsion, or ego function. Physiologists posit problems of withdrawal, metabolism, or target organ effects. Sociologists see processes of social regulation, peer pressure, and/or environmental forces. Politicians, lawyers, and law enforcement agents view addiction problems as involving controlled substances, criminals, and/or deterrence. At present, no single theory dominates thinking in the field of addictive behaviors or informs clinical interventions comprehensively. "Nonetheless, current theory and practice, despite the extreme diversity and often strident discord in the field, reflect a growing consensus on the importance of using scientific methods in both research and practice, and on modeling the older, established scientific disciplines" (Burglass & Shaffer 1981, xxi).

Paradigms, Assessment, and Interventions

Many implications of the paradigm concept extend far beyond the ebb and flow of history and affect clinical practice directly—for example, the strategies that determine the conduct of assessment and psychotherapy. Recently, the concept of paradigm has been applied to the practice of clinical services as a miniature world view that shapes a practitioner's understanding of the phenomenon to be assessed and treated (Sederer 1977; Gambino & Shaffer 1979; Shaffer & Burglass 1981; Shaffer & Gambino 1979, 1983; Shaffer & Kauffman 1985; Shaffer & Neuhaus 1985; Shaffer 1986b). An operating paradigm serves as an *a priori* template through which the clinician views patients and their problems; this template organizes information and suggests which questions to ask and which data are important, thus generating verifiable hypotheses. In addition, ". . . while paradigms provide sets of assumptions by which the person interprets experience, paradoxically, they operate so automatically that their proponents do not seriously question or challenge their inadequacies . . . this is the blinding function of paradigms" (Shaffer & Gambino 1979, 300). Thus, practitioners generally do not recognize the extent to which they are committed to viewing the world through a particular perspective.

Clinical observers often find what they are looking for, and do not see that which does not interest them. In addition, because of their particular clinical persuasion(s), therapists often unknowingly communicate their expectations for patient performance; this sequence of events directly influences the clinical setting and whether patients will consider certain material important enough to be discussed and examined. For example, psychoanalysts look for and find unconscious material such as unresolved Oedipal conflicts and drive/affect defenses and ignore reinforcing events that might develop a conditioned response pattern. Similarly, social psychologists attend to environmental, cultural, and familial influences and typically disregard metabolic disturbances.

Theoreticians are not the only ones affected by conceptual paradigms and models. Diagnosticians also form implicit attitudes, hunches, and observations (that is, tacit knowledge) even before a patient actually presents for evaluation. The available data may or may not support these implicit impressions. To illustrate, if the referral source is a probation officer, a preconceived notion of illegal behavior and/or antisocial personality may bias the assessment. If the patient stumbles as he enters the office, it may be indicative of a toxic condition, lameness, poor eyesight, or something else.

Brown (1987) and Oldman (1978) remind us that we can view gambling from diverse perspectives that are capable of biasing our judgment. For example, we can understand gambling as the result of a physical predisposition that increases personal vulnerability to excess (Carlton & Manowitz 1987; Carlton & Goldstein 1987). Similarly, gambling can become excessive as a result of mental illness, acquired dependence, social learning, or economic influences (for example, Eadington 1987). Most likely, however, gambling and the other addictions are the result of interactive multidimensional causes that include biological, psychological, and sociological influences. To integrate opposing views, Jacobs (1987) proposed an interactive model of addiction that combines some of the more narrow biological-psychological unidimensional views. Although his work represents an important step toward the development of multidimensional models, Jacobs did not place great weight on the social setting factors (Lesieur & Klein 1987; Rosecrance 1988; Zinberg 1984; Zinberg & Shaffer 1985) that influence the development, maintenance, and recovery from addictive behaviors.

Explanations and Assumptions. Unless articulated, theoretical and clinical explanations that guide our understanding of addictive behavior risk being (1) ignored or (2) taken as "facts" which may or may not be accurate. A simple puzzle can readily illustrate this phenomenon.

The nine dots shown in figure 1–1 are to be connected using four straight lines, never taking your writing instrument from the paper. If you are not familiar with this puzzle, take a moment and try to solve it before continuing with the text or turning to the solution (figure 1–3) at the end of this chapter.

Most people try to solve this problem with certain unarticulated assumptions accepted as "fact;" unquestioned conditions interpreted as facts make the solution to the nine-dot problem impossible. Frustrated with this problem, those who fail to solve it actually confirm their unarticulated

Figure 1–1. Nine-dot puzzle

assumptions as "facts" by continually invoking them at every attempt. The fundamentally incorrect assumption that interferes with solving the problem is a self-imposed condition that the solution must be found within the boundaries of the square. However, the instructions to this puzzle do not include that condition. When unarticulated assumptions are taken as "fact" and not accurately identified as tentative, the failure to solve problems does not reside within the nature of the task, but rather with the attempted solution (Watzlawick, Weakland & Fisch 1974).

Very few people solve the nine-dot problem without some assistance, in spite of the simplicity of the solution. If nine dots in space are capable of eliciting assumptions that interfere with the solution to a paper and pencil puzzle, then it should be obvious that the assumptions elicited by gamblers, substance abusing and, perhaps, abusing human beings, with all of the associated "acting out" behavior patterns, are capable of totally confusing and/or restricting our capacity to resolve our feelings and interventions regarding addictive behaviors.

Scientific Development and the Addictions: The Evolution and Revolution of Paradigms

The diversity of models and explanatory mechanisms postulated as responsible for the development of the addictive disorders, and the wide range of competing theories offered to guide the course of treatment, compete for scientific and clinical popularity (for example, Lettieri, Sayers & Pearson 1980). When a particular theory gains widespread support and ascends to momentary popularity because of its explanatory power without an integrative perspective with which to judge its efficacy, the field gradually loses interest, and the model loses its attraction. The debates that develop between competing theories raise serious questions about legitimate methods, problems, and standards of solution; these disagreements serve to define competing schools of thought rather than to facilitate resolution among the competing conceptual parties. Debates such as these characterize and are hallmark of a scientific preparadigm period (Kuhn 1962). Though the concept of paradigm relates primarily to the physical sciences, it is applicable to the current state of affairs in the addictions. In the absence of a paradigm, it is difficult to agree on what are the important parameters of addictive disorders. Furthermore, the evidence intended to support the specific constructs that comprise our knowledge about addictive behaviors—such as risk-taking, sensation seeking, dependence, tolerance, neuroadaptation, character disorder and so on—is often clouded because experts have difficulty agreeing on what data are, in fact, important. "In the absence of a paradigm all of the facts that could possibly pertain to the development of a given science are likely to seem equally relevant" (Kuhn 1962, 15). During a preparadigm period, controversy continues without a foreseeable end. More importantly, without an operative paradigm, the health care community does not have any generally agreed-upon standards for determining the utility of one approach versus another or the efficacy of any theory to explain the observed phenomena. Thus, without such guidelines in place it is no wonder that clinicians do not energetically endorse the findings generated by researchers! Furthermore, these conditions impede our understanding of the nature of the field and serve to block efforts at teaching and training in the human services in general and the addictions in particular.

The Conceptual Crisis

There is a crisis of concepts and explanatory categories in the addictions, in general, and in the field of compulsive gambling in particular. Before examining the nature of this crisis within the gambling field, it is important to understand epistemological crises, or crises of knowing, and establish how and when these occur.

Macintyre (1980) suggests that to understand epistemological crises most simply we should consider the events of ordinary, day-to-day life. Consider, for example, someone who believed that she or he was highly valued by his or her employer and colleagues but is suddenly fired; consider someone who is proposed for membership in a club by members who are believed to be close friends and supporters who is then blackballed; or finally, consider someone who has fallen in love and wants to know how the loved one "really" feels, or alternatively, someone falls out of love and feels the need to know how he or she could have been so wrong in earlier judgments about the loved one. For each of these people, the relationship of what *is* to what *seems* becomes critical. These individuals encounter the difficulties associated with the process of inferring the presence of generalizable, "invisible" feelings, thoughts, motives, and so on to others from the behaviors that they have observed occur in the past. The capacity to make generalizations such as these is valuable if not necessary to the maintenance of subjective beliefs that enable us to reliably predict the future behavior of those around us and therefore provide a modicum of environmental stability.

In each of the examples above, what was taken as unequivocal evidence (that is, the inferred motives or feelings) that pointed in one particular direction turned out to be information that had meaningful alternative interpretations. The awareness of meaningful alternative explanations for the same evidence can be paralysing. Given the seemingly infinite number of interpretations that are available to each of us during the course of our day-to-day social lives, we could barely act if every alternative interpretation required careful consideration. This problem is magnified even more by the existence of human error, deception, irony, ambivalence and self-deception. During the course of routine social activities, defense mechanisms such as denial operate to reduce the conflict associated with confusing environmental information. When denial mechanisms break down and alternative explanations of our existence become unavoidable, a crisis has occurred.

In science, when anomalous data are ignored, denied, or suppressed, current ways of knowing are maintained and a crisis averted. However, when findings that differ from the conventional view cannot be ignored or explained by that perspective, a crisis has occurred. In the addictions, we are in the midst of a crisis of categories. Several examples will illustrate this crisis: the research of Davies (1962), Sobell & Sobell (1973, 1976), and Rosecrance (1988) challenge the dominant notion that the only treatment outcome possible for alcoholics and compulsive gamblers is total abstinence; Peele (1986) questioned both the research and logic that accepted a genetic component or predisposition to alcoholism and other addictions; Shaffer (1985) suggests that the addiction as disease model is simply a metaphor for a commonly observed process and that this metaphor should not be casually substituted for a primary biological process.

Taken together or separately, these positions, representative of numerous other anomalous findings, both reflect and fuel the conceptual crisis in the addictions. As a result of the shifting conceptual tides, even champions of the disease model (for example, Pace 1984) alter their positions so that more adaptive and behavioral approaches become acceptable (Dickerson 1987). The conceptual crisis in the addictions generates a crisis of knowing and therefore a revolution of scientific knowledge.

Crises, Revolutions, Paradigms, and Preparadigms. We can ask whether the addictions field is in a preparadigm stage of development with all of the inherent conceptual problems or, alternatively, in a state of paradigmatic revolution characterized by the crises of conflicting conceptual positions and competing anomalous research findings. Confusion arises because the intense polarization of views associated with a paradigmatic revolution is also characteristic of preparadigm conceptual conflicts. This matter cannot be resolved decisively but is a question that only history can answer. For example, students of the alcohol field might argue that the 175-200–year history (Levine 1978) of workers viewing alcoholism as a "disease" is evidence of an accepted paradigm. However, this motif is dominant primarily in the United States and not around the world. Can a provincial model be acknowledged as paradigmatic for other addictive behaviors, such as heroin dependence? Alternatively, is the absence of widespread acceptance of "addictive disease" as a conceptual explanation for gambling evidence that a conventional paradigm has not been accepted in the addictions and that a preparadigm period still exists?

For purposes of this chapter, it is unnecessary to resolve this debate. Time will judge these trends and determine whether a model (for example, addictive disease, public health, etc.) truly is a paradigm or just surfaces briefly as an historical aberration in the context of a larger scientific trend. It is important, however, to recognize that conceptual crises mark both preparadigm debates and revolutionary polarizations.

Although Kuhn (1962) limited his use of crises to paradigmatic revolutions, crises of knowing are currently evident in the addictions and are characteristic of both paradigmatic revolutions and pre-paradigm conflicts. Preparadigmatic debates can only occur once in the development of a scientific discipline, while revolutions occur repetitively at variable intervals and continue for indeterminate lengths of time. Figure 1–2[5] and the discussion that follows illustrate this issue further.

As figure 1–2 depicts, science evolves from a preparadigm to normal science stage of development; this phase of scientific development is evolutionary. The intense competition among various theoretical positions in the absence of an accepted paradigm characterizes evolutionary science. The emergence of a dominant paradigm with its inherent conventional wisdom is the result of rigorous research and scientific debate. Continued research tends to confirm the conventional wisdom; yet some anomalous research findings are almost always identified. If researchers and theorists find the anomalous findings flawed, the dominant paradigm is confirmed and further entrenched. If, however, the anomalous findings are replicable, revolutionary science begins and a scientific crisis begins to develop. This crisis can be resolved by (a) the determination that the alternative view is inadequate; (b) the suppression of the alternative position; or (c) the acceptance of an alternative paradigm. The following discussion examines the evolution and revolution of science in the addictions.

---

[5]This figure is derived from Kuhn (1962) and adapted from Sobell & Sobell (1984).

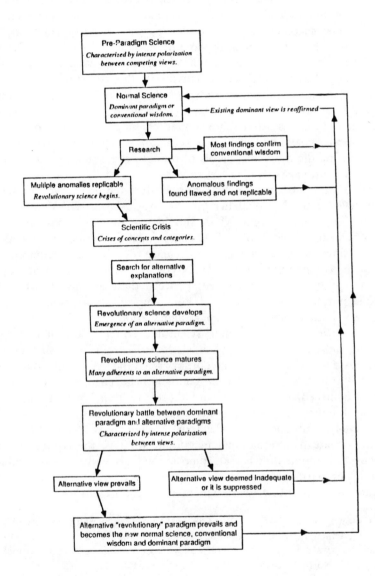

Figure 1–2.

From Shaffer, H. (1986). Conceptual Crises and the Addictions: A Philosophy of Science Perspective. *Journal of Substance Abuse Treatment*, 3, 285–286.

The Crisis of Knowing in the Addictions. Every idea about the phenomenon of addiction derives from the particular perspective and frame of reference of the individual(s) who formulate it. As we have seen, for example, pharmacologists, physiologists, psychologists, psychiatrists, and others differ in their formulations of the etiology of addiction. Furthermore, as an intellectual activity, scholarship in the addictions is a relatively new endeavor. Intellectual activity in the addictions field molds current conceptions and explanations of the phenomena under examination; however, because of the preparadigm stage of scientific development in the addictions, this scholarship is marked by deep debates over legitimate methods, goals, and standards of solution. These controversies and conflicts define the different schools of thought rather than produce agreement or resolution.

For example, Booth (1988) reported that representatives of parent groups believed the National Institute of Drug Abuse (NIDA) was failing to do its job. They thought NIDA should say and do things differently. Charles Schuster, director of NIDA, complained that critics do not understand the slow and cautious nature of science (Booth 1988). Parent groups have an important political agenda. NIDA and scientists have an equally important program. The differences between these groups identifies their roles and purposes, but not grounds for compromise or resolution. These events are characteristic of a preparadigm period.

Kuhn (1962) alerts us that scientific thought does not progress smoothly; rather, when existing models fail to account or assimilate new, anomalous research findings, an abrupt, scientific revolution may occur. This revolution is characterized by conflicts between those who subscribe to the established, older views, and those "radicals" who propose that new and different explanatory systems replace the existing view. Sobell & Sobell (1984), embroiled with Pendery, Maltzman & West (1982) in a scientific debate of international magnitude (that is, the controversy surrounding the notion of whether some individuals with alcohol problems may fully or partially recover without abstinence), described the conflict associated with scientific revolution in the alcohol field as follows:

> As shown in Fig. 1–2, any field begins with a preparadigmatic period, during which there are competing schools of thought. Eventually a prevailing view emerges, and Kuhn call this dominant paradigm 'normal science.' Normal science is the textbook science, the most commonly accepted explanation of a phenomenon. Moreover, most scientific activity occurs within the context of normal science, where scientists of like view seek to answer research questions within the context of an accepted paradigm. An unusual feature of the alcohol field is that *the present normal science did not have an empirical basis.* Basically, it derived from lay theories . . . merged with scientific speculation. . . . The important

point is that the traditions to be defended, so-called conventional wisdom, did not have their roots in scientific research (p. 436–437).

The conflict inherent in the preparadigm stage of scientific development in the addictions creates a crisis of categories (Burglass & Shaffer
1981). Questions and concerns regarding the adequacy of existing categories to explain the present stage of research in the addictions field precipitated this crisis. Progress in any scientific field takes place when the
explanatory categories employed are capable of clarifying, explaining, and
generating an understanding of the phenomenon under investigation; typically, these categories are validated by the research that follows. However,
new ideas emerge from the research that was stimulated by existing categories. These new concepts question the earlier generative categories and
the postulates upon which they rest. The outcome is a crisis of categories.
Kuhn (1962) suggested that these scientific crises are necessary preconditions for the emergence of novel theories. He noted that scientists respond
to categorical crises by *not* doing certain things, for example, "Though
they may begin to lose faith and then to consider alternatives, they do not
renounce the paradigm that has led them into crisis. They do not, that is,
treat anomalies as counterinstances, though in the vocabulary of philosophy of science that is exactly what they are" (Kuhn 1962, 77).

In the field of alcohol and drug addiction, for example, experts continue to struggle and debate the medical model with addictive disease as
its focal point. Gambling authorities struggle with the same conceptual
crisis. For example, Blume (1987) suggests that individual and social advantages make the medical or disease concept of compulsive gambling the
". . . preferred conceptualization at our present state of knowledge" (p.
237). On the other hand, Dickerson (1987) argues that there are sufficient
data to suggest that it is inappropriate to apply the medical model to
compulsive gambling. Further, he believes that the divisive debate that
continues to plague the alcohol field will not emerge among workers in
the gambling field. Rosecrance (1985) holds that attempts to conceptualize
excessive gambling as a disease is equivalent to "medicalizing deviance."

In the mature sciences, this type of conceptual crisis is rapidly resolved by referring to the set of rules of method and practice that serve to
guide the field: an operative paradigm. "The decision to reject one paradigm is always simultaneously the decision to accept another, and the
judgment leading to that decision involves the comparison of both paradigms with nature *and* each other" (Kuhn 1962, 77). It is precisely because gambling lacks an prevailing paradigm that the field is in crisis with
regard to the basic categories by which it gathers data and assembles ideas
into theory. It has neither an accepted paradigm with which to compare
new alternatives nor does it have well-articulated options that are ready to

ascend to the position of dominant paradigm. Thus, the various discipline-specific ideas and theories neither disprove nor invalidate one another. These perspectives simply coexist; each has its loyal adherents; each pursues its particular version of truth about excessive gambling in its own way. For example, experts still debate whether compulsive or pathological is the correct adjective to describe immoderate gambling.

Absent the ordering function of a paradigm, elementary structure can be obtained by categorizing ideas according to the source discipline, special interest group, or individual responsible for the introduction of the concept to the field. Although this simplistic solution is heuristically useful, permitting ideas to be organized, clarified, compared, and contrasted, this approach does not begin to resolve the crisis of categories extant in the addictions field. One of the reasons for this failure is the tendency to equate reductionism and classification with explanation.

Reductionism and the Addictions. Humans love to classify. Most of us spend a lifetime classifying things in our environments to make sense of, and understand, our lives. This tendency has been responsible—since Aristotle—for the trend of reductionism in science. For example, scientists often explain things at one level by describing things at a more microlevel of analysis: psychologists often defer explanations of the mysteries of the "mind" to physiologists who defer to biologists who defer to chemists who defer to physicists. Paradoxically, physicists often explain complex and confusing physical events by deferring to psychologists and their explanations of perception and the "mind."

In the addictions, the trend of reductionism, paralleled by advancing technology, can be illustrated simply by the wide range of models that attempt to explain addictive behavior during the last one hundred years. These explanations for compulsive gambling include, for example, weak "will," moral deprivation, ego deficits, social impoverishment, interactive psychosocial factors, behavioral and social learning, metabolic deficiencies, and endorphin and other central nervous system imbalances. Although these accounts are reductionistic and categorical (rather than dynamically interactive), these models are useful in helping us understand the specifics of a great many different areas; currently, addictive behaviors are among those that seem to defy satisfactory explanation in spite of our capacity for classification.

The Addictions and Compulsive Gambling
As Immature Fields of Inquiry

Conceptual crises are very common among immature fields. Ravetz (1971) describes as *immature* those fields of human inquiry whose theory, methods, and practices have yet to attain the rigor and consistency of the physical sciences. The study of gambling behavior is just such a new and immature field of endeavor.

In the absence of an operative paradigm, the addictions field lacks facts. We can agree that there are units of knowledge about addictive behavior and substance use/abuse in particular; however, there are no facts that can be considered as a particular sort of assertion about addictive behavior that may—albeit imperfectly—correspond to its actual state (Burglass & Shaffer 1981). "Not all facts are, or become genuine scientific knowledge; they must survive lengthy and rigorous processes of testing and transformation. These take place in the course of the evolution of the different components of a solved problem" (Ravetz 1971, 192).

Ravetz proposed that for an assertion to attain fact status it must possess three properties: significance, stability, and invariance. An assertion has significance if it is noticed by someone and judged to be of at least potential interest and value for the field. Recognition of this type assumes that the assertion is fundamentally intelligible for at least some subset of workers in the field. The landscape of scholarship in the addictions is littered with assertions that would be considered insignificant, perhaps even incomprehensible, by at least some of the workers in the field. Consider Wikler's masterful theoretical analysis of the conditioning factors that influence the development and maintenance of drug dependence and abstinence. As a physician and researcher, Wikler first published his ideas in a medical journal. To comprehend his arguments one required at least a fundamental level of knowledge of pharmacology, physiology, and learning theory—both classical and instrumental. Typical physician readers did not possess the skills necessary to develop a working knowledge of Wikler's concepts; thus, for most front-line workers in the field, these assertions remained unintelligible and therefore insignificant.

The stability of an assertion refers to its capacity for reproduction; that is, to generate other ideas, to further specify existing problems, or to define new problems or subproblems. For example, consider the long life and many progeny of Rado's (1933) application of psychoanalytic theory to the phenomenon of drug addiction. His analyses of the compulsive aspects of drug use have provided an enduring motif for many subsequent theorists and practitioners in psychoanalysis as well as other fields of endeavor. Rado's ideas of tense depression, compulsion, and dependence have demonstrated the properties of stability and significance for a large group of researchers and clinicians in the addictions' field.

Ravetz (1971) defined the property of invariance as follows:

> We have seen how science advances through the investigation of problems; how each problem is concerned with the drawing of conclusions about certain classes of intellectually constructed things and events; and how these classes, existing only through the determination of their properties, change even in the course of the investigation of a single problem.

When a solved problem has been presented to the community, and new work is done on its basis, then the objects of investigation will necessarily change, sometimes only slightly, but sometimes drastically. In a retrospect on the original problem, even after a brief period of development, its argument will be seen as concerning objects which no longer exist. There is then the question of whether it can be translated or recast so as to relate to the newer objects descended from the original ones, and still be an adequate foundation for a conclusion. If not, then the original conclusion is rejected as dealing with non-objects, or as ascribing false properties to real objects. But if such a translation or recasting is possible, then the original solved problem is seen to have contained some element which is invariant with respect to the changes in the objects of investigation (pp. 188–189).

Gendreau & Gendreau (1970) traced the history of the "addictive personality" through its various manifestations and expressions in personality theory and as a model in theory derived from other paradigms. The use of drugs (and now other substances) to the point of dependence has long been held as evidence of underlying personality predispositions among drug users; these concepts of personality defect, disposition, or configuration have been useful ideas, historically valued among drug treatment providers and researchers. Nevertheless, professionals reject the idea of an addictive personality because it refers to a nonobject (Gendreau & Gendreau 1970, 1971). Consequently, the concept of addictive personality fails to attain fact status for lack of the property of invariance.

Some Consequences of Addiction Theory

The field of gambling behavior is growing theoretically. The objects of investigation and theory are constantly and rapidly changing. The task of a theoretician is similar to that of the captain of a slowly sinking ship: keep it afloat until support can be found or renovations completed. Within the context of this ever-changing landscape, few assertions become facts. Libraries are filled with research reports, theoretical statements, and philosophical manifestos. Undoubtedly, each of these is the product of hard work, considerable expense, and occasionally inspiration. Rarely, however, can one find any facts. Occasionally, various combinations and permutations of ideas gain ascendancy on the basis of merit or facilitation by a constellation of economic, political, and cultural forces and momentarily enjoy popularity. None can validly claim to be determining and defining for the entire field, however.

Clinical Implications of an Epistemology of Gambling

As clinical practice follows theory—implicitly and explicitly—patient compliance and treatment progress often follow their epistemology of personal disorder (Shaffer 1987). A variety of clinical implications are associated with the way in which excessive gamblers "know" and "understand" their gambling behavior. Some patients enter treatment with the notion that they suffer from some "sickness" and, as a result, will comply most readily with treatment regimens that focus on the nature of their "disease." Others, however, view their difficulties as a "problem in living," "weak will," or poor decision making. Typically, these patients have been considered to be victims of the "disease of denial." While in some cases patients do evidence massive denial, it is also true that many simply do not subscribe to the typical treatment regimen of self-help groups and their reliance on a higher power. For each of these patient groups, it is helpful for the health care provider to ask, "Is it useful to refer to this condition or complaint as a disease?" The disease concept can be applied instrumentally, as a useful metaphor (Shaffer 1985). Later in treatment the clinician may find that the disease metaphor can be redefined or applied differently; shifts in patient world view are not uncommon during the conduct of psychotherapy.

The disease concept can serve as a useful map to guide both clinician and patient through a complex territory; it should not be confused, however, with the territory. Further, the disease map may not represent a topography of personal distress that is understood by certain patients. When clinicians fail to distinguish maps from territories, they risk eating menus instead of meals and can find themselves prescribing medication for the treatment of spring fever.

Addiction Theory and the Generation of Ideas

Addiction theorists have tended to develop minitheories quite different from the megatheories that characterized the early years of psychology, psychiatry, and the other social sciences. With very few exceptions, multifactorial models of addiction have not been developed. This situation is curious considering the recognition documenting and endorsing the efficacy of model building for the development of psychological theory (for example, Chapanis 1961; Lachman 1960; Simon & Newell 1963). Distinct groups of related ideas have been creatively combined, and even, on rare occasions, integrated across disciplinary boundaries. As a result, the addictions is replete with psychopharmacological, sociopolitical, neurophysiological, neurobehavioral and other hybrid ideas and theories about substance dependence and phenomena addictive. Shaped by conceptual crisis, the conjoined words appear to represent some form of unarticulated, unacknowledged paradigm. Yet no explicit paradigm exists to provide the context for the merger of all of the discipline-specific paradigms presently responsible for the generation of ideas about addictive behavior.

In the absence of a paradigm, many subtle and often unarticulated influences affect ideas in the addictions. These influences are responsible for the growth of knowledge in an immature field such as compulsive gambling. They affect the shape of the landscape against which scientific progress thrives or suffocates. Consequently, the next section will examine briefly some of the more important determinants that affect the development of new ideas in the field of gambling behavior.

Factors That Affect the Generation of Ideas and Concepts in the Addictions

Scientific, Technical, and Practical Problems in the Addictions

Ideas arise from the experience of clinicians and researchers who provide services and investigate the behavior of excessive gamblers. Addictions treatment research addresses three formal types of problems: scientific, technical, and practical. To illustrate, scientific problems include the study of the brain's biochemical activities during "risk taking" behaviors; technical problems include the development of effective, long-acting, orally administered anti-depressant; practical problems include the treatment of compulsive gambling patients in an outpatient setting.

Scientific and technical problems are typically investigated by researchers trained in the disciplines that formulate the terms of these problems. Practical problems are usually approached by treatment practitioners who use a multiplicity of unarticulated paradigms and who represent a tremendous diversity of interest and perspective. Existing knowledge in the addictions, in general, and compulsive gambling, in particular, comes more from clinical experience than from direct research. This restricted view is complicated by the nature of the practical problems typically encountered in the addictions; for example, the economic and political aspects of addictions treatment demands a merge of research and clinical intervention. The result rarely results in benefits for either endeavor. Furthermore, the process of funding influences research addressing all three types of problems, as well as clinical practice.

Funding

With few exceptions, funding for gambling research is centrally located and resides within the government.[6] While the centralization of funding sources *could* facilitate long-range planning and therefore facilitate the

---

[6]Private foundations have yet to recognize the important contributions that gambling research can make to understanding both compulsive behaviors and a variety of other human disorders.

development of comprehensive solutions, governmental funding—applied through the mechanisms of contracts and grant awards—is typically short term. As a result, generated ideas evidence little continuity. In addition, there is little continuity of either the programs or the people responsible for the expression or realization of these ideas. Consequently, ideas tend to be less than fully developed or verified. Pelz (1967) suggested that maximal scientific achievement is likely to be realized in those research environments that manage to maintain a "creative tension" between sources of challenge and security. Although the addictions field contains numerous challenges to its workers, little security is available beyond the comforts and stability derived from the pursuit of specialized research within relatively narrow areas. Under these less than optimum conditions, it should not be surprising that few ideas or concepts attain fact status.

Given that funding sources typically reside within the boundaries of the government, political forces influence the funding process almost as much as the merit of proposed scientific projects. The trend of the past decade to decentralize the process of federal funding requires the involvement of state, county, municipal, and other regulatory agencies. This development adds further layers to a complex problem, therefore, compounding the difficulties associated with the grant application and award procedures.

Competition for federal funds is keen among the field's diverse interest groups; each special interest group has its own agenda for research and interventions that is guided by its own particular conception of the problem and the field. The magnitude of the complexities associated with the funding process acts to reward only the most diligent applicants. Not surprisingly, the better formulated and more conventionally or elegantly articulated proposals are often sponsored by the most diligent applicants who also just happen to be in the degree-holding professions. Therefore, the less traditional, alternative, or counterculture proposals are often at a disadvantage stylistically; despite their merits, these proposals often fail to win funding.

Researcher/Administrator Issues

Researchers, as principal investigators, are often obliged to administer their own projects. This is a task for which many of these scientists are ill-suited by experience, training, or inclination. Expected to produce a steady stream of reports and publications as evidence of their competence and enduring activity, demanding organizational tasks plague these researcher/administrators. They tend to have little remaining time or energy for reflective thinking, conceptual construction, or other creative endeavors. It is no surprise then that federally funded research projects, or "products," as these have come to be known, contribute little to the advancement of the addictions field (Booth 1988). Readers interested in this phenomenon should see Wachtel (1980), who has identified a parallel problem in psychology. When the task of research becomes the gaining and maintaining of contracts and grants, the survival of the "laboratory" ascends to prominence at the expense of the development of ideas.

Research-Treatment Interactions

Funding sources in the addictions prefer to support research activities that are conducted in a clinical context. As a result, patients tend to become subjects in research projects and research subjects become patients in treatment programs. This situation often leads to conflicts of purpose and method; the consequence can be a compromise of treatment protocols by research needs as well as a restriction placed upon research design by treatment considerations. In both cases, the results are less than desirable. Patients may suffer unnecessarily and researchers may evaluate their ideas in less than a critical and scholarly manner.

Conclusions

A crisis of concepts and categories exists in the body of knowledge associated with the phenomenon of the compulsive gambling. This crisis is characterized by (a) the absence of an accepted paradigm; (b) the consequent paucity of facts; and (c) the lack of integration between research, theory, and practice. Popular or folk beliefs about gambling suggest that there are many facts—for example, that all excessive gamblers associate with gangsters or that gambling and prostitution follow one another.

Contrary to the casual and unsystematic observations that tend to generate these views, careful examination of the gambling field reveals little conceptual agreement among experts. Few beliefs, assertions, or ideas achieve fact status. When scrutinized by scientific principle, some common-sense beliefs do occasionally yield positive results from reasoning that is less than scientific. The confusion that results from the consequence of this phenomenon is, in part, responsible for the crisis of categories in the addictions. In addition, many of these common-sense beliefs generate confidence about conservative views of addictive behavior.

In the absence of a paradigm, it is difficult to agree on the important parameters of compulsive gambling. Furthermore, the research intended to support constructs such as compulsion, addiction, "chasing," and so on is clouded because experts in the field of addictions have great difficulty agreeing on what factors comprise the important data. These conditions of conceptual crisis impede our understanding of addictive behavior and block efforts at teaching, training, and acquiring knowledge relevant to treatment interventions. In spite of this chaos and confusion, it is in immature fields such as gambling that we find the greatest challenges to research and practice.

Earlier I suggested the possibility that science may not have as much to contribute to our understanding of the addictions as we might expect. Consider the following comments made by the distinguished physicist Victor Weisskopf (1977), past president of the American Academy of Arts and Sciences:

> Although science can study and may be able to explain every human experience, it does not always illuminate those aspects that are considered most relevant . . . Just as the quantum state is destroyed when observed with some sharp instrument, so too the significance of certain experiences, especially those relating to . . . human relations may yet be lost when subject to scientific analysis . . . Science and technology comprise some of the most powerful tools for deeper insight and for solving the problems we face—some of these problems, indeed, were created by the thoughtless application of those very tools. But science and technology are only one of the avenues toward reality: others are equally needed to comprehend the full significance of our existence. We will need all approaches to deal with the predicaments of humanity that prevent so many of our fellow human beings from having a life worth living (pp. 410–411).

According to B.F. Skinner (1983), scientists and compulsive gamblers have more in common than either group suspects. "All scientific work pays off on a variable ratio schedule of reinforcement. So do hunting, fishing, exploring, prospecting, and so on. You never can tell when you are going to be reinforced, but reinforcements do keep turning up. The dedicated scientist is exactly like a pathological gambler. He's been hooked by a system, but in a way which is profitable for everyone. The scientist is fascinated by what he does, just as the gambler is, but nobody is taking his shirt. He's getting something out of it, and so is society" (p. 39).

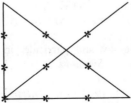

Figure 1–3.

References

Abraham, K. 1960. The psychological relation between sexuality and alcoholism. In *Selected Papers of Karl Abraham*. New York: Basic Books.

Blume, S.B. 1987. Compulsive gambling and the medical model. *The Journal of Gambling Behavior, 3*, 237–247.

Blume, S.B., & Lesieur, H.R. 1987. Pathological gambling in cocaine abusers. In A.M. Washton & M.S. Gold (eds.) *Cocaine: A Clinician's Handbook*, 208–213. New York: The Guilford Press.

Booth, W. 1988. War breaks out over drug research agency. *Science, 241*, 648–650.

Brecher, E.M., and the Editors of Consumer Reports. 1972. *Licit and Illicit Drugs*. Boston: Little, Brown & Company.

Brown, R.I.F. 1987. Models of gambling and gambling addictions as perceptual filters. *The Journal of Gambling Behavior, 3*, 224-236.

Burglass, M.E., & Shaffer, H. 1983. Diagnosis in the addictions I: Conceptual problems. *Advances in Alcohol and Substance Abuse, 3*, No. 1/2, 19–34.

———. 1981. The natural history of ideas in the treatment of the addictions. In H. Shaffer and M.E. Burglass (eds.) *Classic Contributions in the Addictions*. New York: Brunner/Mazel.

Carlton, P.L., & Goldstein, L. 1987. Physiological determinants of pathological gambling. In T. Galski (ed.) *The Handbook of Pathological Gambling*, 111–135. Springfield, Illinois: Charles C. Thomas.

Carlton, P.L., & Manowitz, P. 1987. Physiological factors as determinants of pathological gambling. *The Journal of Gambling Behavior, 3*, 274–285.

Chapanis, A. 1961. Men, machines, and models. *American Psychologist, 16*, 113–131.

Cotler, S.B. 1971. The use of different behavioral techniques in treating a case of compulsive gambling. *Behavior Therapy, 2*, 579–584.

Davies, D. L. 1962. Normal drinking in recovered alcoholic addicts. *Quarterly Journal of Studies on Alcohol, 23*, 94–104.

Dickerson, M. 1987. The future of gambling research—learning from the lessons of alcoholism. *The Journal of Gambling Behavior, 3*, 248–256.

Dole, V.P., & Nyswander, M.E. 1965. A medical treatment for diacetylmorphine (heroin) addiction. *Journal of the American Medical Association, 193*, 80–84.

———. 1966. Rehabilitation of heroin addicts after blockade with methadone. *New York State Journal of Medicine, 66*, 2011–2017.

Eadington, W.R. 1987. Economic perceptions of gambling behavior. *The Journal of Gambling Behavior, 3*, 264–273.

Fleming, A.M. 1978. *Something for Nothing: A History of Gambling*. New York: Delacorte Press.

Freud, S. 1928. Dostoyevsky and parricide. In J. Strachey (ed.) *The complete psychological works of Sigmund Freud*, (1961), *21*, 1975–1996, Standard Edition. London: Hogarth.

Gambino, B., & Shaffer, H. 1979. The concept of paradigm and the treatment of addiction. *Professional Psychology, 10*, 207–223.

Gendreau, P., & Gendreau, L.P. 1970. The "addiction-prone" personality: A study of Canadian heroin addicts. *Canadian Journal of Behavior Science, 2*, 18–25.

————. 1971. Research design and narcotic addiction proneness, *Canadian Psychiatric Association Journal,* 16, 265–267.

Goldstein, A., & Goldstein, D.B. 1968. Enzyme expansion theory of drug tolerance and physical dependence. In A. Wikler (ed.) *The Addictive States.* Baltimore: Williams & Wilkins.

Jacobs, D. 1987. A general theory of addictions: Application to treatment and rehabilitation planning for pathological gamblers. In T. Galski (ed.) *The Handbook of Pathological Gambling,* 169–194. Springfield, Illinois: Charles C. Thomas.

Khantzian, E., & Shaffer, H.J. 1981. A contemporary psychoanalytic view of addiction theory and treatment. In Lowinson, J. and Ruiz, P. (eds.) *Substance Abuse: Clinical Problems and Perspectives.* Baltimore: Williams & Wilkins (refereed chapter).

Kuhn, T.S. 1962. *The structure of scientific revolutions.* Chicago: University of Chicago Press.

Lachman, R. 1960. The model in theory construction. *Psychological Review,* 67, 113–129.

Lesieur, H.R. 1979. The compulsive gambler's spiral of options and involvement. *Psychiatry,* 42, 79–87.

————. 1984. *The chase: Career of the compulsive gambler.* Cambridge, Massachusetts: Schenkman Publishing Company.

Lesieur, H.R., Blume, S., & Zoppa, R. 1986. Alcoholism, drug abuse, and gambling. *Alcoholism: Clinical and Experimental Research,* 10, 33–38.

Lesieur, H.R., & Klein, R. 1987. Pathological gambling among high school students. *Addictive Behaviors,* 12, 129–135.

Lettieri, D.J., Sayers, M., and Pearson, M.W. (eds.), 1980. *Theories on Drug Abuse: Selected Contemperary Perspectives.* National Institute on Drug Abuse, Research Monograph 30. Rockville, Maryland: U.S. Dept of Health & Human Services.

Levine, H.G. 1978. The discover of addiction: Changing conceptions of habitual drunkenness in America. *Journal of Studies on Alcohol,* 39, 143–174.

Lindesmith, A.R. 1947. *Opiate addiction.* Bloomington, Indiana: Principia Press.

Macintyre, A. 1980. Epistemological crises, dramatic narrative, and the philosophy of science. In G. Gutting (ed.) *Paradigms & Revolutions.* London: University of Notre Dame Press.

Martin, W.R. 1968. A homeostatic and redundancy theory of tolerance to and dependence on narcotic analgesics. In A. Wikler (ed.) *The Addictive States.* Baltimore: Williams & Wilkins.

Oldman, D. 1978. Compulsive gamblers. *Sociological Review,* 26, 349–370.

Pace, N.A. 1984. *Guidelines to safe drinking.* New York: McGraw-Hill.

Peele, S. 1984. The cultural context of psychological approaches to alcoholism: Can we control the effects of alcohol? *The American Psychologist,* 39, 12, 1337–1351.

————. 1985. *The meaning of addiction.* Lexington, Massachusetts: Lexington Books.

————. 1986. The implications and limitations of genetic models of alcoholism and other addictions. *Journal of Studies on Alcohol,* 47, 63–73.

Pelz, D.C. 1967. Creative tensions in the research and development climate. *Science, 157,* 160–165.

Pendery, M.L., Maltzman, I.M., & West, L.J. 1982. Controlled drinking by alcoholics? New findings and a reevaluation of a major affirmative study. *Science, 217,* 169–174.

Price, D.J. DES. 1970. Citation measures of hard science, soft science, technology, and nonscience. In C. Nelson & D. Pollock (eds.) *Communication among Scientists and Engineers.* Lexington, Massachusetts: D.C. Heath.

Rado, S. 1926. The psychic effects of intoxicants: An attempt to evolve a psychoanalytic theory of morbid cravings. *International Journal of Psychoanalysis, 7,* 396–413.

Rado, S. 1933. The psychoanalysis of pharmacothymia (drug addiction). *The Psychoanalytic Quarterly, 2,* 1–23.

Ravetz, J.R. 1971. *Scientific knowledge and its social problems.* New York: Oxford University Press.

Rosecrance, J. 1985. Compulsive gambling and the medicalization of deviance. *Social Problems, 32,* 275–284.

———. 1988. *Gambling without guilt.* Pacific Grove, California: Brooks/Cole Publishing.

Rosenthal, R. 1987. The psychodynamics of pathological gambling: A review of the literature. In T. Galski (eds.) *The Handbook of Pathological Gambling.* 41–70. Springfield, Illinois: Charles C. Thomas.

Sederer, L.I. 1977. The importance of seeing psychiatry as more than a science. *Psychiatric Opinion, 14,* 27–29.

Shaffer, H.J. 1982. How did addictive behavior become the object of clinical assessment? From natural history to clinical practice. *Bulletin of the Society of Psychologists in Substance Abuse,* 1:159–162.

Shaffer, H.J. 1983. Integrating theory, research, and clinical practice: A perspective for the treatment of the addictions. *Bulletin of the Society of Psychologists in the Addictive Behaviors,* 2:34–41.

Shaffer, H.J. 1983. The natural history and social ecology of addictive behaviors. *Advances in alcohol and substance abuse, 3:*1–6.

———. 1984. How substance abuse becomes the target of clinical intervention: The impact of Sandor Rado. *Journal of Substance Abuse Treatment, 1*(1), 59–60.

———. 1985. The disease controversy: Of metaphors, maps, and menus, *Journal of Psychoactive Drugs, 17*(2), 65–76.

———. 1986. Conceptual crises and the addictions: A philosophy of science perspective. *Journal of Substance Abuse Treatment, 3,* 285–296.

———. 1986b. Assessment of addictive disorders: The use of clinical reflection and hypotheses testing. *The Psychiatric Clinics of North America, 9,* 385–398.

———. 1987. The epistemology of addictive "disease": The Lincoln-Douglas debate. *Journal of Substance Abuse Treatment, 4,* 103–113.

Shaffer, H.J. & Burglass, M.E. (eds.) 1981. *Classic Contributions in the Addictions.* New York: Brunner/Mazel.

Shaffer, H., & Gambino, B. 1979. Addiction paradigms II: Theory, research, and practice. *Journal of Psychedelic Drugs, 11,* 207–223.

———. 1983. Addiction paradigms III: From theory-research to practice and back. *Advances in Alcohol and Substance Abuse, 3*, No. 1/2, 135–152.

Shaffer, H., & Kauffman, J. 1985. The clinical assessment and diagnosis of addiction I: Hypotheses testing. In Bratter, T., & Forrest, G. (eds.), *Alcoholism and Substance Abuse: Strategies for Clinical Intervention*. New York: The Free Press.

Shaffer, H., & Neuhaus, C. 1985. Testing hypotheses: An approach for the assessment of addictive behaviors. In Milkman, H., & Shaffer, H. (eds.) *The Addictions: Multi-disciplinary Perspectives and Treatments*. Lexington, Massachusetts: Lexington Books, 1985.

Shaffer, H., & Zinberg, N.E. 1985. The social psychology of intoxicant use: The natural history of social settings and social control. *Bulletin of the Society of Psychologists in Addictive Behaviors, 4*, 49–55.

Simon, H.A., & Newell, A. 1963. The uses and limitations of models. In Marx, M. (ed.) *Theories in contemporary psychology*. New York: Macmillan.

Skinner, B.F. 1983, August. Interview with B.F. Skinner. *APA Monitor*, 39.

Sobell, M.B., & Sobell, L.C. 1973. Individualized behavior therapy for alcoholics. *Behavior Therapy, 4*, 49–72.

———. 1976. Second-year treatment outcome of alcoholics treated by individualized behavior therapy: Results. *Behavior Research and Therapy, 14*, 195–215.

———. 1984. The aftermath of heresy: A response to Pendery et al.'s critique of "individualized behavior therapy for alcoholics. *Behavior Research and Therapy, 22*, 413–440.

Szasz, T. 1974. *Ceremonial chemistry: The ritual persecution of drugs, addicts, and pushers*. New York: Doubleday/Anchor Press.

Taber, J.I. 1987. Compulsive gambling: An examination of relevant models. *The Journal of Gambling Behavior, 3*, 219–223.

Wallack, L., & Winkleby, M. 1987. Primary prevention: A new look at basic concepts. *Social Science and Medicine, 25*, 923–930.

Watzlawick, P., Weakland, J., Fisch, R. 1974. *Change. Principles of problem formation and problem resolution*. New York: W. W. Norton.

Wachtel, P.L. 1980. Investigation and its discontents. Some constraints on progress in psychological research. *American Psychologist, 35*, 399–408.

Weisskopf, V.F. 1977. The frontiers and limits of science. *American Scientist, 65*, 405–411.

Wikler, A. 1973. Dynamics of drug dependence. Implications of a conditioning theory for research and treatment. *Archives of General Psychiatry, 28*, 611–616.

Wolkowitz, O.M., Roy, A., & Doran, A.R. 1985. Pathological gambling and other risk-taking pursuits. *Psychiatric Clinics of North America, 8*, 311–322.

Wray, I., & Dickerson, M. 1981. Cessation of high frequency gambling and "withdrawal" symptoms. *British Journal of Addiction, 76*, 401–405.

Zinberg, N.E. 1984. *Drug, set, and setting: The basis for controlled intoxicant use*. New Haven: Yale University Press.

Zinberg, N.E., & Shaffer, H. 1985. The social psychology of intoxicant use: The interaction of personality and social setting. In Milkman, H., and Shaffer, H. (eds.) *The addictions: Multidisciplinary concepts and treatments*. Lexington, Massachusetts: Lexington Books.

2

A General Theory of Addictions: Rationale for and Evidence Supporting a New Approach for Understanding and Treating Addictive Behaviors

Durand F. Jacobs, Ph.D.

Overview

A general theory of addictions is proposed, using the compulsive/ pathological gambler as the prototype subject. Addiction is defined as a dependent state acquired over time by a predisposed person in an attempt to relieve a chronic stress condition. Two interacting sets of factors are said to predispose persons to addictions: an abnormal physiological resting state, either hypertensive or hypotensive, and childhood experiences that have produced a deep sense of personal inadequacy and rejection. All addictions are hypothesized to follow a similar three-stage course, (that is, discovery, resistance to change, and exhaustion). After finding support for these propositions in an exploratory study of compulsive gamblers, a matrix design was applied to collect similar information from different kinds of addicts and normals.

As predicted by the general theory, a common dissociative-like state was found to prevail among compulsive gamblers, alcoholics and compulsive overeaters while indulging in their respective addictive behaviors that significantly differentiated them from normative samples of youth and adults who also indulged in the same activities and substances. This condition has been termed an "altered state of identity." A major objective of this line of theory-directed investigation is to develop a screening instrument that will identify high-risk youth so that early intervention may prevent the development of addictive patterns of behavior. This chapter outlines the author's rationale for developing a general theory of addictions and offers evidence from a new line of inquiry that supports a central proposition of the theory. These findings may broaden understanding of the motives that drive addictions and thereby supplement current methods for diagnosing and treating this general class of behaviors. Optimally, the work reported here will stimulate further research to explore whether dissociative-like reactions are to be found in still more forms of addictive behavior and, if so, how these phenomona seem to be related to other dimensions in this area of study.

Background

"At present, no single theory dominates clinical thinking in the field of addictive behaviors"
—Milkman & Shaffer (1985)

This observation reflects a continuing need for theories that hold promise for directing attention to productive new concepts. These in turn may illuminate new and useful information in this area of inquiry.

Similarities among different kinds of addicts have long been recognized. Clinicians have frequently commented on the similarities in backgrounds, course, treatment, and prognosis among persons with different kinds of addictive behavior patterns (Taber 1982). Persons suffering from more than one addictive behavior who join a second (or third) self-help group such as Alcoholics Anonymous, Gamblers Anonymous, Overeaters Anonymous or Sex Anonymous have been quick to notice striking similarities between themselves and members of these presumably disparate groups. Yet, the tendency among scholarly researchers has been to examine each type of addiction as a separate entity, and to attempt to develop a distinct explanatory schema for each (Walker & Lidz 1983). As a consequence, reports dealing with alcoholism, heroin, and other drug addictions, eating disorders, compulsive gambling, and other addictive forms of behavior tend to be found in distinct literatures with little cross-reference to one another.

When I first proposed and began testing a general theory of addictions in 1980 (using the compulsive gambler as the prototype subject) there had been little systematic searching for common denominators among various addictions that might argue for their being treated as a unified class of behavior (Jacobs & Wright 1980). Indeed, the first concerted attempt to present a systematic analysis of the common elements among different forms of addictive behaviors waited until the publication of *Commonalities in Substance Abuse and Habitual Behavior* (Levison, Gerstein & Maloff 1983). This book reported the outcome of a series of studies initiated by the National Institute on Drug Abuse (NIDA) in 1976. The intent was to gather and evaluate relevant scientific evidence that might indicate the extent to which many aspects of excessive substance use and other habitual activities might have common biological, psychological, and/or sociological roots.

In a series of meta-analyses a group of distinguished researchers gathered the scattered literature that might reveal underlying common processes in three areas: sociocultural commonalities, psychological commonalities, and biological commonalities. While a wide range of habitual behaviors was considered, compulsive gambling was not, since "scientific evidence was simply insufficient to warrant intensive committee study" (Levison, Gerstein & Maloff 1983, preface). After balancing evidence supporting either similarities or differences among addictive forms of behavior, the editors concluded that, "In general, scientific knowledge does not at present provide the basis for a comprehensive theory of excessive, habitual behavior encompassing the available sociocultural, psychological and biological evidence" (page XVI). However, they acknowledged that "compelling and useful regularities do arise when researchers are guided by a coherent scientific frame of reference," and encouraged investigators to follow the research directions that emerged from a commonalities perspective.

Despite the guarded conclusions set forth by Levison et al., there are a number of important reasons why efforts should continue to explore the utility of theory building and testing to determine whether the extensive array of addictions may be regarded as a single unified class of behavior (Jacobs 1982a, 1982b, 1984). Should this prove to be, it could redirect the current flow of scarce dollars from multiple and often redundant projects into a powerfully focused and cost-effective program of coordinated research aimed at accelerated understanding of this major multifaceted health and social problem, and toward finding new methods for broadly based prevention and treatment programs. It could stimulate a reindexing of the presently scattered literatures into a single compendium with comparable subject matters that draw from writings about various kinds of addictive behaviors. This could turn up information already known about one kind of addiction that could be valuable to those immersed in studying another. If there were sufficient reasons to consider addictions as a unified class of behaviors, it could facilitate the design of uniform core training programs for professionals and support personnel. It would encourage and justify economical conjoint treatment and rehabilitation programs that would capitalize on addressing common problems among different kinds of addicts and gain in robustness through the diversity of participants, while still recognizing issues that require separate focus and more differentiated applications.

Four objectives have guided the general theory of addiction presented here. The first is to identify common elements that prevail across three very disparate groups of addicts: (a) alcoholics who ingest a toxic substance; (b) compulsive overeaters who ingest a life-sustaining substance; and (c) compulsive/pathological gamblers who pursue an activity that does not involve an ingested substance. The second is to identify significant differences that emerge among these groups. The third is to highlight and further explore puzzling inconsistencies within and between these groups. The fourth is to compare these three groups of known addicts with normative samples of adolescents and adults that include abstainers, users, and abusers of each type of substance or activity under study.

The strategy selected for testing the general theory of addictions is a matrix approach. Extensive comparable information was collected and analyzed about populations of compulsive (pathological) gamblers, alcoholics, and compulsive overeaters who are characterized by excessive behaviors over which they had shown lapses of control (Jacobs, Marston & Singer 1985). The matrix design also included data from adolescents and adults who had responded to the same basic Health Survey instrument (Jacobs 1986). To the best of my knowledge this approach is the first in which information regarding similar indices has been collected and systematically compared across several different types of addicts, as well as normative samples. This strategy is designed to produce further refinements in theory development. The ultimate goal is to construct descriptive models that will provide a better understanding of the addictive process, as well as facilitate early identification and prompt intervention for persons at high risk for developing addictive patterns of behavior.

An Alternative View of the Etiology and Course of Addictive Behavior

The general theory of addictions emphasizes the presence of two sets of interacting *predisposing* factors that are held to determine whether an individual is at risk of maintaining an addictive pattern of behavior. The first of these two sets of predisposing factors is *a unipolar physiological resting state* that is chronically and excessively either depressed or excited. This lifelong persistent state of hypo- or hyperarousal is believed to predispose the individual to respond to a rather narrow "window" of stress-reducing, but potentially addictive, substances or experiences. The second set of predisposing factors is of a *psychological nature*. The theory predicts that these reactions arise from family, developmental, and interpersonal experiences in childhood and early adolescence, and convince these persons that they are inferior, unwanted, unneeded, and/or generally rejected by parents and significant others. Indeed, the theory proposes that the essential reinforcing quality that maintains the chosen addictive pattern is that, while indulging in it, the individual finds escape from painful reality and experiences wish-fulfilling fantasies of being an important personage, highly successful, powerful, and/or admired. This condition has been termed a "state of altered identity." It is theorized to be the common goal of every form of addictive behaviors, regardless of the means used to attain it. The altered state of identity is hypothesized to be the end product of a dissociative process.

For purposes of testing this central feature of the general theory of addictions, evidence for experiencing a "dissociative-like state" was operationally defined as a subject responding affirmatively to each of the following four questions about his or her subjective experiences during or immediately following a period of indulgence (Jacobs 1980, 1982). The first question reflected a blurring of reality testing: "After (activity noted) have you ever felt like you had been in a trance?" The second question measured a shift in persona: "Did you ever feel like you had taken on another identity?" The third question was designed to capture an out-of-body experience: "Have you ever felt like you were outside yourself—watching yourself (doing it)?" The fourth question inquired about the presence of amnesia: "Have you ever experienced a 'memory blackout' for a period when you had been (doing the given activity)?" When responding to these questions, the subject must stipulate: "never," "rarely," "occasionally," "frequently," or "all the time."

The theory further predicts that *both* sets of predisposing factors must coexist and exercise their respective effects before an individual will maintain an addictive pattern of behavior *in a conducive environment*. Viewed in this light, only a limited segment of the population need be considered at risk for any given addiction. Moreover, even with persons in this group the propensity may remain latent, *unless* they encounter and perceive the above mix of pleasurable results from a chance triggering event in their daily lives that is of sufficient clarity, novelty, and intensity to motivate them to deliberately arrange and diligently pursue future experiences of this type (Thomas & Chess 1984).

On the basis of the interaction of these two sets of predisposing factors, Jacobs proposes that, theoretically, one can predict the probable emergence and course of all addictive patterns, as they progress through three common sequential stages (figure 2–1).

The author suggests further that by applying appropriate assessment procedures one should be able to estimate an individual's relative position in the progression of stages noted above. With such information in hand, it then becomes possible for clinicians to determine the *level of readiness* of a given addicted person either to doggedly cling to or to consider rejection of the addictive pattern. All such predictions would be tempered

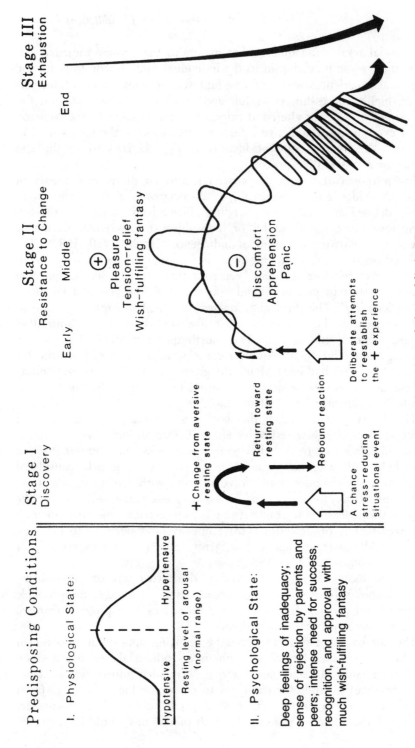

Figure 2–1. Onset and Course of the Addictive Process

Source: Durand F. Jacobs, Ph.D., Redlands, California, 1980.

by considering the facilitating or inhibiting influences of situational factors in the addicts' here-and-now environment (Peele 1986).

Definitions of Addiction

The Standard Medical Dictionary (Dorland 1974) defines addiction as "the state of being given up to some habit, especially strong dependence on a drug." Subdefinitions refer to alcohol, drug, opium, and (interestingly enough) polysurgical addiction—that is, the habitual seeking of surgical treatment. In the context of this definition four criteria are listed as being characteristic of an addictive state: "1) an overwhelming desire or need (compulsion) to continue use of the drug and to obtain it by any means; 2) a tendency to increase the dosage; 3) a psychological and usually a physical dependence on its effects; 4) a detrimental effect on the individual and on society."

Peele (1977) has proposed redefining the historical biologically rooted term "addiction" so that it may be dealt with in a much broader, measurable, and socially relevant manner. He proposes (1979) that "an addiction exists when a person's attachment to a sensation, an object, or another person is such as to lessen his appreciation and ability to deal with other things in his environment or in himself so that he has become increasingly dependent on that experience as his only source of gratification" (p. 56). In an article on alcohol addiction, Cummings (1979) makes the point that "addiction is not merely popping something into one's mouth, but a constellation of behaviors that constitute a way of life" (pp. 1121–1122). Compulsive gambling has been referred to as the "purest addiction," because no external substance is introduced into the biological system (Custer et al. 1975).

My approach to addiction tends to espouse the breadth of Peele's approach, the specificity of criteria listed in the medical definition (but without anchoring the concept to drugs), and Cummings' observation that over an extended period of time addictive behavior comes to dominate one's way of life.

Addictive patterns of behavior may involve substances such as food, alcohol, other licit and illicit drugs, as well as activities such as, but not limited to, gambling, overeating, sex, firesetting, overspending, and overwork. The function of virtually any addictive pattern of behavior as an acquired defense against enduring present or anticipated physical and psychic pain is an aspect stressed by Jacobs that has been given far less emphasis in other treatises on addiction. In a chapter describing what he had characterized as the "Chronic Pain Personality Syndrome," Jacobs (1980) refers to this syndrome as being composed of "a tightly knit set of learned behaviors directed to defending the patient against the phobic-like fear that his level of pain may worsen (p. 93)." In this view, addiction is much like a double-bind phenomenon that may follow the behavioral paradigm of a complex approach-escape-avoidance mechanism. On the one hand it traps the person into an escalating pattern of immediate gratification through greater and more frequent exercise of the "addicted" behavior. (Also see Donegan, Rodin, O'Brien & Solomon 1983).

More subtly, the addict's extended personal experience with the painful series of ups and downs during and between his periods of indulgence fuels a growing sense of apprehension, a sense that even the most extreme exercise of addictive behavior may not prevent the anticipated catastrophe that he dreads will happen when his addictive source is unavailable, or worse. When it inevitably fails to produce its previous positive effects (figure 2–1, late Stage II). The anticipated catastrophe referred to goes far beyond experiencing a brief period of aversive "withdrawal" (Custer et al. 1975) that may or may not follow sudden cessation of the addict's use pattern. Rather, Jacobs suggests that the threat of termination or actual collapse of the addictive pattern precipitates a profound anxiety state of debilitating proportions (figure 2–1, Stage III). The accompanying increase in dysphoria often triggers suicidal behavior (Custer et al. 1975); Jacobs et al. 1985).

Jacobs (1980, 1982) has defined addiction as a "dependent state acquired over an extended period of time by a predisposed person in an attempt to correct a chronic stress condition." Viewed in this light, addictive patterns of behavior may be conceptualized as a form of self-management or self-treatment. This perspective offers some advantages when engaging addicts in treatment. While recognizing the influence of predisposing and driving physiologic and psychologic factors, it holds the patient responsible for acquiring and/or strengthening more adaptive alternatives to replace the maladaptive and damaging efforts previously made to cope with the perceived stress condition.

At this point it is useful to consider at greater length the two coexisting and interacting *predisposing factors* that are held to potentiate and maintain an addictive pattern of behavior.

Physiological Predisposition

First, there is *a physiological arousal level that is perceived as chronically hypotensive or hypertensive.* The literature has referred to a minority of persons at either extreme of the normally distributed range of resting arousal levels as "reducer" or "augmenter/enhancer" types (Petrie 1967, 1978; Ogborne 1974). Either of these extreme arousal states is held to be aversive (Petrie 1978). Consequently, one would expect that those at either pole would attempt to seek and engage in activities that would make them feel better.

Meyer (1987) argues that the "actual aim of dependent people is an immediate change in their emotional state toward an intensified well-being, a satisfaction or euphoria or complete turn-off from the outside world" (p. 102). Based on his research findings, he describes gambling as a "release mechanism which facilitates an increase in physiological arousal levels" (p. 102).

Petrie (1978) offers a persuasive array of evidence from perceptual, kinesthetic, and neurophysiological experiments with normal and clinical populations to support her contention that because of their constitutional makeup, persons found to be at the extreme ends of the "perceptual reactance" spectrum tend to manifest very different forms of social behavior. The "reducer" tends subjectively to decrease the intensity of what is perceived; the "augmenter" to increase the intensity of what is perceived from both the internal and external environment. While not concerned with the problem of addictions per se, Petrie did report that alcoholics (found earlier to be augmenter types) were "particularly susceptible to a pronounced change toward the reducing end of the spectrum after (consuming alcohol)" (p. 38). Barnes (1983) also reports stimulus augmenting in alcoholics.

At the other extreme of the physiological arousal spectrum, Petrie (1978) reports that juvenile delinquents were significantly more pronounced reducers than control subjects. Petrie related these findings to complaints of delinquents that they suffered from chronic boredom, monotony, isolation, and enforced inactivity. A delinquent girl was said to justify her association with peers who had run afoul of the law by explaining she "hung around with those kids because they were always doing something. Regular people don't do nothing" (p. 87). Like Petrie (1978), Gorsuch & Butler (1976) also view extreme arousal states as strong motivators for social behavior. They suggest a cognitive state of boredom is related to mental anguish and may predispose youth to experimentation with potentially addictive behaviors. They observe that internal-sensation-seeking individuals seem to require greater stimulation than is available from their environments. Consequently, experimentation with potentially addictive substances and activities (such as gambling) may relieve the distress caused by the lack of adequate external stimulation.

The clinical histories of compulsive gamblers are replete with themes similar to those recounted by Petrie's young delinquents, plus reports of the unexcelled pleasure ("high") of sustained "action" afforded by gambling and gambling-related activities. In Jacobs' theoretical framework most problem gamblers would be expected to fall within the hypotensive (reducer) category, consistent with their frequent reports of feeling bored, numb, dead inside, and finding life dull and empty except when gambling. "For them, the excitement of gambling replaces their depression and boredom with exhilaration and a feeling of being 'acutely alive,'" (Jacobs 1984, 120).

Zuckerman (1969) speaks of a prevalent trait of sensation seeking or arousal seeking as a human characteristic. "The more orderly, safe, and predictable man's environment becomes, the more he seems to crave change, excitement, novelty, and adventure" (p. 154). His Sensation Seeking Scale (SSS) is based on the assumption that individuals differ in a reliable fashion in their optimal levels of stimulation for arousal. Zuckerman believes that the broad range of experiences captured in the SSS appear to be aspects of a single motive. "This motive has been conceived of as the need to maintain 'an optimal level of stimulation' in order to maintain an 'optimal level of arousal' (p. 162). Predating Jacobs' view of gambling behavior, Zuckerman (1969) had suggested that arousal plays an important role in maintaining gambling activity. In Zuckerman's opinion (1969) gambling is a form of sensation seeking "in which individuals risk loss of money for the positive reinforcement produced by states of high arousal during the period of uncertainty, as well as the positive arousal by winning" (p. 211).

Anderson & Brown (1984) examined sensation seeking in a sample of gamblers who reported betting regularly. Their comparison of the sensation seeking scores of twelve male undergraduate students and twelve experienced gamblers found no significant differences. Kuley & Jacobs (1988) have argued that a confounding variable in the Anderson and Brown study was the lack of control on age. (Zuckerman [1979] has pointed out that sensation seeking scores are found to correlate negatively with age). Anderson & Brown (1984) reported their samples of gamblers were aged twenty to fourty-eight years, while the controls ranged from twenty-one to twenty-eight years. (The mean age of each group was not reported).

Kuley & Jacobs (1988) took pains to control for both age and education in their study of the relationship between dissociative-like experiences and sensation seeking scores among social and problem gamblers. Problem gamblers were operationally defined as those who responded "yes" to seven or more of the Gamblers Anonymous Twenty Questions, and who said they had gambled an average of two days or more a week for the past six months. Those termed social gamblers were operationally defined as those who responded "yes" to fewer than seven of the Gamblers Anonymous Twenty Questions, and who said they had gambled two days or fewer in the previous six months. All subjects completed the Sensation Seeking Scale V (Zuckerman 1979). On the Gamblers Anonymous Twenty Questions, problem gamblers responded "yes" to an average of 12.17 questions. The average score for the social gamblers was 1.90 (p. >.001). Results of a t-test found that the total sensation seeking scores of problem gamblers were significantly greater than those of social gamblers. Problem gamblers also scored significantly higher than social gamblers on the disinhibition, boredom susceptibility, and experience seeking subscales of the SSS. These results offer substantial support to Jacobs' theoretical position that problem gamblers suffer from abnormally hypotensive arousal levels that provoke them to seek (or create) and attempt to maintain high levels of external stimulation.

Zuckerman (1979) earlier had found that individuals who score high on the boredom susceptibility subscale tend to demonstrate "extreme restlessness under conditions when escape from constancy is impossible" (p. 103). In the Kuley & Jacobs study (1988) four of the five sensation seeking scores correlated significantly with the number of days subjects reported gambling in the previous six months. Moreover, the disinhibition and boredom susceptibility subscales were significantly correlated with the percent of income that subjects reported spending on gambling activities. The latter results are consistent with those reported by Anderson & Brown (1984), who noted that sensation seekers tended to make larger bets in a real gambling situation. Subjects in the Kuley & Jacobs study (1988) who admitted to a greater number of adverse consequences as a result of their gambling behavior (as measured by their scores on the Gamblers Anonymous Twenty Questions) also tended to score significantly higher on the boredom susceptibility and disinhibition subscales, as well as the total sensation seeking score. Correlations between the Twenty Questions and sensation seeking scores were highly significant (p. <.001). Kuley & Jacobs' findings (1988) replicate research data reported by Jacobs (1982) and the U.S. National Gambling Commission Survey (Kallick et al. 1979). Both studies found that "excitement" and "escape from a humdrum existence" were major motives for gambling.

Not all reducers and enhancers are prone to acquiring an addiction, according to my theory. The persistence of what is subjectively perceived as an aversive physiological arousal state is only one of the two necessary predisposing conditions for developing an addiction.

The second precondition that theoretically must exist before the stage is fully set for acquiring an addictive pattern of behavior is *a childhood and adolescence marked by deep feelings of inadequacy, inferiority, and low self esteem, and a pervasive sense of rejection by parents and significant others.* Such feelings would be expected to stimulate behaviors and activities that would produce relief from this psychological distress. Several alternatives would be available to persons in such unhappy and frustrating circumstances. These might first include responding adaptively by increasing efforts that would gain recognition and acceptance. A second reaction would be to retaliate with angry and aggressive acting-out behaviors of a delinquent or antisocial type. The work of Kaplan (1977) is precisely illustrative of this type of defensive reaction. Kaplan tested his "general theory of deviant behavior" in a longitudinal study of junior high school students. Central to his theory is a "self-esteem motive," according to which a person engages in deviant activities to restore a sense of worth damaged by experiences in his or her family or peer group. Kaplan's findings are endorsed as supporting his hypothesis that negative self-feelings are predictive of deviant behaviors, including involvement in potentially addictive activities (Capuzzi & LeCoq 1983).

A third much less frequent reaction to feeling inferior and rejected would be to pretend not to care and/or to conceptually leave the offending field through escape into wish-fulfilling fantasies wherein one is successful, powerful, loved, and admired.

The general theory predicts that persons with a chronically abnormal arousal state who *also* tend to respond to feelings of inferiority and rejection by flight into denial and compensatory fantasy are at the highest risk for acquiring an addictive pattern of behavior. Such persons would be particularly vulnerable during adolescence, a developmental period when high levels of both physiologic and psychosocial stresses prevail. Given these interacting predisposing conditions *in a conducive environment*, Jacobs' theoretical position is that whatever the potentially addictive substance or activity chosen, its continued use into a frank addictive pattern of behavior will depend largely on its possessing the following three attributes:

1. *It Blurs Reality Testing.* Specifically, one's attention is temporarily diverted from the chronic aversive arousal state. This may occur as a result of the physiologic affects of an ingested substance, and/or by the manner in which an activity (such as gambling) so completely concentrates one's attention on a series of specific here-and-now events that coexisting aversive aspects of one's physical, mental and/or social life situation are "blurred out" (also see Goffman 1961; Sullivan 1956; Hilgard 1977; Sanders 1986).

2. *It Lowers Self-Criticism and Self-Consciousness.* This is accomplished through an internal cognitive shift that deflects preoccupation from one's self-perceived inadequacies (Sanders 1986). Often this is supported and reinforced by the special circumstances that prevail where the addictive pattern of behavior is ordinarily pursued—such as with peers in a bar, gambling casino, race track, restaurant or party. Each of these environs tends to accord acceptance, even encouragement, to behaviors that would be frowned upon or rejected in other company or in other settings.

3. *It Permits Complimentary Daydreams about Oneself.* These wish-fulfilling fantasies—which surface as a natural aftermath of (1) and (2)—

serve to facilitate the *assuming of an altered identity* wherein, while indulging in the chosen potentially addictive behavior, one perceives his or her self-image as greatly enhanced and his or her related social interactions and performances as highly successful.

Whether the addictive pattern of behavior is practiced in solitary or in social settings, as the number and intensity of these three attributes increase, so does the likelihood that the person will actually "cross over" into a frank dissociative-like state. The relative frequency, intensity, and extent of measures suggested to tap this dissociative-like state may well constitute key pathognomic "hard signs" that will differentiate potential and actual addicts from those who indulge in an abusive manner. Jacobs has proposed (1984, 121) that, theoretically, it is the intent to achieve and act out an altered state of identity that distinguishes the "true addict" from the superficially similar excesses of the abuser. Abusers seek only to reduce stress, while retaining their identity and continuing in their social and occupational roles. For instance, documented high-use levels of extremely potent drugs over an extended period of time did not produce addictive patterns of behavior among large numbers of returning Vietnam veterans (Robins 1973, 1974, 1978).

The Central Importance of an Altered State of Identity for Understanding Addictive Behaviors

In the context of the general theory of addictions an addictive substance or activity is conceptualized as a means to an end. At least during the early and middle to late stages of the addictive career, it serves a friendly gatekeeper function. At a certain level of indulgence (either physiologically, neurochemically, psychologically, and/or via some as-yet unknown combination of these mediators) it permits the person to become so detached from reality and so engrossed in subjective fantasy that he or she assumes an altered state of identity. An altered state of identity is hypothesized to be the end product of a self-induced dissociative condition. When in this state the individual finds it easy to create and act out roles consistent with his or her now modified (idealized?) self-image. Those who have experienced this (alleged) altered state of identity report believing they somehow become "more so" with regard to positive features of their personality, physical appearance, social graces, sexuality, and/or competent functioning. Concurrently, they feel "less so" about what they had perceived as their negative or deficient features. This improvement in subjectively perceived psychological well-being also is said to be accompanied by reduced awareness of previous physical discomfort. While individual reports vary, aspects of this same mix of experiences are said to occur whether the addictive behavior is practiced under social or solitary conditions. Theoretically, with reality testing compromised by the action of the addictive substance or activity, and inhibitions and self-criticism progressively reduced as the level of preoccupation with and indulgence in the addictive behavior increases, self-delusion becomes easier and the individual is freed to generate and even to act out roles that heretofore have been only fantasies. This central premise in the general theory is a direct outgrowth of my years spent listening to the stories told by many different kinds of addicts about how much better they felt and how their interactions with others seemed much improved at those times when they were indulging.

Dissociation: A Many Splendored Thing

All of us are different people at various times, dictated by the roles we play as worker, spouse, parent, amateur sportsman, teacher, social activist, and so on. (Hilgard 1986). Each role permits—sometimes demands—us to be a very different person than that portrayed and experienced in alternate roles. For the most part as we shift from role to role, we carry our memories around with us and thereby maintain a sense of integration and continuity in our lives. There are instances, however, when the varying roles may lose communication with each other. At such times (which would be expected to be relatively infrequent among the general population), Hilgard (1986) believes it is appropriate to refer to the bifurcated roles as becoming "dissociated." Jacobs' four criteria for a dissociative-like state parallel Hilgard's description of "neo-dissociation" (1986) in many respects. According to the general theory of addictions, the altered state of identity, achieved through a "dissociative-like" process, is positioned somewhere between the normal role shifting experiences and functional amnesias of everyday life (Hilgard 1986, 84) and the clinical phenomena of functional fugue states and multiple personalities. Goffman (1961) speaks eloquently about the more familiar portion of this middle ground: "When an individual becomes engaged in an activity, whether shared or not, it is possible for him to become caught up by it, carried away by it, engrossed in it—to be, as we say, spontaneously involved in it. A visual and cognitive engrossment occurs, with an honest unawareness of matters other than the activity, what Harry Stack Sullivan (1956) called 'selective inattention' occurs, *with an effortless dissociation from all other events, distinguishing this type of unawareness both from suppression and repression.*" (p. 38; italics added).

"Under such circumstances, persons can be so engrossed in an encounter that it is practically impossible to distract their attention; in such cases *they can hardly feel ill at ease.* Since we have this capacity to become engrossed, *how is it we do not more often use it to avoid dysphoria?*" (p. 43; italics added).

". . . something in which the individual can become unselfconsciously engrossed is something *that can become real to him*" (p. 80; italics added), ". . . to embrace a role is to disappear completely into the virtual self available in the situation, to be fully seen in terms of the image, and to confirm expressively one's acceptance of it. *To embrace a role is to be embraced by it*" (p. 106; italics added).

It is not too great a conceptual leap from the pleasant and relatively innocuous "engrossments" described by Goffman to the threshold of what may turn out to be a continuum of ever more insular and counterproductive dissociative states. The key to how each of these may be entered and maintained is beyond our current knowledge—and outside the scope of this chapter. However, Jacobs predicts that somewhere in that largely unexplored "middle ground" between normal reverie and total disengagement from reality exists a unique kind of dissociative experience that incorporates an altered state of identity. His general theory reserves this kind of dissociative state to that minority of predisposed persons who reveal themselves by their dogged pursuit of one or another addictive pattern of behavior.

It is important to note that, while the general theory proposes a marked transformation in the addict's self-image and behavior when indulging, this does not mean there is a total dissociation from his former "customary" self. Even while fully engrossed in the altered identity, like an accomplished actor in a play, the addict does not *totally* disengage from his former self. Jacobs proposes that a demonstrable conscious channel of awareness remains open between the customary self and the altered self throughout the entire transition into, during and after the period of addictive experience. Consciousness of one's usual and customary self-state is not fully relinquished when one becomes involved in the addicted-self state, and vice versa. (See Hilgard 1986, "A neo-dissociation interpretation of divided consciousness," p. 216 ff.).

The general theory postulates that, once established, a given individual's addictive pattern of behavior represents that person's deliberately chosen means for entering and maintaining a dissociative-like state. The general theory recognizes that, as with dissociative states in general, an element of functional amnesia, or memory blackouts, is to be expected. Typically, however, such memory losses also are expected to be incomplete and, even then, to be volitionally reversible to some extent.

The issue of partial amnesia is key both for Hilgard (1986) and for the general theory. Amnesia is considered the sine qua non of any dissociative state. However, repeated clinical observations have shown that the memory blackouts of addicts are both incomplete and to some extent retrievable, either spontaneously over time or with some prompting. This effectively counters any argument that the "forgotten material" was repressed. Hilgard (1986) has conclusively demonstrated that amnesias following a hypnotically induced dissociative period later can be breached either spontaneously by the subject or with some gentle probing by the practitioner. When describing these experiments, Hilgard (1986) introduces the concept of a "hidden observer" to explain the continuing co-conscious presence of the awake individual even when that individual is experiencing a dissociative (that is, hypnotic) episode. One of Jacobs' "dissociative" items directly addresses this issue. It is, while indulging, "Have you ever felt like you were outside yourself—watching yourself (doing it)?"

Jacobs' theory does not propose that the addict's altered state of identity is a form of multiple personality or a full-blown fugue state. This would be an erroneous and oversimplified interpretation of what is believed to be happening. However, when predicting that addicts become engrossed in a dissociative-like state (with or without the use of some substance) as a necessary step toward assuming an altered identity, one confronts a set of conditions that has not been fully explored in the past. These phenomena are expected to lie somewhere between the clinically well-defined dissociative reactions of the classic fugue state or multiple personality and the familiar occurrences in everyday life wherein persons find themselves in such a pleasant state of reverie that they temporarily ignore or deny the facts of their usual reality. Hopefully, the general theory of addictions may provide added impetus to the seminal work of the Hilgards and others by opening a new arena for investigating dissociative phenomena.

Experimental Evidence Supporting the General Theory of Addictions

Closest to Jacobs' position on the role of dissociation in addictive behaviors is that recently developed by Sanders (1986). She defines dissociation as "a personality trait that is characterized by modifications of connections between affect, cognition, and perception of voluntary control over behavior, as well as modifications in the subjective experience of affect, voluntary control, and perception" (p. 95). She devised the Perceptual Alteration Scale (PAS) as a means for operationally measuring dissociation. She found that the PAS discriminated between college students who had normal eating habits from those who were binge eaters. *She concludes that the binger seeks food as a means of reducing already high levels of affect* (italics added; also see Petrie 1978). However, eating further heightens anxiety and dissociation is triggered. Consequently, "dissociation is not a cause for bingeing, but is triggered by the same high levels of anxiety that lead to bingeing" (p. 99). Certain subtests of the PAS indicate that low self-esteem has a role in triggering dissociation. This finding would be consistent with the general theory.

The work of Marston, Jacobs, Singer et al. (1988) provides more substantial support to the stance taken by the general theory. Namely, that addictive behaviors not only lead to relief of anxiety, but also serve as a bridge to a dissociative-like state. These researchers studied characteristics of adolescents at risk for compulsive overeating. Students designated to be "at risk" were those who had scored above the cutoff point set by Overeaters Anonymous on their scale for assessing compulsive overeating. When responding to the four items that Jacobs operationally defines as representing dissociative-like experiences, the "at risk" students were said to demonstrate *"the defensive effectiveness of overeating* in their significantly more frequent reports of dissociative experiences while eating" (p. 59, italics added). At-risk students were found to be significantly more likely than their classroom peers to experience themselves "as a different person," as "in a trance," and as "being outside of themselves" while overeating. The at-risk students rated their present life quality as significantly poorer than did their peers, and they also reported themselves as getting along less well with the person they felt most close to. Only the male at-risk subgroup reported a higher frequency of gambling than their male peers (p. <.02).

A study by Kuley & Jacobs (1988) comparing groups identified as social and problem gamblers replicates and extends earlier findings of Jacobs, Marston & Singer (1985) that had indicated an extremely high prevalence of dissociative-like reactions while gambling among known compulsive gamblers. Kuley & Jacobs (1988) found that problem gamblers reported a significantly greater number of dissociative-like experiences than social gamblers on each of the four "dissociative" questions (p. <.01). Fifty-four percent of gamblers reported they felt like a different person "occasionally" to "all of the time" when gambling, in contrast to 10 percent of the social gamblers. Forty-three percent of the problem gamblers reported they felt "in a trance" "occasionally" to "all the time" after a period of gambling, as compared to 3 percent of the social gamblers. Thirty-three percent of the problem gamblers "felt outside themselves" "occasionally" to "all the time" when gambling, in contrast to 4 percent of the social gamblers. Finally, 50 percent of the problem gamblers reported that they experienced memory blackouts "occasionally" to "all the time" following an episode of gambling. Only 3 percent of the social gamblers reported this experience.

Kuley & Jacobs (1988) also noted highly significant correlations (p. <.001) between high scores on each of the four "dissociative" items and high scores on the Gamblers Anonymous Twenty Questions (See Stein, this volume, for the G.A. Twenty Questions). This is the first documented evidence that subjects who admitted to more real-life problems as a result of their gambling behavior on the Twenty Questions also tend to report a higher frequency of dissociative-like experiences. Moreover, the average number of days a week subjects reported gambling correlated highly with the frequency of dissociative-like experiences. Correlations between extent of gambling and each of the dissociative-like experiences ranged from .46 to .60 (p. <.001). The highly significant correlations between dissociative-like reactions with (a) an independent listing of gambling related problems and (b) accounts of the extent of real-life gambling behavior lend impressive support to the theory's contention that problem gamblers can be confidently discriminated from social gamblers by the nature of their answers to four rather simple, nonincriminating questions about what happens to them when they gamble.

Prevalence of Dissociative-Like Experiences Among Addicts and Normals When Indulging

In 1981 a questionnaire was constructed to initiate a program of research designed to test selected aspects of the general theory of addictions (Jacobs 1980). Over a four-year period data were collected anonymously from known groups of compulsive gamblers, alcoholics and compulsive overeaters and compared with responses from normative samples of adolescents and adults. In all, more than four hundred addicts and more than one thousand normals were surveyed. This report is limited to discussing the responses of each of these groups to the four "dissociative" items. A summary of results is presented in table 2–1.

Additional information on the median age and sex distribution of the addict groups is as follows: compulsive gamblers: median age forty-six years, 10 percent females; alcoholics: median age forty-six years, 12 percent females; compulsive overeaters: median age thirty-eight years, 67 percent females. The addict samples were drawn from available inpatient treatment settings and self-help groups. It is recognized that these samples may or may not be representative of their counterparts in other geographic locales, treatment settings, or in other self-help groups.

The median age and sex distribution of the normative samples is as follows: adults: median age sixty-four years, females 15 percent. The adult sample was drawn from available veterans and service club groups in the Inland Empire area of Southern California. The adolescent sample was composed of a broadly representative (though not scientifically controlled) selection of ninth- to twelfth-graders from four high schools in the Inland Empire area of Southern California. The students had a median age of 16.5 years, females 55 percent. The same caveat noted above for the addict group applies to the unknown representativeness of the normative

Table 2–1
Dissociative-like Reactions Experienced by Addicts and Normals When Indulging in Gambling, Drinking and Overeating
(type of indulgence)

Dissociative-like reactions reported "occasionally" to "all the time":*	When gambling			When drinking			When overeating		
	Gamblers N=121	Adults N=168	Adolescents N=843	Alcoholics N=203	Adults N=168	Adolescents N=843	Overeaters N=83	Adults N=168	Adolescents N=843
Trance	79%	5%	2%	62%	17%	29%	41%	5%	7%
Different person	79	21	5	73	36	39	44	21	13%
Outside self	50	8	2	34	12	23	30	7	10
Blackout	38	4	1	73	15	21	14	4	2
Median dissociative score:	64%	6%	2%	67%	16%	26%	35%	6%	8%

* Reactions reported "rarely" are not included above

samples that participated in this study. It is hoped that this partial report of findings will stimulate replication studies that will throw more light on the relationships between demographic, historical, psychosocial, physiological, diagnostic, and response to treatment variables and the experiencing of dissociative-like reactions such as those reported here. Displayed in table 2–1 are the proportions of known addicts, adults, and high school students who responded that they had experienced each of the "dissociative" items "occasionally," to "all the time," when gambling, drinking, and/or overeating. The reader is alerted that the normative samples of adults and high school students were asked to indicate the extent of their dissociative-like experiences when indulging in *each* of an array of potentially addictive behaviors. On the other hand, the earlier samples of addicts had been asked only to report their dissociative-like experiences when indulging in their particular type of addictive behavior: that is, compulsive gamblers when gambling, alcoholics when drinking, and compulsive overeaters when overeating.

Results

As predicted, moderate to high frequencies of each type of dissociative-like experience were reported by each addict group. Compulsive gamblers and alcoholics consistently reported a higher incidence of these reactions than did compulsive overeaters (p. ≤ 01). Each of the three addict groups reported significantly more (p. ≤ 001) dissociative-like reactions on each indicator than did normative groups. Normative groups reported dissociative-like reactions most often when drinking, next when overeating, and least when gambling. High school students reported significantly more dissociative reactions when drinking than did adults (p. ≤ 01). Adults reported significantly more dissociative-like reactions than high school students while gambling (p. ≤ 01). These findings provide impressive support to the general theory's major prediction. Namely, that when indulging, persons known to be addicted to different substances or activities will tend to share a *common* set of dissociative experiences that, by virtue of the relative frequency of their combined occurence, will clearly differentiate them from nonaddicts.

Figure 2–2 portrays the differences between known addicts and the two normative groups to the question, "Did you ever feel like you had been in a trance when . . . (gambling/drinking/overeating)?" Four out of five compulsive gamblers (79 percent) reported that they had this experience "occasionally" to "all the time" when gambling, as do 62 percent of the alcoholics when drinking, and 41 percent of the compulsive overeaters when overeating. Compulsive gamblers reported experiencing a trance-like state significantly more often (chi square = 48.03, p. ≤ .001), than did the

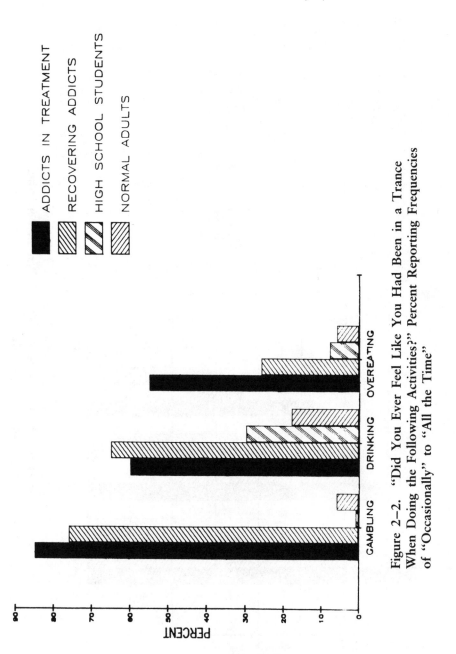

Figure 2–2. "Did You Ever Feel Like You Had Been in a Trance When Doing the Following Activities?" Percent Reporting Frequencies of "Occasionally" to "All the Time"

Figure 2–3. "Did You Ever Feel Like You Had Taken on Another Identity When Doing the Following Activities?" Percent Reporting Frequencies of "Occasionally" to "All the Time"

other two addict groups. As noted above, all three addict groups reported this experience far more frequently than did either of the normative samples (p. ≤ .001).

Figure 2–3 compares the responses of the three addict groups and the normative samples to the question, "Did you ever feel like you had taken on another identity when . . . ?" Four out of five compulsive gamblers (79 percent), 73 percent of the alcoholics, and 44 percent of the compulsive overeaters reported having this experience "occasionally" to "all the time" when indulging in their respective addictive behaviors. Compulsive gamblers and alcoholics reported this experience significantly more often (chi square = 49.75, p. = .0001) than did compulsive overeaters. Again, the normative samples reported this experience far less frequently than did the addict groups.

Figure 2–4 compares the addict groups with the normative samples with regard to their responses to the item, "Did you ever feel like you were outside yourself—watching yourself (doing it)?" This out-of-body experience was reported less frequently than the preceding two dissociative-like reactions by all subjects. Compulsive gamblers reported this experience most frequently (50 percent), followed by alcoholics (34 percent), and compulsive overeaters (30 percent). Normative groups reported this experience far less frequently than did addicts.

Figure 2–5 compares the responses of the addict and normative groups to the question, "Did you ever experience a memory blackout for a period when you had been indulging?" Alcoholics reported this experience most frequently (73 percent). In dramatic support of the central dissociative (that is, amnestic) element proposed by the general theory of addictions, 38 percent of the pathological gamblers and 14 percent of the compulsive overeaters also reported memory blackouts "occasionally" to "all the time" when indulging in their respective addictive forms of behavior. Alcoholics and gamblers reported this behavior significantly more often than did the overeater group (chi square = 159.5, p. = .0001). This experience was relatively rare among the normative sample.

It is of interest that on the *combined dissociative score* (table 2–1) the overeater group was significantly lower than either the alcoholic or gamblers group, who did not differ from one another (chi square = 30.14, p. = .0001).

Table 2–1 details the responses of each of the addict and normative groups to the four dissociative questions. In general, feeling like one had taken on another identity and feeling like one had been in a trance while indulging were the more frequent kinds of dissociative-like reactions experienced by both addicts and normals. Except for the extremely high frequency of blackouts reported by alcoholics following drinking episodes, the remaining addict groups, as well as the normative groups, reported

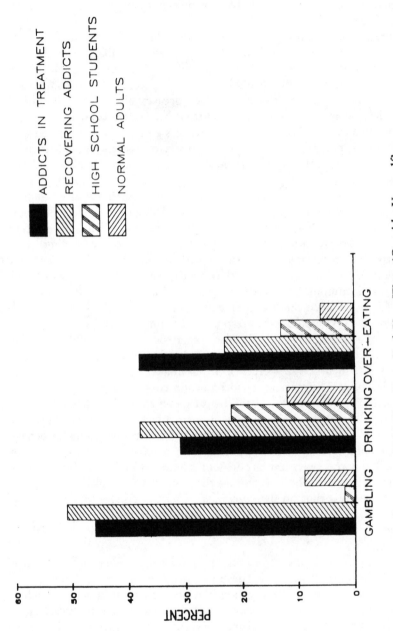

Figure 2–4. "Did You Ever Feel You Were 'Outside Yourself' Watching Yourself Doing the Following Activities?" Percent Reporting Frequencies of "Occasionally" to "All the Time"

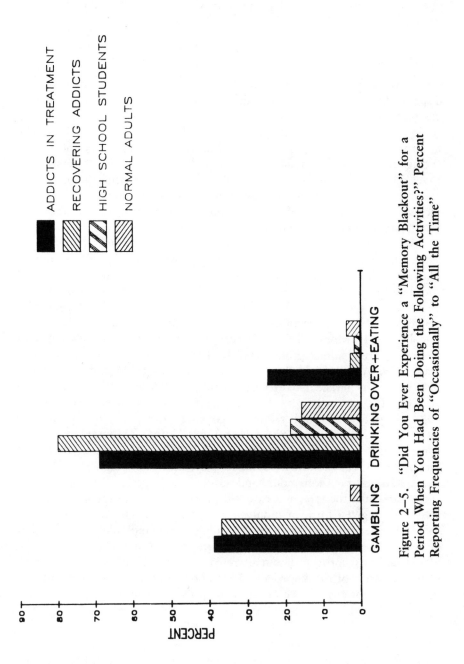

Figure 2–5. "Did You Ever Experience a "Memory Blackout" for a Period When You Had Been Doing the Following Activities?" Percent Reporting Frequencies of "Occasionally" to "All the Time"

out-of-body experiences and memory blackouts less often than trance or feeling like one had taken on another identity.

Conclusions

One may confidently conclude from this study that addicts of markedly disparate types share a common dissociative-like experience when indulging that clearly sets them apart from normal groups of adolescents and adults who also indulge in the same types of substances or activities. The findings that addicts reported a significantly higher frequency for experiencing dissociative-like reactions when indulging than did normals may have clinical as well as forensic utility for differentiating addicts from nonaddicts (that is, other excessive indulgers or abusers) who present themselves or who are referred by families, employers, or the courts to health professionals for evaluation and treatment.

Further research undoubtedly will explore the incidence and prevalence of dissociative-like reactions among still other types of addicts. These findings also open the door to a series of studies designed to correlate the relative presence of dissociative-type phenomena with a variety of other dimensions. These might include assessing the relationships between dissociative reactions and stage or course of an addictive career (Jacobs 1984; Moran 1970; Custer 1982); age and sex distributions among different addict groups (Jacobs 1985); sensation seeking (Zuckerman 1979; Anderson & Brown 1984; Wolfgang 1988; Kuley & Jacobs 1988); arousal level changes when indulging (Brown 1984; Dickerson et al. 1987; Blaszczynski et al. 1986); a neurological substrata (McConaghy 1980; Roy et al. 1988) reducer/augmenter correlates among different kinds of addicts (Petrie 1978); scores on Twenty Question inventories constructed by self-help groups such as Gamblers Anonymous (Kuley & Jacobs 1988), Alcoholics Anonymous, Narcotics Anonymous, Sex Anonymous, Overeaters Anonymous, and so on.

Meanwhile, the type and extent of dissociative-like experiences associated with a given form of indulgence may serve as clinical "hard signs" for early identification of high-risk adolescents and adults before they become enmeshed in an addictive pattern of behavior. The ultimate goal of the author's entire program of research is to augment and encourage systematization of the knowledge base about addictions, so that one day timely interventions can be designed to prevent them.

Epilogue

In a published critique of the general theory of addictions, Johnson (1985) encouraged pursuing this particular line of investigation for several reasons: the theory is based largely on an empirically supportable behavioral framework; the major terms are clearly defined; it concentrates on the obsessive and purposeful nature of the behavioral pattern so typical of the addict; and it offers a high degree of testability in specifying the preconditions necessary for addiction to occur and in proposing the series of stages through which all addicts are expected to pass. Johnson stated, "Perhaps the most compelling feature of the theory is its parsimony . . . seemingly out of control behaviors of all sorts, are explainable by the same set of principles and operating rules . . . Perhaps the greatest benefit to be derived from the particular parsimony of this theory is that it encourages researchers to look at the similarities in seemingly dissimilar practices to distill out what may be the essence of addictions" (p. 306–307).

In his lengthy critique, Johnson pulls no punches in declaring that the general theory has its share of shortcomings as well. These must stand or fall on the results of subsequent testing. Still he offers the opinion that, "compared to other theories of addiction, the ratio of strengths to weaknesses is unusually high in this general theory of addictions" (p. 308).

Johnson concludes (p. 309), "The general theory of addictions . . . is a thought provoking and promising step in the progressive study of abusive and addictive behavior. Hopefully, researchers in prevention as well as in treatment of the various addictions will be affected by the conceptual insights afforded by the theory and begin to consider its ramifications in the design and execution of their longitudinal studies, for it is only through prospective longitudinal research that the potential of the theory can be explored."

REFERENCES

Anderson, G., & Brown, R. 1984. Real and laboratory gambling, sensation seeking, and arousal. *British Journal of Psychology, 75,* 401–410.

Barnes, G. 1983. Clinical and pre-alcoholic personality characteristics. In B. Kissin and H. Begleiter (eds.) *The Pathogenesis of Alcoholism.* Vol. 6. New York: Plenum Press. (Also see Buchsbaum 1976; Sokis & Shagass 1974).

Blaszczynski, A. P., Winter, S. W., & McConaghy, N. 1986. Plasma endorphin levels in pathological gambling. *Journal of Gambling Behavior, 2,* 1, 3–14.

Brown, R. I. F. 1984. *The integration of arousal and sensation seeking factors in the explanation of gambling and gambling addictions.* Paper presented at the Sixth Conference on Gambling and Risk Taking, Atlantic City, New Jersey, December.

———. 1986. Gambling addictions, arousal, and affective decision-making explanations of behavioral reversions or relapses. *International Journal of Addictions.*

Capuzzi, D., & LeCoq, L. L. 1983. Social and personal determinants of adolescent use and abuse of alcohol and marijuana. *Personnel and Guidance Journal,* Vol. 62 (4), 199–205.

Cummings, N. A. 1979. Turning bread into stones: Our modern antimiracle. *American Psychologist, 34,* 1119–1129.

Custer, R., Glen, A., & Burns, R. 1975. *Characteristics of compulsive gamblers.* Paper presented at the Second Annual Conference on Gambling, Las Vegas, Nevada.

Custer, R. L. 1982. An overview of compulsive gambling. In P. Carone, S. Yoles, S. Keiffer & L. Krinsky (eds.) *Addictive Disorders Update.* New York: Human Sciences Press.

Dickerson, M. G., Hinchy, J., & Fabre, J. 1987. Chasing, arousal, and sensation seeking in off-course gambling. *British Journal of Addictions, 82,* 673–680.

Donegan, N. H., Rodin, J., O'Brien, C. P., & Solomon, R. L. 1983. A learning-theory approach to commonalities. In P. Levison et al. (eds.) *Commonalities in Substance Abuse and Habitual Behavior.* Lexington, Massachusetts: D. C. Heath & Company.

Dorland's Illustrated Medical Dictionary (Twenty-fifth Edition) 1974. Philadelphia, Pennsylvania: W.B. Saunders.

Goffman, E. 1961. *Encounters.* Indianapolis, Indiana: Bobbs-Merrill Company.

Gorsuch, R. L., & Butler, M. C. 1976. Initial drug abuse: A review of predisposing social and psychological factors. *Psychological Bulletin, 83,* 120–137.

Hilgard, E. R. 1977, 1986. *Divided Consciousness: Multiple Controls in Human Thought and Action.* New York: Wiley & Sons.

Jacobs, D. F., & Wright, E. T. 1980. *A program of research on the causes and treatment of addictive behaviors: Using the compulsive gambler as the prototype subject.* Loma Linda, California: Veterans Administration Hospital. Unpublished.

Jacobs, D. F. 1982a. *Factors alleged as predisposing to compulsive gambling.* Paper presented at the Annual Convention of the American Psychological Association, Washington, D.C.

———. The Addictive Personality Syndrome (APS): A new theoretical model for understanding and treating addictions. In W. R. Eadington (ed.) *The Gambling Papers: Proceedings of the Fifth National Conference on Gambling and Risk Taking.* Reno, Nevada: University of Nevada.

———. 1984. Study of traits leading to compulsive gambling. In *Sharing Recovery Through Gamblers Anonymous.* Los Angeles, California: Gamblers Anonymous Publishing, Inc.

Jacobs, D. F., Marston, A. R., & Singer, R. D. 1985. Testing a general theory of addictions: Similarities and differences between alcoholics, pathological gamblers and compulsive overeaters. In J. J. Sanchez-Soza (ed.) *Health and Clinical Psychology.* Amsterdam, The Netherlands: Elsevier Science Publishers B.V.

Jacobs, D. F. 1980. Holistic strategies in the management of chronic pain. In F. McQuigan, et al. (eds.) *Stress and Tension Control.* New York: Plenum.

Jacobs, D. F., Marston, A. R., & Singer, R. D. 1985. Testing a general theory of addictions: Similarities and differences between alcoholics, pathological gamblers, and compulsive overeaters. In J. J. Sanchez-Sosa (ed.) *Health and Clinical Psychology.* North Holland: Elsevier Science Publishers B.V.

Jacobs, D. F. 1986. A general theory of addictions: A new theoretical model. *Journal of Gambling Behavior*, 2, 1, 15–31.

—————. 1987. A general theory of addictions:. Application to treatment and rehabilitation planning for pathological gamblers. In T. Galski (ed.) *Handbook of Pathological Gambling* (169–194). Springfield, Illinois: Charles C. Thomas.

—————. 1988. Evidence for a common dissociative-like reaction among addicts. *Journal of Gambling Behavior*, Vol. 4 (1), Spring, 27–37.

Johnson, C. A. 1985. Discussion and critique of a General Theory of Addictions. In J. J. Sanchez-Sosa (ed.) *Health and Clinical Psychology (306–310)*. North Holland: Elsevier Science Publishers B.V.

Kallick, M., Suits, D., Dielman, T., & Hybels, J. 1979. *A Survey of American Gambling Attitudes and Behavior*. Ann Arbor: University of Michigan Survey Research Center.

Kaplan, H. B. 1977. Antecedents of deviant responses: Predicting from a general theory of deviant behavior. *Journal of Youth and Adolescence*, 6, 89–101.

Kuley, N. 1986. *Avoidance learning in pathological gamblers: A test of optional arousal theory*. Doctoral dissertation. San Diego, California. Unpublished.

Kuley, N. B., & Jacobs, D. F. 1988. The relationship between dissociative-like experiences and sensation seeking among social and problem gamblers. *Journal of Gambling Behavior*, Vol. 4, (3), 197–207.

Levison, P. K., Gerstein, D. R., & Maloff, D. R. (1983). *Commonalities in substance abuse and habitual behavior*. Lexington, Massachussetts: D. C. Heath & Company.

McConaghy, N. 1980. Behavior completion mechanisms rather than primary drives maintain behavioral patterns. *Activitas Nervosa Superior* (Praha), 22, 138–51.

Marston, A., Jacobs, D., Singer, R., Widaman, K., & Little, T. In press. Adolescents apparently invulnerable to drug, alcohol, and nicotine use. *Adolescence*.

Meyer, G. 1987. The stimulating effect of gambling. *Suchtgefahren*, 33, 102–109.

Milkman, H. B., & Shaffer, H. F. 1985. (eds.) *The Addictions: Multidisciplinary Perpectives and Treatments*. Lexington, Massachusetts: D. C. Heath & Company.

Moran, E. 1970. Gambling as a form of dependence. *British Journal of Addictions*, 64, 419–428.

Ogborne, A. 1974. Two types of heroin reactions. *British Journal of Addictions*, 39, 237–242.

Peele, S. 1977. Redefining addiction I: Making addiction a scientifically and socially useful concept. *International Journal of Health Services*, 7, 103–124.

—————. 1979. Redefining addiction II: The meaning of addiction in our lives. *Journal of Psychedelic Drugs*, 11, 289–297.

—————. 1986. The implications and limitations of genetic models of alcoholism and other addictions. *Journal of Studies on Alcohol*, Vol. 47, (1).

Petrie, A. 1967; 1978. *Individuality in pain and suffering*. Chicago: University of Chicago Press.

Robins, L. N. 1973. *A followup of Vietnam Drug Users*. Washington, D.C.: U.S. Government Printing Office.

—————. 1974. The Vietnam user returns. *Final Report: Special Action Office,*

Monograph Series A, No. 2. Washington, D.C.: U.S. Government Printing Office.

———. 1978. The interaction of setting and predisposition in explaining novel behavior: Drug initiations before, in, and after Vietnam. In D. Kandel (ed.) *Longitudinal Research on Drug Use: Empirical Findings and Methodological Issues,* 179–196. New York: Hemisphere-Halsted Press.

Roy, A., Adinoff, B., Roehrich, L., Lamparski, D., Custer, R., Lorenz, V., Barbaccia, M., Buibotti, A., Costa, E., & Kinnoila, M. 1988. Pathological gambling: A psycho-biological study. *Archives of General Psychiatry, 45,* 369–373.

Sanders, S. 1986. The Perceptual alteration scale: A scale measuring dissociation. *American Journal of Clinical Hypnosis,* Vol. 29, (2), 95–102.

Sullivan, H. S. 1956. *Clinical Studies in Psychiatry* (38–76 and 63–64). New York: Norton.

Taber, J. I. 1982. Group psychotherapy with pathological gamblers. In W. R. Eadington (ed.) *The Gambling Papers: Proceedings of the Fifth National Conference on Gambling and Risk Taking.* Reno: University of Nevada.

———. 1984. Gambling behavior. In R. J. Corsini (ed.) *Encyclopedia of Psychology,* (Vol. 2, 43–46). New York: Wiley.

Thomas, A., & Chess, S. 1984. Genesis and evolution of behavioral disorders: From infancy to early adult life. *American Journal of Psychiatry.* 141:1, 1–9.

Walker, A. L., & Lidz, C. W. 1983. Common features of troublesome habitual behaviors: A cultural approach. In P. Levison et al. (eds.) *Commonalities in Substance Abuse and Habitual Behavior.* Lexington, Massachusetts: D.C. Heath & Company.

Wolfgang, A. K. 1988. Gambling as a function of gender and sensation seeking. *Journal of Gambling Behavior, 4,* 71–77.

Zuckerman, M. 1969. Theories of sensory deprivation I. In J. P. Zubek (ed.) *Sensory Deprivation: Fifteen Years of Research. New York: Appleton-Century Crofts.*

———. 1979. *Sensation Seeking: Beyond the Optimal Level of Arousal.* New Jersey: Lawrence Erlbaum Associates.

3

A Developmental Approach to Understanding Compulsive Gambling Behavior

Sharon A. Stein, Ed.M., M.A.

Introduction

The questions that most plague researchers and treatment providers who study compulsive gambling behavior are these: Why do compulsive gamblers continue to engage in behavior that is so clearly harmful to themselves? Why do they continue to spend money at the very thing that caused their financial troubles in the first place? Even more puzzling, when certain gamblers recognize that they are losing money at a rate that produces severe financial difficulties that may lead to prison or death, why do they continue to gamble? These questions all point out the irrationality, at least economically, of compulsive gambling behavior.

Several models from psychological theory attempt to answer why gamblers continue to gamble despite terrible cost to themselves and their families. This chapter draws upon Piaget's (1954/1957) interactive theory of cognitive development to integrate various existing models of compulsive gambling. As will be shown, the "irrationality" of compulsive gambling has an order to it that makes sense to compulsive gamblers at the time each bet is placed. A new epistemology regarding gambling behavior must be developed for compulsive gamblers to discontinue their destructive behavior pattern.

Thanks are extended to Blase Gambino, Howard Shaffer, and Michelle Bowdler for comments on earlier drafts of this chapter.

Preparation of this chapter was supported, in part, by a contract (#2322905893) from the Massachusetts Department of Public Health.

Requests for reprints should be sent to Sharon Stein, Center for Addiction Studies, Department of Psychiatry, Harvard Medical School at the Cambridge Hospital, 1493 Cambridge Street, Cambridge, Mass. 02139.

Models of Compulsive Gambling Behavior

As noted by Rosenthal (1987), three major types of theoretical models have attempted to explain compulsive gambling: the psychodynamic or Freudian, which views the problem as being within the gambler's psyche or personality (Freud 1928; Bergler 1958; Rosenthal 1986); the behavioral, which explains compulsive gambling by schedules and contingencies of reinforcement (Skinner 1974; Dickerson 1979, 1984); and the physiological or psychobiological, which looks for measurable biological differences between compulsive gamblers and noncompulsive individuals to explain excessive gambling behavior (Carlton & Goldstein 1987; Jacobs 1987; Roy, Adinoff, Roehrich, Lamparski, Custer, Lorenz, Barbaccia, Guidotti, Costa & Linnoila 1988). One can also add the sociological perspective as a fourth explanatory perspective. However, sociologists tend to observe compulsive gambling behavior without interpreting it as being necessarily "compulsive" or even necessarily destructive or irrational, preferring instead to assume that gamblers gain certain satisfaction or pleasure out of the activity, otherwise they would not do it (Oldman 1978; Herman 1976; Campbell 1976; Rosecrance 1988). As will be discussed, the definition of behavior as "out of control" depends greatly on who is viewing the behavior. The sociological perspective seems to be more descriptive than interpretive, using gamblers' descriptions of their own behavior (Oldman 1978; Rosecrance 1988; Lesieur 1984), whereas the psychological models are used mainly by providers of treatment, and take an outside, interpretive viewpoint.

Each of the psychological models of compulsive gambling looks in a different "place" to find the source of the destructive gambling behavior. As a result, none of the models can make much use of the information the other models offer. Psychodynamic theory suggests that the compulsive gambler has an unconscious wish to lose (Bergler 1958). Behavioral theories argue that the variable-ratio schedule of reinforcement that occurs in gambling is the one of the most elusive and compelling patterns of rewarding behavior, and that gamblers are "reinforced" to act the way they do (Skinner 1953, 1974; Knapp 1976; Dickerson 1979). While psychodynamic theory looks to an internal source for the repetitive, excessive behavior, behavioral theory looks for external, environmental sources. Both theories agree that self-destructive gambling behavior is compulsive and that compulsive gamblers cannot "voluntarily" control their behavior. However, psychodynamic theory places the source of the compulsive behavior inside the gambler's head; physiological theories place the source within the gambler's body; and behavioral theories place the source within the game itself. As Shaffer (this volume) points out, the field of compulsive gambling is in conceptual crisis because the very same data, the behavior of compulsive gamblers, yields multiple causal interpretations.

A Developmental Approach

This chapter proposes an alternative way of viewing compulsive gambling behavior that incorporates key aspects of psychodynamic, behavioral, and sociological perspectives. Although the physiological model will not be taken up here, the proposed developmental approach has implications for a physiological model as well. Compulsive gambling behavior may be viewed as a symptom of a cognitive developmental delay in the transition from adolescence to adulthood. Using the Piagetian stage model of development as a theoretical starting point, this chapter argues that compulsive gamblers appear to use ways of thinking regarding their gambling and themselves that are normally abandoned by mature adult thinkers.

The self-enclosed system of options and involvement (Lesieur 1979, 1984) describes the limited way compulsive gamblers view solutions to their financial problems. Because this cognitive system is closed to creative problem-solving strategies, the limited system of the compulsive gambler is likely to be demonstrably delayed compared to normal adult cognitive development. The problem-solving strategies that compulsive gamblers use to gain pleasure or diminish pain through gambling are equivalent to those used by developmentally normal early adolescents, as will be shown below.

The developmental model that follows can also explain how long-term recovery from compulsive gambling occurs as compulsive gamblers escape the closed system of options and involvement (Lesieur 1979, 1984). To escape the closed system, recovering gamblers undergo a developmental change that involves the interaction of both gamblers' understanding of their gambling behavior, and a supportive environment of people who share similar beliefs. The result of this interaction is that gamblers will learn to abstain from or control their gambling. Just as an interaction of the gambler's internal belief system about gambling and the external environmental factors of the game itself originally causes the compulsive gambling behavior, new internal and external factors interact to contribute to recovery.

This internal change can best be understood as a developmental stage change. During recovery, compulsive gamblers come to understand their behavior and the way their behavior affects, or does not affect, the outcome of a bet in a completely different way. One result of this new epistemology is that placing bets becomes less desirable. This developmental approach to compulsive gambling is basically consistent with Custer's (1982, 1987) model of compulsive gambling and recovery. The additional information the developmental model adds is that compulsive gambling is not radically inconsistent or aberrant from normal adult development. This developmental model also can explain why recovery can occur at any "phase" in a gambler's career, not just after a desperation phase. It can also explain why some formerly "compulsive" gamblers may be able to learn to gamble in a controlled way after they change their ways of thinking and their motivation for gambling (Rosecrance 1988).

The remainder of this chapter proceeds in two parts. First, before presenting the Piagetian developmental model, it is important to give a generally agreed-upon definition of compulsive gambling behavior, and to discuss the issues that surround the definition. Descriptions of compulsive gambling behavior are taken from Gamblers Anonymous Twenty Questions and the American Psychiatric Association's (1987) *Diagnostic and Statistical Manual*, Third edition, Revised (DSM-III-R) diagnostic manual, to provide a picture of prototypical compulsive gambler. Secondly, the general description of observed behavior in compulsive gamblers will be explained according to an adapted version of the Piagetian developmental model.

Descriptions and Definitions of Compulsive Gambling Behavior

Throughout this chapter, the terms "compulsive gambling," "pathological gambling," and "addiction to gambling," will be used interchangeably to describe the same phenomenon as defined below. Since various models of compulsive gambling are currently used to explain the same prototypical behavior, it is difficult to come to an agreed-upon "picture" of compulsive gambling behavior. The word "compulsive" seems to be the source of conflict for many clinicians and researchers, because it implies an inability to control behavior, whereas the term "pathological" gambler is considered to be more descriptive (Knapp & Lech 1987). Many clinicians observe gamblers who are well in control of their behavior at certain times and in certain situations. However, most models agree that there is a *problem* for a gamblers who end up losing more money than they wish to (Oldman 1978). Rosecrance (this volume) also recognizes the problem for gamblers who spend more money on gambling than they can afford to lose.

The only behavior defined here as "compulsive gambling behavior" is that in which gamblers engage despite their stated intention not to. Whenever there is a conflict between a gambler's stated intention, such as to not gamble, or to not gamble more than X amount, and the actual behavior, which violates the intention, this behavior can be considered "compulsive." Typically, when an individual looks back on the failure to act according to the earlier intention, the individual feels some remorse or regret. This definition of compulsion is different from behavior in which people truly change their minds and act differently from an earlier stated intention.

This simple definition of compulsion has the advantage of being embedded within the standard diagnostic instruments that currently define compulsive gambling, as will be shown. It also has an advantage because both the treatment provider and the compulsive gambler can share a common perspective on the gambler's behavior. If a gambler states some intention to limit or stop gambling, and then violates it, then at least a part of the gambler's "self" is out of the control of another part of the self. The fact that the gambler has stated an intention to limit gambling opens the possibility of shared reflection on the behavior from the point of view of both the treatment provider, or recovering G.A. member, and the gambler who is still gambling destructively. This shared perspective can grow, and as the gambler recovers, he or she will look back on the earlier gambling behavior as self-deceptive and "compulsive."

Some readers may argue that this definition is too narrow. For example, Custer & Milt (1985) say compulsive gambling behavior may be recognized by a winning and a losing phase early in a compulsive gambler's career, before negative consequences have started to occur. Gamblers in the early phases are not likely to say they want to stop, because they see no reason to. Custer and others may argue that the behavior of these early gamblers is "compulsive" even before these gamblers say they want to stop, and these gamblers are in a strong state of denial. My response is that this label is useful neither to the gambler nor to the treatment provider, because there is no common understanding between the two of the gambling behavior as destructive or compulsive. Until gamblers recognize the self-destructiveness of their behavior and have some desire to change it, no development, or change, can occur.

However, compulsive gamblers in the early phases can be taught to see the consequences and the destructiveness of their behavior. Those in the social environment around destructive gambling can help to educate these gamblers about the costs of gambling. Spouses, children, or coworkers, who will not tolerate destruction to themselves, may be able to educate gamblers about the costs of excessive gambling. As the social costs increase, such as when the gambler is fired or the spouse leaves, the compulsive gambler may begin to have a desire to stop, or at least control the gambling. As will be shown below, the Twenty Questions of Gamblers Anonymous, and the *Diagnostic and Statistical Manual*, Third edition, Revised, (DSM-III-R), of the American Psychiatric Association (1987), all contain this shorter definition of compulsive gambling within their diagnostic criteria.

Gamblers Anonymous Twenty Questions

Twenty Questions were developed by Gamblers Anonymous to help problem gamblers diagnose themselves and decide whether they need help.

This list identifies particular behaviors and situations in which the proto-typical compulsive gambler is engaged in or involved. Most compulsive gamblers will answer yes to at least seven of the following questions (Custer & Custer 1978):

1. Do you lose time from work due to gambling?
2. Is gambling making your home life unhappy?
3. Is gambling affecting your reputation?
4. Have you ever felt remorse after gambling?
5. Do you ever gamble to get money with which to pay debts or to otherwise solve financial difficulties?
6. Does gambling cause a decrease in your ambition or efficacy?
7. After losing, do you feel you must return as soon as possible and win back your losses?
8. After you win, do you have a strong urge to return and win more?
9. Do you often gamble until your last dollar is gone?
10. Do you ever borrow to finance your gambling?
11. Have you ever sold any real or personal property to finance gambling?
12. Are you reluctant to use "gambling money" for normal expendi-tures?
13. Does gambling make you careless of the welfare of your family?
14. Do you ever gamble longer than you had planned?
15. Do you ever gamble to escape worry or trouble?
16. Have you ever committed, or considered committing an illegal act to finance gambling?
17. Does gambling cause you to have difficulty sleeping?
18. Do arguments, disappointments, or frustrations create within you an urge to gamble?
19. Do you have an urge to celebrate any good fortune by a few hours of gambling?
20. Have you ever considered self-destruction as results of your gam-bling?

The questions, when viewed as twenty aspects of the compulsive gam-blers' "predicament" (Shaffer 1987), point out the cycle of negative and positive reinforcement for gambling behavior. Gambling is conceived of by the compulsive gambler as the only way to escape a financially desperate situation. Lesieur (1984) has called this phenomenon of throwing good money after bad "chasing." As questions 5, 7, 15, and 18 all emphasize, compulsive gamblers use gambling to escape bad situations, whether financial or emotional. However, compulsive gamblers also use gambling as a reward after positive experiences. Questions 8 and 19 emphasize that gambling is used to celebrate happy or rewarding occasions, so that gambling itself is seen as both to gain monetary rewards and as an inherently positively rewarding, or reinforcing, activity.

As compulsive gamblers become deeper in debt and despair, the options for getting out of debt appear more and more limited. Gambling becomes the only option for getting out of a financial mess, and yet is the main source of the financial debt in the first place (Lesieur 1984). Question 1 asks whether the gambler has missed time from work to gamble. Certainly any compulsive gambler would, since work takes too much time for too little a reward. The only option for making money fast enough to keep ahead of the loan sharks or police is to win it gambling, or steal it, or borrow more money. Work takes too much time.

It is probably at this point in most compulsive gamblers' careers, when gambling is recognized to be at once the main source of trouble and the only solution to financial problems, that compulsive gamblers may say they want to stop. Questions 4, 13, and 20 reveal that the compulsive gambler may have had glimpses of time when they gambled more than intended, or noticed that gambling was becoming self-destructive. This moment of having "conflicted desires" is important because it means that the closed system of options and involvement (Lesieur 1979, 1984) has begun to disintegrate. This conflict of motives will be explored more fully below.

The DSM-III-R offers a fairly concrete, behavioral definition of pathological gambling consistent with the criteria for substance dependence disorders. According to the DSM-III-R, at least four of the following diagnostic criteria must be met to identify the pathological gambler:

1. Frequent occupation with gambling or obtaining money to gamble;

2. Frequent gambling of large amounts or over a longer period than the individual intended;

3. A need to increase the size or frequency of bets to achieve desired excitement;

4. Restlessness or irritability if unable to gamble;

5. Repeated loss of money by gambling and returning another day to win back losses (chasing);

6. Repeated efforts to reduce or stop gambling;

7. Frequent gambling when expected to fulfill social or occupational obligations;

8. Sacrifice of some important social, occupational, or recreational activities given up to gamble;

9. Continuation of gambling despite an inability to pay mounting debts, or despite other significant social, occupational, or legal problems that the person knows to be exacerbated by gambling.

The DSM-III-R criteria highlight many of the same behaviors as the Twenty Questions. The pathological gambler seems to be caught in a behavioral trap because of the repeated efforts to relieve symptoms, which in turn create more symptoms. Point 8 mentions that compulsive gamblers often act in ways contrary to the expectations of the culture, as stated in most city, state, and federal laws, as well as social norms. This implies that pathological gamblers do not share quite the same values as the society around them does. Points 2 and 6 state that pathological gamblers may act in ways contrary to the verbal desires that they express during earlier points in time. These two points will be discussed more fully later, under compulsive gambling as a "conflict of motives," and compulsive gambling as "loss of control."

Compulsive Gambling as a "Conflict of Motives"

The DSM-III-R criteria points 2 and 6 mention that pathological gamblers appear to act in ways they do not really intend. This suggests that at one point in time gamblers want to control their gambling, but at a later point make the crucial decision to go beyond their own original limit. This decision is a temporary resolution of a conflict of motives, because for a brief period, the impulse to gamble has won out over the impulse to refrain. As Custer & Milt (1985) discuss, at the moment of choice the decision to gamble is egosyntonic. However, the conflict of motives is sure to return in the form of regret when more money is lost. As long as the gambler has some knowledge that gambling is partly to blame for financial difficulties, a conflict will be present.

This type of conflict is most evident in the behavior of those who enter treatment for gambling. Most gamblers who enter gambling treatment programs have in some way asked for help with their addiction, thereby stating a desire to stop, but have not yet demonstrated control or abstinence prior to entering treatment. To a nonaddicted person, this seems contradictory. "Why don't these people just stop gambling?" Such behavior is baffling to our culture, which relies heavily on the concept of personal responsibility. One consequence is the reliance on simple explanations for the behavior, such as to call it being "out of control," or "a disease." This view resolves the problem of individual responsibility for many laypersons, but as will be shown next, it poses important issues for the treatment provider.

Personal Responsibility and "Loss of Control"

One of the central assumptions that any model of compulsive or addictive behavior must address is whether the authors of the model believe that the compulsive gambler or addict has "lost control" (Marlatt 1985; Shaffer 1986). The term "loss of control" entails a judgment of one person by another regarding the other's inability or unwillingness to control themselves. That an individual is "out of control" is an assessment by the nonaddicted treatment provider, or by the recovering gambler, and often is *not* shared by the compulsive gambler who is to be "helped." Oldman (1978) had an interest in "how the idea of compulsion can come to form part of how some people theorize about the gambling activities of themselves and others (p. 349)." Paradoxically, gamblers who are able to admit that they want to stop their destructive gambling but cannot see how to do it feel trapped, but they have taken the first step to freeing themselves of the compulsive gambling trap. To admit that there might be another solution to a problem that one just has not discovered yet is the first step toward finding the solution.

The theoretical model that the treatment provider holds of who is responsible for the problem of compulsive gambling, and how that person can best be helped, will determine what happens in the interaction between the two (Brickman, Rabinowitz, Karuza, Coates, Cohn & Kidder 1982). This interaction is important and its outcome can result in an epistemological change for compulsive gamblers, in which they may look back on their previous behavior as "out of control," just as recovering gamblers in GA, or recovering alcoholics in AA look back on their previous behavior as "unmanageable." (Gamblers Anonymous 1984; Alcoholics Anonymous 1939). The problem with most models of responsibility is that they view the compulsive gambler as a holistic being who is either completely responsible or completely not responsible for the gambling behavior. If we think of the term "responsibility" as literally being "able to respond," the compulsive gamblers' behavior is "response" gone awry, because there seems to be no other alternative than to gamble. In my view, the compulsive gambler is only "out of control" because at the precise moment of choosing to bet, the gambler does not see that it is necessary or worthwhile not to bet. This fact is especially significant if the gambler earlier has recognized that gambling is not in his or her best self-interest, but at the moment of choice thinks it is. Part of the environmental support of treatment is to provide examples of other ways to respond in that crucial moment of choice, as well as to create internal motivation for stopping or controlling gambling behavior.

This interaction between the self, or parts of the self, and the environment, between things that are in and out of one's control or understanding, is the essence of what makes all human beings develop and evolve. The seemingly contradictory behavior that compulsive gamblers exhibit when they claim to want to avoid the negative consequences of gambling, but still do not change their behavior, can be explained by developmental stage theory. The fact that a conflict exists within each individuals' mind indicates that the individuals are in the process of changing a theory about their behavior, or the way they understand their behavior. The conflict can become a crisis of understanding for the individual, which creates an opportunity for growth (Kegan 1982). With proper environmental support that continues to point out the adverse and destructive consequences of the compulsive behavior, the crisis can become a turning point and the compulsive behavior begins to stop (Shaffer & Jones 1989). The individual may then learn a new way to manage his or her destructive behavior, which becomes classified by the individual's new epistemological theory as "compulsive." As will be defined later, the crisis and turning point seem to occur for individuals as their thinking and problem-solving strategies become transformed from strategies that use concrete operations to those that use full formal operations.

Piaget's Development Stage Model as Applied to Compulsive Gambling Behavior and Recovery

Jean Piaget spent most of his life observing the way children change, grow, and develop more and more complex problem-solving abilities. The general Piagetian stage model consists of six demonstrable stages of human development from birth to adulthood. Piaget (1937/1954) observed that as children learned to solve problems, their abilities were stratified across broad stage measurements, each of which were characterized by progressively more complex structures of thought, and problem-solving capacity. These broad stage measurements also roughly corresponded to age, but there could be variation among children of the same age. The first period, which covers three cognitive stages, Piaget observed, occurs before a child is two years old. This is called the sensory-motor period, in which children learn to grasp and coordinate objects as units separate from themselves. The other three stages Piaget (1937/1954) observed are the following: the stage of preoperational actions, or intuitive intelligence, in which children learn to name objects and make simple inferences about objects, such as that paint is wet and dogs have fur, occurs from approximately ages two to six years old. The stage of concrete intellectual operations, in which children coordinate dimensions in the physical and social world lasts from approximately age six to age fourteen; and finally, the stage of formal operations, in which adolescents and adults coordinate complex abstract concepts occurs for individuals age fourteen and older. For example, to fully understand in a game of roulette the relationship between a bet, its outcome, and the probability of winning or losing (Oldman 1974) requires formal operational stage thinking.

Each higher stage of understanding is developed through the process of "disequilibrium." Piaget (1937/1954) discovered that when a child perceives evidence that appears to be contradictory with his or her way of understanding the world, the conflict results in a disruption, or disequilibrium, of the child's way of making sense of how the world operates. This set of limitations in thinking that make up the child's epistemology Piaget called a "stage." One can observe behavior in which children solve problems using certain rules, and the children cannot solve problems that require more complicated rules than the child is capable of using. Stage is a measure of the complexity of the rules used by children and adults in solving problems (Commons, Stein & Richards 1987). The finite sets of rules of a particular stage are also used as individuals assimilate information from the environment. If the information from the environment is not contradictory to the way an individual understands it, there is no conflict. However, when disequilibrium occurs, it creates a crisis for the individual. If the contradictory information cannot be denied or regarded as false, the individual must change, or "accommodate," the way he or she thinks in order to make sense of the new information. This in turn, allows the finite system of rules to be expanded, so that more complicated ways of understanding behavior are allowed.

The term "stage" has a very technical meaning. According to Piaget, each transformation is like a Copernican revolution, in which an individual becomes decentered from his own actions. What was formerly an action that coordinated objects is transformed to become itself an object to be coordinated at the next higher stage (Commons, Stein & Richards 1987). This process for individuals is analogous to Kuhn's (1962) revolutions in science. Each new paradigm in science incorporates the older paradigm it has replaced; for example, Einstein's physical system incorporated Newtonian physics. Similarly, each earlier stage's rules of knowing are incorporated into the new, more complex stage, for an individual.

How Piagetian Stage Development Applies to Compulsive Gambling

A limited way of understanding the environment is built around gambling for the compulsive gambler (Custer 1982; Lesieur 1984). Gambling is considered a way to celebrate happy events, and to escape from negative events. Custer's (1982, 1987) model of compulsive gambling and recovery lists phases in the gambling cycle which lead to a crisis: the winning phase, a period of losing, and a desperation phase. Finally a crisis occurs in which compulsive gamblers face their destructive behavior and begin the road upward to recovery.

In Piagetian terms, this crisis, or "disequilibrium," occurs for the gambler when gambling, which was formerly perceived as a pleasure and an escape from pain, is itself understood to be the very source of great financial loss and emotional pain. This sudden realization is a true example of disequilibrium, in the same way that children undergo disequilibrium as they grow and develop. To develop a new way of understanding gambling behavior, compulsive gamblers must give up what they formerly thought—for example, that each bet was going to be the winning one, that luck had blessed them and singled them out to be winners. Each of these beliefs must be understood as being illusory. With the new understanding, formerly compulsive gamblers realize that the winnings occurred only because of pure chance, and not because of some special skill or special pact with fate that they possessed. This transformation, from being omnipotent, skillful, and powerful over games of chance, to being a mortal without superhuman gifts, occurs for gamblers in recovery. The game itself becomes transformed from existing on a moment-to-moment basis with each bet an opportunity, to becoming a series of losses with few gains. The gambler must view his total debit and credit sheet from the time his "career" began rather than at each bet as an isolated chance for instant riches. The emotional and intellectual change that occurs is consistent with a Piagetian stage change from using concrete operational thinking regarding gambling to using formal operational thinking.

Compulsive Gambling Results from Poor Problem-Solving Strategies

Most economic or utility theories of rational economic behavior assume that individuals act in accordance with their own self-interests, are goal-oriented, and rational (Eadington 1987). Although rational economic theory accepts that not everyone has the same goals, once a goal has been stated, then failure to act in a way to attain it is irrational. This section shows how using a concrete operational strategy in gambling will not result in maximal utility for the behavior performed, but a formal operational strategy will.

People who repeat a behavior to gain a desired end that is self-destructive behave in ways that a rational theory of choice cannot satisfactorily explain (Herrnstein 1988). Rational theory assumes an individual will choose to allocate behavior between alternatives in such a way as to maximize the total utility from the alternatives. In the case of gambling, a "rational" person would gamble only enough to gain the pleasurable sensation from gambling, whether it be the thrill of the game, or the winning of money, and would cease to gamble when the chance of incurring the negative side effects of gambling more than one can afford become sufficiently likely. However, to act in this way, the gambler must view the consequences of either placing a bet or not placing a bet from an "objective" viewpoint. This view must take in the possibilities of both outcomes, losing or winning, and be able to justify placing the bet with full knowledge of the consequences. This ability to hold in one's mind all possible outcomes, and understanding that the decision to bet yields with it a specified probability for each possible outcome, requires formal operational thinking in Piaget's scheme. This mental action is equivalent to isolating a causal variable among a matrix of possible causal variables by tracing each possibility of the variable to its outcome, which was one of the problems Piaget used to assess formal-operational ability.

Without this "objective" viewpoint from which one can weigh and evaluate hypothetical outcomes, an individual is literally powerless to resist a short-term reward (such as making a bet with the belief that this one will be the lucky win) over a reward that is farther away in (saving the money that could be bet to keep from losing it). Ainslie (1975, 1982, 1984) calls the reward that is nearer in time for behavior "specious" because it always looks better at the moment of choice than the reward that is farther away in time for an opposite behavior. This discounting of the long-term reward will occur unless one can hold constant the time element and simply compare the two rewards for behavior independently of the time they are to be given. The task of holding one variable constant while comparing it to others in relation to an outcome requires formal operational stage reasoning (Richards & Commons 1984).

An example of a compulsive gambler in action explains how the timing of rewards can influence behavior. A man may start a night of gambling intending to leave the casino when he has one hundred dollars left. This intention is highly motivated because he knows he has to pay a loan shark at least one hundred dollars the next day, and could be physically hurt if he does not pay. He ends up gambling away everything, which is inconsistent with his stated intentions. As soon as he made a bet in which he came close to losing more than the amount he was willing to lose, the man continued to gamble because the belief that this particular bet would win was more valued at the moment he made it than the more distant in time but highly valued reward of avoiding a beating from a loan shark. In this case, the behavior motivated by specious or short-term reward has life-threatening consequences.

Given only that the amount of the reward for not making the bet (that is, saving the one hundred dollars and avoiding a beating) is bigger than the amount of the reward for placing the bet (with the belief he will win), the man would not place the bet. However, because the reward for placing the bet is very close at hand, and the reward for paying the loan shark is eight hours in the future, a person using concrete operations (that is, action causes reward) will place the bet. The time delay between the rewards for the two behaviors makes the man unable to resist unless some other constraint appears, such as a friend who physically keeps him from placing the bet or holds the money for him.

Ainslie (1984) states that two highly motivated behaviors can be viewed as having two separate interests, or reward groups, one smaller and earlier in time, and one delayed. The reinforcement effectiveness of a given reward increases at a hyperbolic rate as the time draws near for the reward to be given. When a conflict between a smaller, earlier reward and a larger, delayed reward occurs, the short-term reward looks like a much better alternative than the long-term reward at the moment of choice. The point on the plot in figure 3–1 where the curves cross is the point at which the smaller reward takes on greater motivational effectiveness than the opposite behavior.

The matching law (Herrnstein 1961, 1970) predicts that when an organism is faced with two alternatives, it will choose to act in a ratio of the two that matches the reinforcement gained from the combination of alternatives. This equation can be written as follows:

$$\frac{B1}{B1 + B2} = \frac{R1}{R1 + R2} \tag{1}$$

B1 is the number of responses of type 1, (for example, the gambler's placing a bet with his last one hundred dollars) and B2 is the number of responses of type 2, (for example, not placing the bet.) Similarly, R1 is the amount of reinforcement obtained by making response type 1, (the amount of pleasure or avoidance of pain received from placing the bet) and R2 is the amount of reinforcement for making response type 2 (the amount of pleasure or avoidance of pain by saving the one hundred dollars). Because the reward for betting (including whatever reinforcer accompanies it for the individual) is always closer in time than the reward for not making a bet, the delay in time plays a role in discounting the perception of the reward.

The matching law can be rewritten so that the amount, frequency, and delay of the rewards for two opposite behaviors, such as placing a bet or not placing one, are explicit in the equation (Ainslie 1975, 1982, 1984). The equation is as follows:

$$\frac{B}{B'} = \frac{A}{A'} * \frac{R}{R'} * \frac{T-t}{T'-t} \tag{2}$$

Where t is the moment the choice is made; B is the behavior to obtain one alternative, and B' is the behavior to achieve the other; A's are the amounts of the rewards for each alternative, R's are the rates of the rewards, and T's are the times the rewards become available.

From the plot in figure 3–1, we can see how someone who enjoys the effects of betting because of the belief that he will win, and is not *at the same time* aware that the good feelings (or relief from pain) of the moment could lead to destructive consequences, is virtually powerless to resist placing a bet at the point where the lines cross. When the desire for both behaviors (betting and not betting) is very strong, the conflict is excruciating for an individual.

For the gambler to avoid the trap of the specious reward when faced with losing his last one hundred dollars, he must use formal operational stage reasoning. The gambler must weigh the consequences of the risk of losing against the chances of winning to see which is bigger, independently of the time factor that discounts the risk of losing. With time held constant, and a realistic view of the chances of winning, the gambler would be acting against his other own self-interest to place the bet. However, for a gambler using concrete operations, who is not thinking about all of the possible future consequences of his present behavior, it seems logical and rational to place the bet.

Given that a gambler using concrete operations has an inability to choose not to bet when the opportunity is nearby, how do any compulsive gamblers manage to abstain from betting? How does development to formal operational thinking occur? The next section will discuss possible answers to that question.

Developing Formal Operational Strategies for Gambling Behavior

The problem of "weakness of the will" for the gambler using concrete operations is clear. As long as the larger reward of living an economically more stable life by not gambling is far in the future, the specious reward of making the "big win" right now will be a stronger motivator for behavior. This is true no matter how large the motivation for not gambling. The task then becomes controlling the environment so that the specious reward of placing a bet is never very nearby in time. However, this is very difficult to do. Most gamblers can find some way of making a bet if they so desire. What needs to happen is that one must learn to change the motivation for gambling, the desire for a stable, pleasant life

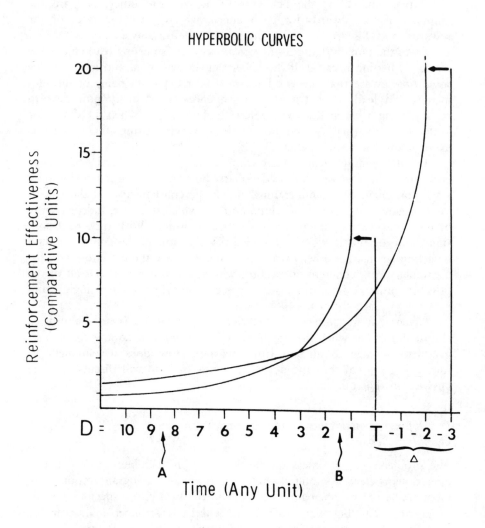

Figure 3–1.

From Ainslie (1984)

must become more important than making a big win, to somehow prove that one is powerful over fate and chance. Custer & Milt (1985) also emphasize that the compulsive gambler's values change as they progress in recovery.

Motivational Conflict Generates Development

When two highly motivated behaviors are contradictory, as in the motivation to place a bet, or not to place a bet, they cannot both occur at the same time. Each behavior must compete for expression. Even though the gambler's temporary change of preference explains the existence of both behaviors, these behaviors are expressed by the same person, which is why the person feels conflict about wanting both of them. The only factor that allows them both to exist is the time difference. When holding time constant, one behavior (betting one hundred dollars) cannot occur with the opposite behavior (saving one hundred dollars) within the same person. The task, therefore, for the gambler *who is also equally or more motivated to stop gambling*, is to hold time constant whenever he feels the desire to gamble. By doing this, the gambler can say, "For this day only, what do I want more, to place a bet or not place a bet?" If the reward for gambling is perceived to be greater than the reward for not gambling, then abstinence will win out. The slogan from Gamblers Anonymous, "One day at a time," is applicable. Members are encouraged to alter the slogan to "one minute at a time" if needed.

The task of holding one variable in an equation constant while comparing two or more additional variables requires formal operational stage reasoning. Instead of seeing gambling or not gambling as two separate things to be controlled, compulsive gamblers' must transform their view to see the whole *relationship* between gambling and not gambling as one object. By restructuring this view, gamblers can see that whenever they place a bet with the belief that this bet will be a winner, they cannot control their ability to stop betting. The present and future rewards for opposite behaviors become viewed as part of one package. Therefore, taking one bet with the hope of winning this one time, when repeated, becomes the first behavior in a chain leading toward total destruction. When viewed this way, the behavior of taking one bet becomes something one is highly motivated to avoid.

With the developmental stage change to formal operations for compulsive gamblers, the perceived reward for gambling behavior is also changed. Just as the recovering gambler can see the first bet as a step in a chain of repeated betting behaviors that should be avoided, the hoped-for "reward" of a big win is no longer the main motivation in life. The gambler now sees that the reward for behavior is not simply a good feeling for a moment while a bet is placed, but the concept of living a longer, healthier life by avoiding a higher probability of bankruptcy, prison, or death is even more richly rewarding and longer lasting.

Gamblers Anonymous as Environment That Supports Development

Because there is no cultural norm or rule in this society that says any normal adult would need to abstain from making fast money, and in fact this ideal is encouraged by American society, it is very difficult for gamblers to quit gambling by themselves even though they may feel conflict about their gambling behavior. When the formal operational stage solution to the problem of whether to gamble is externally supported by the social environment, the gambler's behavior is very likely to change. Gamblers Anonymous is a program of men and women who encourage one another to stop their formerly compulsive and destructive gambling behavior.

The first step of Gamblers Anonymous is phrased to transform gamblers perception of their gambling behavior: "We admitted we were powerless over gambling, that our lives had become unmanageable." The admittance of powerlessness by the gambler reveals how powerful the specious reward really is, and simultaneously makes it less desirable. Why place a bet if the reality is that you are powerless over the outcome? Also, because the other members in GA have admitted their powerlessness over gambling, validity is created for the entering gambler's perception of his or her own powerlessness.

The only requirement for membership in Gamblers Anonymous is the desire to stop gambling. Membership in the program itself supports nongambling behavior because the desire to stop is the only requirement. Unlike religious or political organizations that actively promote their cause, the public relations policy of GA is based on attraction rather than promotion. Therefore, people who join the program are those who already have some desire to stop gambling and have been unable to.

Support for the desire to stop gambling is already present when a potential member walks through the door to a meeting of GA. All that members of the program must do is encourage the quitting behavior. Older members of the program know that the newcomer's act of coming to a meeting must immediately be reinforced. They greet the newcomer and offer him or her coffee. As the older members tell of their former behavior, the newcomer is encouraged to identify the behaviors they share. One slogan of GA is "identify, do not compare." The newcomer listens to the stories of the older members who were just like him before they joined GA. By seeing how the older members changed through taking part of this program, the newcomer is given the hope that he too may change his behavior. In GA this is called the power of example. Psychologists call it learning through observation.

Not all compulsive gamblers recover by joining twelve-step programs like GA. It may be true that some formerly compulsive gamblers can recover naturally and spontaneously without any sort of formal intervention or support group, as cocaine addicts have been demonstrated to do (Shaffer & Jones 1989). Similarly, not everyone must have abstinence as the goal of their recovery. Rosecrance (this volume; 1988) has found that some individuals diagnosed as compulsive gamblers can later develop the ability to gamble in a controlled way with peer support.

Abstinence Versus Controlled Gambling

Earlier, abstinence was portrayed as the goal of the gambler who enters GA. The requirement is that one has a desire to *stop* gambling, not just cut down or control one's gambling. Given how highly reinforcing gambling is for those diagnosed as compulsive gamblers, abstinence is probably necessary at least for the period when individuals are struggling to make sense of the relationship between gambling and its consequences. However, with the developmental model suggested above, it seems theoretically possible for a person who can reflect on the relationship between a bet and its outcome to develop controls over his or her behavior. Control means that the formerly compulsive gambler can learn to bet only a limited amount, and this limit cannot be exceeded without creating a potentially dangerous situation. The limit does not have to be abstinence, necessarily. However, many recovering gamblers say that betting small, limited amounts of money has no excitement for them, so it makes no sense for them to try to bet in a social or controlled way.

Similarly, even members of GA who choose never to gamble again, need to make a distinction for themselves between risk-taking behavior and gambling (Thomas Cummings, personal communication, December 12, 1988). As Zinberg notes (this volume), recovering gamblers cannot possibly cease all risk-taking behavior in the same way that alcoholics can completely stop drinking alcohol. However, recovering gamblers who use formal operational reasoning when deciding whether to take a risk are not likely to become compulsive. Decisions made under uncertainty that take into account the possible losses and gains for each option, as well as the probability of each option occurring, are made on a rational, not compulsive, basis.

Development of the Self: Holistic or Fragmented?

While making the argument that formal operational reasoning is a requirement for recovery from compulsive gambling, we have avoided another complicated issue. Many compulsive gamblers exhibit high intelligence in decision making, intelligence that would be considered formal operational in situations other than gambling. Compulsive gamblers are thought to have higher-than-average IQs (Custer & Milt 1985). It seems odd that gamblers would not apply their high intelligence to areas regarding gambling behavior, to assess whether making a bet is a wise option. However, compulsive gamblers seldom keep track of winnings or losses (Custer & Milt 1985) which would contribute to their making formal operational decisions in their gambling choices.

Research remains to be done on whether the self develops in a fragmented or a holistic way, and how much environmental variables contribute to the developmental stage of a person's decision-making strategies. Gardner's (1983) notion of multiple intelligences points to the idea that one can be at a higher stage in one area of life and a lower stage in another. Other developmental stage theorists believe that the self is holistic, and that the stage of problem solving in one area transfers to another area of a person's life (Piaget 1937/54; Kegan 1982). At least for compulsive gamblers, it appears that different parts of the self develop at different rates, and that one part of the self can be operating at a higher stage than another part of the self, as when one part wants to stop gambling and the other part continues to do it. However, the environmental conditions surrounding gambling behavior may somehow be associated with people using a lower stage of problem solving than they are normally capable of. Future research should collect data on the developmental stage of gambling strategies for compulsive gamblers in and out of a gambling environment, and in different problem-solving domains, to shed light on these questions.

Conclusion

Why do compulsive gamblers continue to gamble despite destructive consequences? This chapter argues that at the moment before a compulsive gambler chooses to place each bet, placing the bet appears to be a better choice than not placing it. To realize the destructiveness and irrationality of compulsive gambling, the gambler must undergo a change in perception so that placing a bet no longer appears to be the best decision at each moment of choice. The change in understanding of gambling behavior that recovering compulsive gamblers experience is a developmental stage change from concrete to formal operational strategies in Piaget's (1937/54) theory.

This developmental model of compulsive gambling behavior has an advantage of incorporating aspects of psychodynamic and behaviorial theories of compulsive gambling. Psychodynamic theories are concerned with human beings' internal drives and ego structures, while behavioral theories are concerned with humans' behavioral responses to rewards or punishment from the environment. The developmental model conceptualizes human beings in constant interaction with the environment—both as active beings who shape the environment and passive beings who are shaped by it. The internal factors are the individual's mind set, the way he or she conceptualizes the behavior. The external factors are the responses the environment makes to the individual's behavior, such as the outcome of the bet whether it be positive or negative.

Compulsive behavior is the result of a combination of internal (cognitive and emotional) and external (environmental) factors. When either factor is changed, such as when gamblers realize they really have no control over the whims of fate, they are powerless over gambling; or such as when gamblers are physically barred from any gambling activity, the behavior will stop.

The fact that either alternative will stop the compulsive behavior explains why there are seemingly opposite views about how to treat compulsive gambling. Some treatment providers for compulsive gambling claim that the gambler must cease all contact with gambling activities (Nora, this volume; Blume 1987). This is understandable, because abstinence from gambling stops the environmental influences—the positive and negative reward system that seems to control the gambler's behavior. But internal states also contribute to the compulsive gambler's predicament. Others have the view that controlled gambling is possible when gamblers learn to understand their gambling behavior and change their bad strategies and *motivation* in gambling (Oldman 1978; Rosecrance 1988). More research regarding internal cognitive stage and external environmental influences should be carried out to determine more effective strategies for treating compulsive gambling.

References

Ainslie, G. 1975. Specious reward: A behavioral theory of impulsiveness and impulse control. *Psychological Bulletin 82*, 463–96.
———. 1982. A behavioral economic approach to the defense mechanisms: Freud's energy theory revisited. *Social Science Information 21*, 735–79.

————. 1984. Behavioral economics II: Motivated involuntary behavior. *Social Science Information* 23, 735–79.

Alcoholics Anonymous. 1939. New York: Alcoholics Anonymous World Services Inc.

American Psychiatric Association. 1987. *Diagnostic and statistical manual of mental disorders.* 3rd Edition., rev. Washington D. C.

Becker, H. S. 1960. Notes on the concept of commitment. *American Journal of Sociology* 66, 32–40.

Bergler, E. 1958. *The psychology of gambling.* New York: International University Press.

Blume, S. B. 1987. Compulsive gambling and the medical model. *Journal of Gambling Behavior* 3(4), 237–247.

Brickman, P., Rabinowitz, V. C., Karuza, J., Coates, D., Cohn, E., & Kidder, L. 1982. Models of helping and coping. *American Psychologist* 37(4), 368–384.

Campbell, F. F. 1976. Gambling: A positive view. In W. R. Eadington (ed.) *Gambling and society* (218–228). Springfield, Illinois: Charles C. Thomas.

Carlton, P. L., & Goldstein, L. 1987. Physiological determinants of pathological gambling. In T. Galski (ed.) *The handbook of pathological gambling* (111–122). Springfield, Illinois: Charles C. Thomas.

Commons, M. L., Stein, S. A., & Richards, F. A. 1987, April. *A general model of stage theory: Stage of a task.* Paper presented at the meeting of the Society for Research in Child Development, Baltimore, Maryland.

Custer, R. L. 1982. Pathological gambling. In A. Whitfield (ed.) *Patients with alcoholism and other drug problems.* New York: Year Book Publishers.

————. 1987. The diagnosis and scope of pathological gambling. In T. Galski (ed.) *The handbook of pathological gambling* (3–7). Springfield, Illinois: Charles C. Thomas.

Custer, R. L., & Custer, L. F. 1978. Characteristics of the recovering compulsive gambler: A survey of 150 members of Gamblers Anonymous. Paper presented at the Fourth National Conference on Gambling, Reno, Nevada, December 1978.

Custer, R. L. & Milt, H. 1985. *When luck runs out.* New York: Warner Books, Inc.

Dickerson, M. G. 1979. FI schedules and persistence at gambling in the UK betting office. *Journal of Applied Behavior Analysis,* 12, 315–23.

Dickerson, M. G., & Weeks, D. 1979. Controlled gambling as a therapeutic technique for compulsive gamblers. *Journal of Behavior Therapy and Experimental Psychiatry,* 10, 139–41.

Dickerson, M. G. 1984. *Compulsive gamblers.* London: Longman.

Eadington, W. R. 1987. Economic perceptions of gambling behavior. *Journal of Gambling Behavior* 3(4), 264–273.

Freud, S. 1928. Dostoyevsky and parricide. In Strachey, J. (ed. and trans.) *The complete psychological works of Sigmund Freud,* Standard Edition. London: Hogarth Press, 1961, vol. XIX, 157–170.

Gamblers Anonymous 1984 (3rd Edition) Los Angeles: Gamblers Anonymous Publishing.

Gardner, H. 1983. *Frames of mind.* New York: Basic Books.

Herman, R. D. 1976. Motivations to gamble: The model of Roger Caillois. In W. R. Eadington (ed.) *Gambling and society* (207–217). Springfield, Illinois: Charles C. Thomas.

Herrnstein, R. J. 1961. Relative and absolute strength of response as a function of frequency of reinforcement. *Journal of the Experimental Analysis of Behavior,* 4, 267–272.

———. 1970. On the law of effect. *Journal of the Experimental Analysis of Behavior,* 13, 243–266.

———. 1988. Lost and found: One self. *Ethics* 98 566–578.

Jacobs, D. 1987. A general theory of addictions: Application to treatment and rehabilitation planning for pathological gamblers. In T. Galski (ed.) *The handbook of pathological gambling* (169–194). Springfield, Illinois: Charles C. Thomas.

Kegan, R. 1982. *The evolving self.* Cambridge, Massachusetts: Harvard University Press.

Knapp, T. 1976. A functional analysis of gambling behavior. In W. R. Eadington (ed.) *Gambling and society* (276–294). Springfield, Illinois: Charles C. Thomas.

Knapp, T. J., & Lech, B.C. 1987. Pathological gambling: A review and recommendations. *Advances in Behavior Research & Therapy* 9, 21–49.

Kuhn, T. S. 1962. *The structure of scientific revolutions.* Chicago: University of Chicago Press.

Lesieur, H. R. 1984. *The chase: Career of the compulsive gambler.* Cambridge, Massachusetts: Schenkman Publishers.

———. 1979. The compulsive gambler's spiral of options and involvement. *Psychiatry: Journal for the Study of Interpersonal Processes,* 42, 79–87.

Marlatt, G. A. 1985. Part I. Relapse prevention: General overview. In G. A. Marlatt & J. R. Gordon (eds.) *Relapse prevention: Maintenance strategies in the treatment of addictive disorders.* New York: The Guilford Press.

Oldman, D. 1974. Chance and skill: A study of roulette. *Sociology* 8, 407–426.

———. 1978. Compulsive gamblers. *Sociological Review* 26, 349 370.

Piaget, J. 1954. *The construction of reality in the child.* (Margaret Cook trans.) New York: Basic Books. (Originally published in French in 1937.)

Piaget, J., and Inhelder, B. 1958. *The growth of logical thinking from childhood to adolescence.* (Anne Parsons and Stanley Milgram trans.) New York: Basic Books. (Originally published in French in 1955.)

Richards, F. A., & Commons, M. L. 1984. Systematic, metasystematic, and cross-paradigmatic reasoning: A case for stages of reasoning beyond formal operations. In M. L. Commons, F. A. Richards, & C. Armon (eds.) *Beyond formal operations: Late adolescent and adult cognitive development* (92–119). New York: Praeger.

Rosecrance, J. 1988. Active gamblers as peer counselors. *International Journal of the Addictions* 23(7), 751–766.

Rosenthal, R. J. 1986. The pathological gambler's system for self-deception. *Journal of Gambling Behavior* 2(2), 108–120.

———. 1987. The psychodynamics of pathological gambling: A review of the literature. In T. Galski (ed.) *The handbook of pathological gambling* (41–70). Springfield, Illinois: Charles C. Thomas.

Roy, A., Adinoff, B., Roehrich, L., Lamparski, D., Custer, R., Lorenz, V., Barbaccia, M., Guidotti, A., Costa E., & Linnoila, M. 1988. Pathological gambling: A psychobiological study. *Archives of General Psychiatry 45*, 369–373.

Shaffer, H. J. 1986. Conceptual crises and the addictions: A philosophy of science perspective. *Journal of Substance Abuse Treatment 3*, 285–296.

———. 1987. The epistemology of "addictive disease:" The Lincoln-Douglas debate. *Journal of Substance Abuse Treatment 4*, 103–111.

Shaffer, H., & Jones, S. 1989. *Quitting cocaine: The struggle against impulse.* Lexington, Massachusetts: Lexington Books.

Skinner, B. F. 1953. *Science and human behavior.* New York: Appleton-Century-Crofts.

———. 1974. *About behaviorism.* New York: Alfred A. Knopf.

Part II
Models of Treatment for Compulsive Gambling

4

The Applicability of the Twelve-Step Model to Compulsive Intoxicant Use and Other Compulsive Behaviors

Norman E. Zinberg, M.D.

I t was a rare stroke of genius that resulted in the development by two alcoholics of the basic concepts of self-help and the Twelve Steps to recovery (Robertson 1988). Beginning with the idea that alcoholics, by committing themselves to help others in their struggle, could save themselves, Bill and Dr. Bob built up a forceful set of organizational principles (Alcoholics Anonymous 1939). The power of Alcoholics Anonymous to provide an accepting social support network for people who could and would tell their own stories was recognized early, as was the efficacy of the disease concept in dealing with the guilt and stigma of being branded an alcoholic. Yet, even while AA was growing and gaining recognition, the professional mental health community, with the exception of a few far-sighted supporters, was antagonistic toward the self-help movement. Gradually, however, professionals are beginning to acknowledge the importance of self-help (Vaillant 1983; Mack 1981; Bean 1975; Zinberg 1977; Tiebout 1943; Khantzian, forthcoming). At the same time, they are recognizing the ingenuity of the organizational principles of AA and seeing the similarity between them and some of the principles of psychodynamic psychiatry (Bean 1975; Zinberg 1977; Tiebout 1943; Khantzian, forthcoming). This has made it easy for most inpatient programs for intoxicant users to include self-help as an important component in an overall program. The formation of Narcotics Anonymous, modeled on AA's principles, which seemed a logical step because of the similar nature of the problems, shows a further recognition of the force of AA's organizational principles.

These events of the last few years have in retrospect a stunning logic; they have arisen from well-known American tendencies to jump on the bandwagon and look for answers, as well as from the growing attention being paid by the media to sufferers who appear out of control. As a result, many kinds of difficulty usually classified as compulsive behavior disorders, such as compulsive eating or not eating, gambling, and sexuality, have begun to be regarded as similar to the compulsive ingestion of intoxicants. Certain similarities are obvious. The sense of compulsion, the longing, the fear of deprivation, the loss of interest by sufferers in their own well-being, and in that of others, and the denial of all these can look frighteningly similar to an overwhelming intoxicant dependency. Thus self-help organizations have been formed around these complaints, and many have adopted the Twelve-Step model of AA (CompCare 1987; Hollis 1985; Larsen 1985; Milkman & Shaffer 1985; Peele 1975; Phelps & Nourse 1986; Slater 1983; Diamond 1988; Lesieur 1984; Custer & Custer 1987; Gamblers Anonymous 1984).

Nevertheless, despite these similarities between other compulsive behaviors and the problems engendered by intoxicants, certain differences exist that have important theoretical and clinical implications for the use of the Twelve-Step model. To throw light on these implications, I will first describe some of the dynamics implicit in the AA model. Then I will point out the theoretical differences between the use of the First Step by AA and by groups dealing with other compulsive behaviors. Finally, I will discuss the therapeutic advantages and disadvantages of applying the Twelve Steps to these other compulsive behaviors.

Dynamics

AA has shown from the beginning that admitting the possibility of alcoholism is very different from accepting the fact that one is an alcoholic (Bean 1981). Nevertheless, the admission of alcoholism is the first breach in the powerful defense of denial. Next comes the understanding that AA's attack on the psychological defense system must be kept within limits. An all-out assault is made on the denial of alcoholism, but denial in other areas is accepted and even encouraged. "Alcoholics can't afford resentment" is a good example. AA also recognizes, as did Freud, (Freud 1963). That certain "helpful" relationships may be so dependency-inducing as to be self-defeating. Many psychiatrists who have tried to treat alcoholics have found, to their sorrow, that they could not put up with the continual drunken phone calls and pleas for help. AA states that the alcoholic's relationship is to the *organization and its principles*, not to individuals. Consequently, anyone can go out on Twelve-Step work, not just one particular individual with special skills.

Twelve-Step work functions to relieve the guilt and sense of weakness engendered by all the help that individuals have received from AA. Although they appreciate the welcome, the acceptance, and the social support, many people find it hard to accept so much without feeling guilty—without feeling that they are only takers. Twelve-Step work allows them to pay back their obligations and to pass on to others what has been given to them. From the beginning AA has recognized that in the process of helping others, recovering drinkers are enabled to hold on to their own sobriety. Moreover, the act of providing rather than passively receiving builds self-esteem.

By seeing individuals as always recovering and never recovered, AA balances the alcoholic's twin phobias of drunkenness and sobriety. When sober, alcoholics fear desperately that they may drink again and further impair their bodies, their relationships, and their dignity. Yet they also fear a life in which they will never again feel the flush of well-being that followed the first drink. AA leaves that possibility open. The drinker is only recovering and is only doing that "one day at a time." The struggle against drinking goes on with the relief that sobriety brings, but there is always the possibility, if the going gets too tough, that the magic potion will be available.

The last subtle dynamic of AA is its way of avoiding judging. Despite their denial and forgetfulness, alcoholics rage at themselves. The concept of alcoholism as a disease heuristically relieves these savage judgments. The "last house on the street" accepts people on any terms and urges sufferers to do the same: to accept themselves as ill and to relinquish personal blame without giving up all sense of responsibility (Zinberg 1977).

Use of the First Step: Powerlessness

People attending AA meetings often mention their first drink. Their response to it varies, for, as we know, some drinkers drink alcoholically almost from the beginning while others take many years to get into trouble. But the first drink has significance because it was something they had never experienced before. Certainly there was preparation for it. This culture teaches a great deal about ingestion through family life, books, and the media (Zinberg 1984). But hearing about it and doing it are two different things. Actually to feel the sensation in one's body, to test one's capacity to deal with these new, strange sensations, to imagine the effects they are having on one's interactions with others, are potent learning experiences. And too little is made of the fact that one must *learn* to feel "high." It is not an automatic response to what is happening in one's body (Zinberg 1974). The experience must be organized and put into a learned context that has social as well as personal psychological determinants (Weil et al. 1968). Some people, of course, never do. They either drink to unconsciousness or become abstinent or so abstemious that they avoid any fear of intoxication. Most others do learn, more or less, how to organize the experience, although the degree to which they like it varies widely.

None of this is true of the other compulsive behaviors. Eating starts at the beginning of life, and we have little doubt, whether we are Freudians or not, that children from the earliest time have an inherent sensuality that occupies their consciousness. Likewise, risk taking begins at an extremely early time: the first cry is a bet on getting a response; the first step is a precarious gamble. These are indigenous experiences, not the product of a much later exogenous ingestion. Years before the first eating binge, the first sexual vehemence (disquietude), or the act of putting money on the line, the individual's body and psyche have begun to handle kindred experiences. The sensations are constantly familiar. Complex and automatic responses, developed both psychologically and physically, place the exciting stimuli into contexts. Inhibitions or preferences grow around certain foods, sensations, and fears. Thresholds that regulate perception and decree what can be noticed are in place, as are thresholds regulating discharge (Goodwin 1971). There already exist, before a certain experience becomes a compulsive pattern, overt conflicts about that experience because so many aspects of it are viscerally known. What child hasn't eaten too much or too little? What child hasn't been stimulated or frightened after taking a chance? Afterward he or she must struggle with the internal consequences of these everyday adventures. And, above all, these experiences are part and parcel of everyday living. They are here and will always be here. They will not and cannot be put aside.

The First Step of AA states: "We admitted we were powerless over alcohol—that our lives had become unmanageable" (Alcoholics Anonymous 1934). Whatever the capacity of the other steps to relieve guilt and to balance phobias, this numbing realization is basic: "I cannot ingest like other people. If I do, I will slide helplessly down the same well-worn, tortured path. A day at a time, I will not touch it." The struggle posed by this step is to stop the behavior. It further indicates that such a possibility can be accomplished. But the same is not true of the other compulsive behaviors. Even though individuals' lives may have indeed become unmanageable because of their affliction, there is no possibility of powerlessness or of making actual abstinence the task. Rather, the task is to regain control over regulatory mechanisms that have gone awry (Zinberg 1984). Each sufferer must become a controlled user—a goal which, according to AA, is impossible for the alcoholic. Yet, obviously, people must eat, encounter sexual impulses, and sustain risks. Thus they cannot be "powerless" in the presence of their compulsion, as intoxicant addicts can and must be. In fact, what is indicated is a process that insists on the exercise of internal capacities on a continuing basis. Living without binging, when one is eating several times a day, requires different psychological muscles from those required by the one who wants to go on a hunger strike.

Therapeutic Implications

Although the First Step may not be applicable to compulsive behaviors other than those surrounding the ingestion of exogenous substances, other aspects of the self-help system are not only useful but may even be essential. A social support system that accepts a sufferer with the full understanding of what he or she has been through is a powerful aid (Robertson 1981). All compulsive behaviors exact a painful toll in guilt and a sense of being unfit to exist in the everyday world. The feeling that one's controls are gone, and that in the grip of a compulsion one may do things that are hateful and embarrassing, puts self-esteem and self-respect at risk. To acknowledge to a group (or to listen to another's acknowledgment) that one has awakened again and again in a strange bed with a strange person, or has pawned a spouse's heirloom for money to place a bet, may lead to the realization, "I am not alone in my problem." Here are people who understand, accept, and insist that one need not be helpless and hopeless.

The sense of community that grows up in such groups is hard to convey to those who have not experienced it. It partakes of the loyalty to a country, a school, an ethnic group, an organization, or a family. But probably even closer is the sense of shared experiences described by soldiers, policemen, and others in combat, where truly "the enemy of my enemy is my friend." These experiences transcend the usual social boundaries of class, economic circumstances, education, and values. But I suspect identification with others in experiences that are degrading and socially unacceptable goes even deeper. Sufferers from these disorders feel cast out of ordinary social structures. Even soldiers and similar groups coalesce in part around the social approval of their cause, or at least of each other. Until finding self-help, those people in the grip of compulsive behaviors despise their own difficulty and that of others because they cannot believe that anyone else is as badly off as they are.

All self-help groups deal with denial of the particular condition systematically and vigorously (Bean 1981). Like AA, they recognize that other denials can wait. The obsessive behavior is so destructive in itself that it overshadows lesser emotional conflicts and self-consciousness. Members of these groups recognize that reaching out to other sufferers is crucial to their own struggle with personal demons and, less consciously, they appreciate the relief from guilt and from the sense of being a taker that is engendered by actively providing rather than just passively receiving. The "one day at a time" philosophy that balances the fear of never again having the "thrill" that comes from satisfying the compulsion against the horrid fear of what it is doing to one's life is just as characteristic of and as effective with gambling, eating, and sex as it is with intoxicants. And, above all, the significance of avoiding judging and providing a "last house on the street" pervades all the groups.

But even here problematic differences begin to emerge. AA rests heavily on the disease concept. In part this is used as a heuristic device to relieve guilt and find a new way of looking at responsibility. Recently, however, with the discovery that a genetic loading factor may be active in alcoholism, the concept has acquired a literal truth (Goodwin 1971; Goodwin et al. 1973; Peele 1986). This is enhanced by the effect of the ingestion of an exogenous substance to which one may be "allergic." For example, Orientals actually flush when they are given alcohol, which indicates a complex physiological response (Wolff 1972, 1973). Obviously, compulsive abusers of eating, risk taking, and sex, like intoxicant abusers, encounter a world where others can enjoy in moderation the same behaviors that render them helpless. But it is hard to think of these other desires as a kind of allergy. Despite this society's preoccupation with intoxicants, the "highs" resulting from their use differ from what all of us have dreamed of in connection with the other compulsive desires. The others are much more universal and therefore less aberrant. Haven't most people hoped that a forgotten uncle would will them $1 million, or that the glamorous lady or gentleman would come down from the screen and make them feel fully sexually realized, or that the day's hunger would be gluttonously assuaged by the meal of their dreams? When these behaviors are out of control, people who are not in trouble do separate themselves psychologically from their fantasies, but it is easier to see the behaviors themselves as an aberration of character than as an allergy or a "disease." This attitude may change over time as it has with alcohol, but right now the application of the disease concept to the other compulsive behaviors lacks verisimilitude, which is, of course, a crucial factor in recovery.

Alcoholics and most other drug users are surrounded by people who do (sometimes successfully, sometimes not successfully) what they have begun to learn they never can do: ingest in a controlled way. Alcoholics can go to a group that says, "Abstinence is for us the only way." Those with other kinds of compulsive problems cannot do this. Wherever they go, even in their self-help experience, they cannot concentrate simply on stopping. Their dilemmas continue to be "How?" "When?" "Under what circumstances?" These much more complex questions cannot be answered by a simple "No." Not only can such individuals *not* accept powerlessness, but powerlessness is eventually the enemy.

Why not simply accept this reaching of Step One as another heuristic device and not make a fuss about the differences with intoxicant users? The answer to this question takes us back to the idea of verisimilitude, or to put it another way, to an inner sense of conviction or authenticity. One of Freud's great imaginative leaps was his understanding of the concept of transference (Freud 1963). Above all—whether they achieve it or not—therapists want to avoid pretense. To the extent that this is possible, they try not to agree, as people do regularly in ordinary social situations, that shadow is substance (Zinberg 1987). All the odd and intense reactions that people have to their therapists are important to work with; but the fear, the resentment, the affection, the lust could not and should not be taken at face value. The importance of these reactions in the therapy is authentic; the reality, whatever that means, is not.

In therapy, this insistence on a sense of inner conviction is carried much further. Patient and therapist try not to accept superficial intellectualization as an authentic representation of understanding. In "parlor" psychiatry or with inexperienced therapists, quick and facile connections are made. For example, the therapist may show that the patient's resentment at the therapist's misunderstanding of the point of an anecdote stands for an irrational fury stemming from the patient's childhood rage at parents' misunderstanding. But for such connections to mean anything they require many convincing, emotionally charged repetitions in other areas of the patient's life. Not only is there the recognition that for something to be emotionally convincing a person must see the highly individual, automatic, personally repetitious ways of perceiving as consistent and "true" for the sake of what we call "therapy," but there is also a subtle psychosocial understanding between therapist and patient that in their working together they do not accept as "true" anything that does not have the quality of emotional conviction (Zinberg 1987).

I would argue that the self-help movement relies deeply on just that sense of emotional conviction. There is no pretense in the accepting, nonjudging nature of the group, which is dealing with people who are deeply sensitive to pretense because their denial or pretense to themselves has required smelling it out in others. Just as in therapy, it takes time and working through for the person who tries a self-help group to acknowledge that here it is different. It is hard to believe that when he or she "tells it like it is," there will not be the shunning and distaste that sufferers feel about themselves.

It is not enough to show that the tasks of Gamblers Anonymous, Overeaters Anonymous, and Sexuals Anonymous differ from the task of AA, and that this realization will make it easier for participants to avoid the inner emotional split and inner disbelief that come from pretending that something (in this case, powerlessness) that is being attempted as possible is not. Rather, it is essential to understand that such pretense is not necessary. The self-help concept has enough to offer without slavishly repeating the AA credo. The steps can be changed and modified to fit the particular conditions so that they will become and feel more direct and therefore authentic. Bill and Dr. Bob muddled around, using their knowledge of their condition, to find steps that were specific and effective. To do the same for other similar but not identical conditions is a valid challenge.

References

Alcoholics Anonymous. 1939. New York: Alcoholics Anonymous World Services, Inc. 1939.

Bean, M. H. 1981. Denial and the psychological complications of alcoholism, in *Dynamic Approaches to the Understanding and Treatment of Alcoholism.* Edited by Bean, M. H., & Zinberg, N. E. New York: The Free Press, 55–96.

———. 1975. *Alcoholics Anonymous: A.A. Psychiatric Annals;* 5:3–64.

CompCare. 1987. *Hope and Recovery: A Twelve-Step Guide for Healing from Compulsive Sexual Behavior.* Minneapolis: CompCare Publishers.

Custer, R. L., & Custer, L. S. 1987. *Characteristics of the Recovering Compulsive Gambler: A Survey of 150 Members of G.A.* Unpublished paper.

Diamond, J. 1988. *Looking for Love in all the Wrong Places: Overcoming Romantic and Sexual Addictions.* New York: G.P. Putnam's Sons.

Freud, S. 1963. Introductory lectures on psychoanalysis (1916–1917), in *Complete Psychological Works,* standard ed, vol. 16, London, Hogarth Press.

Goodwin, D. W. 1971. Is alcoholism hereditary? *Arch Gen Psychiatry* 25:545–549.

Goodwin, D. W., Schulsinger, F., Hermansen, L., Guze, S. B., & Winokur, G. 1973. Alcohol problems in adoptees raised apart from alcoholic biological parents. *Arch Gen Psychiatry* 28:238–243.

Hollis, J. 1985. *Fat is a Family Affair.* San Francisco: Harper & Row.

Khantzian, E. J., & Mack, J. E. Alcoholics Anonymous and contemporary psychodynamic theory, in *Recent Developments in Alcoholism,* vol. 7. Edited by Galanter M. Accepted for publication.

Larsen, E. 1985. *Stage II Recovery: Life beyond Addiction.* New York: Harper & Row.

Lesieur, H. 1984. *The Chase: Career of the Compulsive Gambler.* Cambridge, Massachusetts: Schenkman Publishing Company.

Mack, J. E. 1981. Alcoholism, A. A., and the governance of the self, in *Dynamic Approaches to the Understanding and Treatment of Alcoholism.* Edited by Bean, M. H., & Zinberg, N. E. New York, The Free Press, 128–162.

Milkman, H. B., & Shaffer, H. J. 1985. *The Addictions.* Lexington, Massachusetts: D.C. Heath & Company.

Peele, S. 1986. The implications and limitations of genetic models of alcoholism and other addictions. *J Studies on Alcohol* 47: 63–73.

———. 1975. *Love and Addiction.* New York: New American Library.

Phelps, J. K., & Nourse, A. E. 1986. *The Hidden Addictions and How to Get Free.* New York: Little, Brown & Company.

Rapaport, D. 1958. *Theory of ego autonomy: A generalization.* Bull Menninger Clinic 22:13–35.

Robertson, N. 1988. *Getting Better: Inside Alcoholics Anonymous*. New York: William Morrow & Company.

Sharing Recovery through Gamblers Anonymous. 1984. Los Angeles: Gamblers Anonymous Publishing, Inc.

Slater, P. 1988. *Wealth Addiction*. New York: E.P. Dutton.

Tiebout, H. M. 1943. Therapeutic mechanisms of Alcoholics Anonymous. *Am J Psychiatry* 100:468–473.

Vaillant, G. E. 1983. *The Natural History of Alcoholism: Course, Patterns, and Paths to Recovery*. Cambridge, Massachusetts: Harvard University Press.

Wolff, P. H. 1973. Vasomotor sensitivity to alcohol in diverse Mongoloid populations. *Am J Human genetics* 25:193–199.

———. 1972. Ethnic differences in alcohol sensitivity. *Science* 175:449–450.

Weil, A. T., Zinberg, N. E., & Nelsen, J. 1968. Clinical and psychological effects of marihuana in man. *Science* 162:1234–1242.

Zinberg, N. E. 1987. Elements of the private therapeutic interview. *Am J Psychiatry* 144:1527–1533.

———. 1984. *Drug, Set, and Setting: The Basis for Controlled Intoxicant Use*. New Haven: Yale University Press.

———. 1977. Alcoholics Anonymous and the treatment and prevention of alcoholism. *Alcoholism: Clinical and Experimental Research* 1:91–101.

———. 1974. *"High" States: A Beginning Study*. Special Studies Series #3. Washington, D.C., Drug Abuse Council, Inc.

5
Pathological Gambling and Problem Gambling: Problems of Definition and Diagnosis

Richard J. Rosenthal, M.D.

Introduction

Prevalence studies of pathological gambling, as well as data on treatment outcome, can only be as good as our definition of the disorder, and confusion exists. There is a shift in the patient population, brought about by the change from DSM-III to DSM-III-R. Various terms, such as "problem gambling," "excessive gambling," and "potential pathological gambler" differ in meaning from one investigator to another. Some professionals continue to deny that compulsive gambling even exists, or argue that the numbers claimed are greatly exaggerated and include mostly undisciplined or unlucky social gamblers.

In May of 1987, one year before this study, DSM-III-R was introduced. How has it been received by clinicians? Is it actually used to diagnose the pathological gambler, or do therapists rely more on intangibles, such as their experience or "gut feeling"? Or are GA criteria, the Twenty Questions, being used? From a practical standpoint, how do the criteria in DSM-III-R differ from those in DSM-III? Is it the improvement we had hoped it would be, and what are its limitations or shortcomings?

DSM-IV will be introduced in 1993. The International Classification of Diseases (ICD-10) will publish its tenth revision in the early 1990s, and American psychiatry is hoping to be a major influence. With regard to the section on pathological gambling, this is the time to evaluate our criteria, and for researchers and clinicians to make their opinions known. This chapter was written to nudge the debate.

First, let us quickly review. In 1980, largely through the efforts of Robert Custer, the American Psychiatric Association first recognized pathological gambling. Table 5–1 lists the criteria as they appeared in DSM-III. We note that there is an introductory statement about the chronic and progressive nature of the disorder; there is a criterion of exclusion ruling out the antisocial personality; however, the emphasis is on damage and

Table 5–1
DSM-III Criteria for Pathological Gambling

A. The individual is chronically and progressively unable to resist impulses to gamble.

B. Gambling compromises, disrupts, or damages family, personal, and vocational pursuits, as indicated by at least three of the following:

1. Arrest for forgery, fraud, embezzlement, or income tax evasion because of attempts to obtain money for gambling

2. Default on debts or other financial responsibilities

3. Disrupted family or spouse relationship because of gambling

4. Borrowing of money from illegal sources (loan sharks)

5. Inability to account for loss of money or to produce evidence of winning money, if this is claimed

6. Loss of work because of absenteeism to pursue gambling activity

7. Necessity for another person to provide money to relieve a desperate financial situation

C. The gambling is not caused by Antisocial Personality Disorder.

From American Psychiatric Association, DSM-III, 1980

disruption. The individual gets in trouble; his or her life is destroyed by gambling.

Appearance in the *Diagnostic and Statistical Manual* does not mean everything has been settled. Inclusion prompts research and criteria are refined in subsequent volumes. Decisions are not always made on scientific grounds; there are cultural and political influences. With regard to pathological gambling, to see how changes were made from DSM-III to DSM-III-R, it is helpful to examine an intermediate step, the rough draft for the proposed revisions, which was circulated in 1985. We see how the criteria emphasize the addictive nature of the gambling disorder. Table 5–2 shows the proposed changes, and to clarify what was done, I have taken the earlier section of the draft on substance dependence, and presented the two sets of criteria side by side.

They are close to identical. Instead of "substance use" or "intoxication" the word "gambling" has been substituted. Note that item number three is tolerance, and number four, withdrawal. When we go from this early draft to DSM-III-R as we know it today (see table 5–3), number nine is expanded to make it more like its counterpart under substance dependence. The number of criteria needed for a diagnosis drops from six out of nine to four out of nine, again bringing it closer to substance dependence. A last-minute change in the latter, perhaps for reasons of comprehension, brings a rearrangement of items. The ordering of criteria has been changed for substance dependence, not for pathological gambling, so the borrowing is less obvious in the final version of DSM-III-R.

Thus we see a major shift from DSM-III to DSM-III-R with regard to the diagnosis of pathological gambling. It is not just that we can now diagnose the problem earlier. The emphasis is on pathological gambling as an addiction. Criteria include tolerance and withdrawal, thereby suggesting a physiological basis for the disorder. This, even though we are now

Table 5–2
Comparison of Proposed DSM-III-R Criteria for Substance Dependence and Pathological Gambling

Psychoactive Substance Dependence	*Pathological Gambling*
1. Frequent preoccupation with seeking or taking the substances	1. Frequent preoccupation with gambling or obtaining money to gamble
2. Often takes the substance in larger amounts or over a longer period than he or she intended	2. Often gambles larger amounts of money or over a longer period than intended
3. Tolerance: need for increased amounts of the substance to achieve intoxication or desired effect, or diminished effect with continued use of the same amount	3. Need to increase the size or frequency of bets to achieve the desired excitement
4. Characteristic withdrawal symptoms (see specific withdrawal syndromes in Psychoactive Substance—induced Organic Mental Disorders)	4. Restlessness or irritability if unable to gamble
5. Relief substance use: often takes the substance to relieve or avoid withdrawal symptoms	5. Repeated loss of money gambling and return another day to win back losses ("chasing")
6. Persistent desire or repeated efforts to cut down or control substance use	6. Repeated efforts to cut down or stop gambling
7. Often intoxicated or impaired by substance use when expected to fulfill social or occupational obligations, or when substance use is hazardous (for example, doesn't go to work because hung over or high, goes to work high, drives when drunk)	7. Often gambles when expected to fulfill social or occupational obligations
8. Has given up some important social, occupational, or recreational activity to seek or take the substance	8. Has given up some important social, occupational, or recreational activity to gamble
9. Continuation of substance use despite a significant social, occupational, or legal problem or a physical disorder, that the individual knows is exacerbated by the use of the substance	9. Continues to gamble despite inability to pay mounting debts

From American Psychiatric Association, DSM-III-R in Development, 1985

Table 5–3
DSM-III-R Criteria for Pathological Gambling

Maladaptive gambling behavior as indicated by at least four of the following:

1. Frequent preoccupation with gambling or with obtaining money to gamble
2. Frequent gambling of larger amounts of money or over a longer period of time than intended
3. A need to increase the size or frequency of bets to achieve the desired excitement
4. Restlessness or irritability if unable to gamble
5. Repeated loss of money by gambling and returning another day to win back losses ("chasing")
6. Repeated efforts to reduce or stop gambling
7. Frequent gambling when expected to meet social or occupational obligations
8. Sacrifice of some important social, occupational, or recreational activity to gamble
9. Continuation of gambling despite inability to pay mounting debts, or despite other significant social, occupational, or legal problems that the person knows to be exacerbated by gambling

From American Psychiatric Association, DSM-III-R, 1987

talking about addiction, not to a substance, but to an activity. I have discussed the notion of addiction as it pertains to gambling elsewhere (Rosenthal 1986),[1] and will turn now to an examination of the DSM-III-R criteria from the point of view of the diagnostician and therapist. I will relate the experience of thirteen clinicians, beginning with my own.

Critique of DSM-III-R

Most pathological gamblers are easy to diagnose, and particularly so when they are in the more advanced stages; that is, when they are most apt to be coming to us for help. It is in the questionable cases that formal criteria are important, and there, when most needed, DSM-III-R is not up to the task. The criteria are too subjective and ambiguous.

Several criteria are particularly troublesome. Item number 5, for instance, is a compound sentence linking two phrases either of which can be true independent of the other. I suspect it is meant to inquire, not about

---

[1] Among other points I note the derivation of the word *addiction*, literally "to speak to someone" (the same root as dictate, diction, and dictionary). It comes to us from early Roman law. Up until about 500 A.D. someone in debt would appear before a judge, and since most people were illiterate, his sentence would be spoken to him. He would be given in slavery to the person he couldn't pay. So, not only do we learn that addiction is, literally, enslavement, but it suggests that the primary or earliest addiction may have been, not some form of drug dependence, but gambling.

losing, but about chasing. This should be clarified, and perhaps what is needed is a more precise definition of chasing.

Numbers 7 and 8 seem to me identical, and when I have read them to patients they look at me blankly or tell me I'm repeating myself. This may illustrate one of the hazards of borrowing criteria from another disorder. If we are talking about substance dependence it makes sense to distinguish the person who takes drugs at work, or who drives while intoxicated, from the person who misses work altogether. For the race track, poker, or casino gambler, the distinction becomes meaningless.

Number 9 appears to duplicate 7 and 8, or at least to so overlap it, that a problem in just one area will give a person two or probably three affirmative responses. Nine is also extremely vague and subjective. What constitutes "significant social problems?" For an answer I turned back to the section on substance dependence (p. 168), and learned that family arguments over the substance or activity are sufficient to earn one an affirmative response to number nine.

Number 4 consists of "restlessness or irritability if unable to gamble." This is meant to represent withdrawal. Since many professionals consider this the hallmark of addiction, it will be discussed at some length. In my experience withdrawal has been relatively insignificant both in the course of treatment and as a diagnostic criterion. There may be depression when the person stops gambling. This may be an underlying depression against which the gambling had defended. Alternatively, it may be that once the individual stops gambling he begins to recognize how destructive his behavior had been. He experiences guilt about the people he has hurt, and about his lying, cheating, and stealing. This may present initially, not as manifest depression and guilt, but with somatic complaints. The relationship between hypochondriasis and feelings of guilt and depression which are not yet conscious is well-known. Or we may find reactions to the loss of an important symptom. Gambling, and perhaps particularly the omnipotence, are mourned.

I have found rather dramatic physical symptoms, including those that might appear to mimic withdrawal—chills and sweating, muscle cramps and gastrointestinal disturbances, and flulike symptoms. These were unrelated to length or intensity of the gambling, and even occurred in at least two instances while the person was still gambling. These symptoms were clearly related to change, and to the emergence of guilt and other depressive anxieties.

As far as I know there is only one study of withdrawal symptoms among pathological gamblers. Wray & Dickerson (1981), on the basis of retrospective questionnaires given to GA members, reported that on cessation of gambling one third of their respondents experienced mild disturbances of mood and behavior—irritability, restlessness, depressed mood, poor concentration, and obsessional thoughts. By the latter, I assume they meant "cravings." One wonders why only a third showed symptoms. You would think that giving up something as important as their gambling would produce some disturbance. After all, even chronic headache sufferers sometimes respond to the loss of their painful symptom with depression or anger. Are Wray & Dickerson's findings a function of recall, or of the gambling pattern, or does it say something about the psychological makeup of their subjects? This is clearly an area for further study, and one of the inpatient programs would be an ideal place to carry it out.

I will shift now from a discussion of the specific items to some general observations. It is important to distinguish the political motivations for diagnostic criteria from those factors that are clinical or scientific. For example, Custer (see Delaware Council newsletter, vol. III, no. 4, 1988, p. 2; also personal communication) has acknowledged that inclusion of category C of DSM-III, the exclusion of antisocial personality, is no longer necessary, in that its purpose has been accomplished. Initially it was included to counteract a myth or stereotype people had about pathological gamblers. In other words, it served an educational purpose.

So, too, it seems, does the identification of pathological gambling with psychoactive substance dependence in DSM-III-R. By borrowing the criteria of tolerance and withdrawal, and paralleling one disorder with the other, we are trying to educate alcohol and drug abuse counselors to look for gambling problems, and we are emphasizing the concept of cross-addiction. These are certainly worthwhile goals, and maybe when we accomplish them, we will move on, and again change our criteria. However, such an approach will be at the expense of our credibility.

Granted, there are clear advantages to an alliance with the field of alcohol and drug dependence. In addition to the educational one, it seems to make funding for treatment easier to come by. It also makes sense to patients. A pathological gambler I recently saw had been heavily involved in both casino gambling and the commodities market, but was able to stop those activities although he continued to purchase one lottery ticket a week. He did so until he considered the addiction model, and came to see that ticket as the equivalent of the alcoholic's first drink. Thinking of gambling as a drug, he told me, made him realize that even a little bit was no good for him.

However, there may be a down side to all this. I believe we are seeing the beginning of a backlash against the acceptance of alcoholism and drug dependence as diseases. There is the recent Supreme Court decision about alcoholism, books such as Herbert Fingarette's *Heavy Drinking: The Myth Of Alcoholism As A Disease* (1988), and what I think we can expect next: a revolt on the part of insurance companies against payment for inpatient treatment programs for alcohol and drug dependence. So, if we continue trying to establish the validity of pathological gambling by claiming it is a disease *just like alcoholism,* we may find ourselves on a limb destined for pruning.

These are political considerations. More important is my questioning the applicability of the criteria, and an impression that there is something lazy about the transposition. An earlier paper (Rosenthal 1986) suggested that pathological gambling was both an addiction *and* a compulsion.[2] For some patients it is more one than the other. But if we really believe that pathological gambling, because of the absence of any ingested substance, will help us shed light on the whole process of addiction, and help with a general theory of addiction, then DSM-III-R is going about it backwards. Rather than assume that gambling is just like the other addictions, we need to pool our collective experience and describe what makes it unique. What do pathological gamblers do that other gamblers do not, and at what point do they cross the line?

The diagnostic and statistical manual is more than just a how-to book, to be used to satisfy insurance companies and the courts, and assist in the compilation of data. It determines how people will think about these disorders. This brings me to my second general issue. I believe one should be able to say concisely what pathological gambling is, not according to points scored on a questionnaire, but with a few easily stated characteristics. This would allow us to say why a gambler did not fit the criteria, or to explain to someone why he or she did. It is essential for teaching.

DSM-III attempted to do this. It began with a partial definition: pathological gambling is a chronic and progressive disorder. It then offered a series of questions, all aimed at meeting a single criterion, that of disruptiveness in the person's external life. Lastly, there was a criterion of exclusion, that he or she not have an antisocial personality. DSM-III had four criteria that could be tersely summarized: It is chronic and progressive and occurs in a person who is not antisocial, and it will disrupt the major areas of his or her life. This person will get in trouble because of gambling.

DSM-III clearly had its faults. Henry Lesieur (1984) has delineated some of them, such as its middle-class bias, its lack of recognition that many pathological gamblers are self-employed, and its exclusion of individuals with antisocial personality disorder. DSM-III-R also is flawed. How much, one may wonder, does any of this matter? Is the diagnostic and statistical manual actually used by clinicians when faced with a gam-

---

[2]Those features characteristic of compulsion include a) magical thinking and omnipotence; b) alternating submission to and defiance of authority; c) competitiveness and emphasis on power games; d) repetitive, reassuring rituals; e) preoccupation with numbers, odd and even.

bling problem? And how is it used? To what degree does it influence thinking? I decided to conduct an informal survey.

Informal Survey

I made a list of the clinicians I thought had the most experience diagnosing and treating pathological gamblers. When I asked colleagues for suggestions, the same names recurred. I eliminated those who had been involved in the planning of DSM-III-R, as well as a few who work together. Twelve names remained. They were scattered throughout the country, and represented all the major treatment programs. While the number is small, it is an influential group. There are few therapists in the country with a special expertise in this area. Furthermore, all twelve are involved in training others in diagnosis.

My survey was begun eleven months after DSM-III-R was released, and was conducted by telephone over a two-week period. I explained I was interested in diagnostic procedures, and wanted to know how they went about the evaluation of a questionable case. I was particularly interested in their experience with DSM-III-R. All twelve subjects were fully cooperative. That in itself may be remarkable, since these are all extremely busy individuals, and the interviews took between half an hour and an hour and a half. They generously shared their experience, and even put up with my overly persistent efforts to pin them down. I tried to take them through a hypothetical case, to see not only what sort of questions they asked, but what kind of assumptions were made. Did they actually do what they thought they did? Could we conceptualize the model with which they worked?

I was surprised at the amount of data they brought together, and the variety of instruments used. These are listed in table 5–4. Eight of the twelve use what one subject referred to as a "damage inventory." This is an inquiry into the various areas of functioning, to see how gambling has affected one's career, family, and so on. It is a kind of informal application of DSM-III criteria, and was, along with the GA Twenty Questions, the method most often used by those interviewed. Of the six who use the South Oaks Gambling Screen, four emphasized that they use it just as a screening instrument, and not for specific diagnosis. Several subjects liked it for research.

When asked what tools they most relied on when faced with a diagnostic dilemma, they gave the answers summarized in table 5–5. Eight of the twelve again stressed damage and disability (the "damage inventory"); six emphasized loss of control, as measured by inability to stop and a disregard for the consequences; two looked at the history for progression. We note that two believed the personality organization was crucial, while

Table 5–4
Used in Diagnostic Assessment
of Pathological Gambler

- DSM-III-R (6)
- DSM-III (5)
- "damage inventory" (8)
- GA Twenty Questions (8)
- South Oaks Gambling Screen (6)
- gambling history
- family history
- personality factors and organization
- interview with family members
- irrational beliefs
  (such as money will solve all problems)
- Custer and Glen's "soft signs"
- criteria for impulsive disorder
- pragmatic test
  (can he or she quit for a month?)
- psychological testing
  (MMPI, Millon)
- written autobiography
- addictions questionnaire

N clinicians = 12

Only the first five items were quantified. These were specifically volunteered by the subjects, although to some extent all took a gambling history, a family history, and made some attempt at personality assessment.

Table 5–5
Most Relied On

- damage and disability (8)
- loss of control (6)
  - inability to stop
  - disregard for consequences
- GA Twenty Questions (3)
- DSM-III-R (2)
- DSM-III (1)
- progression (2)
- personality organization (2)
  (narcissistic, obsessive-compulsive)
- need to exclude antisocial personality (2)

two others felt it important to exclude the antisocial personality. Three of the twelve turned to the GA Twenty Questions, two relied on DSM-III-R, and one on DSM-III.

One would expect that which were regarded most highly would conform closely to the individual's conceptualization of the disorder, and for the most part this was true. When asked for a definition, eight of the twelve subjects (although not the same eight as in the previous paragraph; two were different) emphasized the damage and disability caused by gambling. The most commonly offered definition was of a chronic and progressive disorder, characterized by loss of control, intense involvement, and causing great damage to the gambler's life and to those who care about him. Two people emphasized the cognitive distortions and impaired judgment, and three the gambler's need to escape pain. It was noteworthy that of the six who use DSM-III-R, three of them conceptualize the disorder according to DSM-III models. Two were not aware that they were doing so.

Eight of the twelve subjects accept the notion of pathological gambling as an addiction, although, interestingly, none mentioned tolerance or withdrawal in their conceptualization of it. One expressed confusion as to what the addiction was; based on her clinical experience she believed the importance attached to the excitement, or "action," had been greatly overstated in the literature. It is significant that, given the thrust of the new criteria, five of the eight still prefer to think along DSM-III lines. What of the other four? One believed pathological gambling to be more of a compulsion than an addiction. A second felt that impulsive aspects should have been emphasized. The other two thought it an addiction, but significantly different from those that were chemically induced; they wished to see personality factors emphasized.

What was the attitude toward DSM-III-R? I was surprised to learn that of the six who were using it, all had been doing so from the time of its release. I had expected a time lag, although there is no research on this with regard to any psychiatric diagnoses, or to previous manuals (personal communication, Robert Spitzer). The six subjects were equally divided as to how they used it: two read it to the patient from the book, two presented it as a written questionnaire, and two were sufficiently familiar with DSM-III-R to work in the criteria, in their own words, in an otherwise unstructured interview. It was these latter two subjects who were the only ones to rely on DSM-III-R exclusively for diagnosis. Not surprisingly, they were the only two who felt it represented a great improvement over DSM-III.

What about the other four who used it? Three of them viewed DSM-III-R as an improvement, but only for political, that is, educational, reasons; they felt that to stress the similarity to other addictions would leave out too much that was unique about pathological gambling. Two of the four used it only in forensic evaluations, alongside a number of other instruments. One did not regard the new criteria as an improvement over DSM-III. The third used DSM-III-R only after he had taken a complete history and essentially already finished his assessment. He would then go over each of its criteria with the patient, as an educational and therapeutic device. He felt, however, that too much was left out for it to be a satisfactory diagnostic tool. The fourth individual was the only one to use both DSM-III and DSM-III-R. He also favored DSM-III-R for political reasons, but was critical of it clinically; he was the one who thought of the disorder as more compulsion than addiction.

Exactly 50 percent of those interviewed regarded DSM-III-R as an improvement over DSM-III, although they were not, as one would expect, the six who were using it. One of those who made use of it, as previously noted, did so for forensic reasons, but did not regard it as an improvement, while one of the others, who did not use it, thought of it as an improvement, and expected to be using it in the near future. (He was the only nonuser who anticipated changing his diagnostic criteria.) It should be remembered that only two of the twelve thought it an improvement for clinical reasons.

Three of the subjects were not sufficiently familiar with DSM-III-R to have an opinion on it. This may seem surprising but perhaps should not. The question is not how long it takes someone to begin using a new diagnostic manual, but whether he or she will be using it at all. While there is very little research on this subject (personal communication, Robert Spitzer), one study is relevant. V. Chowdery Jampala et al. (1986) surveyed American psychiatrists in 1984 about their attitudes and practices with respect to DSM-III. This was four years after it had been introduced. Based on a questionnaire mailed to a thousand psychiatrists, he found that the majority generally approved of it, yet, in practice, a whopping 48 percent of patients receiving official DSM-III diagnoses did not satisfy all the necessary criteria. Many psychiatrists were using DSM-III as "a convenient source of labels for diagnoses already made without using this specific system." Actually, he surmised, given the bias in such studies against subjects reporting socially unacceptable phenomena, the figure of 48 percent was probably an underrepresentation of the true prevalence of such practices. He also found that whether or not psychiatrists used DSM-III was partly a function of whether they were required to do so. A full 41 percent of those in private practice said they would stop using DSM-III if it were not required. In discussing the various reasons for this, Jampala stresses the importance of having diagnostic criteria that are easy to use and that make sense to the clinician.

What were the perceived strengths of the new criteria for the diagnosis of pathological gambling? Turning to table 5–6, we note that three of our twelve subjects perceived DSM-III-R as easier to read and remember

Table 5–6
Perceived Strengths of DSM-III-R Criteria
for Pathological Gambling

Viewed as improvement over DSM-III (6)

1. likes similarity with other addictions (alcohol, drugs) (5)
   - "political advantages" (3)
   - easier to read, remember (3)
   - easier for teaching (3)
   - easier to work out treatment plan (1)

2. easier to make diagnosis (1)

3. allows earlier diagnosis (1)

4. more specific criteria (1)

5. likes simpler language (1)

6. likes inclusion of antisocial personality (1)

---

than DSM-III. This was attributable to their background in the addictions field. They also found the criteria easier to teach to counselors and therapists, and one found it more adaptable for the working out of treatment plans. Altogether five approved of the change involved in making it parallel to the other addictions. One thought the criteria now made it easier to make a diagnosis, and another emphasized that diagnoses could be made earlier. One believed the criteria to be more specific, and also liked the simpler language.

Table 5–7 summarizes the perceived weaknesses. When it came to specific items, their criticisms were not dissimilar from mine. Three of those interviewed thought that restlessness and "withdrawal" were seldom seen and too insignificant to be useful in diagnosis. Two subjects found item number 5 a compound question and hence too confusing to score. Others guessed that chasing was the important criterion, but at least one felt it needed to be defined. Three of the clinicians found numbers 7 and 8 indistinguishable, and one of them assumed it a misprint. Only two of the twelve could explain the difference, but gave it a different interpretation than the one I presented. They informed me that number seven refers to those social and occupational activities one has to do; they are obligations. Number 8, on the other hand, refers to activities one would have previously enjoyed. Number 8, therefore, would indicate a deeper involvement in gambling. Interestingly, one of the two who thought she understood numbers 7 and 8 considered them the weakest and least significant of the nine criteria. Several subjects also noted that number 9 covered much of the same ground as 7 and 8, hence constituting a kind of double or triple jeopardy, in which one problem could easily result in affirmative responses to three criteria.

Table 5-7
**Perceived Weaknesses of DSM-III-R Criteria
for Pathological Gambling**

1. specific criteria
   - item #4 too insignificant or seldom seen (3)
   - item #5 a double question (2)
     (confusing)
     • chasing needs to be defined (1)
   - items #7, 8 too similar (3)
     • not too similar but the weakest criteria (1)
   - item #9 too much overlap with #7, 8 (2)
     • lumps together too many things specific for gambling (1)
2. too hard to remember (3)
3. ambiguous answers (1)
4. disapprove of gambling lumped with other addictions (2)
5. too much left out (5)
   - DSM-III (2)
   - compulsion (1)
   - impulsive (1)
   - personality factors (2)
   - soft signs (1)
   - exclusion of antisocial personality (2)

Although only three complained that the criteria were too difficult to remember, several others immediately went for their manuals when questioned; two were unaware of slipping into DSM-III criteria when they thought they were discussing DSM-III-R. Two of the twelve disapproved of gambling being lumped with the other addictions. The biggest failing, however, was felt to be how much had been left out; four attributed this to the need to conform to the other addictions. They were not always able to specify what they would have wanted to add, although two favored a return to some of the DSM-III criteria, while others wanted more emphasis on compulsion, or impulsive behavior, or various personality factors. Two, interestingly, wanted to put back the exclusion of the antisocial personality.

All twelve of those interviewed agree, that in the vast majority of cases, the diagnosis of pathological gambling is easy to make. I leave this section with some regret that I have not conveyed either the struggle of these subjects to improve their skills, or the complexity with which they are looking at personality factors, family dynamics, and traumatic life events in the histories of their pathological gamblers. They will have to report their own findings, and I encourage them to do so. Suffice it to say that none of the twelve is completely satisfied with DSM-III-R. In fact, only two viewed it as clinically superior to DSM-III. I have already given my own critique. Now I would like to suggest another way of approaching the diagnosis.

Toward DSM-IV

Pathological gambling, as I have recently begun considering it, seems to have four characteristics: 1) progression; 2) an intolerance of losing; 3) preoccupation; 4) a disregard for consequences. Under these four headings, in tables 5–8 through 5–11, I have listed some of the items which would be associated with them. These have not been validated or tested; however, most of them will be familiar to those involved in diagnosing and treating the disorder. The first of the categories, *progression*, as summarized in table 5–8, includes the notion of tolerance. The gambler cannot quit while ahead, and will frequently continue until he has lost all his money. A corollary is that he can never win enough. He will wager for longer periods of time, and bet more than expected. He will increase the size of his bets, or the odds he goes up against, needing greater risks to produce the desired amount of excitement.

The second category is *intolerance of losing*. Chasing, of course, is a phenomenon known to all who work with pathological gamblers. Henry Lesieur (1984) has described it quite movingly. What I think is not sufficiently appreciated, however, is the degree to which the intolerance of losing, and the whole phenomenon of chasing, may be rooted in the underlying personality structure of the pathological gambler. Lesieur, for example, wrote in another, now classic, contribution, *The Compulsive Gambler's Spiral of Options and Involvement* (1979), that chasing is behavior learned from other gamblers. "The major message from the compulsive gamblers' friends is that chasing works." Meanwhile, the noncompulsive gambler is supposedly learning from *his* friends that chasing is stupid, and so he is not motivated to try it. This gives it a wholly logical explanation, but of course there is nothing logical about the phenomenon. It is borne out of desperation.

Table 5–8
Progression

1. Cannot quit while ahead
   - continuing as long as there is money left
   - after a win can't wait to come back and play again
   - one cannot win enough
2. Gambles for longer periods of time and wagers more than expected
3. Needs to bet larger amounts, and take greater risks, to produce the desired amount of excitement

While Lesieur calls our attention to often-overlooked social aspects of gambling, it is also true that there are many solitary pathological gamblers who are neither emulating nor influenced by other gamblers. Therapists can verify this, as well as the experience of having witnessed chasing phenomena arising status ascendi in gamblers already in treatment. But we also have a kind of control group. Many of us have treated individuals with narcissistic personality disorders, and have found that even though many of them were not pathological gamblers, or even gamblers, that they, nonetheless, chased. They are unable to accept a loss. There are three characteristics to their response: 1) there is an inordinate amount of shame and guilt associated with failure; 2) their self-worth, and even their right to exist, is equated with success, often at seemingly arbitrary ventures; 3) desperation leads to a sense of omnipotence in which there is seemingly nothing they cannot do. I have reflected some of these beliefs in the six items listed in table 5–9.

When not gambling, the pathological gambler may be preoccupied with thoughts about gambling. This *preoccupation* constitutes the third category, summarized in table 5–10. He may be reliving past gambling experiences, handicapping, or planning his next venture, or thinking of ways to get money to gamble. He lies to cover up the extent of his involvement. He gambles as an expression of anger, or when feeling misunderstood. In fact, gambling is thought of as the way to solve problems, financial or otherwise, and is turned to in order to relieve boredom or restlessness.

Cravings are a phenomenon in need of study. Some recovering gamblers have overwhelming and persistent urges to gamble that last for a long time; others will have them only intermittently, in situations that call forth a defensive need to return to gambling; a third group reports no cravings at all, doesn't seem to miss gambling, and in therapy will focus on other topics.[3]

Table 5–9
Intolerance of Losing

1. Losing not thought of as "part of the game," but as something personal
2. Chasing—after a loss must return as soon as possible and win back one's losses
3. When losing will abandon one's gambling strategy and try to win back one's losses **all at once**
4. The belief that if one wins back one's losses, one needn't feel guilty about gambling
5. Losses are concealed—there is shame about losing
   – one cannot account for money lost
6. Self-worth equated with gambling outcome; to lose is to be despicable or worthless

---

[3]This last group is so lacking in any cravings that to regard abstinence as an indication of treatment success seems almost cheating. Yet these people have not been misdiagnosed.

Table 5–10
Preoccupation

1. When not gambling is preoccupied with reliving past gambling experiences, handicapping, or planning the next gambling venture, or thinking of ways to get money with which to gamble

2. The presence of a persistent urge to gamble—"cravings"

3. Gambling thought of as the way to solve financial problems—there may be a fantasy of a "big win"

4. Gambling thought of as the solution to other problems
   – gambles as an expression of anger, or when feeling misunderstood
   – turns to gambling when restless or bored

5. Will lie—to family, employer, therapist—to protect and conceal the extent of one's involvement with gambling

Does the presence of cravings reflect the individual's love of gambling, its psychic importance and his defensive need for it, and/or membership in some particular subtype of pathological gambler?

My fourth category, *disregard for the consequences*, is the one most familiar to previous users of DSM-III. Table 5–11 lists three items that, like the ones appearing under each of the other categories, are focal points for the information I gather in making my diagnostic assessment. These items also raise questions. For example, I wonder about the difference between the gambler who actually engages in illegal activities, such as forgery or embezzlement, and those who think about doing so, but seek help before crossing that line. What I wish to emphasize, however, is how these categories structure my approach, allowing me to say why someone is a pathological gambler, and what got them in trouble, and maybe why they sought therapy. It allows some basis for comparison.

In addition to the diagnostic criteria, which emerge during a thorough gambling history, I look at ancillary factors, and predisposing factors. Ancillary factors, as their name suggests, are not necessary for a diagnosis

Table 5–11
Disregard for Consequences

1. Has borrowed under false pretenses or beyond one's means, sold possessions, or gone without necessities to get money for gambling

2. Has committed or considered illegal acts, such as forgery, fraud, theft, or embezzlement to finance gambling

3. Has jeopardized (or lost) marriage, job, or career because of gambling

but supplement the essential criteria. All twelve of those interviewed in the preceding section were unanimous in their belief that the gambling was a symptom of low self-esteem, a sense of not being in control of one's life, and a need to avoid pain. Personality problems, they agreed, were significant in most cases, and *preceded* the gambling.

Some of the *ancillary factors* I list in table 5–12 are common to all the addictions, while others seem specific for the pathological gambler. You will notice some overlap between factors, and that there has not been an attempt to arrange them in order. This is a list that is evolving.

In addition, I look at *predisposing factors*, and here I differ somewhat from those published in DSM-III-R and reprinted in table 5–13. The one I am most critical of is gambling exposure during adolescence. While pathological gamblers tend to attach greater significance to their early gambling experiences, adolescent gambling is a rather normal and universal phenomenon, at least it is for boys. Boys actually begin gambling much earlier, during latency or preadolescence, pitching pennies, flipping base-

Table 5–12
Ancillary Factors

1. Self-worth equated with financial and material success (corollary: money will solve all problems)
2. All-or-nothing thinking: things are black or white, good or bad; one is a winner or loser
3. Fear, avoidance of intimacy
4. Believe nothing they do is ever good enough (life is a series of no-win situations)
5. Concern with appearances, with "looking good" to others; an emphasis on the trappings of status (excessively generous or extravagant)
6. An inordinate amount of anger
7. Very competitive
8. Problems (also pain, guilt, all uncomfortable feelings) are to be avoided
9. Excessive omnipotence (fantasies of power and control that defend against helplessness and other intolerable feelings)
10. An intolerance of uncertainty
11. Feels unlovable, and at the same time *entitled* ("angry for love")
12. Resents authority; also responsibility, obligations, necessity (will procrastinate)
13. Wants to turn the tables, to make others feel as he or she does
14. Doesn't know how to handle success
15. Shame at not being in control, or if forced to acknowledge limitations
16. Easily restless or bored

Table 5–13
Predisposing Factors (DSM-III-R)

1. Inappropriate parental discipline (absence, inconsistency, or harshness)
2. Exposure to gambling activities as an adolescent
3. High family value placed on material and financial symbols
4. A lack of family emphasis on saving, planning, budgeting
5. Female pathological gamblers are more apt to have a husband with alcohol dependence or who is often absent from home

Table 5–14
Predisposing Factors

1. Emphasis on social status in family
2. A particularly critical or rejecting parent with whom the gambler identified
3. Father either a failure or very successful; and competitive
4. A neglecting or inconsistent mother, or one who clearly preferred a sibling
5. Family history of alcoholism or compulsive gambling
6. Physical defect, or some other developmental or medical problem causing shame or humiliation

ball cards, and playing marbles.[4] My list of predisposing factors is presented in table 5–14.

For completeness' sake, I include a list of *exacerbating factors*. These are the events that might set off a binge or be the stimulus for a gambler's deterioration. It might have occurred years before, yet be the external factor ultimately responsible for the person coming to you in such desperate straits. The list is well-known, and includes 1) a death or divorce; 2) the birth of a sibling or child; 3) some physical illness or threat to one's life; 4) a job or career disappointment; or, paradoxically, 5) success.

Problem Gambling

The term "problem gambler" appears in the literature in varying and contradictory ways. Frequently it is used to describe someone whose gambling falls short of the diagnostic criteria, but who is assumed to be at an earlier stage. Such individuals are referred to as early or "potential" path-

---

[4]Sirgay Sanger said that in his experience treating children, this difference between the sexes is disappearing, with girls now showing more of an interest in early gambling games (Symposium on Compulsive Gambling, sponsored by the Massachusetts Council and the Harvard Center for Addiction Studies, June 3 and 4, 1988).

ological gamblers. Sometimes these problem gamblers exist only statistically, defined by a score on the DSM-III, the DSM-III-R, or the South Oaks Gambling Screen, which is below the number of affirmative responses needed to be considered "pathological."

On other occasions the term "problem gambling" is used more inclusively, to refer both to pathological gamblers and to those in the lesser category. Again, this can be defined statistically, by questionnaire response, or can refer loosely to anyone with a gambling problem.

A third meaning makes "problem gambler" synonymous with "pathological gambler." The former is sometimes used when an author is deliberately seeking to be vague; the term "excessive gambler" may be used for the same purpose. Elsewhere the choice is made for aesthetic or literary reasons, as when "pathological gambler" has already appeared twice in the paragraph, and the author wishes to avoid repetition.

I suggest that with all these meanings the term has become something of a wastebasket. It is time we fill in this wasteland by describing those other kinds of gambling problems that are not compulsive or pathological. The difficulty in doing this is that these are people who don't usually come to us for help. These problem gamblers don't go to therapists, and are even less likely to be seeking admission to our treatment centers.

There has been some attempt at classification; notably Custer's relief and escape gambler and his serious social gambler, and Vicki Abt's obsessional gambler, come immediately to mind. Now that the shift to DSM-III-R is permitting earlier diagnosis, it is essential that we reexamine these types to see where in the continuum they fit.

We'll start with the easiest, Custer's *serious social gambler*. The name is accurate; this is a social gambler, for whom gambling is entertainment. While he hopes to win, he accepts losing as a natural part of the game. However, he takes his gambling seriously, and plays regularly, with concentration and intensity. Custer (1985, 25), writes that there are gambling widows, just as there are golf or tennis or football widows, but that it does not go beyond that: "Serious social gamblers are generally attentive to their families, spending time with them and being involved in their problems and pleasures. If they are not, it is not because of their preoccupation with gambling."

This is a rather idealistic portrayal. I'm sure there are many golf or football widows who feel neglected. There is a spectrum of involvement, and as we approach upper limits, the preoccupation does take away from family relationships. Note that we are still talking about people whose gambling is controlled. Money allotted for, and spent on gambling, is well within their means. When they are ahead they do not keep playing until their winnings have been lost, nor do they chase their losses. In fact, alongside the tremendous importance attributed to gambling in their lives, is this emphasis on control.

Abt et al. (1985) has referred to them as obsessive gamblers, and while I have elected not to use her term, I wholeheartedly recommend her description of the phenomenon. What I do not like about her name for it is that, first, "obsessive" refers to thoughts, not actions, and clearly we are talking about behavior here, and second, because obsessive or obsessional thoughts are, by definition, not in control. I prefer to think of them as either *habitual* or *control* gamblers.[5]

They will go to the race track and bet every race, but see to it that they have enough money left so they can come back the next day and continue. Unlike pathological gamblers, who are in rebellion against rules and authority, habitual gamblers like order and conformity in their lives. They may work at occupations like accounting, where just such traits are valued. However, for various reasons they find real life too uncertain and insecure for them. They do not feel in control. Gambling offers them an escape—and a solution. As Abt has noted, "The attraction of (such) gambling is not risk but certainty; it is an escape into order (p. 122)."

In addition to his greater involvement, and this emphasis on control, I find two additional features frequently distinguishing the habitual gambler from his serious social cousin: first, gambling has become the focus of his identity. He thinks of himself not as an accountant or husband, but as a gambler. (You might learn about this by inquiring what he would like as his epitaph.) Secondly, he is frequently a system player, with a fantasy of becoming a professional gambler. The relationship between the different types of gamblers is diagrammed in figure 5–1.

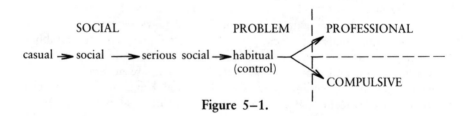

Figure 5–1.

---

[5]The latter (control gambler), of course, would be the obvious name, and my hesitation stems from the need to avoid confusion. Most pathological gamblers, at one time or another, like to think of themselves as control or controlled gamblers.

Dostoyevsky (1866; letters and other writings) described what he called the "aristocratic" or "superior" gambler who is in control of his emotions. He, himself, believed that by controlling his feelings, essentially not caring, he would be guaranteeing success at the roulette table. Edmund Bergler (1958), in his classification of compulsive gamblers, includes this type of "superior" or "unexcited" gambler.

Since the habitual gambler does not appear in the professional literature, a clinical illustration may be useful:

Mr. M. came to me with a most serious problem: he had lost the ability to gamble! Following a traumatic incident, a little over a month before, in which he thought a gun had been pointed at him, then fired, he became extremely anxious. It turned out to be a hoax, and at no time had he been in danger. When he learned this afterward, the anger he felt brought no relief, but an intensification of his symptoms. He couldn't stop reliving the incident, and kept looking over his shoulder, expecting to see the gunman. He couldn't concentrate, developed a tremor, had severe insomnia, and worst of all for him, no longer looked forward to his daily visits to the track. When he did go, it was without his previous sense of pleasure and satisfaction.

He was a habitual gambler, and the race track was where he felt most alive, yet to the people who knew him, he was an extremely successful, talented, and prolific writer. His personal life was another story. He had been married three times and had numerous girlfriends, yet he admitted never having let anyone get close to him. He acknowledged chronic feelings of emptiness, and for that reason, could not stand being alone. There had been a lifelong avoidance of emotional conflict.

He described himself as a coward who hid behind a facade of un-flappability. What he was most fearful of was any kind of physical or emotional confrontation. This would most particularly mean violence, but would also include any kind of face-to-face confrontation in which he did not know what the other person would say or do. When he had to break up with a girlfriend, he would so fear any emotional reaction from her that he would have a friend fly out from New York to do it for him. Needless to say, this fear of emotion had inhibited the development of any real intimacy in his relationships.

His problem seemed rooted in his parents' frequent arguments when he was growing up. In response to criticism by the patient's father, or whenever she was made angry, his mother would have "screaming fits" in which she would get hysterical and complain that she couldn't breathe. The patient would believe her, and be terrified of her dying. Father, meanwhile, would be egging her on, laughing.

Since the age of twelve, he has been infatuated with gambling, not in the manner of a pathological gambler, which he most clearly is not, but in an extremely controlled fashion. While this is his primary interest—his one goal in life is to beat the horse races, and this is far more meaningful than any professional accomplishments—it is just one of a number of ways in which he demonstrates mastery and control over exciting, unpredictable, competitive, or aggressive activities. These invariably involve him as a spectator rather than as a participant.

Mr. M. never writes under his own name. He has remained unknown to the public while fostering the careers of others. He remains hidden from view, as he does in his own life, ghost writer, publicist, promoter, but never actor. The strongest clue to his peculiarly counterphobic lifestyle was found in his dreamlife. There were recurrent dreams which had been present for as long as he could remember—that is, up until the traumatic incident, when they had been replaced by typical anxiety dreams in which he felt helpless and out of control. What were these earlier counterphobic dreams? What for anyone else would have been nightmares, had for him a paradoxical effect. Dreams and fantasies of the most extreme violence had regularly soothed him to sleep. He would dream of trains crashing, cars hitting head-on, one person attacking and killing another. Always he would be watching and enjoying it; he would cheer them on, and feel satisfaction at the outcome. He was never involved as actor or acted upon—he was always a spectator.

All of that changed the night of his trauma, when the dream seemed to become real. It was as if his trusted characters, suddenly refusing to play the game, turned on him. His defenses temporarily broke down, when his illusion of safety and control proved false.

Mr. M.'s experience may be more dramatic than one usually encounters; more often the habitual gambler comes at the insistence of a spouse or family member, who thinks he or she is dealing with a compulsive gambler. Sometimes the relative is a member of AA or one of the other twelve-step groups, and is on a campaign to eliminate all addictive and compulsive activities from the family. Sometimes, gambling may be the presenting complaint, but not the problem, and one soon realizes there are control issues between husband and wife. The relationship is a symbiotic or parasitic one, with a lot of primitive projection and projective identification; one partner, usually the husband, turns to gambling to create a new identity and a world he can control. Frequently, when the gambler gets involved in therapy, and the relationship starts to improve, the spouse will find an excuse for ending treatment.

We turn now to Custer's *relief and escape* gambler, a type I must admit having difficulty understanding. From the description in *When Luck Runs Out* (1985), it was not at all clear whether the author was including pathological gamblers, particularly when he mentions how, after a period of years, "relief and escape become a way of life" (p. 30).

He describes the relief from anxiety, depression, anger, boredom and loneliness; how gambling alters self-perception, by allowing the person to feel powerful and important; and how it provides an escape from difficulties and crises. He compares the use of gambling to that of alcohol, where gambling has the same mood-altering and perception-altering effects. While this is undoubtedly true, these are the same dynamics found in our pathological gamblers, who also are seeking relief and escape. Clearly the dynamic use to which gambling is being put is not an essential feature.

Custer distinguishes two subtypes: the explosive and the quiet (see figure 5–2). As an example of the *explosive* relief and escape gambler he describes a man who periodically rebels against his pervasive sense that he can never be good enough. "There was something inside of me that continued to put me down and made me feel just the way my father had made me feel—a nothing and a nobody" (p. 32). His father had never been interested in him. Gambling allowed him to let off his anger, and to feel important. (Again, we note, the description would fit many pathological gamblers.)

Custer clarified (personal communication) that what he wished to emphasize was the binge aspect of such gambling. A typical example would be the "high roller" who goes to Las Vegas two or three times a year, and loses what others would consider a lot, but for him is maybe ten percent of his income. What is significant is that he knows he is going to lose and he has a good time doing it. Another name for this might be the *episodic excessive* gambler. When the episodes occur increasingly closer together, we start to suspect we are dealing with a pathological gambler.

Custer's other subtype is the *quiet* gambler, the person who gambles for its analgesic rather than euphoriant effect. His clinical illustration (pp. 30, 31) is of a rather depressed woman who gambles daily in search of oblivion. Here his analogy with alcohol seems particularly apt. Such people are gambling dependent, the equivalent of the person who is drunk every day but who goes to work and takes care of his obligations, kind of a low-level alcoholic who, if he does not develop cirrhosis or other physical problems, will continue without obvious progression or loss of control. It should be noted that each of Custer's examples of relief and escape gamblers was significantly depressed or dysphoric, and in need of psychotherapy.

Since these problem gamblers—the habitual or control gambler, the episodic excessive or explosive, and the analgesic or quiet gambler—rarely

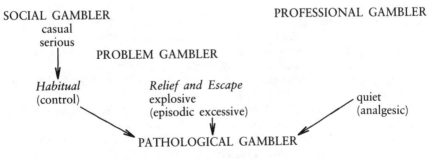

Figure 5–2.

come to us, why is it important that we recognize and discuss them? First, because as we are successful in educating the public about gambling problems, we will be seeing more and more of them. As I hope I have conveyed, many of these people are in need of help. Second, and perhaps more relevant given the topic of this paper, they can assist us in clarifying our definition of pathological or compulsive gambling.

These problem gamblers may seem at times as involved with gambling as the pathological gambler, and they show many of the same dynamics— they gamble to escape, from depression and other intolerable feeling states, from the uncertainties and insecurity of their lives; they may be seeking control, and do so in an alternative world, which they create in a casino or race track; and they solve their problems omnipotently, resulting in a temporary sense of triumph or grandiosity.

Despite these similarities, there are crucial differences. If we think back to the four characteristics of the pathological gambler listed in the previous section, one can appreciate what is missing. Problem gamblers do not show progression, their response to winning and losing is different, and they don't chase.

Clearly, problem gamblers have personality and coping problems and turn to gambling as a solution, which is not to say that they may not eventually become pathological gamblers. It is important to know where these other types fit. This is essential if we are to understand what the pathological gambler is like early in his or her career, and if we are to acknowledge those people who gamble heavily, even excessively, without becoming pathological.

References

Abt, V., Smith, J. F., & Christiansen, E. M. 1985. *The Business of Risk: Commercial Gambling in Mainstream America.* Lawrence: Univ. Kansas.

American Psychiatric Association 1980. *Diagnostic and Statistical Manual of Mental Disorders,* third edition. Washington, D.C.: APA.

American Psychiatric Association Work Group to Revise DSM-III 1985. *DSM-III-R in Development,* draft 10/5/85. Washington, D.C.: APA.

American Psychiatric Association 1987. *Diagnostic and Statistical Manual of Mental Disorders,* third edition revised. Washington, D.C.: APA.

Bergler, E. 1958. *The Psychology of Gambling,* rpt. 1970. New York: Int. Univ. Press.

Custer, R., & Milt, H. 1985. *When Luck Runs Out: Help for Compulsive Gamblers and Their Families.* New York and Oxford: Facts on File Publ.

Dostoyevsky, F. M. 1866. *The Gambler.* In *The Gambler/Bobok/A Nasty Story,* trans. J. Coulson. London: Penguin

Fingarette, H. 1988. *Heavy Drinking: The Myth of Alcoholism as a Disease.* Berkeley: Univ. Calif.

Jampala, V. C., Sierles, F. S., & Taylor, M. C. 1986. Consumers Views of DSM-III: Attitudes and Practices of U.S. Psychiatrists and 1984 Graduating Psychiatric Residents. *American Journal of Psychiatry, 143*: 148–153.

Lesieur, H. R. 1979. The Compulsive Gambler's Spiral of Options and Involvement. *Psychiatry, 42*: 79–87.

———. 1984. *The Chase: Career of the Compulsive Gambler.* Cambridge, Massachusettes: Schenkman Publ.

Rosenthal, R. J. 1986. Chance, Luck, Fate, and Destiny: Toward a Developmental Model of Pathological Gambling. Keynote address of the Second Annual Conference on Gambling Behavior, sponsored by the National Council on Compulsive Gambling, November 20, 1986.

Wray, I., & Dickerson, M. G. 1981. Cessation of High Frequency Gambling and 'Withdrawal' Symptoms. *British Journal of Addiction, 76*: 401–405.

6

Inpatient Treatment Programs for Pathological Gamblers

Rena M. Nora, M.D.

Introduction

Within the past two decades, a number of events and developments evolved that led to significant changes in the legal, social, and professional-medical approaches to the problem of compulsive gambling in this country. Some of these are: (a) establishment of legalized gambling in forty-seven states with rapid expansion of gambling facilities; (b) availability of incredible amounts of money and instant credit, (c) advances in technology such as the wonders of simulcasting and computerized slot and jackpot machines; (d) increased accessibility by way of modern transportation by land, by sea, and by air; (e) a growing number of sophisticated forms of gambling opportunities including stock and commodity options; (f) formal recognition by the American Psychiatric Association in 1980 of pathological gambling as an impulse control disorder and its inclusion in the Diagnostic and Statistical Manual of Mental Disorders, Third Edition (the 1987 revision of this classification, DSM III-R, acknowledges compulsive gambling as an addictive disorder with diagnostic criteria and associated clinical features remarkably similar to alcoholism and other psychoactive substance dependence); (g) increased public awareness through education and counseling as with employee assistance programs; (h) increased interest by local and state legislative officials regarding the psychosocial impact of legalized gambling in the community; and (i) some improvements in the payment system for mental health care services. Findings of research recently conducted by the National Council on Compulsive Gambling indicate that 80 percent of adult Americans engage in some form of gambling as an exciting pastime or as a recreational diversion. However, there is a growing population of about 3 to 10 million vulnerable individuals who fit the criteria for pathological gamblers. There is a commensurate need for appropriate services and resources for the diagnosis, treatment, and rehabilitation of compulsive gamblers and their families.

Current treatment approaches to pathological gambling include inpatient, outpatient, residential care, halfway homes and the use of freestanding or contract treatment units. Factors that determine the type of care for a patient may include not only the severity and complexity of gambling related problems but also the accessibility and availability of treatment providers and facilities. Most health professionals, even those in the mental health field, have virtually no training in the diagnosis and treatment of compulsive gambling. In 1988, there were only about twenty treatment facilities in the United States established specifically for the treatment of compulsive gambling.

Inpatient Treatment Programs

Many compulsive gamblers can and do recover using only outpatient care and/or self-support groups such as Gamblers Anonymous, Gam-Anon, and Gam-Ateen. However, there are indications for considering the inpatient treatment approach: (1) significant disturbed behavior or ideations relating to suicide, violence, or intent to commit a crime; (2) severe target symptoms of anxiety, panic, or fear of psychological decompensation; (3) existing comorbidities such as medical or psychiatric complications that require careful monitoring and supervision (including severe dissociative-like symptoms of sleep deprivation following several days of continuous and uncontrolled gambling); (4) need to perform diagnostic tests for primary and differential diagnoses that cannot be accomplished on an outpatient basis without undue hardship; (5) patient has become so overwhelmed and devastated by family pressures, work problems, financial problems, and legal predicaments, and may temporarily require a well-structured, secure, and safe environment; (6) patient has reasonably tried outpatient care but was unsuccessful. The first three indications may constitute psychiatric emergencies. In my experience, patients who chose to participate in an inpatient program learn early to accept the concept of themselves as sick patients in need of treatment. They also appreciate sooner the value of a new lifestyle that does not include gambling. The program provides a good foundation for the patient's recovery and ensures a proper introduction to Gamblers Anonymous and other self-help groups. Patients also benefit by the medical orientation of a hospital setting and exposure to didactic sessions on alcoholism and other psychoactive substance dependance. The latter is important since current surveys indicate that approximately 15 to 20 percent of compulsive gamblers are dually addicted to alcohol.

The first inpatient treatment program for pathological gambling was started by Dr. Robert L. Custer and Dr. Alida Glen in 1972 at the

Veterans Administration Medical Center in Brecksville, Ohio. Since then, other inpatient programs were developed in other VA medical facilities in Miami, Florida; Brooklyn, New York; Loma Linda, California; and Lyons, New Jersey. New programs were established in recent years such as the Taylor Manor Hospital in Ellicot City, Maryland, the Philadelphia Psychiatric Institute in Pennsylvania, and the New Hope Foundation in Marlboro, New Jersey. Dr. Custer and his associates provided consultation and initial staff training for most of these facilities. This in part may explain the similarities in the organization, philosophy, and function of these treatment centers.

Program elements and features commonly shared by most of the inpatient programs are best memorized using the acronym THERAPIES: T—Team approach provided by a well-trained and well-qualified multidisciplinary staff; H—"Here and now" focus pertaining to the patient's behavioral repertoire and problems; E—Educational modules on compulsive gambling and other addictive disorders; R—Restitution of all gambling-related debts and review of financial problems; A—Abstinence from gambling activities; P—Physical problems attended to and physical fitness emphasized; I—Individual, group, marital, and family therapies are considered highly important; E—Evaluation and management of characterological defects and maladaptive coping skills; S—Self-support groups as Gamblers Anonymous and others are recognized as integral parts of the program.

The following discussion describes the inpatient program for compulsive gamblers at the VA Medical Center in Lyons, New Jersey.

Treatment Setting

The Compulsive Gambling Rehabilitation Unit (GRU) was established at Lyons, VA Medical Center in 1984 as a six-bed section of the Alcohol Dependence Treatment Program. This unit maintains a length of stay of twenty-one days. The basic management principle of using existing staff, space, and resources was given careful consideration to accommodate budget constraints and to maintain cost-effectiveness. Feasibility and needs assessment studies conducted before the establishment of the program indicated a small projected number of patients during the initial years of operation. The use of the six-bed section follows the "accordion" approach to effective use of beds. This allows flexibility to increase or decrease the census of the program according to the need for beds. When the GRU census is low, the beds are made available for patients admitted to the alcohol program. Efforts are made to consistently maintain reasonable occupancy rates for the entire floor with fifty-two beds.

Program Management

Administration

The care and supervision of patients in the GRU is provided by a multi-disciplinary treatment team. The core members of the treatment team consist of a psychiatrist, a nurse, a social worker, and a psychologist. Representatives from other disciplines, such as the chaplain, dietician, recreation, and rehabilitation therapists, vocational and peer counselors also participate in the patient's overall treatment planning and also implementation. The use of volunteer services and visits by members of Gamblers Anonymous are extremely valuable. In-service training sessions for the treatment team were conducted during the year before the program started. These sessions focused on the diagnosis, treatment, and rehabilitation of compulsive gambling. Propensity for compulsive gamblers to have dual or cross-addictions was recognized. The existing staff of the alcohol program learned quickly. They had less difficulty in understanding and accepting implementing treatment principles specific to compulsive gambling because of their basic orientation and familiarity with approaches to addictive disorders.

Admission and Intake

All patients admitted to the program are interviewed and screened by the treatment staff. Referrals from outside the state may be evaluated and processed by the staff psychiatrist via telephones when necessary. The DSM-III-R diagnostic criteria is used as the basis for screening. Patients with active and significant alcohol or psychoactive substance dependence are encouraged to participate in the alcohol or drug program prior to their entry to the GRU. Most of those who seek inpatient treatment have more serious problems than patients who seek outpatient treatment. Patients who are actively suicidal or who require special observation and supervision are cared for in another psychiatric ward and are transferred to the GRU only when their clinical condition has been stabilized. During the first two to three days of hospitalization, the patient receives a complete medical, psychological, and social assessment, including medical history and physical examination, as well as routine and appropriate laboratory tests. A battery of psychological tests includes the South Oaks Gambling Screen (SOGS), the Minnesota Multiphasic Personality Inventory (MMPI), the Clinical Analysis Questionaire (CAQ), and Beck's Depression Inventory (BDI). When appropriate, Dexamethasone Suppression Tests and other tests are done. Baseline information is useful not only as a clinical tool for diagnosis and treatment; such data may be extremely useful for research and educational purposes.

Treatment

Individual and group therapy sessions, didactic lectures, group discussion, and attendance at GA meetings constitute the core of the program. Compulsive gamblers and patients in the alcohol program participate jointly in recreational activities, as well as stress management and relaxation exercises. Techniques used in cognitive-behavior therapy are useful. Patients are encouraged to write their autobiography, as this relates to their gambling problem. Patients are also instructed to make a list of their "character defects" and maladaptive behavior patterns. They then develop alternative strategies and priorities that will enable them to maintain a good recovery and to lead a satisfying life that is gambling-free. Opportunities for marital and family therapy are available. The spouses are strongly encouraged to join the Gam-Anon self-help group. The family members are often the hidden victims of compulsive gambling and they require appropriate attention and support.

Financial Matters

Pathological gambling is a complex disorder. Comprehensive treatment should include dealing with the financial crisis, legal problems, loss of a job, and loss of family and social support system. Members of GA with expertise in financial matters may be invited to sit down with the patient and the spouse to conduct a "pressure group" session. This meeting focuses on the realistic accounting of all debts and obligations to creditors. Reasonable ways of how best to repay or settle financial obligations are discussed. Efforts are made at full restitution, no matter how many months or years it may take to accomplish this. In some situations, patients may have to consider either changing jobs or developing "safety" systems that could be built into their work situation to minimize the dangers of handling large amounts of cold cash.

Gamblers' Strengths

Compulsive gamblers are basically competitive, energetic, success-driven, intelligent, and resourceful individuals. Many had successful and brilliant careers before the onset of devastation caused by their compulsive gambling. These positive attributes and skills can have useful and practical therapeutic implications.

Other Program Activities

As a program that provides unique and specialized care to compulsive gamblers, the unit becomes the hub of education and training activities for medical students, residents, and other health professionals. There are ample opportunities for conducting interesting and worthwhile research projects. Since the treatment of compulsive gambling is still a new and rapidly growing field, the staff are frequently invited to give educational presentations to other professionals or the community. Active involvement in television, radio, and other media presentations is one of the functions of the staff that promotes good public relations, enhances community service, and stimulates referrals of patients to the program. On certain occasions, the professional staff have participated in legislative hearings and special meetings which deal with the problems of compulsive gambling.

Aftercare Planning

Discharge planning begins on day one of the program. Most patients, however, are too distraught or too overwhelmed to come up with a reasonable goal during their initial stay. By the second week, however, most of the patients are able to think more clearly and to make more specific plans for their return to the community. The importance of abstinence and involvement in Gamblers Anonymous and other self-help groups are repeatedly emphasized. Some patients who have been rejected by their families may need assistance in getting temporary placement in boarding or halfway homes. Followup of individual therapy on an outpatient basis may be appropriate for some patients; others choose to continue with GA meetings only. In any case, the patient is strongly urged to make contact with the treatment staff either in person or by phone on the ninetieth day of his or her abstinence from gambling. This serves as a positive reinforcement for recovery and indicates our interest in his or her progress. A meeting with the spouse or family on the day of discharge provides opportunities to clarify questions and reinforce realistic aftercare plans. Such a meeting could have a profound effect on the morale of the patient and the family.

Additional Considerations

In addition to the above descriptions of the various aspects of inpatient programs for compulsive gambling, the following comments may be noteworthy:

- Comprehensive care is the basis for the inpatient program for compulsive gambling. Services and care are geared toward healing of the whole person. Attention is given not only to the patient's disability or weakness but more importantly to his or her strength, capabilities, and skills.

- Treatment of compulsive gamblers can produce substantial economic savings in terms of decrease in absenteeism, maintenance of satisfactory job performance, reduced incidences of stealing, forging of checks, and embezzlement. Even if the program brings about only a temporary remission from gambling, improvement in the quality of life of the patient and that of his or her family is well worth it and goes beyond dollars and cents.
- A new inpatient program may start with a small number of beds, which could expand when the need arises. When established as a subsection of another addictive disorder unit, the program can better survive its initial years, especially when the combined units are served by the same staff and resources are shared.
- Maintenance of a high standard of care requires a treatment staff who keeps informed with current and innovative treatment approaches. Attendance at various conferences, workshops, and activities such as GA conclaves enable staff to keep abreast with state-of-the-art issues and prevents "professional burnout."
- Effective program evaluation on a yearly basis and regular monitoring of potential problems may result in timely corrective actions and appropriate modification of policies that have impact on patient care.
- Studies on treatment outcome following participation in the GRU programs are important and indicators usually include the status of the patient's abstinence, his or her efforts at restitution of debts, and the overall quality of life functioning.

A compulsive gambler is a total human being whose complex needs may require complex interventions. It may be that no one treatment program can meet the needs of all compulsive gamblers. There is a growing trend to recognize various subtypes of compulsive gamblers who may require different treatment approaches. Significant clinical research and demographic studies on compulsive gambling are painfully slow in coming. However, we now have some amount of knowledge and understanding of this devastating illness that could serve as a theoretical framework and basis for helping the compulsive gamblers on their way to recovery.

Bibliography

Bannister, G. 1977. Cognitive and Behavior Therapy in a Case of Compulsive Gambling. *Cog. Ther., Res.* 1:223.

Beck, A. T. 1970. Cognitive Therapy: Nature and Relation to Behavior Therapy. *Behav. Ther.* 1:184.

Custer, R. L. 1984. Profile of a Pathological Gambler, *J. Clinical Psychiatry*, 45:12 (Sec. 2) December.

Greenberg, H. R. 1980. Psychology of Gambling, *Comprehensive Textbook of Psychiatry*, Third Edition, 3274–3282.

7

Clinical Observations of Family Members of Compulsive Gamblers

Joanna Franklin, M.S., C.A.C.
Donald R. Thoms, M.S.

T he history of treatment of the family of the compulsive gambler begins in 1960 with the formation of Gam-Anon. This self-help group is patterned after Al-Anon, the support group for the loved ones of alcoholics. Not until 1971 did the professional mental health community begin treatment of pathological gambling. The Veterans Administration began this first treatment program in Brecksville, Ohio. Though involved with family members from day one, the Brecksville program was limited in its ability to focus on the treatment needs of the family members. The V.A. designed a twenty-eight-day therapeutic stay for the pathological gambler, and because of the inpatient design of the program, ongoing family therapy was precluded by both geographical and fiscal constraints.

Since these pioneering days of gambling treatment, much has been learned. The advent of state-funded treatment programs has allowed mental health practitioners to examine more closely the dynamics of the pathological gambler's family, while they participated in long-term outpatient therapy. In many state-funded programs the spouse of the pathological gambler has been treated as a primary client, often without the gambler being involved in the treatment process. Group therapy for the spouse of the gambler was formed to meet the therapeutic needs of not just the current gambling crises but also the long-standing issues of depression, isolation, marital discord, poor parenting, and poor communication skills.

In 1979 Maryland began the first "open to the public" treatment program, meaning one was not required to be a veteran to seek help. This treatment program is at Taylor Manor Hospital, in Ellicott City, Maryland. In 1982 New York passed similar legislation creating, initially, two outpatient programs: St. Vincent's North Richmond Community Mental Health Center's Gamblers' Treatment Center, on Staten Island, and the Rochester Health Association's Gamblers' Treatment Program in Rochester, New York. Since their initial funding, New York has begun to expand treatment services to Queens, Manhattan, and in Buffalo at Buffalo Jewish

Family Services Gamblers Treatment Program. There are approximately forty-five treatment programs for compulsive gamblers and their families at this time. The availability of services to local populations has allowed treatment providers to collect information first-hand from family members as they become actively involved in the therapeutic process over an extended time. The observation of hundreds of families have lead us to develop a profile of the spouse of the compulsive gambler. (See table 7–1 for profile of spouse.) More often than not the spouse who joins in the therapeutic process with the gambler is a wife and the identified gambler

Table 7–1
A Potential Profile of a Spouse of a Male Compulsive Gambler

1. Passive dependent
2. Poor self-image/self-concept
3. Unrealistic expectations of a husband and marriage
4. Rescue fantasies/mold into fantasy image
5. Impressed by gambler's outgoing behavior
6. Psychologically and physically abused
7. Denial as strong as gambler
8. Family history of gambling or alcohol or substance abuse
9. Often contemplating separation/divorce
10. Fantasizing having an extramarital affair
11. Unable to manage kids
12. Feeling trapped
13. Poor interpersonal skills
14. Inconsistent discipline with children/feeling inadequate as a parent
15. Inconsistent message to husband/demanding at times
16. Often the enabler
17. Poor assertiveness skills
18. Allies with children against husband
19. Angry—resentful, depressed, anxious, confused, guilty
20. Often a spender/nothing but the best
21. Appearance most important
22. Physically neglectful
23. Few friends
24. Lack of sexual desire
25. Unresolved issues in father/daughter relationship
26. Grew up feeling inadequate
27. Experienced emotional deprivation
28. Frequently physical ailments
29. Codependent
30. Adult child of an alcoholic

is a husband. Though current research indicates that a growing number of gamblers seeking help are female, the following information is reflective of the female spouses seen at both the St. Vincent's gambling treatment program in New York, and the Taylor Manor gambling treatment program in Maryland.

The Effects of Compulsive Gambling on the Family

Though we are speaking in general terms, and there are always exceptions to any rule, the following profile outlines not just some common characteristics of the spouse of a male compulsive gambler but also many of the clinical areas with treatment implications.

As is the case with the drug addict and the alcoholic, the gambler and the spouse go through a progressive decline, or worsening of symptoms, until a bottom is "hit" and the rebuilding phase of the disorder begins. For the spouse this includes seven phases. The first is the denial phase. (See figure 7–1.) During this time the spouse has occasional worries, usually keeps concerns to herself, considers the gambling as temporary and is usually easily reassured. The extent of gambling is often hidden from the spouse, and at this time, she appears as a colluder, silently agreeing not to confront the tiring excuses put forth by the gambler. When the issue of unpaid bills arises, a growing financial crisis usually begins the stress phase. During this period, the spouse experiences rejection from her gambling husband, arguments increase, she makes more demands upon the gambler, and attempts to control his gambling. This leads inevitably to bailouts and increased isolation from her support system as she avoids those who are advising her to "leave the guy," divorce, or press legal charges. Rather than follow through with such severe consequences she begins to lie and distance those who may inquire about her circumstances. In some cases her depression increases to a point where it now becomes evident to family, friends, and children. She becomes ineffective at work and as a parent.

In the second phase, the desperation of the spouse as gambling continues and finances worsen, leave the spouse frequently seeking bailouts, making excuses to creditors, family, friends, employers, employees, and creating explanations for the children about their father's absence or uncaring behavior. But she has not directly addressed the fact that life has become unmanageable. The emotional and economical needs of the family are being neglected. This frustration the spouse feels as gambling continues, debts increase, and lies and avoidance compound, leaves her emotionally and physically exhausted. The spouse feels distress, confusion, resentment, anxiety, and in the more severe cases, immobilization and impaired thinking. In the third phase, rage and panic often fill the heart of the spouse, who is at a loss for any way to affect her husband's pathology. Shortly after this phase comes "the bottom" for the spouse. By the time she hits bottom in the fourth phase, she may feel helpless and hopeless, may be abusing substances (specifically alcohol and pills), considering divorce, suffering from depression, and in the extreme, considering suicide.

Origins of the Characteristics of the Gambler's Spouse

Some of the characteristics of the spouse appear to have developmental origins. Poor self-image and self-concept seem to frequently coincide with a family history of gambling, alcohol, or substance abuse. Frequently the adult children of alcoholics, these spouses contend with unresolved conflicts with their fathers that affect their lives. Experiences of emotional deprivation as a child leave the spouse searching for rescue fantasies and eager to mold her spouse into her ideal image of a husband. Many of these women enter into adult relationships with long histories of being victims and martyrs. Many have spent much of their childhood and adolescence as saviors in the family and find themselves trapped in a passive-dependent relationship.

Often the enabler's passivity leads to inconsistent discipline with children and increasing feelings of inadequacy as a parent. For example, harsh punishments for minor rule infractions generate feelings of guilt and remorse. To modify these feelings, Mother then finds herself being overly permissive with her children, and frequently allows them to cross generational lines. In an attempt to control the gambler she often allies the children against her husband. Consequently, children find themselves trying to parent their father. Children inquire about his absences, neglecting behavior and make efforts to pressure Father into pleasing Mother by not gambling, being home, and fulfilling his emotional and financial obligations to the family. The spouse has succeeded in aligning the children with her but there is no power in numbers when trying to combat the gambling disorder. The result is further alienation within the couple, and between parents and children, distancing on the part of the gambler, and often, increased gambling in his attempt to reinstate himself within his own family.

The spouse soon finds herself unable to manage her children, whose fears and anxieties lead to inconsistent academic performance and under- or overachieving as well as tendencies toward substance abuse, sexual promiscuity, and gambling. This contributes to feelings of frustration, anger, resentment, confusion, guilt, and depression on the part of the spouse and family.

We often see inconsistent messages given to the gambler. At times the spouse places great importance on appearances. The assumption is that if things "look good" they will "be good." If the family can have the nice house, furniture, car, and so forth, then life will take on the qualities of the material possessions and stability will be not only financial but also emotional. The spouse has made a normal life her goal, so if things look normal then perhaps they will become normal. So when her husband has had a lucky day at gambling and brings home winnings, all celebrate and enjoy the good fortune. This reinforcement encourages the gambler to be the hero at home by bringing home the prize. But of course when the gambler returns from gambling and has lost, he receives resentment, anger, and rejection that send him quickly back into action in search of not just the lost money but more importantly, the lost respect, affection, and acceptance that being the winner have come to represent. Eventually the spouse comes to hate those few winning episodes as much (if not more) as the losing ones because they have come to represent a continued lifestyle of neglect to her emotional needs, the loss of her coparent, and an ever worsening cycle of pain, deceit, and abandonment.

During the early stages of this losing phase for the gambler, the spouse is in denial over what she sees. The thought of having selected a mate that has some of the same characteristics of her father is a frightening one. Denial takes over and the spouse tries to convince herself and her family and friends that this is not as bad as it seems, that her husband will stop his destructive gambling and return to the family. But as time continues so does the cycle of compulsive gambling and the impulse disorder begins to rule the lives of not just the gambler but also all who care and try to help him. Early efforts to ask that the gambling ease up give way to demanding and pleading and the spouse experiences herself as once again, as in childhood, unable to control the disruption in her life. She believes herself to be inadequate and ineffective at making a normal life for herself and her family.

Should the spouse be in her second marriage, perhaps having divorced her first husband because of a drinking or substance abuse problem, she is now beginning to believe she will never have the kind of normal, happy marriage she has always wanted. She may even think she is responsible for her husband's gambling activity and blame herself for the current state of the marriage, which is often stated when initially engaged in treatment. Should the gambler counterattack in an attempt to defend against his spouse's accusations, he would accuse her of not being the kind of wife he needs, of being a nag, a poor mother, and so forth. Such arguments

Table 7–2
The Other Woman

The other woman invades your mind every day; she chains your soul leaving me no chance to touch it. Your every motive in life includes only her. Your obsession with her steals your honesty, making it easier to lie than breathe, taking with it your laughter and tears. She consoles you the best and even satisfies your lust, always leaving no room for me. Even when you're not with her she's on your mind and devours your every breath. She's exciting; I'm boring.
I, as your wife, concede—I cannot compete. She will always survive leaving you alone to die a loser . . . Miss "Gamble" always wins!

By Connie (Wife of a Compulsive Gambler)

underline the poor interpersonal communication skills common in such relationships.

The spouse (and the gambler) have poor assertiveness skills. They try to effect change by manipulating each other. They each have such sensitivity to rejection that they have spent many years as "people pleasers," and have an exceptionally difficult time trying to effectively communicate their thoughts, emotions, needs, and desires.

As the exhaustion phase takes over the life of the spouse, she finds herself feeling psychologically abused, with few friends, physically neglectful, and with a lack of sexual desire. She may complain of increased physical ailments, and perhaps fantasize about having an extramarital affair. The spouse's feelings of lowered self-worth are supported by the common belief that her frequently absent spouse, who has shown no interest in sex lately, must be having an affair with another woman. She has great difficulty believing that the only other woman the typical compulsive gambler is interested in is "lady luck." This is illustrated in verse from a wife of a compulsive gambler.

Diminished libido, a common occurance among depressed and highly stressed gamblers, only increases mistrust and further alienates the couple.

The Effects of Compulsive Gambling on Children of Gamblers

A look at the children of the compulsive gambler yields a profile affected by both mother and father. (See table 7–3.) Many children of such disrupted homes have severe role conflict. Some have taken on the family role of scapegoat, some of peacemaker, and others carve out their niche in the family system as the overresponsible child. Often with growing feelings of anxiety, anger, and/or depression, these children feel responsible for the emotional climate in the home. Without a direct way to affect

Table 7–3
A Potential Profile of a Child of a Compulsive Gambler

1. Role conflict
   a. Scapegoat
   b. Put in middle
   c. Overresponsible
2. Depressed/anxious/angry
3. Poor social skills
4. Inconsistent academic performance/under- or overachiever
5. Family mascot
6. Feeling responsible for emotional climate
7. Alignment with mother
8. Protector of mother
9. Denies gambler's negative activity
10. Consistently disappointed
11. Tendency:

Alcoholic	Overeating	Isolation
Drug	Physically abusive	Gambling
Sexual promiscuity	Poor grades	

12. Overachievers
13. Sense of specialness
14. Always looking for positive feedback from gambler
15. Very physically active
16. Project anger and depression on peers
17. Poor interpersonal skills
18. Fear of abandonment
19. Doesn't want to be like gambler
20. They seek other adult males as role models

their family system, children begin acting out their conflicting emotions in a variety of ways. Inconsistent academic performance with under- or overachieving has already been mentioned, as has substance abuse and gambling behavior.

Growing up in a home with progressively worsening discord and turmoil, children of compulsive gamblers do not get a chance to witness effective interpersonal skills and consequently have poor skills themselves. An underlying fear of abandonment sends them searching for positive feedback from the gambler. Looking for father's approval seems to be an attempt to increase their sense of importance. Children who try to emotionally connect with their father also sometimes feel a need to deny the gambler's negative activity.

Much like the children of any addicted parent, these children have a long history of disappointment. Father and Mother make promises that are never kept and trust diminishes as the children learn not to believe what they hear and begin to use defenses against worsening psychic pain and frustration. Commitments to attend that ball game, birthday party, or special show all end in broken promises as the gambling disorder progresses. As children are solicited by Mother to align with her against this "bad father," they begin to make efforts to protect Mother. This crossing of generational lines takes the form of scolding father, correcting him, trying to shame him into some kind of compliance with mother's wishes, creating a wedge between not just husband and wife but father and children as well. Many a spouse entering treatment has told about having one or more children sleep with her while her husband is away gambling. Children and mother seek out each other for the security and comfort they both lack.

Some children take on the role of family mascot, trying to represent those values and ideas important to their perception of the family. Many children are very physically active and on the go all the time. They are involved in school, sports, games, friends, and perhaps a job, as if the activity is a kind of escape from their disrupted home life. While trying to be socially accepted by their peers, poor social skills often leave these children with few, if any, close friends. They frequently project their anger and depression on to peers. Many times these offspring promise themselves they will never be like their gambling fathers, that they will treat their families differently when they grow up. In an effort to ensure this they reach out to other adult males as role models. Many times their attempts to improve their situation in fact contribute to the disruption at home fueling neglect, resentment, and anger.

Treatment Issues Involving Families of Compulsive Gamblers

Clearly the treatment plan of any compulsive gambler is incomplete if it does not address the needs of the family. To assess such needs it has become common practice in both private and state-funded treatment programs to have them involved in the treatment process. The engagement of family as early as the assessment and evaluation phase is critical. Typically the compulsive gambler will sabotage his initial spouse contact; even if he does not, the spouse will, because of her own denial of pathological participation. The longer the therapist delays contact the more difficult it will become to engage the spouse and children in treatment. This may result in more sabotaging during the client's re-entry into the family system. Treatment proceeds in a four-part manner.

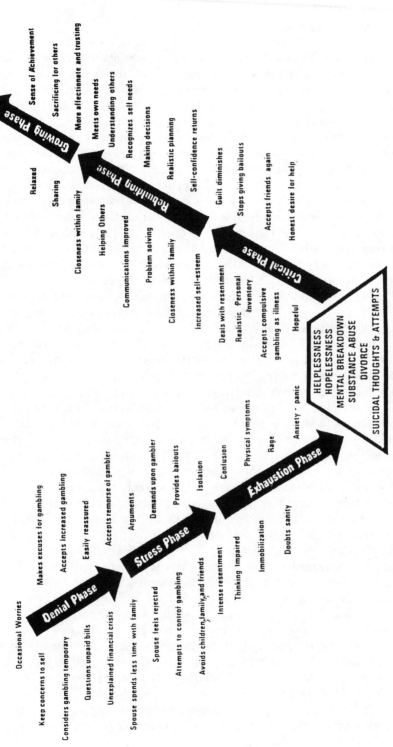

Figure 7–1. A Chart on the Effects of Compulsive Gambling on the Wife

From Wexler, S. *A chart on the effects of compulsive gambling on the wife.* Paper presented at the Sixth National Conference on gambling and Risk-Taking, Atlantic City, December 1984.

The first part focuses on the informational/educational needs of the spouse and family. While collecting a history from the spouse during the first few sessions, two things are accomplished. The first is that the spouse gets to vent her pent-up anger, fear, hurt, and frustration. The second achievement is one of validating information put forth by the gambler. No one is better able to accurately describe the home/financial situation than the spouse. Though she often does not know the full extent of the gambling or indebtedness, she does know the family circumstances, and can contribute to the picture a substantial amount of valid information.

The second area of treatment to pursue is one of separation. Optimally, the spouse is by this time a new member of Gam-Anon. As such she is learning she is not responsible for her husband's gambling, and in fact is only responsible for herself and the care of her children. Concurrently, the treatment focus is reviewing the spouse's developmental issues and addressing her Adult Children of Alcoholics concerns. As the spouse begins to see herself as the product of her childhood, recognizes her own pathological involvement and increases her own self-awareness. She then can take an active role in modifying her own behavior. We find the "steps" within the Gam-Anon program and the practical experiences shared the most helpful support system to the gambler's spouse.

The third area of treatment focus is most frequently ongoing with the previous two areas. Crisis intervention for the spouse usually requires immediate attention on the part of the treatment team. Though the team may not directly address every area of need, each area must be identified and either addressed or referral made to the appropriate agency. Legal advice, for example, is rarely available in the treatment setting, but often the treatment team can evaluate whether legal counsel is necessary and make recommendations. If essentials such as food, rent, medical needs, utilities, and so on have been addressed, then treatment can continue with the list of patient needs prioritized and dealt with in a systematic manner using community and agency resources.

The final area of treatment for the spouse and family is perhaps the most difficult and time consuming, but likewise the area with the highest potential for productivity. So far each member of the couple has usually been seen individually to address his or her needs as they are perceived. Then comes the time for the couple to begin addressing their joint issues face to face. Couple or marital therapy, though not required in most treatment settings, is often necessary. Though the style and format differ not just from program to program but also from therapist to therapist. Areas frequently addressed either directly by the family therapist or adjunctively include: couples' communication skills building; assertiveness training; effective parenting; productive problem solving or "fair fighting;" codependency issues; trust issues; management of finances; separation and divorce; reentry sabotaging; excessive spousal expectations; sexual problems; and parenting skill building.

The reentry phase of family treatment is a critical area. While the initial crisis may have been resolved or some closure has been accomplished, it is now time to reintegrate the gambler into the family system. He has been absent physically and emotionally during his active gambling days, which in many cases can be years. He's missed milestones in his children's development and has not participated to any great degree in their lives. In many cases he has missed birthdays, anniversaries, and significant social events. Family anger is significant. Over the years they have developed a variety of coping skills, some healthy and some unhealthy.

The recovering gambler through his individual treatment is prepared to take on more responsibility. Within the context of family therapy he begins his return, which is typically met with resentment and resistance. The resistance may be aggressive and/or subtle. Statements regarding his previous behavior are often brought up in anger by his family. The children may not want to surrender their roles as caretakers, mediators, and facilitators. The spouse, after being the only involved parent and responsible adult, also may resist the gambler's involvement. Blatant remarks such as, "I liked you better when you gambled," or "Where were you when I really needed you?" often feed the anxiety and inadequate feelings the recovering gambler may already have about reinvolving himself with this family. The mother's alignment with the children becomes difficult to penetrate. Now the recovering gambler who often seeks rejection to rationalize his return to gambling and become irresponsible begins to withdraw from the family. It takes a skilled professional to recognize these possible dynamics and balance this dysfunctional system to achieve a successful reentry. These areas may be served by referring the couple to local community seminars, courses or workshops, or they may be a part of the agencies' services. Often the couple can benefit most from having that third party available to them as they begin the first phase of recovery—the critical phase. The therapist, sometimes functioning more as a sounding board, or referee, facilitates the couple's efforts to effectively communicate and resolve conflicts.

This process may be a time-limited six-to-twelve-week period or it may be a long-term group experience with other couples addressing the same issues. Whatever the means, the end is a common one. Each member of this marital dyad has undergone serious pain, suffering, hurt, anger, and guilt. Only in the working through of their emotional needs and marital conflicts can they hope to put the gambling disorder behind them and pursue productively realistic expectations. Successful treatment may be defined by goals set by the treatment professionals with the family.

Such goals may include improved parenting skills, enhanced communication skills, abstinence from gambling, and crisis resolution.

The use of family therapy to explore and clarify family structure, enhance family contact and explore boundaries as they relate to family member roles, is extremely valuable to the recovery process of the compulsive gambler and to the dysfunctional family system. What is clear is the effective use of many forms of family therapy, such as systems approaches, structural interventions, Bowen Theory, and conjoint therapy have all (in the hands of an experienced professional) been productive, successful techniques in accomplishing these goals. Though more research on follow-up and outcome is necessary to further define the needs of the family and the most productive interventions to meet those needs, what does not have to be proven is the need for gambling treatment to routinely include family treatment.

8
Controlled Gambling: A Promising Future

John Rosecrance, Ph.D.

Introduction

Increasing legalization and growing public acceptance have led to significant increases in gambling participation. In 1986 the nation wagered an all-time record $198 billion (Christiansen 1987). Gaming industry projections show no signs of market saturation and continued gambling growth seems assured (Rosecrance 1988). Americans have become more pragmatic about gambling and no longer view it from an ethical perspective (Kusyszyn 1984). Separating gambling from moral condemnation has allowed it to be seen as a legitimate social activity; and in the process the base of potential participants has been broadened. Many new gamblers have not had time to develop informal coping strategies for dealing with the problematic nature of the activity. This is especially true of middle-class gamblers who, in many instances, are being introduced to gambling without a full appreciation of the risks. Until Americans become more sophisticated and knowledgeable, it is safe to assume that as gambling participation increases so will the incidence of problem gambling.

Problem gambling, which I define as the losing of an excessive amount of money, is becoming an all-too-familiar behavior pattern. Problem gamblers are increasingly being identified as compulsive or pathological (the terms are used synonymously) and their behavior diagnosed as symptomatic of a progressive illness. The disease model has been accepted as a legitimate explanation for inappropriate gambling. Sheila Blume (1987, 240) recently delineated the model as it applies to excessive gambling:

1. A behavior pattern that is reliably and repeatedly harmful to the individual and/or others.

2. The pattern must be characteristic for the individual and outside of full conscious control.

3. The behavior and accompanying internal state must follow a predictable course common to other individuals, yielding describable signs, symptoms, stages of development, and patterns of harm.

Those who incur excessive losses are seen as having lost control because of their compulsion to gamble. Therapeutic intervention is needed to correct the compulsive condition and to enable the gambler to regain control of his or her life. The perception that losing gamblers need correction and treatment by professional counselors is part of the medicalization of a variety of behaviors, such as excessive drinking, overeating, child abuse, narcotics use, and impotence (see Conrad and Schneider 1980). A leading figure in the compulsive gambling field defines this phenomenon as:

> . . . an addictive illness in which the subject is driven by an overwhelming, uncontrollable impulse to gamble. The impulse persists and progresses in intensity and urgency, consuming more and more of the individual's time, energy, and emotional and material resources. Ultimately, it invades, undermines, and often destroys everything that is meaningful in a person's life (Custer & Milt 1985, 40).

Advocates of a compulsion model have been strengthened by the inclusion of pathological gambling in DSM-III (American Psychiatric Association 1980, 291). It was classed as a disorder of impulse characterized by "a chronic and progressive failure to resist impulses to gamble."

Statistics regarding the incidence and prevalence of compulsive gambling are illusive. After conducting a national survey, University of Michigan researchers (Kallick et al. 1979) concluded that 0.77 percent of the population (approximately 1.1 million) were probable compulsive gamblers. Gamblers Anonymous, citing no particular methodology, has concluded that there are between 6 million and 9 million compulsive gamblers (Dunne 1985, 11). Using preliminary data from local studies, compulsive-gambling researchers (Culleton 1985; Lesieur 1985; Taber et al. 1986) have concluded that the national figure should be established at 2 million to 3 million probable compulsive gamblers. Most recently, Rachael Volberg has undertaken a nationwide prevalence study that may shed some light on this subject (Volberg & Steadman 1988). Notwithstanding a lack of hard data, compulsive gambling advocates maintain that since "each compulsive gambler affects the life of ten to twenty relatives, friends, and fellow workers, we have 20 to 30 million people who are an at-risk population"(Dunne 1985, 15). In point of fact, there is little empirical or theoretical justification for extrapolating from compulsive gamblers to an "at risk population." In this instance, it would seem that a medical contagion model is being used for a condition (compulsion gambling) that has not been empirically demonstrated as a contagious disease. There is consensus among proponents of a disease model that pathological (or its putative counterpart, compulsive) gambling is a major health problem, the consequences of which have yet to be fully identified (Miller 1986).

Treatment Goals

The treatment goal in nearly all compulsive-gambling-intervention programs is total abstinence. Traditional treatment approaches involve counseling to develop insight and continuing group therapy to maintain the resolve to live without gambling (Lesieur 1984). The benefits of group therapy in resolving problem gambling are described by researchers:

> Group therapy enables the therapist to overcome the obstacles and problem noted previously. Fellow gamblers, because they know the facades and lies the neophyte has constructed, are able to show the gambler the other problems that need to be addressed aside from the monetary ones. In addition, identification with the group helps reduce the sense of isolation and alienation that compulsive gamblers feel (Lesieur & Custer 1984, 155).

This perspective assumes that knowing about problems through personal experience is sufficient to create and maintain a desire for change—an assumption that has yet to be demonstrated empirically.

At present, group therapy for problem gamblers means attendance at Gamblers Anonymous meetings (Greenberg 1980). Regular participation in Gamblers Anonymous is considered by many to be "the most important step a compulsive gambler can take toward recovery" (Custer & Milt 1985, 199). Gamblers Anonymous members are considered the "true experts" (Martinez 1983; Lesieur & Custer 1984; Custer & Milt 1985; Allcock & Dickerson 1986; Brown 1986) in helping compulsive gamblers. The following statement from a Gamblers Anonymous pamphlet clearly reveals its proselytizing mission:

> Throughout history untold suffering and humiliation has been the lot of countless thousands of men and women due to their addiction for playing games of chance for money. Today, with the formation of a fellowship called Gamblers Anonymous, a bright new page has been unfolded in man's struggle against this insidious problem (Livingston 1974, 148).

Advocates of a compulsion model currently have exclusive maintenance of public sponsored treatment programs for problem gamblers (Rosecrance 1985). This dominance has evolved from the general acceptance accorded to medical explanations of this behavior pattern. Media accounts of compulsive gamblers have increased significantly (Greene 1982; Berkow 1984; Mansfield 1984; *New York Times* 1984). These accounts invariably assume that Gamblers Anonymous is the best hope for overcoming compulsive gambling. The response of Ann Landers to a writer who claimed that gambling was destroying his life is representative:

> Dear Hurting: Gambling, like alcoholism and drug addiction, is an illness. In the case of all three, the best approach is a self-help group. Nothing is as effective as the emotional support of people who share the problem. I strongly recommend Gamblers Anonymous (*Tahoe Daily Tribune* 1987).

The Efficacy of Traditional Treatment Methods

While the sincerity of Gamblers Anonymous cannot be doubted, its overall effectiveness can be seriously questioned. The single goal of abstinence has definite limitations, and in some cases is counterproductive to the effective treatment of problem gamblers (Scodel 1964). A homogeneous goal for a heterogeneous population is an invitation to failure. It is axiomatic that no treatment approach can be uniformly applied to diverse groups. For many gamblers it would appear that abstinence is unrealistic. Although attendance at Gamblers Anonymous meetings may result in a temporary remission, the recurrence of gambling activities is common. When this happens, those gamblers who have internalized the concept that they can no longer hope to control their gambling often engage in self-defeating gambling binges. During these sprees they make little effort to control their gambling, preferring instead "the voluptuousness of giving oneself up for lost" (Halliday & Fuller 1974, 24). Several researchers have pointed out the high dropout rate of those attending Gamblers Anonymous meetings (Moody 1972; Ashton 1979; Lester 1980; Brown 1984, 1986; Preston & Smith 1985). Some individuals and groups simply do not feel comfortable at GA meetings. For example, minority group members and women rarely join Gamblers Anonymous (Brown 1986). It is apparent that attendance at Gamblers Anonymous meetings is not a panacea for problem gambling.

The public and professional acceptance accorded the medical model is more of a sociopolitical accomplishment than a scientific development. Virtually all investigators who have studied gambling groups in natural settings find little ethnographic evidence of either compulsive or pathological behavior. Field researchers studying such diverse groups as horse players (Newman 1972; Kusyszyn & Kallai 1975; Rosecrance 1982), poker players (Martinez & LaFranchi 1969; Zurcher 1970), and casino gamblers (Oldman 1972, 1978), have rejected compulsion as an adequate explanation for problem gambling. The medical model of problem gambling, developed from a clinical perspective, focuses upon those persons who are attempting to discontinue their gambling activities. Such a model overlooks the coping mechanisms and self-control techniques of the vast majority of gamblers who participate regularly. In many cases problem gamblers, by changing strategies, are able to reverse a pattern of progressively larger losses. In light of serious questions regarding the efficacy of the medical model, and the single-treatment goal it espouses, a new perspective on problem gambling is urgently needed.

Another Perspective

David Oldman, after conducting an observational study of roulette players, from his vantage point as a croupier, identified the central issue in dealing with problem gambling:

> Perhaps the most important message for those who gamble, or wish to control gambling, or wish to help those in trouble through gambling, is that this particular mechanism whereby one reaches a crisis point is a consequence not of personality defect but of a defective relationship between strategy of play on the one hand and a way of managing one's finances on the other (1978, 369-70).

Even though Oldman's research is relatively unknown in the United States, his findings are very important because they run counter to prevailing assumptions about problematic gambling. He rejects the notion of an uncontrollable compulsion and instead locates the source of problem gambling in inappropriate gambling strategies. Such a perception of troubled gambling offers the possibility of teaching gamblers to become more controlled in their betting. This perspective deserves serious consideration by all those who operate treatment programs. Although the possibility of a problem gambler becoming a controlled gambler is anathema to advocates of a medical model, there is ethnographic evidence to substantiate such a transformation.

While conducting research with several nativistic gambling groups I have, on many occasions, observed seriously troubled gamblers develop coping skills that helped them to maintain participation in an acceptable manner (Rosecrance 1986). In so doing, the troubled gamblers learned how to become controlled gamblers. Additionally, English (Rankin 1982) and Australian (Allcock & Dickerson 1986) researchers have successfully implemented controlled-gambling programs. The Australian experience is particularly noteworthy since controlled gambling has been part of a comprehensive treatment package for over five years. Teaching excessive losers to develop and use appropriate (nonproblematic) strategies is a difficult process. Counselors who currently administer gambling treatment programs in this country generally are unable to effectively help their clients develop new gambling strategies. This inability stems from four basic factors:

1. Lack of knowledge concerning appropriate gaming strategies and or money management.
2. An inability to develop empathy for gamblers who want to maintain participation.
3. The fact that inappropriate strategies are manifested outside of a counseling setting.
4. Failure to be aware of sources that could aid gamblers in developing appropriate strategies.

While these factors are limiting, they can be overcome. The purpose of this chapter is to demonstrate that Oldman's prescription for dealing with "compulsive" gambling can be implemented in an actual treatment regimen. In addition, evidence will be presented that a successful controlled gambling program is currently in operation. The source of this control, in many cases, comes from other gamblers.

Peer Counseling

An integral component of my approach toward problem gambling is the use of active gamblers as counselors. Elsewhere (Rosecrance 1988), I have argued that such an approach would tap a valuable resource—successful gamblers. Successful in this context does not mean that the gamblers necessarily are able to consistently win money, but rather that their gambling is not problematic. Just as ex-gamblers are able to help those seeking abstinence, active and controlled gamblers can help those seeking to develop appropriate gambling strategies or money management practices. This perspective does not accept the traditional assumption that it is necessary to permanently discontinue participation to overcome problem gambling or that members of Gamblers Anonymous are the only acceptable peer counselors.

Based upon ethnographic studies of several gambling groups (Rosecrance 1982, 1985, 1987) I have concluded that gambling acquaintances often provide significant help in coping with problem gambling. Active gamblers can provide valuable sources of empathetic understanding and objective appraisal. Those who gamble regularly face specialized contingencies that frequently are unsharable with nongamblers. Sustained gambling is disconcerting because the rewards are intermittent and relatively unpredictable. Financial rewards are typically gained in a fluctuating cyclical pattern; the rate of return at a particular point in time cannot be assured. Even sophisticated betting strategies developed over long periods cannot guarantee a financially rewarding rate of return. The intermittent distribution of wins and losses is psychologically, financially, and socially unsettling. In many instances, the difficulty in coping with these negative contingencies can only be understood by other gamblers.

Mutual understanding among participants allows them to relate on both a cognitive and emotional level. The initiation of empathetic contact is often prefaced by the statement, "Hey, I've been there too." By this opening gamblers assure one another that they understand the problematic aspects of gambling. A similar emotional response pattern has been described as occurring "when the two people have both similar past learning experience and share similar locations in the present structure of interaction" (Baldwin 1983). Empathetic appreciation of the troubled gamblers' situation can be a valuable tool in suggesting methods to alleviate the current difficulties without permanently discontinuing gambling. Strategies such as temporarily distancing oneself from the gaming setting (in gambling argot, an "early out"), decreasing the size of wagers until winning patterns develop, changing one's overall approach, specializing in a particular type of wagering, eschewing certain wagering situations, placing a specified amount of winnings in an inviolate trust, doing something practical (buying a new car, fixing the house, making advance house payments) with winnings, changing to less risky wagering propositions, or implementing voluntary control by a third party, are all examples of alternatives that gamblers offer acquaintances with problem gambling. Often these same strategies have been implemented by the gambling "adviser" and he or she has some firsthand experience with how they work. Those particularly adept at aiding troubled gamblers are commonly known as "gambling shrinks."

Regular gamblers often serve as devil's advocates or sounding boards to objectively assess a prospective bet. In so doing they provide a touchstone of reality that helps disoriented gamblers regain the proper perspective. When contemplating large wagers, gamblers routinely seek corroboration from other participants. This process, in some cases, allows gamblers to "talk down" an unusually disturbed bettor who may be considering a foolhardy wager. The comment of a veteran sports bettor illustrates this phenomenon:

A buddy saves me four or five grand a year by criticizing my crazy bets. I'm usually so stubborn that I still bet the same teams, but I cut my bets so much that I don't get hurt when my weird hunches lose—and they usually do.

The perspective that gambling acquaintances can aid in overcoming gambling problems is contrary to other studies that emphasize the pejorative aspect of betting relationships. In his study of off-track gamblers, Zola (1963) depicted gambling buddies as those who egged each other on to make ever-larger and increasingly foolhardy wagers. Scott, in his work on horse players, indicated: "In the final stage of an addict's moral career he becomes enmeshed in a web of relations with other addicts" (1968, 82). After studying compulsive gambling, Lesieur (1984) concluded that other gamblers act as enablers by helping the compulsive find sources of money to continue gambling in spite of obvious signs of out-of-control behavior. While these observations undoubtedly reflect certain situations, they do not represent the totality of betting relationships. On the contrary, Hayano (1982), Herman (1967), and D'Angelo (1984), while studying poker professionals, horse players, and sports bettors respectively, describe the positive and sustaining aspects of gambling relationships. In these studies gamblers helped each other maintain controlled participation by offering positive and rational suggestions. My own longitudinal observation, developed over a thirty-year gambling career, is in agreement with the latter body of research.

Developing a Controlled-Treatment Plan

A major problem facing treatment regimens that use active participants is how to harness the gamblers' nativistic talent in a structured program. To achieve this it is essential to transfer their informal and implicit skills to a formal regimen. The first step is establishing a group of controlled gamblers who are willing to share their coping skills. These gamblers would not suggest actual bets, but rather would help to develop appropriate gaming and money management strategies. They would be peer counselors, and not tipsters. In such a program the counselor would serve as both consultant and teacher. Initially, peer counselors would work closely with program organizers to suggest an appropriate gaming strategy. If the gambler agrees to try the new strategy, counselors would facilitate its implementation in the real world of gambling. There are no norms operating in gambling environments to discourage or prohibit peer counseling.

The identification of prospective counselors requires a comprehensive recruitment campaign to bring controlled gamblers into the program. The profile of an "ideal" counselor would be an experienced gambler with a social science background who has overcome problem gambling and who is willing to help other bettors. Surprisingly, many gamblers do fit this profile. Once a few dedicated counselors are located and become part of the treatment program they would be able to recruit others, and the list of available counselors hopefully would become self-generating. Those selected must be in control of their own gambling and be willing to learn some basic counseling techniques. They must be available to take phone calls from problem gamblers and to meet with them. Those who serve as counselors would of course profit from the experience. It is an axiom that peer counselors themselves often gain valuable insight and develop an enhanced self-image through their counseling efforts (Empey 1982). I have firm commitments from several controlled gamblers willing to serve as counselors when peer counseling is actually implemented.

After a list of peer counselors has been developed, the next task is to make problem gamblers and treatment officials aware of and receptive to this new resource. If clients are classified as appropriate candidates for a controlled gambling regimen, they would undertake a reappraisal of their inappropriate gambling patterns. Peer counselors who participate in the same gambling game as the subject would be especially helpful in this process, because they are familiar with specific strategies applicable to their mutual activity. Most gamblers specialize by concentrating their efforts upon one gaming activity. Taking stock of gaming strategies should be done with reference to self-control techniques, such as keeping precise records of daily wagers (Dickerson & Weeks 1979), specifying exactly how winnings are to be distributed (Rankin 1982), and establishing a precise unit of wager (Beyer 1978).

Those who operate gambling-treatment programs at VA hospitals, mental health facilities, addiction centers, or other locations must be informed that peer counseling for controlled gambling is available. At present these treatment centers, almost without exception, are heavily invested in the medical model and consider abstinence the only treatment goal. They have established close working relationships with Gamblers Anonymous and generally require their clients maintain a continuing association with that group (Greenberg 1980). Gamblers Anonymous members are *adamantly* opposed to the idea of controlled gambling:

> With reference to gambling, the delusion that we are like other people, or presently may be, has to be smashed. We have lost the ability to control our gambling. We know that no real compulsive gambler ever regains control. All of us felt at times we were regaining control, but such intervals—usually brief—were inevitably followed by still less control, which led in time to pitiful and incomprehensible demoralization. We are convinced to a man that gamblers of our type are in the grip of a progressive illness. Over any considerable period of time we get worse, never better (Gamblers Anonymous n.d.:1-2).

Conventional treatment counselors must be convinced that controlled-gambling programs with peer counselors are not designed to displace Gamblers Anonymous and their established network of more than four hundred chapters in the United States. However, current treatment programs by demanding abstinence often cause delays in seeking treatment (Lester 1980) since troubled gamblers are reluctant to permanently give up an activity that serves as an important source of excitement and camaraderie in their lives. At present gamblers assume that if they want treatment they must first agree to give up gambling (Martinez 1975). Therefore only desperate losers are willing to seek help. It seems wasteful to discourage all but the most severely troubled from seeking assistance. Controlled programs, by offering an alternative approach, are capable of reaching gamblers who have not yet hit "rock bottom" but who nevertheless are experiencing serious problems related to gambling. Referral to a controlled program is not tantamount to disavowing either the medical model or abandoning Gamblers Anonymous, but instead is an alternative treatment for a multivariant population. Professional counselors should welcome the possibility of considering another treatment goal for problematic gamblers. Just as total abstinence is not a panacea for all problem gambling, neither is controlled gambling.

The criterion of success in a controlled treatment program involves an evaluation of the subject's gambling patterns. If the gambler continues to demonstrate excessive losses, the program has not achieved its purpose. On the other hand, if gamblers have been able to alter their gaming strategies to the point where they are winning or (more likely) their losses are within acceptable parameters, the program will have succeeded. This type of pragmatic criterion is free of the assumption, prevailing in traditional treatment approaches, that gaming is a frivolous activity. Conventional programs (demanding abstinence) typically view time spent gambling as nonproductive and wasteful. Controlled gambling programs make no such assumption. If gamblers want to spend *their* time in off-track betting parlors, casinos, or paper parlors, they should not be automatically dissuaded. Under the right circumstances, many problem gamblers can learn to gamble responsibly.

Whenever I have raised the issue of controlled gambling, compulsion advocates have replied (in what seems tautological reasoning) that gamblers who overcome severe problems are not "true" compulsives. I have completed a research project that definitively belies that contention. While the data from the project are not completely analyzed, and will be the subject of future articles, the preliminary findings are worth briefly reporting.

Recently I conducted several field observations of a group of gamblers who have overcome serious gambling-related problems. Dr. Howard Sartin operates a handicapping school for horse race gamblers in Southern California. His approach involves psychological and practical tips for selecting winning horses. The Sartin approach encourages gamblers to share their skills (often through computer interface) to develop more rational betting strategies. At his center I interviewed more than fifty gamblers. Several of them, prior to entering the group, met *all* the DSM-III criteria for pathological gamblers. They had lost businesses, homes, spouses, and financial resources all to gambling. Some had served time in jails or prisons for gambling-related thefts. Several had attended Gamblers Anonymous meetings. No one could deny they had been "true" problem gamblers. However, after changing their betting strategies and money managing practices (through the assistance of Dr. Sartin and others in the group) most had been able to overcome their problem gambling, and were now managing participation in an acceptable manner. Not all had become winning gamblers (although some had advanced to this level) but they were able to keep losses within manageable parameters. I contend that similar helping (while not formally structured) often is available within the social worlds of gambling.

Summary

In this chapter, I have presented a preliminary plan for developing a controlled-gambling-treatment program. A major component of the program featured the use of active gamblers as peer counselors. The kind of treatment advocated was an attempt to operationalize Oldman's (1978) hypothesis that troubled gambling is a problem of defective wagering strategies. Abstinent gamblers who are members of Gamblers Anonymous have been considered as experts in aiding problem gamblers. Based upon personal experience and ethnographic studies, there is every reason to believe that controlled gamblers could be equally effective in counseling those seeking assistance with problem gambling. In the real world of gambling, acquaintances currently provide valuable informal assistance to troubled gamblers. The treatment program I advanced would attempt to harness such nativistic assistance to a formal program.

The first stage of the proposed treatment program would involve the recruitment of peer counselors into an organized group. Troubled gamblers could then avail themselves of the peer counselors and receive instruction in self-help techniques. The treatment program depicted in this chapter is a new and untested approach. To my knowledge, there has never been a formally recognized effort to use active gamblers as peer counselors. However, preliminary data from a study of the Sartin group indicate that large numbers of troubled gamblers can become controlled gamblers by the use of self-help techniques. Considering the projected increases in problem gambling and the questions concerning the efficacy of current treatment programs, it seems essential to consider other alternatives. The use of peer counselors in a controlled-treatment program is one such alternative.

Optimally, those currently operating gambling treatment centers will seriously question whether their reliance upon one treatment goal is in the best interests of problem gamblers. While controlled gambling certainly will not work for everyone, it can help some. It is an idea that offers promise.

References

Allcock, C. C., & Dickerson, M. 1986. *The Guide to Good Gambling.* Wentworth Falls, Australia: Social Science Press.

American Psychiatric Association. 1980. *Diagnostic and Statistical Manual III.* Washington, D.C.: American Psychiatric Association.

Ashton, N. 1979. Gamblers disturbed or healthy. In D. Lester (ed.) *Gambling Today.* Springfield, Illinois: Charles C. Thomas.

Baldwin, J. 1983. Social behaviorism on emotions: Mead and modern behaviorism compared. University of California, Santa Barbara: Working paper.

Berkow, I. 1984. Schlicter: Caught up in something big. *New York Times,* February 5:20.

Beyer, A. 1978. *My $50,000 year at the races.* New York: Harcourt Brace.

Blume, S. 1987. Compulsive gambling and the medical model. *Journal of Gambling Behavior* 3:237–248.

Brown, R. I. 1984. Gamblers Anonymous' view of its own success rate as a baseline for the comparisons of treatments of compulsive gambler. Paper presented at the Sixth National Conference on Gambling and Risk-Taking, Atlantic City.

———. 1986. Dropouts and continuers in Gamblers Anonymous: Life-Context and other factors. *Journal of Gambling Behavior* 2:130–140.

Christiansen, E. M. 1987. The 1986 gross annual wager part I: Handle. *Gaming and Wagering Business* 8 (July): 7–14.

Conrad, P., & Schneider, J. W. 1980. *Deviance and Medicalization.* St. Louis: Mosby.

Culleton, R. P. 1985. *A Survey of Pathological Gambling in the State of Ohio.* Philadelphia: Transition Planning Associates.

Custer, R. L., & Milt, H. 1985. *When Luck Runs Out.* New York: Facts on File Publications.

D'Angelo, R. 1984. The social organization of sports gambling. Paper presented at the Sixth National Conference on Gambling and Risk-Taking, Atlantic City.

Dickerson, M., & Weeks, J. D. 1979. Controlled gambling as a therapeutic technique for compulsive gamblers. *Journal of Behavior Therapy and Experimental Psychiatry* 10:139–141.

Dunne, J. A. 1983. The president's message. *National Council on Compulsive Gambling Newsletter* 1:2.

———. 1985. Increasing public awarenes of pathological gambling behavior. *Journal of Gambling Behavior* 1:8–17.

Empey, L. T. 1982. *American Delinquency.* Homewood, Illinois: Dorsey Press.

Gamblers Anonymous. n.d. *Gambling Pamphlet.* Los Angeles: Gamblers Anonymous Publishing.

Greenberg, H. 1980. Psychology of gambling. In H. Kaplan, A. Freedman, & B. Sadock (eds.) *Comprehensive Textbook of Psychiatry III.* New York: Williams & Wilkins, 3274–3283.

Greene, J. 1982. The gambling trap. *Psychology Today* 16 (9):50–55.

Halliday, J., & Fuller, P. (eds.) 1974. *The Psychology of Gambling.* London: Allen Lane.

Hayano, D. M. 1982. *Poker Faces.* Berkeley: University of California Press.

Herman, R. 1967. Gambling as work: A sociological study of the race track. In R. Herman (ed.) *Gambling.* New York: Harper & Row, 87–106.

Kallick, M., Suits, D., & Hybels, J. 1979. *A Survey of American Gambling Attitudes and Behavior.* Ann Arbor: Institute for Social Research, University of Michigan.

Kusyszyn, I. 1984. The psychology of gambling. *Annals of American Academy of Political and Social Sciences* 474:133–145.

Kusyszyn, I., & Kallai, C. 1975. The gambling person: Healthy or sick? Paper presented at the Second Annual Conference on Gambling and Risk Taking, Lake Tahoe.

Lesieur, H. R. 1984. *The chase: Career of the compulsive gambler.* Cambridge, Massachusetts: Schenkman.

———. 1985. Editor's introduction. *Journal of Gambling Behavior* 1:3–7.

Lesieur, H. R., & Custer, R. L. 1984. Pathological gambling: Roots, phases, and treatment. *Annals of American Academy of Political and Social Sciences* 474:146–156.

Lester, D. 1980. The treatment of compulsive gambling. *International Journal of the Addictions.* 15(2):201–206.

Livingston, J. 1974. *Compulsive gamblers.* New York: Harper & Row.

Mansfield, S. 1984. Addicted to a losing bet. A compulsive gambler struggling to quit puts her cards on the table. *Washington Post,* January 17: C 2.

Martinez, T. 1975. A review of Gambling: Hazard and Reward. *Society* 12:88–89.

———. 1983. *The Gambling Scene.* Springfield, Illinois: Charles C. Thomas.

Martinez, T., & La Franchi, R. 1969. Why people play poker. *Transaction* 6:32–52.

Miller, W. 1986. Individual outpatient treatment of pathological gambling. *Journal of Gambling Behavior* 2:95–107.

Moody, G. 1972. The facts about the money factories. *London Churches Council on Gambling* 1:64–86.

Newman, O. 1972. *Gambling: Hazard and Reward.* London: Athlone Press.

New York Times. 1984. Clinic to treat compulsive gamblers. February 5:20.

Oldman, D. 1974. Chance and skill: A study of roulette. *Sociology* 8:407–426.

————. 1978. Compulsive gamblers. *Sociological Review* 26:349–370.

Preston, F. W., & Smith, R. W. 1985. Delabeling and relabeling in Gamblers Anonymous: Problems with transferring the Alcoholics Anonymous paradigm. *Journal of Gambling Behavior* 1:97–105.

Rankin, H. 1982. Control rather than abstinence as a goal in the treatment of excessive gambling. *Behavior Research Therapy* 20:185–187.

Rosecrance, J. 1982. The regulars: A study of inveterate horse players. Master's paper, Sociology Department, University of California, Santa Barbara.

————. 1985. Compulsive gambling and the medicalization of deviance. *Social Problems* 32:275–284.

————. 1986. Why regular gamblers don't quit: A sociological perspective. *Sociological Perspectives* 29:357–378.

————. 1987. The social world of sports betting. *Arena Review* 11:15–24.

————. 1988. Active gamblers as peer counselors. *International Journal of the Addictions* 23 (7):751–766.

Scodel, A. 1964. Inspirational group therapy: A study of Gamblers Anonymous. *American Journal of Psychotherapy* 18:1115–1125.

Scott, M. B. 1968. *The Racing Game.* Chicago: Aldine.

Taber, J. I., Collachi, J., & Lynn, E. 1986. Pathological gambling: Possibilities for treatment in northern Nevada. *Nevada Public Affairs Review* 2:39–42.

Tahoe Daily Tribune. 1987. Ann Landers Column. February 2:10.

Volberg, R., & Steadman, H. 1988. Refining prevalence estimates of pathological gambling. *American Journal of Psychiatry* 145:502–505.

Zola, I. 1963. Observations on gambling in a lower-class setting. *Social Problems* 10:353–361.

Zurcher, L. A. 1970. The friendly poker game: A study of an ephemeral role. *Social Forces* 49:173–186.

Part III
Public Policy Implications for Compulsive Gambling

9

Policy Implications of Prevalence Estimates of Pathological Gambling

Rachel A. Volberg, Ph.D.
Henry J. Steadman, Ph.D.

Although Gamblers Anonymous has been established for thirty years and treatment programs for pathological gamblers have been available for fifteen years, there have been few studies of the prevalence of pathological gambling in the general population. The first prevalence study was done in 1974 as part of an effort to investigate the general phenomenon of gambling in the United States (Commission on the Review of the National Policy Toward Gambling 1976). Other prevalence studies, such as one done in Minnesota in 1983 and one in Connecticut in 1986, consisted of several questions included in surveys on very different topics (Steinberg, private communication; Minnesota Department of Human Services 1986).

Despite the absence of reliable prevalence data, publicly funded treatment programs have been established since 1980 in several states, including Maryland, Massachusetts, Iowa, New Jersey, and New York. In these states, the National Council on Compulsive Gambling and its affiliates, mental health practitioners, and members of Gamblers Anonymous and Gam-Anon played critical roles in convincing key legislators to allocate funds to state agencies for the establishment of treatment programs. The effectiveness of these groups is evidenced by the significant increase in size and structure of these treatment programs since their establishment, still without reference to empirical data. Rather, decisions have been made through a political process that remains uninformed, for the most part, about the nature and the extent of the problem of pathological gambling.

In contrast to this general situation, we were asked in 1985 by the New York Office of Mental Health to conduct an evaluation of the state's compulsive gambling treatment programs after these programs had been operating for three years. The evaluation continued for three years and

This work was partially supported by NIMH Grant MH-44295. Some material was adapted from papers appearing in the *American Journal of Psychiatry* 145 (1988: 502–505) and the *Journal of Gambling Behavior* (forthcoming).

included the collection and analysis of uniform data on all clients in these programs as well as several specialized research initiatives. One such initiative was a prevalence survey of pathological gambling in the general population. We felt this type of prevalence survey was important to determine the volume and the distribution of need in the New York State population. We hoped that by developing a clearer picture of the extent of pathological gambling in New York State, as well as of the types of people entering newly established treatment programs, we could help refine the state's efforts to provide services for people affected by pathological gambling.

This chapter describes the results of the New York State prevalence survey as well as another recent effort to conduct a prevalence survey of pathological gambling in the general population. After discussing the results of these surveys, we will address several important methodological issues that have been raised concerning the prevalence surveys that have been carried out to date. Finally, we will suggest the importance that prevalence surveys of pathological gambling should have for a variety of audiences concerned with the funding of treatment programs for pathological gamblers and their families.

The New York State Prevalence Survey

The prevalence survey of pathological gambling that we carried out in 1986 as part of the evaluation of state-funded treatment programs in New York was based on the South Oaks Gambling Screen, developed by Lesieur and his colleagues (Lesieur & Blume 1987). The South Oaks Gambling Screen is a twenty-item scale in which all the items are weighted equally. Weighted questions concern behaviors identified in the American Psychiatric Association's *Diagnostic and Statistical Manual* (1980) as diagnosable criteria of gambling pathology. Items include hiding evidence of wagering activity, arguments with family members over wagering, and borrowing money to wager or to pay gambling debts.

For the telephone survey, several questions on wagering activities and demographics were added to the South Oaks Gambling Screen. The instrument was also translated into Spanish for interviewing Hispanic respondents. Respondents were contacted and interviewed by Fact Finders, Inc., a survey research firm. Respondents were randomly selected and the entire sample was stratified to proportionally represent the New York counties on the basis of 1980 census figures. One thousand interviews were completed, forty-three of them in Spanish.

Twenty-eight of the New York State respondents (2.8 percent of the sample) scored three or four points on the South Oaks Gambling Screen. According to the scale used in this instrument, these respondents were classified as "problem gamblers." Another fourteen of the respondents (1.4 percent of the sample) scored five or more points on the South Oaks Gambling Screen. These respondents were classified as "probable pathological gamblers." Among the respondents in the New York study, significant differences (p<.05) between the sample as a whole and the respondents classified as problem and probable pathological gamblers were found on several dimensions.

Sex: Men constituted 44 percent of all respondents but 64 percent of the problem and probable pathological gamblers (chi-square = 6.49, df = 1, p = .01).

Age: While 22 percent of the entire sample was under the age of thirty, 38 percent of the problem and probable pathological gamblers were in this age group (chi-square = 8.81, df = 2, p = .01).

Ethnicity: While 23 percent of the entire sample was nonwhite, 43 percent of the problem and probable pathological gamblers were nonwhite (chi-square = 8.86, df = 1, p<.01).

Income: Problem and probable pathological gamblers were also overrepresented among those earning $25,000 or less. While 45 percent of the total sample earned $25,000 or less each year, 61 percent of the problem and probable pathological gamblers earned $25,000 or less each year (chi-square = 14.13, df = 4, p<.01).

Education: While 18 percent of the total sample had not graduated from high school, 34 percent of the problem and probable pathological gamblers had not graduated from high school (chi-square = 6.81, df = 1, p<.01).

Employment: While 7 percent of the entire sample was unemployed, 21 percent of the problem and probable pathological gamblers were unemployed at the time the survey was done (chi-square = 13.62, df = 1, p<.01).

Regional Differences: There were regional differences in the distribution of respondents in the total sample when compared with respondents in the diagnostic categories. While 42 percent of the entire sample resided in the New York City region, 55 percent of the problem and probable pathological gamblers resided in the New York City region.

The reason for the importance of these data was recently articulated by Rosecrance (1988). As he pointed out, most recent studies of pathological gambling use similar sources of information—that is, patients seeking treatment or members of Gamblers Anonymous. Reliance on information from these sources has led to a highly selective view of pathological gambling. Pathological gambling is widely believed to affect primarily upper middle class and middle class white men in their forties and fifties. Pathological gamblers are believed to be highly employable and to have had fairly stable family lives until their gambling problems escalated.

However, the problem and probable pathological gamblers identified in the New York survey did not fit such a profile. They were significantly younger than the clients entering treatment programs in the state. They were also far more likely to be women than were the clients in the state-funded treatment programs. When compared with clients in the treatment programs, the problem gamblers in the New York population identified in the survey were more likely to be black or Hispanic and they tended to have lower incomes and less education.

The Cumulative Clinical Signs Method

There is one approach, in addition to the South Oaks Gambling Screen, that warrants consideration for estimating prevalence rates of pathological gambling. This is the Cumulative Clinical Signs Methods (CCSM), developed by Culleton on the basis of Custer's Inventory of Gambling Behavior. The CCSM has been used in two prevalence studies, one in the Delaware Valley in 1984 (Culleton & Lang 1985) and the other in Ohio in 1985 (Culleton 1985). The CCSM is composed of twenty-eight items clustered into five areas or tests. A positive score on any item in a given test constitutes a positive score on that test. The sum of the test scores yields a respondent's total score. In the Delaware Valley survey, Culleton found that 3.4 percent of the adult respondents (N = 534) scored as "probable pathological gamblers." In the Ohio survey (N = 801), he found that 2.5 percent of the respondents scored as "probable pathological gamblers."

Culleton used odds ratios, which express the odds in favor of having a disease when a certain factor is present and when it is absent, to estimate the number of false positives included in the prevalence rates in the Ohio and Delaware Valley surveys. Based on this method, he calculated that the true prevalence rate in the Delaware survey was 3.3 percent while the true prevalence rate in Ohio was 2.4 percent of the adult population. Based on these figures, there were between 63,700 and 172,900 probable pathological gamblers in the Delaware Valley region in 1984 and between 108,850 and 263,250 probable pathological gamblers in Ohio in 1985.

Comparing the SOGS and CCSM Approaches

In 1987, Culleton undertook a critique of the New York State prevalence survey results. In his critique, Culleton noted that the prevalence rate of 1.4 percent, which we used in New York, was not corrected to account for respondents who scored as false positives on the SOGS scale. The fourteen respondents who scored as probable pathological gamblers in our sample fell into two categories—true pathological gamblers and those who falsely scored as pathological gamblers. As Culleton pointed out, this meant that the prevalence rate was incorrect, since we included an unknown number of false positives in our results. However, we disagree with Culleton that our New York State results are either unreliable or uncorrectable.

There are two cases in which 1.4 percent would be the true figure. The first is to assume that our instrument is perfect and makes no errors. This is what Culleton believed we did. The second approach, and the one that we did take, is to assume that the false positives are equal to the false negatives and that these balance each other out. However, in cases of rare phenomena such as pathological gambling, any instrument will identify more false positives than false negatives and corrections for these cases will not balance each other out.

To correct our estimate of the prevalence of pathological gambling in New York State, Culleton attempted to determine the number of false positives who scored as probable pathological gamblers in the New York survey. He did so by taking the positive predictive value of SOGS from a single pretest (with hospital workers). The positive predictive value of an instrument indicates how many of the positive scores are true positives and how many must be dropped as false positives. The positive predictive value of an instrument is calculated on the basis of the instrument's known sensitivity and specificity. Culleton argued that use of the positive predictive value of the pretest with hospital workers would require us to drop 50 percent of our fourteen cases, leading to a prevalence rate lower than the rate found in the 1974 national study.

In fact, several pretests were done during the development of SOGS to determine the instrument's sensitivity and specificity. The sensitivity of SOGS (its ability to correctly detect pathological gamblers) was extremely high among the members of Gamblers Anonymous (99.5 percent). The specificity of SOGS (its ability to not falsely detect pathological gambling) was also extremely high when the instrument was pretested with university students and hospital workers (98.5 percent for the university students, 99.3 percent for the hospital workers).

Our approach to adjusting the 1.4 percent prevalence rate differs only slightly from that of Culleton. Rather than taking the positive predictive value from a single pretest, we chose to take our measure of sensitivity from the Gamblers' Anonymous pretest and our measure of specificity from the hospital workers pretest. Using these two measures, we constructed a table for given prevalence rates using a sensitivity of 99.5 percent and a specificity of 99.3 percent as follows:

Given that the true prevalence rate is:	the Positive Predictive Value will be:	and the number of true cases is:
0.5%	41.7%	5.8
1.0%	58.9%	8.2
1.5%	68.4%	9.6
2.0%	74.4%	10.4
2.5%	78.5%	11.0
3.0%	81.5%	11.4
3.5%	83.8%	11.7
4.0%	85.6%	12.0

As Culleton pointed out, the positive predictive value of any instrument will vary, depending on what the true prevalence rate in the general population is believed to be. If the true prevalence rate of pathological gambling in the general population were 0.5 percent, then 41.7 percent of the fourteen probable pathological gamblers found in New York State would be true positives and the prevalence rate in New York State would be .58 percent of the general population. However, if the true prevalence rate were 4.0 percent, then 85.6 percent of those fourteen cases would be true positives, which means that the prevalence rate in New York State would be 1.2 percent of the general population. Our best estimate is that the true prevalence rate of pathological gambling in the general population is approximately 1.5 percent, which means we can keep 68.4 percent of our fourteen cases, for a prevalence rate of .96 percent. This means that the range of pathological gambling in New York State is between 43,520 and 204,800 adults among its 12.8 million adult inhabitants (U.S. Bureau of the Census 1986).

The CCSM and the Rule of Independent Probabilities

Having adjusted our original SOGS-based prevalence rates, we returned to assess the utility of the CCSM. In evaluating Culleton's approach, we found one particularly vexing problem with the Cumulative Clinical Signs Method. This was his use of the rule of independent probabilities in calculating the rate of true positives in his Ohio and Delaware Valley samples. It is clear from the text of his article that Culleton bases his calculation of odds ratios on the rule of independent probabilities.

Use of this rule assumes that the tests which comprise the Cumulative Clinical Signs Methods are statistically independent (Fairley & Mosteller 1977). Thus, if the probability that a pathological gambler will score on

Test One is 40 percent and the probability that a control will score on Test One is 10 percent, then the odds are 4:1. If the probability that a pathological gambler will score on Test Two is 50 percent and the probability that a control will score on Test Two is 25 percent, then the odds are 2:1. Under independence, probabilities are calculated on the basis of simple multiplication. Thus, the probability that a pathological gambler will score on *both* tests is 20 percent (40 percent × 50 percent), while the probability that a control will score on both tests is 2.5 percent (10 percent × 25 percent), making the odds 8:1. If the tests are in fact independent, this is an extremely powerful method for distinguishing pathological gamblers from others in the general population. However, if the tests are *not* independent, then it is impossible to use the rule of independent probabilities to calculate the rate of false positives in the sample.

Our impression of the items in the five tests of the CCSM is that they do not appear to be independent. For example, is it reasonable to assume that a positive response to the statement "Since I started gambling, I seem to be less efficient and less ambitious" has absolutely no relationship to a positive response to the statement "I have lost time from work on occasion due to gambling"? It seems to us that if an individual has become less involved and interested in his work as a result of gambling, it is not unreasonable to suppose that he will also take more time off from work to gamble.

If any two items in the five tests are not independent, then the power of the CCSM to differentiate pathological gamblers in the general population declines dramatically. We believe that use of the rule of independent probabilities to calculate the rate of false positives in the Ohio and Delaware Valley surveys is inappropriate because it rests on an assumption about the items contained in the instrument that must still be validated. Since it is impossible to tell what the rate of errors in the CCSM might be, we find it difficult to accept the reported results of the Ohio and Delaware Valley surveys as the only valid estimates of the rate of pathological gambling in the general population.

Testing the Efficacy of SOGS and CCSM Together

In April 1988, with Volberg as the principal investigator, we began work on a three-year, NIMH-funded study in five states, comparing the characteristics of problem and probable pathological gamblers in the general population with those of clients entering treatment programs. Data collection includes prevalence surveys in New Jersey, Maryland, Massachusetts, Iowa, and California. Like the New York State prevalence survey, these surveys will be weighted to reflect the demographics of each state's adult population.

To try to integrate previous approaches to determining the prevalence of pathological gambling, we augmented our survey instrument to collect data comparing responses to SOGS and CCSM. The most discriminant items from each of the CCSM tests were added to the survey instrument. We felt these additional questions would allow us to compare the two available methods for determining the prevalence of pathological gambling to determine whether they identified the same probable pathological gamblers in the general population and, if not, to see on what dimensions those identified differed.

The augmented survey instrument was used to collect prevalence data thus far in New Jersey during June of 1988. We found that while responses to the SOGS questions were highly consistent with the results from New York, the responses to the CCSM items were quite disappointing. For example, just as in New York, 1.4 percent of the New Jersey respondents (N = 1000) scored as probable pathological gamblers on the SOGS, compared to the 1.4 percent found in New York. New Jersey responses to questions about the types of wagering respondents had done were also highly consistent with the results from the New York survey. However, only three New Jersey respondents scored high enough on the CCSM items to be classified as probable pathological gamblers. While all three of these respondents scored as probable pathological gamblers on SOGS items, none of those who scored as probable pathological gamblers on SOGS scored high enough on the CCSM items to be classified as pathological gamblers.

It is possible, of course, that we have done a disservice in using this abbreviated version of the CCSM instrument. One explanation for why so few respondents scored on three or more of the six CCSM items included in the New Jersey survey may be that respondents grew tired of the interview prior to these questions. Another explanation may be that the items we chose, although they were the most discriminant, were not the most appropriate items to have included in conjunction with the SOGS questions. The only solution would be to conduct a survey using full versions of each instrument on two randomly selected groups of the same size from the same state. Unfortunately, since so many of the SOGS and the CCM items are similar, it is questionable whether the benefits of such an approach would outweigh the costs.

Research on the prevalence of pathological gambling is still in its earliest stages. In contrast to Culleton, we feel it is too soon to select a single "method of choice" for research on the prevalence of pathological gambling. Over the next few years, we hope a variety of prevalence surveys can be carried out using different instruments and methods. Such a multiplicity of approaches is necessary to triangulate our efforts and arrive at the best estimate of the prevalence of pathological gambling in the general population.

Discussion

In the end, what purpose does debate about the number of pathological gamblers in the general population serve? Research to date leads us to believe that the prevalence of pathological gambling in the general population is probably at the lower end of a range, between .77 percent (Commission on the Review of the National Policy Toward Gambling 1976) and 3.3 percent of the general population (Culleton, forthcoming). However, on a state-by-state basis, even the lowest of these numbers translates into hundreds of thousands of individuals who are seriously compromised by gambling problems. This number does not include the family members, friends, employers, banks, credit unions, and other individuals and organizations who are affected by the pathological gambler.

Who has used the prevalence estimates of pathological gambling that are now available? Until very recently, the only users of prevalence estimates of pathological gambling have been the Presidential Commission on the Review of the National Policy toward Gambling and the National Council on Compulsive Gambling and its affiliates. The former group was more interested in an indictment of illegal gambling than in the actual costs, social or economic, of pathological gambling. The National Council and its affiliates have used prevalence estimates to directly lobby state legislatures in New Jersey and New York for funds to provide treatment for pathological gamblers and their families. Since the New York State study was completed, and the results published, a substantial number of researchers have contacted us requesting information about our prevalence estimates in New York. Several legislators and private research organizations have also contacted us to explore the possibilities of conducting similar prevalence surveys in other states.

Ultimately, debates about the number of pathological gamblers in the general population, or even about the best way to discover this number, are only important to the extent that they inform the development of legislative policies, treatment programs, and services to pathological gamblers and their families. Programs are needed regardless of the precise number of pathological gamblers in the general population. There are, however, a variety of issues under debate in several arenas where information about the prevalence of pathological gambling in the general population could be of use.

From our perspective, the most important findings to emerge from studies of the prevalence of pathological gambling concern the *types* of individuals in the general population who are most seriously compromised. As we found in New York State, and as Culleton found in his Delaware Valley survey (Culleton, private communication), pathological gamblers in the general population are far more likely to be women, to be young, and to be members of ethnic minorities than the pathological gamblers who enter treatment programs. These groups are the ones most in need of prevention and outreach efforts. These are the people who would most benefit from the establishment of treatment programs in minority neighborhoods, in high schools, and in women's and youth centers rather than in suburban community mental health centers or store fronts in white-collar working areas.

Prevalence data on the types of individuals most seriously in trouble from gambling have relevance for treatment professionals planning services for pathological gamblers and their families. It may be that the kinds of services offered to middle-aged, middle-class, mostly white men and their wives have little attraction to women, youth, and minority pathological gamblers. Treatment modalities (individual and group therapy, peer counseling) that may be effective with the types of pathological gamblers who are entering treatment may not be the most effective ways to treat women, minorities, and youth. Information about the types of people most seriously affected by pathological gambling should enable treatment professionals to develop alternatives to the treatment modalities now in use.

Prevalence data on pathological gamblers in the general population also have relevance for legislators and program administrators concerned with obtaining resources to pay for treatment, prevention, and outreach efforts. The treatment programs now in operation all have different ways of funding their services. Some of these programs are federally funded through the Veterans Administration. Other treatment programs are privately funded and rely on third-party reimbursement to cover the costs of their services. Still other treatment programs are funded by state governments, which appoint one or more state agencies to oversee their efforts. Finally, there are many private mental health practitioners who provide services to pathological gamblers. For all of these providers, as well as for legislators, a critical issue is who should be responsible for paying for these services. Is it the gaming industries, which profit from people's desire to wager? Is it the state governments, which are able to provide funding for vitally needed programs in other areas by legalizing gambling? Is it the gamblers themselves, who engage in these activities, and who might be expected to provide for those of their numbers who become seriously compromised by their gambling activities? Or could it be that a mix of all the interests that profit from wagering could contribute to the establishment and development of treatment programs for pathological gamblers?

There is also the issue of the regulation of gaming and gaming businesses to prevent the need for services for pathological gamblers. It has been suggested by Eadington (1988) that the British and European models of gaming provide a more socially responsible approach than the approaches used in the United States. It might be worthwhile for legislators and policy makers to consider alternatives to the Atlantic City and Nevada models of the casino industry when debating the issue of legalizing casinos in other parts of the United States. It might also be worthwhile to look at how other nations manage legalized gambling, such as lotteries, card games, and horse racing, for ideas on how to prevent pathological gambling rather than waiting until treatment services are needed for those who have become pathological gamblers.

Finally, there is the issue of the relationship of the prevalence of pathological gambling to the availability of legalized gambling in different states. Research on prevalence is still not refined enough to be able to establish a causal relationship between the availability of gambling and an increase in the number of pathological gamblers. However, continued research on the prevalence of pathological gambling must certainly address this issue since it is a question of major concern to state governments considering the development of revenue streams based on legalized gambling as well as to the gaming industries concerned with apportioning responsibility for the development of gambling problems among their consumers.

Conclusion

As we have shown, developing the best estimate of the prevalence of pathological gambling in the general population, as well as the best estimate of the types of individuals most seriously affected, should be of interest to several audiences. Legislators, regulators, and administrators concerned with policy issues should use information about prevalence to decide the appropriate distribution of funds and argue for additional funds for the many social service and health programs needed by pathological gamblers and their families. Treatment professionals and program administrators should value this prevalence data because it is useful in informing their efforts to enroll clients most in need of their services and in tailoring their treatment approaches to a variety of clients.

There is, however, a gap between "should value" and "do value" in both the political and programmatic arenas. In the current environment of the politics of pathological gambling, it is incumbent upon researchers, clinicians, and administrators to be aggressive in moving beyond simply reporting prevalence results and developing sounder measurements. We must also be willing to invest time and intellectual energy in the translation and communication of our findings to decision makers who hold the purse strings and draft the legislation. To stop at less leaves these research initiatives as hollow science.

References

American Psychiatric Association. 1980. *Diagnostic and Statistical Manual of Mental Disorders*, 3rd Edition. Washington, D.C.: American Psychiatric Association.

Commission on the Review of the National Policy toward Gambling. 1976. *Gambling in America*. Washington, D.C.: Government Printing Office.

Culleton, Robert P. Forthcoming. "The Prevalence Rates of Pathological Gambling: A Look at Methods," *Journal of Gambling Behavior*.

———. 1985. "A Survey of Pathological Gamblers in the State of Ohio." Report prepared for the Ohio Lottery Commission. October.

Culleton, Robert P., & M. H. Lang. 1985. "The Prevalence Rate of Pathological Gambling in the Delaware Valley in 1984." Report prepared for People Acting To Help, Philadelphia, Pennsylvania. October.

Eadington, William R. 1988. "Problem Gambling and Public Policy: Alternatives in Dealing with Problem Gamblers and Commercial Gambling." Paper presented at the Harvard Invitational Symposium on Compulsive Gambling, Cambridge, Massachusetts. June.

Fairley, William B., & F. Mosteller (eds.). 1977. *Statistics and Public Policy*. Reading, Massachusetts: Addison Wesley.

Lesieur, Henry R., & Sheila Blume. 1987. "The South Oaks Gambling Screen (SOGS): A New Instrument for the Identification of Pathological Gamblers." *American Journal of Psychiatry* 144:1184–1188.

Minnesota Department of Human Services. 1986. "Treatment of Compulsive Gamblers." Final Report to the Legislature. February.

Rosecrance, John. 1988. *Gambling Without Guilt: The Legitimation of an American Pastime*. Belmont, California: Wadsworth.

U.S. Bureau of the Census. 1986. *Statistical Abstract of the United States, 1986*. Washington, D.C.: Government Printing Office.

Volberg, Rachel A., & H. J. Steadman. 1988. "Refining Prevalence Estimates of Pathological Gambling." *American Journal of Psychiatry* 145:502–505.

10
Problem Gambling and Public Policy: Alternatives in Dealing with Problem Gamblers and Commercial Gambling

William R. Eadington

Introduction

Over the past two decades, many commercial gambling industries in the United States and abroad—casinos, lotteries, on-track and off-track horse race betting, bingo, and others—have evolved in significant ways. In general, commercial gambling has become more sophisticated, more legitimate, more corporatized, and more broadly accepted, in terms of management structure and policy, customer development, and the general public's perception of gambling industries. Legalization of gambling in various forms has occurred in many states and countries, as governments have looked to commercial gambling as a means of raising tax revenue, revitalizing otherwise declining economic areas, crowding out illegal gambling, or just meeting consumer demand for legal gambling activities and related services.

Yet, in spite of the rapid and generally positive changes that have occurred in these industries, one area of serious controversy remains: how much damage does commercial gambling do to individual society members? In spite of considerable attention given to this problem in professional journals and meetings, the magnitude and severity of problem gambling, as it relates to commercial gaming industries, is not well understood (see, for example, Eadington 1982a; Eadington 1985; Eadington 1988). The issue of the individual effects of the presence of commercial gambling on society can be summarized by the following questions: What will increased access to commercial gambling opportunities do to individuals with potential or actual gambling problems, and what can be done at various policy levels to mitigate these problems?

One of the difficulties perceived by those involved in the treatment of problem gamblers is the observation that the more prevalent commercial gambling is in society, the more problems individuals who are prone to excessive gambling will have. Yet it is apparent that commercial gambling is going to continue in a variety of forms in many parts of the country. Thus, from a policy perspective, it becomes important to examine the issue of gambling not in terms of whether it should exist in society (because certainly it does exist and it will), but rather in terms of how private sector and public sector entities linked to commercial gambling can direct their actions to mitigate the severity of gambling related problems.

The purpose of this analysis is to examine some of the policy options available at various institutional levels that deal with the issue of problem gambling in an environment with commercial gambling industries. Self-regulation and constraint within the commercial gambling organization are examined in light of their likely effectiveness and the tradeoffs between organizational goals and the economic impacts of the actions. The effectiveness of statutes and regulations by governmental bodies that deal with the issue, with respect to the tradeoffs on the demand, growth, revenue, profit, and job-creating potential for the gambling industries, is discussed. Finally, methods of cooperation between commercial gambling operators, regulatory authorities, and health service professionals are evaluated in light of how they might mitigate the overall social costs associated with problem gambling.

Definitions and Scope of the Problem

One of the major difficulties inherent in studying problem gambling is that of identifying and then measuring the social costs attributable to problem gambling. The difficulties begin with attempts to define "pathological" or "compulsive" gambling. Probably the best known current definition is the one put forth in the American Psychiatric Association's Diagnostic and Statistical Manual of Mental Disorders (DSM-III-R) (Custer 1988; Lesieur 1988). Though it describes pathological gambling as a degenerative disease with certain common traits and symptoms, there still is considerable dispute within the psychological community as to the applicability of this "medical model" (Dickerson 1988).

The courts have been working with the issue of pathological gambling for the past decade, and they seem to have gotten caught up in the same areas of ambiguity. Though they have expressed willingness to accept expert analysis as to the existence of pathological gambling as an illness or mental disorder, they have been reluctant to allow compulsive gambling as the basis of a defense in nongambling offenses, such as robbery, forgery, or embezzlement (Rose 1988). They are concerned that the acceptance of compulsive gambling as an illness or mental disorder would be an acknowledgement of the loss of free choice by the problem gambler, which would imply a shifting of responsibility away from the individual for his or her actions.

Even if there were a common understanding of what constituted a pathological gambler, there is still no clear litmus test, no on-the-spot equivalent of a blood-alcohol reading, that would allow for the unambiguous classification of a pathological gambler. It is largely an invisible problem, with symptoms quite hard to distinguish from the actions of nonpathological gamblers. Furthermore, if a person is truly a pathological gambler, that person may literally be the last to know. Often, a problem gambler is convinced the reasons he or she is losing are bad strategies, bad money management, or bad luck; an illness or mental disorder is probably far from such a person's conscious mind.

In the reality of the world of commercial gambling, this creates a significant difficulty for either the gambling proprietor or the regulator who is concerned in addressing this issue. If pathological gambling is an invisible problem, how can it be mitigated without interfering with the rights of those who want to gamble and are perfectly competent to make rational decisions with respect to their own gambling? Lacking such clear evidence of identification, the best that can be hoped for is the creation of a gambling environment where the potential for severe damage to an individual from excessive gambling can be mitigated. That environment can be created through the actions of commercial gambling operators, through regulatory or statutory edict, or through mutual cooperation between the gambling industries and regulatory bodies.

Enlightened Self-Interest, Self-Regulation, and the Gambling Enterprise

The following discussion concentrates on casino gaming organizations because of the wide variety of approaches that have been taken to regulate casino operations in various countries throughout the world (Kelly & Eadington 1986; McMillen & Eadington 1986). However, many of the points made can be broadly applied to other commercial gambling organizations.

Assume for the time being that casino operaters became convinced that eliminating pathological gambling within their facility was in their best interests. What implications might follow from this position?

First, the organization would have to train its management staff to identify certain signs of pathological gambling, whether it be the frequent drawing from one's wallet of additional cash, the bouncing of checks, or the anger displayed in the casino's parking lot by large losers. Second, some type of strategic policy would have to be established mapping out how the casino should deal with players with apparent gambling problems. These could range from outright banning of players from the facility, to the casino's providing advice to the problem gambler about the availability of counseling services or of Gamblers Anonymous chapters in the area, to discussions on the realities of the probabilities that govern casino games, slot machines, and devices.

The difficulties of an individual casino's implementing such a policy are obvious. Ideally, such a casino would only want rational pleasure-seeking gamblers who are freely choosing to risk (and usually lose) portions of their discretionary budgets. This would not include those players who over time were clearly depleting their wealth at the expense of their gambling habit. It would obviously be almost impossible for casino management to discern such a sequence of events among casual or occasional visitors to the facility, so attention would have to concentrate on regulars. The casino's management would then have to classify regulars as either normal or pathological, perhaps by estimating the income of gamblers against their rates of loss to see if in fact some individuals are losing to the gambling establishment at a rate fast enough to deplete their wealth. When that is the case, then management would have to make a determination as to the mental state of such individuals. Clearly, this approach leaves a lot to be desired.

But it is possible that seasoned casino personnel can identify many of the degenerate gamblers in their facilities. However, even if they were known to be pathological gamblers, and were then either encouraged to leave or banned from further participation in the casino, it is likely they would wander out the front door of the casino, find its closest competitor, and continue to lose until total financial ruin or psychological "rock-bottom" set in. If this were the case, the only solace for the casino in question would be the knowledge that it "did the right thing" by not directly bringing about the gambler's ruin.

A related line of argument is that by denying individuals who are pathological gamblers access to the gambling within their casino, then management is participating in non-value-maximizing behavior—that is, it is sacrificing profits to fulfill other objectives. If the casino firm is publicly owned, this would lower the market value of that firm's stock. In these circumstances, the firm runs the risk of becoming a takeover target to outsiders who recognize both the undervalued stock and the non-value-maximizing behavior. Should such a takeover transpire, then the asset value of the firm could be increased if the new management forgoes non-value-maximizing behavior and only concentrates on bottom line performance. Even without an actual takeover, management is made aware of the possibility that its attempts to be humane toward pathological and problem gamblers can increase its vulnerability to external forces. Thus, the incentives for any management are to ignore the non-value-maximizing behavior and concentrate on company profits as the primary objective of the enterprise (Schleifer & Vishny 1988).

Another consideration is that, in many gambling establishments, regular gamblers contribute a significant portion to the total revenues of the gambling operation. If it were determined that many of these regulars were in fact pathological (however it is defined), then their removal would threaten revenue generating capabilities, and even possibly the continuing economic viability, of the gambling operation. If indeed this is generally the case, there may be no resolution to the conflict between pathological gambling and commercial gambling operations.

Thus, the traditional lines of argument that would be offered by casinos in competitive environments as to why they should not have to be concerned with the plight of the pathological gambler are:

a) it is difficult to classify a gambler as being pathological;

b) even if gamblers could be correctly identified as pathological, then denial of access to one casino facility would only induce them to gamble and lose elsewhere;

c) any sanctions against pathological gamblers instituted by individual gambling operations would result in lower revenues, lower profitability, and an inherently weaker financial position, thus jeopardizing the economic viability of the operation and perhaps management's position in the organization;

d) pathological gamblers might be too important a source of gaming revenues for casino management to unilaterally exclude them from gambling.

In conclusion, even if one were dealing with private sector gambling organizations who were legitimately concerned with problems of pathological gambling, it would be unrealistic to expect them to be self-regulating in dealing with the issue. On the other hand, it is not out of the question for some, if not many gambling organizations to recognize the image and legitimacy problems that pathological gambling can create for the commercial gambling industry. Thus, if a set of regulations was imposed on the entire gambling industry, so that all competitors would be equally constrained in dealing with problem or pathological gamblers, the likelihood of success would be greater than depending upon self-regulation. Alternatively, in those jurisdictions where casinos are established as franchised monopolies, insulated from direct competition from other casinos and protected from takeovers, they could choose to be more paternalistic and benevolent in their dealings with problem gamblers, though there is no strong reason to suspect that they would choose to do so.

Regulation and Public Policy Approaches to Problem Gambling

If self-regulation of problem gambling by gambling organizations is unrealistic, how effective can the alternative of regulation by governmental bodies be expected to be? A starting point to analyze this question is to examine the practices of jurisdictions in various locations in the United States and in other countries.

Throughout the world, a wide variety of approaches has been tried for dealing with pathological gambling. Often, however, these strategies are easy to implement because the casinos operate in a monopoly subject to strict governmental oversight, and the government is effectively a partner in casino operations because of tax policies and contractual relations. Thus, competitive pressures are quite different than in American casino markets, and there is seemingly less concern over revenue maximization as an organizational objective at the expense of other noneconomic objectives.

Many casinos in other countries use entrance fees and identity checks at the door to the gaming areas. With this type of screen, some restrictions appropriate for the control of the problem gambler are possible. For example, in France, locals are prohibited from playing in the main portion of the casino, and a person can be banned from playing in the casino because of irresponsible gambling. Individuals can also request that the casino ban them from entering in future visits if they fear they will not be able to control their gambling losses in future visits. Also, family members can petition a casino to ban a gambler. Variations of these restrictions are present in some of the German and Austrian casinos.

In general, continental European casinos adhere to a philosophy that casino gambling is parasitic and potentially damaging to local populations because of problem gambling. Therefore, by design, it is made difficult for locals to enter the casino. Furthermore, because it is felt that casinos can do serious damage to any players that overindulge, casino management is apparently conditioned to be more sensitive to such situations and can ban a gambler from entering the casino to protect him from himself. This degree of paternalism, which would be difficult to apply in the United States, is probably caused by a mix of social concern for the potential ruining effects of gambling, and the enlightened self-interest of casino officials who realize that they are involved in a tolerated, though controversial, industry.

The British experience with casino gambling also provides a number of indications on the alternatives available for dealing with problem gambling, and their likely effectiveness. The casino industry in the United Kingdom is strictly regulated in a number of ways to adhere to the philosophy that commercial gambling is only supposed to cater to unstimulated demand for gambling. Therefore, people who want to participate in casino gambling will have to seek it out, and those who do not will not be attracted to it by promotional or marketing efforts. It also reflects an underlying attitude that casinos should not be allowed to entice or exploit those individuals who choose to gamble in British casinos.

Thus, anything that would appear to broaden the general appeal of casino gambling in the United Kingdom is proscribed by law or regulation. For example, the British casino industry is run strictly on a club basis with members and bona fide guests as the only allowed participants at the casino games. Any advertising to the general public is forbidden, and signage on the exteriors of casinos is severely limited. Furthermore, new members of clubs that offer gaming must sign a form that states they wish to gamble; they must then wait forty-eight hours before they are allowed to gamble, for the apparent purpose of discouraging impulse gambling. Alcohol is not allowed at the gaming tables in British casinos, because it might impair judgment when gambling. Live entertainment is not allowed in casino clubs on the basis that it might induce individuals to join the clubs for reasons other than gambling, but then they could be drawn into gambling. Certain "sucker" bets are forbidden at blackjack and craps, and casinos are required to provide printed strategies of good play to players.

However, the most important facet of British regulation is the prohibition against credit. British casinos are allowed to offer check cashing services, but checks must be processed through the drawer's bank within two banking days (Eadington, 1987). Furthermore, violations of credit regulations are taken quite seriously; such violations led either directly or indirectly to a number of major casino companies losing their licenses in London between 1979 and 1981 (Kent-Lemon 1984; Miers 1981).

The American casinos of Nevada and Atlantic City provide a very different approach to the issue of dealing with the problem gambler. For the most part, the problem gambler is officially ignored. Individuals who choose to participate in casino games are assumed to be rational and are held responsible for their own actions, including their gambling losses. Furthermore, instead of the restrictive low-key approach to casino marketing, implicit in continental European casinos and explicit in the United Kingdom, American casinos have become expert at providing various marketing strategies to maximize casino participation by the general public.

Where European and British casinos tend to be invisible, American casinos are relatively unrestricted in terms of their efforts to broaden demand for gambling services through marketing efforts. In Nevada, there is very little restriction placed upon casinos in terms of how they can promote their gaming facilities, and Atlantic City is only slightly more limiting.

Among the practices that have evolved over the years germane to marketing and gambling stimulation are:

a) pricing policies that offer food, hotel rooms, entertainment, convention services, transportation (such as busing), and other activities at prices near or below cost, in the expectation that additional casino revenues from increased levels of business will more than cover the promotional costs;

b) extensive use of complementary services in the casino environment, ranging from free drinks to slot machine and keno patrons to free room, food, and beverage privileges throughout the casino facility for "high rollers" (Swartz 1984);

c) the provision of incentives for cashing paychecks in the casino that run from free drink coupons and "lucky bucks" to free plays on slot machines or free chances at draws on vehicles or other substantial prizes;

d) easily available credit to high-end-of-market casino patrons (Eadington 1987) and bank teller machines available within the casinos;

e) the provision of a wide variety of nongaming activities whose primary purpose is to increase the patronage level in the casino and the overall profitability of the operation. These range from high quality floor shows and big name entertainment to world class boxing matches, car races, and other sponsored sporting events;

f) the organization of gaming oriented events to provide excuses for the casino to invite good players to the casino property and to provide players with additional excuses to visit the casino. These would include such activities as player tournaments covering blackjack, craps, slot machines, keno, and other casino games, as well as organized activities built around major sporting events, such as the Super Bowl or the Kentucky Derby;

g) the identification of important players through observation, credit records, or new player-tracking technologies, and the development of player relations with direct mailings and other personal contact;

h) advertising campaigns emphasizing luck, chance, escapism, inexpensive food, lodging, entertainment, and other themes that potential visitors to casinos find enticing (Hess and Diller 1969);

i) extensive use of signage, lighting, noise, ambience, and other sensory experiences to create a "theme" that allows the player to escape and fantasize while gambling.

Most of these activities form the basis for modern marketing strategies within American casinos. How many are also contributory to problem gambling is clearly debatable. On the surface, some seem clearly more predatory than others. For example, paycheck cashing could be construed as being highly exploitative to individuals with low tolerance for control over their gambling. Also, the serving of complimentary alcoholic beverages at the gaming tables would tend to lower inhibitions and impair judgment, and liberal granting of credit within the casino, or the presence of bank teller machines, would also encourage impulsive individuals to lose more than they otherwise would.

On a policy level, restrictions on those facets of casino marketing would create a direct tradeoff between the revenue-generating capabilities of the gambling operations and the protection of the problem gambler from himself. Furthermore, in markets where casinos already exist, most of the marketing strategies are viewed by casino patrons as desirable services provided by the casino. Indeed, the reason marketing programs are effective is that customers perceive them as attractive, and much of the psychology of patrons in American casinos is to take advantage of the "good deals" the casinos offer. Furthermore, just how significant such restrictions would be is an empirical question for which there is very little available credible data because of the paucity of good empirical work in this area.

It is far more realistic to consider restrictions on the marketing activities of a gambling industry that is just beginning, say, through new legislation, rather than one that has been in existence and has incorporated such practices as part of overall operations. It can be argued that as long as there is excess demand for legal gambling services, gambling industries created through legislation with varying degrees of regulatory control or varying tax rates can be profitable. Different tax rates or different regulatory structures would affect the overall size, tax revenue generating capability, employment implications, and other quantitative aspects of the gambling industry, but it would not necessarily undermine the industry's economic viability (Eadington 1982b).

In terms of jurisdictions' considering creating commercial gambling industries through legislation, a fundamental question deals with the wisdom of such an endeavor. As a matter of strategy, public policy makers should attempt to weigh all social and economic costs and benefits associated with creating a new commercial gambling industry, including among the benefits such things as tax revenue generation, job creation, fulfillment of consumer demand, and economic stimulation. The costs to be considered should include, among other things, the amount of economic displacement that will occur through redirected spending patterns as a result of the new gambling industry, the effects on localized crime rates, and the social costs attributable to problem and pathological gamblers. Regulations and constraints should be developed that reasonably and cost-effectively address these concerns. If, at that point, aggregate benefits do not exceed aggregate costs, or the proposed gambling industry is not economically viable, then creation of a new gambling industry would not be a wise move.

Cooperative Attempts at Dealing with the Problem Gambler

The need to develop broad strategies for dealing with pathological gambling that have a good likelihood of success is going to continue to increase as commercial gambling expands in this country. Clearly, a negative aspect of the spread of commercial gambling in America is the difficulty of the individual who has a gambling problem to escape from places where gambling is offered. When serious gambling could only be found in Nevada, at the race tracks, or through illegal outlets, a problem gambler could relocate himself or herself away from those places where gambling was present. If, however, we are moving toward a situation in which commercial gambling is present in nearly every community in a wide variety of forms, schizophrenic problem gamblers may end up with having no place to hide.

If the plight of the problem gambler in jurisdictions with commercial gambling is going to be successfully addressed, then a number of things must happen. A high degree of understanding of the issues will have to be established among interested groups, institutionalized programs for dealing with problem and pathological gamblers will have to be developed and implemented, and each of the interested groups will have to acquire some sense of the effects of the programs and the constraints on the interests of the other groups. When a better understanding of the realities of problem gambling and commercial gaming is established, effective lines of communication among groups must be developed and cooperative endeavors pursued. Appropriate regulations and constraints on commercial gambling operations and on players will have a much better chance of being implemented and becoming effective if a degree of cooperation exists among the interested groups.

The groups most affected by attempts to deal with problem gambling would be commercial gambling operators, gambling patrons, regulators, and health service professionals. One possible strategy that could be developed would be for regulatory authorities to adopt, as a statement of policy, a position that pathological gambling is an issue of legitimate concern for public well-being, and that actions undertaken by commercial gambling interests should not be inconsistent with that position. Furthermore, an advisory committee to the regulatory authorities could be established to provide information and advice to the regulatory authorities on appropriate policies on problem gambling. Regulatory authorities could then draw from the collective expertise provided by representatives of the various interest groups when making their deliberations.

Certainly, such an approach would not be a panacea to all problems that arise as a result of pathological gambling, but it is probably better than the alternatives of either hoping that self-regulation by commercial gambling industries will adequately deal with the problems as they arise, or proscribing a wide variety of actions by gambling operators based on the judgment of regulators or legislators alone. Perhaps by establishing advisory committees that reach across various interest groups, a deeper level of understanding of conflicting issues could be achieved that will ultimately lead to better public policies toward problem and pathological gambling.

References

Custer, R. L. 1988. Pathological gambling as presented in the American Psychiatric Association's Diagnostic and Statistical Manual-III-Revised. In *Gambling Research: Proceedings of the Seventh International Conference on Gambling and Risk Taking*, University of Nevada Reno, Volume 5, 74–77.

Dickerson, M. 1988. The future of gambling research—learning from the lessons of alcoholism. In *Journal of Gambling Behavior*, Volume 3, Number 4, 248–256.

Eadington, W. R. 1988. *Gambling Research: Proceedings of the Seventh International Conference on Gambling and Risk Taking*, University of Nevada Reno (five volumes).

———. 1987. Credit play and casinos: Profitability, legitimacy, and social responsibility. In *Journal of Gambling Behavior*, Volume 3, Number 2, 83–97.

———. 1985. *The Gambling Papers: Proceedings of the Sixth National Conference on Gambling and Risk Taking*, University of Nevada Reno (five volumes).

———. 1982a. *The Gambling Studies: Proceedings of the Fifth National Conference on Gambling and Risk Taking*, University of Nevada Reno (thirteen volumes).

———. 1982b. Regulatory objectives and the expansion of casino gambling, *Nevada Review of Business and Economics*, fall, 4–13.

Hess, H. F., & J. V. Diller. 1969. Motivation for gambling as revealed in the marketing methods of the legitimate gambling industry. In *Psychological Reports*, Volume 25, August, 19–27.

Kelly, J., and W. R. Eadington. 1986. The regulation of casino gambling in Europe: A comparative analysis. In *Nevada Public Affairs Review*, Number 2, 56–64.

Kent-Lemon, N. 1984. Significant influences on the United Kingdom casino industry since 1960. In *Annals of the American Academy of Political and Social Science*, Volume 474, July, 72–79.

Lesieur H. R. 1988. Altering the DSM-III criteria for pathological gambling. In *Journal of Gambling Behavior*, Volume 4, Number 1, 38–47.

McMillen, J., & W. R. Eadington. 1986. The evolution of gambling laws in Australia. In *New York Law School Journal of International and Comparative Law*, Volume 8, Number 1, 167–192.

Miers, D. 1981. The mismanagement of casino gaming. In *British Journal of Criminology*, Volume 21, January.

Rose, I. N. 1988. A new deal for problem gamblers: Compulsive gambling and the law. In *Gambling Research: Proceedings of the Seventh International Conference on Gambling and Risk Taking*, University of Nevada Reno, Volume 3, 223–252.

Schleifer, A., & R. W. Vishny. 1988. Value maximization and the acquisition process. In *Journal of Economic Perspectives*, Volume 2, Number 1, Winter, 7–20.

Swartz, S. 1984. Want a nifty suite in Atlantic City? Just lose $900,000. In *Wall Street Journal*, December 27, p. 1 ff.

11

State Lotteries: Should Government Be a Player?

H. Roy Kaplan, Ph.D.

There can be little doubt that state lotteries are gaining respectability. From their reemergence in New Hampshire in 1964, they have swept up and down the east and west coasts and across the heartland of the country. From north to south they have penetrated the liberal east to the conservative Midwest, even the southern Bible Belt. By the end of 1988, twenty-seven states and the District of Columbia had lotteries, with more than half the population of the United States residing in them.[1]

The primary rationale for the new legalization of lotteries is to raise funds for states. This was also the justification for their introduction in Europe and England during the sixteenth century. Then, as now, the public balked at higher taxes and the seeming simplicity with which funds could be raised through the "painless tax" of a lottery served as the impetus for their development. In Italy, France, Germany, and England they were used to fund public works projects such as bridges, hospitals, and roads. They also played a vital role in the founding of our country when the King of England granted the Virginia Company of London a charter in 1612 to conduct lotteries to save its struggling settlement in Jamestown (Ezell 1960).

In the eighteenth century lotteries helped defray expenses during the French and Indian Wars, and in 1777 the Continental Congress sponsored a lottery to finance the Revolution. In addition to public works projects, many schools benefitted from them as well, including nearly all the Ivy League universities, but lotteries were banned in the nineteenth century because of fraud and corruption.

Although more state legislatures have managed to overcome reservations about the propriety of governmental involvement in legalized gambling, with a wide array of parimutuel betting and games of chance receiving legislative imprimatur, lotteries are somewhat different. Unlike these other activities, the government is directly involved in the organization, administration, and promotion of lotteries. In the minds of many people, the rationalization for governments' direct involvement seems justified—a pragmatic reversal of Kant's categorical imperative with the ends justifying the means. But is the public's and legislators' confidence misplaced? Now that lotteries have been on the scene for more than two decades, we can begin to assess the economic and social impact they are having on our society.

The Economic Impact of State Lotteries

Lotteries generate money, which has not been overlooked by state legislatures. But what have they accomplished since their reintroduction? How significant an effect have they had on state finances? Outwardly they appear to be an enormous financial success. In 1988 lottery sales surpassed $15 billion, but only slightly more than a third of that will find its way into state coffers. This is because states return approximately 50 percent of gross receipts to players in prizes. Of the remaining money, 10 percent to 15 percent goes for the administration and promotion of the games and to pay vendors who supply tickets and machines. Ticket agents, who normally receive five percent of gross sales, must also be paid, and some states provide incentive bonuses to them as well. This leaves the state with approximately 35 percent of the gross, which makes the lottery a very inefficient form of revenue generation compared to other forms of collections, such as taxes and licenses. The average administrative cost of collecting lottery revenues was found to be 20 percent with a high of 43.4 percent in Maine and a low of 4.6 percent in Illinois. This compares to administrative costs for broad-based taxes of less than 1 percent of net revenue to 1.6 percent to 4.4 percent of total tax revenue (Mikesell & Zorn 1986). These costs are related to the large network of ticket sales agents. California has more than twenty-five thousand of them, while a smaller state like New Jersey has four thousand.

Although hundreds of millions of dollars can be raised through a lottery, their proceeds rarely supply a state with more than 3 or 4 percent of its budgetary needs. A National Science Foundation study pointed out years ago that states could generate the same amount of revenue derived from lotteries by increasing the sales tax rate by half a percent (Weinstein & Deitch 1974). In some states, the error in predicting tax revenues for the coming year's budget exceeded lottery revenues (Kaplan 1984). In 1984 net revenues of state lotteries averaged less than 2 percent of state general revenue from taxes, interest, special assessments, and property sales. When the lottery was compared with twenty-two tax sources, its proceeds ranked ninth or higher in twelve of seventeen states analyzed. Lottery revenue most frequently ranked behind motor vehicle license fees in importance. Even more perplexing is the unreliability of lottery revenues. Between 1978-84, thirteen of seventeen states experienced at least one annual decline in lottery revenue ranging from .8 percent in Massachusetts to 50 percent in Maine (Mikesell & Zorn 1986).

While seemingly large sums of money are generated by lotteries, other, more efficient and effective methods of revenue generation must still be used. For example, New Jersey legalized the lottery in 1970, but that year the state's sales tax was also increased to 5 percent. New Jersey revolutionized the contemporary lottery industry by introducing the daily numbers game and holding regular million-dollar drawings. These innovations dramatically increased lottery revenues but were still insufficient to meet the state's needs, and so casinos were legalized in 1976. Despite a panoply of legalized gambling activities, only 7 percent of its revenue comes from them, and the state recognized their insufficiency and introduced a graduated income tax, also in 1976.

New York provides us with another example of the financial ineffectiveness of lotteries. Its lottery contributed $666.8 million in fiscal 1986-87 on sales of $1.5 billion, but this was equal to only 1.8 percent of the state's $37.3 billion budget. Although lottery revenues were earmarked for education, they were insufficient to meet its immense needs, contributing slightly over 4 percent.

Earmarking of lottery revenues, practiced by twelve of the twenty-two active state lotteries in 1986, is often little more than budgetary shuffling. Funds are frequently moved from one category to another, substituted in like amounts so the expected recipient of a lottery bonanza emerges with the amount the legislature intended it to receive before the existence of the lottery. Education is the most commonly earmarked category for lottery funds, and while it is difficult to trace their impact, some observations can be made about the absolute contribution to state expenditures for education. Table 11–1 attempts to do this by comparing the average amount spent per pupil in the year before lottery implementation with current expenditures. In four of the seven states that earmark some or all lottery proceeds for education, their rank compared to other states declined. This was most noticeable in Michigan, which slipped eight positions. New Jersey remained the same, while Ohio and California improved their positions. But a word of caution must be interjected about the California figures. According to Susan Lange, public relations director for the California Department of Education, in its first year of operation, 1986, the system for lottery funds distribution was not even in place, and in the second year only 50 percent of earmarked funds were received. "There's been less money put into education than before." (Lange 1988) Her sentiments were later echoed by Bill Honig, California superintendent of public instruction. "Education was used to get the lottery passed, but education hasn't benefitted from it." (Freedberg 1988) This happened despite California law, which specifies that lottery revenues "shall not be used as

Table 11-1
Impact of Lotteries on Per-Pupil Expenditures on Education

State	Year Lottery Started	Expenditure per Pupil in Year Prior to Lottery		Rank among States	1986 Expenditure Per Pupil	Rank	Difference
California	1985	$2,912	(1984)	31	$3,573	22	+9
Michigan	1972	$1,134	(1971)	4	$3,789	16	-12
New Hampshire	1964	$440	(1963)	30	$3,115	34	-4
New York	1976[1]	$2,179	(1975)	1	$5,616	2	-1
Ohio	1983[2]	$2,492	(1982)	32	$3,547	25	+7
New Jersey	1971	$963	(1970)	3	$5,544	3	—
Iowa	1985	$3,212	(1984)	20	$3,568	23	-3

*Source: "Public Elementary and Secondary School Estimated Finances," Statistical Abstracts of the U.S. 1965, 1970, 1972, 1976, 1984.
[1]The New York lottery was begun in 1967 but reconstructed in 1976 and funds were then designated for education.
[2]This year marked the designation of funds for education. Though begun in 1974, funds were exclusively dedicated to education in 1983.

substitute funds but rather shall supplement the total amount of money allocated for public education." Legislators' and the public's anticipation of the infusion of lottery funds often results in decreased overall allocations for earmarked categories such as education. In California, for example, the percentage of the state budget spent on education declined from 39 percent in 1984, the year before the lottery introduction, to 37.5 percent in 1987. And voters have become reluctant to approve school tax measures in that state—only 30 percent passed in 1987 (Freedberg 1988).

Many intervening variables affect lottery expenditures and rankings, not the least of which is the prevailing economic climate in states. For example, Michigan's economy experienced a severe downturn during the late '70s and early '80s, which no doubt contributed to its decline in spending for education. It is extremely difficult to trace the effect of lottery funds on earmarked categories, and when added to the general fund, as a majority of states do, that task becomes virtually impossible.

The Social Impact of Lotteries

Generating revenues through legalized gambling is a controversial public policy, especially since the funds are derived from the losses incurred by participants, in contrast to progressive forms of taxation which depend on the creation of wealth.[2] It has been known for some time that lotteries are a regressive form of revenue generation. Brinner & Clotfelter (1975) estimated that lotteries in Connecticut and Massachusetts were equivalent to a state sales tax with a rate of 60 to 90 percent, and Spiro's (1974) analysis of 271 Pennsylvania lottery winners' socioeconomic status revealed that the lottery was highly regressive for people in the $10,000 to $15,000 income bracket.[3]

One of the most heated areas of debate about the social impact of lotteries concerns ticket purchasing. A survey conducted for the National Commission on Gambling in 1974 revealed that over 50 percent of the people in states having lotteries purchased tickets and while middle and upper class people purchased more, poor people were spending proportionately more of their annual income (Gambling in America 1976). Lottery organizations have commissioned numerous marketing studies that invariably conclude that most tickets are purchased by middle and upper income people (see for example Bruskin 1984). But Suits (1982) demonstrated that in Michigan, where per capita sales of tickets were $75, blacks spent more than whites, and the proportion of family income spent on lottery tickets declined almost 12 percent for every 10 percent increase in per capita income. He concluded that the Michigan lottery "is one of the most regressive taxes known and by far the heaviest relative burden on those least able to pay."

Kaplan's (1978) study of lottery winners confirmed the assumption that most players came from working class backgrounds. None of the winners had graduated from college, the average income of male heads of households was $12,000 the year before winning, and nearly all worked in semiskilled or skilled blue collar jobs. Shortly after this, the Connecticut State Commission on Special Revenue found that the state's daily numbers game primarily attracted the poor, the chronically unemployed, and the uneducated, while people with college degrees and incomes over $25,000 largely ignored them (*New York Times*, January 6, 1980: E6).

Recent evidence is even more compelling. Looking at lottery sales information by census tracts in Florida, Halldin & Siemaszko (1988) found that while residents of rich and poor counties were spending equal amounts in proportion to their population in the state during the first four weeks of the new instant ticket game, there were some interesting disparities based on income within counties. When they analyzed ticket purchases in Hillsborough County, where the city of Tampa is situated, per capita sales in poor areas exceeded sales in affluent areas by more than 60 percent ($13.2 to $8.4 per capita). Similarly, Luke (1988) found that in some areas of Detroit eight percent of household income is spent on tickets. Eleven percent of the state's population resides in the predominantly black city, but 28 percent of lottery sales come from there. With a median income of $13,600, Detroit residents spend at the rate of $645 per capita on lottery tickets, primarily the legal numbers game. In Iowa, Shaw (1986) analyzed data compiled by the lottery on instant ticket winners and discovered that people earning less than $10,000 annually purchased 5.3 times more tickets than people in the $10,000 to $25,000 income range and more than seven times the amount of people in the $25,000 to $50,000 range. The poorest group of Iowans spent nine times more on the lottery than the wealthiest group, those earning over $50,000. Though they accounted for only 7.5 percent of the state's income, the lowest earnings group purchased over 26 percent of the instant game tickets.

Clotfelter & Cook (1987a) also analyzed instant ticket winners' incomes focusing on Maryland and Massachusetts by comparing the median income of their zip code areas. They concluded that the games were regressive, with low expenditures on tickets in the top income group. A relatively small proportion of households in each income group purchased a disproportionate share of the tickets and there was heavier play among blacks than whites.[4] The concentration of ticket purchases among a small segment of the population was also found in two California surveys conducted by the Field Institute in 1985 and 1986 (The California Poll 1986).

A decreasing proportion of the population was found to be accounting for a majority of the tickets—12 percent of the adult population purchased 69 percent of them, with blacks and Hispanics more often heavy players. In their forthcoming book, *Selling Hope: State Lotteries in the U.S.*, Clotfelter and Cook present compelling evidence that the top 10 percent of lottery players account for 50 percent of the total money wagered, and the top 20 percent account for two-thirds of the total weekly lottery revenues.

Despite this evidence, lottery administrators continue to contend that sales are evenly distributed among the population.[5] Zip code and sales data are said to be unreliable because they may reflect sales to people who do not reside in the area: tourists, workers, transients. While there may be some validity to this criticism, it is unlikely the discrepancies can be solely discounted by this possibility, nor is it likely that tourists flock to the inner city to purchase instant tickets or that large segments of the nonindigenous population are employed there.

Lotteries have changed greatly since their reintroduction. The early passive games have evolved into more active ones that allow players to select their own numbers, as in state-run daily numbers games and lotto, where players pick numbers in an attempt to match randomly selected ones chosen by the state. While instant tickets are still sold, their share of the total lottery market has diminished considerably. For example, in New York, the instant game accounts for only 4 percent of total sales. But studies seem to indicate that a dual consumer market of lottery players has emerged. It appears that poor people, blacks, and Hispanics prefer to play the instant and daily numbers games, while middle and upper class players prefer lotto. The widespread availability of illegal numbers games among ethnic groups and within the inner cities has been shown to be culturally institutionalized (Light 1977). This may explain the popularity of the instant and daily numbers games among these groups. Although there is no way of knowing exactly how many of the underprivileged population are purchasing tickets, how much they are spending, and what percentage of their expenditures are from discretionary income, a recent study of lottery ticket purchases among Canadians questions the validity of marketing surveys commonly used by lotteries.

For decades there has been controversy over the issue of the low correlation between attitudes and behavior (See Phillips 1971). Aware of the discrepancy between what people say and what they do, Brenner, Montmarquette & Brenner (1987) attempted to gauge the extent of ticket purchases among the public in Canada by comparing information gathered from interviews conducted by Statistics Canada with actual sales information compiled by provincial lotteries. They found as much as 50 percent underreporting of purchases, with the greatest underreporting among the poor. No doubt some of the discrepancy may be accounted for by cross border sales to United States citizens, but the researchers were skeptical that such a large disparity could be explained that way.

In the face of these data, lottery officials remain intransigent, dismissing the charge that lotteries victimize the poor by noting that the poor spend a disproportionate share of their income on all types of consumer goods: food, milk, clothes (Shaw 1986). But should state governments actively promote an activity that may encourage the poor to buy tickets that have little intrinsic worth—at least you can eat food, drink milk, and wear clothes. Proponents of the lottery retort that most people are able to handle their finances rationally and the professed concern for the discretionary spending of the poor is both patronizing and unjustified. However, some disconcerting information about the supposed discretionary nature of the funds used to purchase tickets was revealed shortly after Florida began its lottery in January 1988. In the first two months of operation the state's Department of Health and Rehabilitative Services reviewed the names of $5,000 winners and found 47 who were derelict in their child support payments, totaling more than $100,000. The *Tampa Tribune* (February 6, 1988: 10A) estimated that negligent providers had wagered $2,320,000 on lottery tickets in the first month of the Florida lottery.

Lottery officials are reluctant to refer to ticket purchases as gambling, preferring to call it entertainment, but their promotional campaigns accentuate the former. Clotfelter & Cook (1987b) analyzed lottery advertisements and concluded that they promoted materialistic values and were misleading about the odds against winning. The twenty-two active state lottery organizations spent $156 million on advertising in 1987 in an attempt to increase bettor participation. But how far should they go? That question was raised by the Illinois Economic and Fiscal Commission (1986) when it reviewed the status of the lottery in that state. It was found that inner city blacks were targeted by the lottery's advertising agency because earlier marketing surveys found considerable interest in the lottery among this group. The campaign took the form of billboard advertising bearing such statements as, "Your ticket off Washington Avenue to Easy Street."

In Detroit, Luke (1988) found an intense radio blitz aimed at inner city blacks. He compared two stations with similar Arbitron ratings, one that featured classical music and appealed to white middle and upper class listeners and the other with rock music that appealed to blacks. Fifty advertisements for the Michigan lottery were aired on the classical station during 1987, while seventeen hundred ads were aired on the black-oriented station.

Lotteries and Compulsive Gambling

Another side of the social impact issue, one that has been attracting attention in recent years, concerns the effect of lotteries on compulsive gambling. Officially recognized by the American Psychiatric Association as a psychiatric disorder, compulsive gambling can wreak havoc on individuals, families, and the economy by interrupting normal functioning in life roles. The Commission on the Review of the National Policy on Gambling estimated that 1.1 million Americans are compulsive gamblers, but the National Council on Compulsive Gambling puts the figure much higher—perhaps 3 million adults. Economic losses from work absenteeism, bad debts, and crime have been estimated at over $34 billion annually to our society (Politzer, Morrow & Leavey 1982).

While much of the psychological literature focuses on personality types that may be etiological factors in this syndrome (for example, McCormick et al. 1987), there is general agreement among clinicians that the increased availability of legalized gambling is contributing to increased abuse. The state with the highest number and proportion of compulsive gamblers is Nevada. It has a wide variety of legalized gambling activities, including horse racing and casinos, which, along with sports betting, constitute the three most commonly abused forms of gambling. But there is no lottery in Nevada, although one might liken the casino game keno to a form of lottery. The introduction of Megabucks, the linking of progressive slot machines in different casinos to form multimillion dollar jackpots, is also a form of lottery held among slot machine players. It is conceivable that many compulsive gamblers migrated to Nevada, but it is also probable that the availability and promotion of gambling there has contributed to the problem.

Until recently, lotteries were not thought to be a particularly important factor in the compulsive gambling equation because they lack three key elements that appeal to gamblers: excitement, low odds, and a sense of mastery. Because picking a lottery number is not an intrinsically challenging or stimulating experience and the odds against winning a big jackpot are astronomical (as much as 14 million to one in the six-out-of-forty-nine format used in California, Florida, and Canada), most serious gamblers focus their energies on activities that offer a higher probability of success, such as handicapping a race or football game. But recent developments in the nature of lottery games and prize structures is causing concern among some clinicians. Changes in game formats are related to the sluggish growth of mature lotteries that normally reach a plateau in sales after several years. For example, Pennsylvania, one of the top three lottery sales leaders for most of this decade, generated increased sales of just two percent in 1986 (Davis, Hevener & La Fleur 1987). Although much has been said about the dynamic growth in the lottery industry, most of it has been the result of expansion to new states (for projections on lottery sales and cycles see DeBoer 1986). Consequently, there is increasing pressure on lottery administrations by government officials to bolster sales. Twelve of the twenty-two lottery directorships changed hands in 1986 (including Pennsylvania), signifying the volatility of this politicized position.

To counter the inevitable sales malaise, advertising has become more aggressive, and, more importantly, games are being changed from a static format to a more engaging variety. This trend is exemplified by the emergence of the lotto and daily numbers games. Traditionally low-excitement, passive games where players purchased a ticket and waited to match their numbers with winning numbers drawn at a later date have been replaced by "instant win" scratch-off tickets that reveal outcomes immediately. Despite colossal odds, such as those in Florida's initial game, which offered an eighty thousand-to-one chance of winning $5,000 and 125-million-to-one chance for a million dollars, the public snapped up the tickets; 95 million were purchased in the first week—more than $5 per capita. These tickets function much like miniature slot machines, using concepts of behavior modification pioneered by psychologist B.F. Skinner (1971). Through subtle reinforcement of buying behavior—players have a one-in-four chance of winning something with every ticket purchased—ticket buying is conditioned. While many lottery players may view ticket purchases as a form of entertainment, it is a legitimate question whether state governments should promote such activities.

This question becomes more significant in view of the inherent potential for abuse of lotteries by certain segments of the population. Research on winners (Kaplan 1988a) indicates that lotteries may be tapping non-betting segments of the population, heightening the risk of addictive and pathological behavior among them. Those especially vulnerable are youths, the elderly, the poor, and minorities. We have already seen that the poor and minorities are overrepresented in their frequency of playing and the proportion of money they wager on tickets. The dream of financial security offered by lotteries and illegal numbers finds a special place in the subculture of poverty and despair that pervades the inner cities of our society.

One of the justifications for legalizing state lotteries has been their supposed impact on their illegal counterpart, variously called numbers, policy, or bolita. Such games are prevalent in metropolitan areas, especially the inner cities. But evidence of legal lotteries' inroads into organized crime is sketchy and inconclusive. Law enforcement officers and lottery officials disagree over the effects of legalization. In some cities such as Cleveland, lottery officials contend that the numbers game has been severely affected by the legal daily (Bloomberg 1988). In other areas, such as New York, the numbers game is a thriving enterprise, although one study indicates it does not generate nearly as much revenue as popularly believed (Reuter & Rubenstein 1982). Preliminary findings from research conducted with the assistance of the Metro-Dade Sheriff's Department in Miami, Florida indicates that the introduction of the legal daily numbers game initially cut into its illegal counterpart, but after several weeks the illegal game rebounded as writers expanded their product line, taking bets on the legal number as well (Kaplan & Blount 1989). This is a common practice among illegal numbers writers. A serendipitous finding that emerged from the Miami study was that many people employed in the network of numbers writers and runners are compulsive gamblers who plow their daily profits back in wagers, taking advantage of the 20 percent discount they're given by bankers. In one case, a black female writer whose profit in 1987 was more than six figures finished the year with nothing, living in squalor.

Added to this array of impoverished ethnics who are predisposed through tradition and circumstance to succumb to the temptation to abuse the lottery, both legal and illegal, is a potentially huge reservoir of naive nongamblers for whom the lottery is a first flirtation with gambling. It is known that large numbers of the general population play lotteries, and many elderly, youths, and housewives are among them. Some, perhaps taking a cue from the lottery industry, do not consider playing the lottery gambling. It's entertainment, according to industry officials, and a sizeable proportion of players apparently agree. A recent survey of winners in British Columbia revealed that 35 percent of them did not view the lottery as gambling, and only one-third had ever participated in any other form of gambling activity (Kaplan 1988b). Similar results were obtained among million-dollar winners in Ohio (Kaplan 1988a). This contrasts sharply with the public participation rate of 68 percent reported by the Commission on the Review of the National Policy Toward Gambling in 1974.

As with the poor, the elderly are particularly susceptible to the lure of instant riches, since many of them are on fixed incomes which often place them marginally above the poverty level. The average age of lottery winners is fifty-four, and since winners are representative of players, being randomly selected, this indicates the popularity of lotteries among the older age cohort of our population. One study found that many elderly winners used their winnings for health and nursing home care (Kaplan, 1985).

Other vulnerable people are youths, who are being exposed to various forms of legalized gambling on an unprecedented scale. Lottery advertisements frequently convey the theme of instant wealth and the gratification of materialistic desires through luck and chance. This theme runs counter to the American tradition of industriousness and work and may ultimately change the American work ethic into a no-work ethic. To date there has not been a definitive study of the effect of lottery availability and advertising on the youth of our society. However, Jacobs (1988) found an 11 percent increase in gambling among high school students after the lottery was introduced in California. But intervening variables may have mediated these results, making it difficult to establish causality. Unfortunately, it was not a panel study.

How widespread are lottery-related abuses? In the absence of definitive studies one can only speculate. It is unlikely that lotteries are contributing significantly to the ranks of compulsive gamblers at the present time because of their passive nature. Nevertheless, the mass media periodically report cases of pathological behavior. For example, Valerie Kaczor, a thirty-two-year-old Michigan housewife, was sentenced to prison for writing bad checks and forging money orders to support her $1,000 a day lottery ticket purchases. Over eighteen months she spent $250,000 to $300,000 on tickets (Wagman 1986; Dennis, 1988). Obviously, such behavior is rare, but in view of the widespread availability, promotion, and participation in lotteries it is reasonable to assume that similar cases will occur. The legitimization of activities that were previously illegitimate increases the likelihood that they will be engaged in. In the case of lotteries we not only have the legislative imprimatur of the state stamped on them, but their active promotion as well, often under the guise of a noble cause, such as the improvement of education.

Lacking the ingredients of low odds, a sense of mastery, and excitement, lotteries probably will not contribute proportionately as much to the general pool of compulsive gamblers as other forms of parimutuel wagering, such as horses and sports betting. Still, in absolute numbers of people at risk, especially if one considers less serious forms of abuse such as financial hardships experienced by families who wager scarce resources on tickets, the potential negative effect on society is enormous.

Recent innovations in games signify an important transition in the nature of lotteries in our society. The trend is toward converting traditionally passive activities into more engaging, challenging, active ones. Just as television and the mass media have been used to increase sports betting by offering odds and advice of network aficionados to fans (Kaplan 1983), lotteries are promoted by states as an enjoyable, thrilling, challenging form of entertainment. Rarely are the odds against winning jackpots clearly stated in ads (see Clotfelter and Cook 1989). Instead, a mindset is created among would-be players that attempts to convey the impression that winning is easy and playing may be the best way of solving one's financial problems. This approach has been likened to a form of social control, a modern equivalent of the bread and circuses of the Roman Empire, where the public is preoccupied with promises of instant gratification of materialistic dreams while more direct social action is avoided (Kaplan 1984).

Contributing to these dreams is a burgeoning industry of lottery advisers, soothsayers, charlatans, and con artists who hawk a variety of products ranging from gimmicks and gizmos that randomly select lotto numbers to full-scale computer programs costing over one hundred dollars. A wide variety of lottery magazines, books, and pamphlets offer advice of "experts" on picking numbers, and psychics are having a field day with the gullible who are willing to pay for horoscopes with personalized numbers. One of the contemporary rages among lotto players is known as tracking. Here players chart the occurrence of numbers from previous draws with an eye toward selecting commonly occurring or infrequently picked numbers. It makes no difference to many of them that each drawing is random and independent of all others, especially when winners give testimonials asserting that they used tracking "systems." Obviously, if enough people use such systems the law of averages will yield some winners on a random basis, but logic is not always a strong suit among the naive and desperate. And while most lottery players are able to distinguish fact from fiction and rationally view lotteries as a mild form of entertainment, there will be some who go beyond the pale. Their numbers may increase as new games proliferate and the lottery industry introduces modifications to combat player apathy and capture larger amounts of their money.

Right now, a relatively small percentage of patients are being seen at private therapeutic facilities for lottery-related compulsive gambling problems. For example, Valerie Lorenz, executive director of the National Center for Pathological Gambling in Baltimore, reports that approximately 9 percent of the compulsive gamblers she encounters are having problems with the lottery (Lorenz 1988). One must also remember that these patients are a small percentage of the total population—better-educated and treatment-oriented people. It is not uncommon for such people to be multiple abusers—that is, to be having problems with other forms of gambling as well. Nevertheless, there are indications that the number of people having gambling problems related to lotteries is increasing.

In 1982 the New Jersey Council on Compulsive Gambling established a twenty-four-hour telephone hotline for people with gambling problems. The number of lottery-related calls went from zero the first year to 12 percent in 1985 and 21 percent in 1987 (New Jersey Council on Compulsive Gambling 1988). Some states have begun to sense the possible significance of the compulsive gambling issue and at least nine (New Jersey, Connecticut, Massachusetts, Ohio, Wisconsin, Maryland, New York,

Iowa, and Delaware) have provided funds for research into the phenomenon of gambling, education of the public, and rehabilitation of compulsive gamblers, but the effort has been feeble for the most part.

The lack of enthusiasm among states to endorse and fund such programs may emanate from fear that establishing them would be a tacit admission of their culpability, which might lead to litigation. Regardless, the issue is becoming more salient, as witnessed by the recent formation of a commission to look into compulsive gambling in New Jersey and restrictions on advertising in the enabling lottery legislation in Wisconsin, Missouri, and Virginia. Some of these restrictions, were, however, modified, as in Missouri, when sales slumped and the director resigned.

Conclusions

The lure of lotteries, with their promise of instant riches for the public and "painless" revenue generation for states, will most certainly hasten their adoption. By the year 2000 almost every state will have one, and the multistate lottery, Lotto America, begun in 1988 with Rhode Island, Kansas, Oregon, Iowa, West Virginia, and the District of Columbia, may become the equivalent of a national lottery as other states join. As lotteries spread, so too must come an awareness among officials and legislators of their limitations as revenue-generating mechanisms and as possible sources of negative social and economic impacts on the public. Lottery funds may supplement but cannot supplant traditional, more progressive forms of revenue generation. As questions about the effectiveness and social impact of lotteries increase, spurred by growing aggressiveness to expand markets and adverse public reaction to the specter of pathological gambling, state governments might wish to consider turning the administration of them over to corporations and adopting a regulatory role. This strategy would diminish the moral ambiguity governments are experiencing as they promote activities of questionable fiduciary merit, and may even be antithetical to public welfare. In recent years there has been increased awareness of government's responsibilities in promoting and regulating activities that may be injurious to the public. From seat belts to cigarettes, government has assumed a more proactive and protectionist posture.

Allowing the private sector to administer lotteries has precedent in many foreign countries. In the United States the racing industry can serve as a paradigm. This transfer might enhance the efficiency and effectiveness of lotteries. Government might cease regulating itself, and more importantly, might assume oversight responsibilities it is unwilling and incapable of performing in the lotteries' present configuration. This would also serve the public interest by removing the present reticence among lottery organizations to monitor the social, psychological, and economic effects of lotteries on citizens. Adopting such a model also might lead to increased state revenues as the private sector assumes responsibility for cost containment and depoliticizes key administrative positions.

Notes

1. Arizona, California, Connecticut, Delaware, Florida, Illinois, Iowa, Kansas, Maine, Maryland, Massachusetts, Michigan, Missouri, Montana, New Hampshire, New Jersey, New York, Ohio, Oregon, Pennsylvania, Rhode Island, South Dakota, Virginia, Vermont, Washington, West Virginia, Wisconsin. In the November 1988 elections, referenda were passed permitting the introduction of lotteries in Idaho, Minnesota, Kentucky, and Indiana.

2. For a discussion of the conflict between the state, citizen, and the gambling industry's interests see Abt, Smith & Christiansen 1985.

3. In a forthcoming work Clotfelter & Cook (1989) do not conclude that there is a direct link between increased lottery expenditures and income. However, they do find an inverse correlation between education and lottery expenditures and larger expenditures on tickets by blacks and Hispanics than whites.

4. For more information on the regressivity of lotteries see Suits (1977, 1979), Heavey (1978), and Clotfelter (1979).

5. For example, see the statement of J. Blaine Lewis, Jr. (1988), director of the Connecticut lottery and president of the North American Association of State and Provincial Lotteries.

References

Abt, V., J. F. Smith, & E. M. Christiansen. 1985. *The business of risk.* Lawrence, Kansas: University of Kansas Press.

Bloomberg, Anne. 1988. Director of public relations, Ohio state lottery. Personal communication.

Brenner, G., C. Montmarquette, & R. Brenner. 1987. Expenditures on state lotteries: What do people say and what do they do? An econometric analysis. Working paper no. 8735, University of Montreal.

Brinner, R. E., & C. T. Clotfelter. 1975. An economic appraisal of state lotteries. *National Tax Journal,* 28, 402.

Bruskin, R. H. 1984. New Jersey lottery awareness, purchase, and attitude study prepared for New Jersey State Lottery Commission. (mimeo)

California Poll. 1986. Release no. 1345, The Field Institute, June 6.

Clotfelter, C. T. 1979. On the regressivity of state operated number games. *National Tax Journal,* 32, 543–548.

Clotfelter, C. T., & P. J. Cook. 1987a. Implicit taxation in lottery finance. *National Tax Journal,* 40, 533–546.

_____. 1987b. Op editorial, *New York Times*, August 20, 1987 p. 21

_____. (forthcoming, 1989). *Selling Hope: State lotteries in the United States.* Cambridge, MA: Harvard University Press.

Davis, M. P., P. Hevener, & T. La Fleur. 1987. Lotteries lead the pack; thoroughbred, casinos fare well. *Gaming and Wagering Business*, 8:1, 22, 24–31.

De Boer, L. 1986. When will state lottery sales slow growth? *Growth and Change*, 17, 28–36.

Dennis, J. 1988. *Money for Nothing.* Davison, Michigan. Friede Publications.

Ezell, J. S. 1960. *Fortune's Merry Wheel: The Lottery in America.* Cambridge, Harvard University Press.

Freedberg, L. 1988. California educators see the schools reaping no bonanza from lottery. *New York Times*, October 4, national section, 9.

Gambling in America. 1976. Commission on the review of the national policy toward gambling. Washington, D.C., U.S. Government Printing Office.

Halldin, B., & C. Siemaszko. 1988. Poor give more pay to lottery. *Tampa Tribune*, February 28, Bl & B6.

Heavey, J. F. 1978. The incidence of state lottery taxes. *Public Finance Quarterly*, 6, 415–426.

Illinois Economic and Fiscal Commission. 1986. The Illinois state lottery. A special report.

Jacobs, D. 1988. Comments made about on-going research at the national symposium on lotteries and gambling, Simon Fraser University, Vancouver, Canada, May 26.

Kaplan, H. R. 1978. *Lottery winners: How they won and how winning changed their lives.* New York: Harper & Row.

_____. 1983. Sports, gambling, and television: The emerging alliance. *The Arena Review*, 7, 1–11.

_____. 1984. The social and economic impact of state lotteries. *Annals of the American Academy of Political and Social Science*, 474, 91–106.

_____. 1985. Lottery winners and work commitment: A behavioral test of the American work ethic. *Journal of the Institute for Socioeconomic Studies*, 10, 82–94.

_____. 1988a. Gambling among lottery winners: Before and after the big score. *Journal of Gambling Behavior*, 4, 171–182.

_____. 1988b. Survey of lottery winners in British Columbia. British Columbia Lottery Corporation. (mimeo)

Kaplan, H. R., & W. Blount. 1989. The effects of legalized lotteries on the numbers game. Paper presented at the annual meeting of the American Criminal Justice Society meeting, Washington, D.C., February.

Lange, S. 1988. Personal communication. February.

Lewis, J. B., Jr. 1988. *USA Today*, January 12, 11A.

Light, I. 1977. Numbers gambling among blacks: A financial institution. *American Sociological Review*, 42, 892–904.

Lorenz, V. 1988. Personal communication. November.

Luke, P. 1988. Reporter for Boothe Newspapers Syndicate. Personal communication. March.

McCormick, R. A., et al. 1987. Personality profiles of hospitalized pathological gamblers: The California personality inventory. *Journal of Clinical Psychology*, 43, 521–527.

Mikesell, J. L., & C. K. Zorn. 1986. State lotteries as fiscal savior or fiscal fraud: A look at the evidence. *Public Administration Review*, 46, 311–320.

New Jersey Council on Compulsive Gambling. 1988. News release. April.

Phillips, D. 1971. *Knowledge From What?* Chicago: Rand McNally.

Politzer, R., J. S. Morrow, & S. B. Leavey. 1982. Report on the social cost of pathological gambling and the cost-benefit effectiveness of treatment. The gambling papers: Proceedings of the fifth national conference on gambling and risk taking. Reno: Bureau of business and economic research, University of Nevada.

Reuter, P., & J. Rubenstein. 1982. *Illegal Gambling in New York*. New York: The Policy Sciences Center.

Shaw, B. 1986. Rich stay rich while Iowa's poorest buy lottery tickets. *Des Moines Register*. August 24, 1A & 7A.

Skinner, B. F. 1971. *Beyond Freedom and Dignity*. New York: Alfred A. Knopf.

Spiro, M. H. 1974. On the tax incidence of the Pennsylvania lottery. *National Tax Journal*, 27, 59.

Suits, D. B. 1977. Gambling taxes: Regressivity and revenue potential. *National Tax Journal*, 30, 25–33.

———. 1979. Economic background for gambling policy: The elasticity of demand for gambling. *Quarterly Journal of Economics*, 93, 155–162.

———. 1982. Gambling as a source of revenue. H. E. Brazer & D.S. Laren (eds.) *Michigan's Fiscal and Economic Structure*. Ann Arbor: University of Michigan Press.

Wagman, R. 1986. *Instant Millionaires*. New York: Woodbine House.

Weinstein, D., & L. Deitch. 1974. *The Impact of Legalized Gambling: The Socioeconomic Consequences of Lotteries and Off-track Betting*. New York: Praeger.

12

Compulsive Gambling: Forensic Update and Commentary

Milton Earl Burglass, M.D., M.P.H., M.Div., M.S., F.A.A.F.P.

Introduction

Dysfunctional gambling behavior ("compulsive" or "pathological" gambling) is of exceptional theoretical importance for the criminal law and the forensic mental health disciplines. It requires a reexamination of our fundamental legal postulates, precedents, and assumptions about liability, responsibility, and intentionality. As an *addictive* disorder ("compulsive gambling") in which no exogenous substance is ingested, it raises profound questions about the basic categories by which the addictions field gathers data and assembles its ideas into theory and practice. As an *impulse control* disorder ("pathological gambling") it raises difficult questions about the causal and temporal relationships between a person's impulses and the acts issuing therefrom. The recognition of this phenomenon as a "disease" and the growth of a professional field around it has had significant social and professional consequences (Blume 1988; Scodel 1964), as well as curious and instructive effects on the legal rules.

One may well believe that traditional attitudes of condemnation toward gambling and gamblers render rational and just determinations of the culpability of pathological gamblers charged with a crime more difficult than in cases involving more florid and stable forms of mental dysfunction. The recent rise of a scientific literature on gambling, pathological and otherwise, makes reconsideration of the traditional legal doctrines all the more important, indeed imperative, for those who seek on the one hand to avoid the tragedy of unwitting harshness toward the weak, and on the other, to preserve the innate dignity of the individual by presuming him to be judgmentally autonomous and the author of his actions.

Although there has been much wise legal insight into compulsive behavior in the past, in recent years clinical research has brought into sharper focus such fundamental issues as reaction versus response and compulsion versus decision. The veil has been drawn sufficiently to stir profound and troublesome problems. Questions arise that challenge long-accepted assumptions and standards, suggesting that in the broad field of human activity where compulsive behavior and serious harm concur, the criminal law can be an inefficient engine of severe and indiscriminate oppression. In addition to reflection on the portentous social implications of this challenge, the study of crimes committed by impulse-disordered persons requires analysis of the relevant meanings of traditional principles of culpability, and of the effects of evolving scientific knowledge on their application by legal tribunals. On the one hand, the central issues thus raised chiefly concern the courts' qualified acknowledgment of recent scientific discovery. On the other hand, in the context of modern social theory, the problem involves the positivist thesis that these conceptual difficulties can be eliminated and a correct solution reached only by repudiation of the traditional legal principles of responsibility. There are serious errors both in this thesis and in the prevailing law.

After a brief review of the history of mental defenses in criminal prosecutions, the conceptual and procedural problems of basing such defenses on the disorder of pathological gambling will be reviewed. Finally, the findings and implications of *United States v. Shorter* (1985; 1987), for pathological gambling as a defense in criminal prosecutions, will be examined. An exhaustive analysis of the evolution of the relevant legal rules, doctrines, and principles, a full discussion of the pertinent cases, and a comprehensive review of the conceptual problems in the addictions is clearly beyond the scope of this chapter but is in preparation.

Mental Defenses and Criminal Responsibility

Elements of the Offense

Both common law and statutory crimes require an act or omission in addition to a bad state of mind. Criminal liability further requires that the act be voluntary. However, the meaning of the term "voluntary" has defied any lasting and universally accepted definition. Most modern criminal codifications use adverbial qualifiers such as "knowingly," "willfully," or "intentionally" to designate as voluntary an act performed consciously as a result of effort or determination.

The meaning of "intent" in the criminal law has always been somewhat obscure. See Cook (1917) for a thorough discussion of the various theories of intent embodied in the early common law. Traditionally, intent was defined to include elements of both knowledge and volition. In the modern era, a statutory distinction generally is made between the mental states of knowledge and intent.

The Exculpatory Doctrine in Common Law

The early common law apparently made no concession whatever because of impaired impulse control. Story, in an early case involving intoxication, stressed the merit of "the law allowing not a man to avail himself of the excuse of his own gross vice and misconduct to shield himself from the legal consequences of such crime." (*United States v. Drew* 1828)

As scientifically informed views of human behavior gradually supplanted morally based ones, and in large measure concurrent with the increase in alcohol consumption in all social and economic strata, the common law system evolved what has come to be known as "the exculpatory doctrine," whereby evidence of specified mental conditions (transient, as in intoxication, or perduring, as in traditional insanity) could be introduced in legal proceedings in mitigation of culpability, liability, or responsibility. Such evidence could be introduced in the form of an assertion of a defendant's insanity, or of his lack of the specific intent required as an element of the offense charged. Despite the substantial expansion of the exculpatory doctrine into the criminal law, explicit resistance to it persists in many quarters. The types of cases in which this becomes evident, as well as the legal and social policy reasoning advanced in such cases, illustrate the tenacity of the traditional moral attitudes. Still, the doctrine permitting disproof of intention has been widely accepted and, no doubt, it has functioned to ameliorate the severe operation of the older common law.

The Problem of "Intent"

It is easy to understand the motivation that led judges to rely on the "general intent" principle as the most likely technique to achieve mitigation, and thus to formulate the exculpatory doctrine by reference to it. The earliest cases involved alcohol intoxication. The solid, unavoidable fact was that a harm committed under gross intoxication ought to be distinguished from a like injury by a sober person. The challenge to ethical judgment and to common sense was unmistakable. But the commission of a serious injury by a normal person, combined with traditional moral attitudes stigmatizing intoxication as a vice, indicated with equal clarity the impropriety of complete exculpation. The rules on intent lay closest at hand to provide a means of mediation.

These doctrines, supplying the ultimate support of the exculpatory rule, imply that "specific intent" is distinguishable from "general intent." They signify also that certain crimes require only "general intent," whereas most other offenses require certain "specific" intents. This distinction persists at law, despite the fact that the modern sciences of cognition have yet to formulate a reliable test for discriminating "general" from "specific" intent. Where impulsive or compulsive behavior is involved, as in pathological" or "compulsive" gambling, this distinction is even more problematic.

The policy implicit in the prevailing law represents society's historical vacillation and expedient compromises between the punishment of impulse-disordered offenders in complete disregard of their condition (that is, viewing them as criminals), and the total exculpation frequently suggested by the actual facts at the time the crime was committed (that is, viewing them as patients). A balance, then, has been compounded from a realization, on the one hand, that the moral culpability of an offender acting on impulse or from compulsion should be distinguished from that of one whose decisional act effects a like injury, and from a persistence of the belief, on the other hand, that a person who voluntarily indulges in risk-taking behavior, such as ingesting intoxicants or gambling, should not escape the full consequences thereof. For a comprehensive review of the evolution of the doctrine of "transferred intent" and its application to mental defenses in general and intoxication in particular, see LaFave & Scott (1986, §§ 3.11-3.12; § 4.10).

The Concept of "Partial Responsibility"

In an attempt to resolve these conceptual problems, a substantial medical literature has developed the idea of "partial responsibility." This construction merits examination as regards the treatment of pathological gamblers who commit offenses. The relevant thesis is that the categories "normal" and "incompetent" represent merely heuristic extremes. There is an intermediate zone of persons who are "weak" physically and psychologically— that is, there is an unbroken continuum from "normal" to "incompetent," composed of imperceptible gradations that can be separated only arbitrarily (on the basis of clinical experience). Thus, it is argued, the legal classification is unsound, or, at least, at odds with clinical thinking in the field. Certainly to a nonlegal mind, it must seem highly probable that there are countless persons whose classification within either extreme category does violence to the facts. Hence the claim that there should be a third legally recognized category, "the semiresponsible," has been vigorously asserted. The fallacy of such proposals, however, arises from a failure to grasp the nature of law and the purposes and limitations of legal control. Legal adjudication and the inexorable logic of its method, implied in the issue whether a person falls within the reach of the prescriptions, require a determination that the defendant is responsible or that he is not responsible. All or none. There is no other alternative.

Hence, interpreted not merely as a scientific category, but also as a legally significant one, "semiresponsible" must imply two things: responsibility and a lesser degree of responsibility. In short, it represents no new category; it signifies simply that one of the present legal categories ("normal" or "responsible") is divisible into degrees, ranging from an ideal of maximum capacity to that least degree of capacity that satisfies the accepted, minimum standard of "normality." Accordingly, the utility of the proposed concept is at best questionable.

Pathological Gambling as a Psychiatric Defense

In its most extreme form, a criticism of the prevailing legal rules demands a complete exculpation for all offenders whose crimes are the product of uncontrollable impulse or compulsion. It is therefore important to emphasize that such sweeping legal reform is not supported by expert clinical opinion. On the contrary, opinion in the field is conflicting, contradictory, and inconclusive. Lacking a paradigm, the field attempts to discriminate in terms of the diversity in personality and etiology involved (Burglass & Shaffer 1984; Gambino & Shaffer 1979; Shaffer 1977; Shaffer & Gambino 1979). This state of affairs in the addictions has been attributed to the immaturity of the field (Burglass & Shaffer 1981); the structure of the field's knowledge transfer system (Burglass & Shaffer 1981); and the lack of integration of theory, research, and practice (Shaffer & Gambino 1979). An earlier observation, that "The progress of research in the addictions has been impeded by two misconceptions: first, that all habitual excessive behavior is a disease, and the second, that it is the same disease" (Jellinek & Jolliffe 1940, 143), seems *particularly* relevant to today's heated debate of the "disease model" of addiction and its applicability to pathological gambling.

Classification of Pathological Gamblers

An initial step in resolving these conceptual problems would be for the field to formulate a classification of pathological gamblers and the fact-situations relevant to their behavior(s) that would be defensible empirically and also relevant to the problems of criminal responsibility. On these criteria, pathological gamblers who commit crimes would be (a) normal or diseased, and (b) their gambling behavior, at the time of the commission of the crime charged against them, would be pathological in various degrees. To date, no such classificatory schema has emerged.

What we find in the fact patterns of the legal cases relevant to the problem of pathological gambling is not a total or, at times, even a substantial incapacity to perform simple (or even complex) acts. Nor do we find such a failure of the intellect as to entirely exclude purposeful conduct. Rather, we can observe an apparent blunting of ethical sensitivity sufficient to destroy the understanding of or regard for the moral quality of the act, combined with a drastic, often protracted, lapse of inhibition. Rarely do we find a lapse of conscious awareness of the criminal act itself. Because pathological gambling is a chronic disorder with a recognizable natural history (Custer 1980; Lesieur 1977), these mental elements typically can be identified before, during, and after the crime is committed. In this sense, the disease of pathological gambling is more a *process* than a state, and in its effects it more closely resembles "insanity" of both legally recognized varieties—inability to distinguish right from wrong and irresistible impulse—than it does the *state* of intoxication.

It is recognized clinically that at least some compulsive gamblers who commit crimes are impaired physically and psychologically, so as to be only partially responsible for their misconduct. In this sense, at law they resemble the inebriate, whose reason has been temporarily compromised; and the rules governing intoxication often seem more applicable than do those of insanity. Although, typically, they do not exhibit well-marked psychoses, and only a few may be neurotic (Custer 1982), they are considered abnormal by a number of clinicians (Carlton & Manowitz 1988; Goldstein 1985; Milkman & Sunderwirth 1982; Moran 1979; Wray & Dickerson 1981), albeit in ways of questionable relevance. Hence, for this subgroup of "impaired" compulsive gamblers, the indication would seem to be neither complete exculpation nor normal capacity.

It must be conceded, however, that many (possibly, most) compulsive gamblers accused of crimes are simply criminals who have gambled and/or do gamble to excess, not helpless victims of gambling driven to crime; and that such individuals properly are to be held accountable for their actions and the consequences thereof. Although clinicians in the field, free to apply the concept of a "spectrum" disorder, have grown reasonably comfortable making fuzzy differential diagnoses of pathological gamblers, the courts have enormous difficulty translating the subtle distinctions of a clinical gray scale into the black and white categories of the common law heritage.

In light of the foregoing conceptual problems, one might argue that as applied to pathological gamblers who commit crimes, the legal rules should be expressed not in terms of lack of intent, but in terms of lack of understanding of the ethical quality of the act and/or the ability to control behavior. Indeed, a brief review of the history of the insanity defense reveals just such an evolution in legal reasoning.

The Insanity Defense

The old common law formulation of the"insanity" defense was narrowly defined and moralistic. For a comprehensive discussion of the history of the insanity defense, see *Durham v. United States* 1954. Under the classic *M'Naghten* rule, a defendant would be found insane if it could be established that as a result of a mental defect, the defendant was unable to distinguish between right and wrong at the time he committed the offense *(M'Naghten's Case* 1843).

The *M'Naghten* rule was later modified to include the case of a defendant driven by an irresistible or uncontrollable impulse to commit the crime alleged *(Durham* 1954; *Smith v. United States* 1929).

Over the years federal courts abandoned the insanity defense as defined under the *M'Naghten* rule and the "irresistible impulse" test of *Durham*. A leading example of the court's view of the defense of mental disease or defect was set forth by the Second Circuit in *United States v. Freeman* (1966). Relying on the test for insanity formulated in the American Law Institute's (A.L.I.) *Model Penal Code* (1955, § 4.01) the *Freeman* court upheld the insanity defense where it was shown that as a result of the defendant's mental disease or defect, he lacked the capacity to conform his conduct to the requirements of the law.

This "capacity to conform" approach to the psychiatric defense raised to a new level the problem of defining a "mental disease or defect." In *Freeman*, the Second Circuit emphasized that "an abnormality manifested only by repeated criminal or otherwise antisocial conduct" was not a disease (p. 625). Narcotics addiction, in and of itself, also did not suffice (p. 625). On the other hand, mental retardation has been recognized as constituting a mental defect supporting a mental defense *(United States v. Jackson* 1976). The problem was conceptual, not semantic. And the definition of a mental disease or defect for legal purposes did not depend upon the label assigned by a psychiatrist to a mental condition *(McDonald v. United States* 1962; *United States v. Kohlman* 1972; *United States v. Robertson* 1974). In general, a mental disease or defect for purposes of establishing a legal defense has been limited to those conditions of the mind that substantially affected mental or emotional processes and substantially impaired behavior controls *(United States v. Brawner* 1972). Were the "substantial capacity to conform" test for a mental disease or defect set forth in *Freeman* still the law, a defense of insanity due to pathological gambling would likely prevail in many cases.

The A.L.I. *Model Penal Code* test was adopted by virtually all the United States Courts of Appeals, only to be specifically repudiated by Congress in 1984 in favor of a *M'Naghten*-style statutory formulation. A significant minority of the states have accepted the A.L.I. test, either by statute or by court decision (LaFave & Scott 1986, 465). The statute, drafted in reaction to the attempted assassination of President Ronald Reagan and the subsequent acquittal of his assailant for reason of insanity, eliminates any and all volitional elements of the definition and reverts to a cognition test similar to the nineteenth century *M'Naghten* rule:

> It is an affirmative defense to a prosecution under any Federal statute that, at the time of the commission of the acts constituting the offense, the defendant, as a result of a severe mental disease or defect, was unable to appreciate the nature and quality or the wrongfulness of his acts. Mental disease or defect does not otherwise constitute a defense.
>
> The defendant has the burden of proving the defense of insanity by clear and convincing evidence. (18 U.S.C. § 17)

The *Federal Rules of Evidence* simultaneously were amended to prohibit expert psychiatric testimony on the ultimate jury issue of "whether the defendant did or did not have the mental state or condition constituting an element of the crime charged or of a defense thereto" *(Federal Rules of Evidence* Rule 704). At the federal level, psychiatric testimony is now limited to an explanation of the defendant's diagnosis and the characteristics of the disease or defect.

If the insanity defense is presented to the jury, the court must instruct the jury that it may return one of three verdicts: "guilty," "not guilty," or "not guilty only by reason of insanity." If the defendant is found "not guilty only by reason of insanity" he automatically will be committed to a hospital for a psychiatric evaluation. Subsequently, a hearing will be held to determine whether he is presently suffering from a mental disease or defect, thereby creating a substantial risk of bodily harm to another person or damage to the property of another. At the hearing, the burden of proof by a preponderance of the evidence is on the defendant. If, however, the offense charged involved a substantial risk of bodily injury or serious property damage, the standard of proof at the hearing is by clear and convincing evidence. See LaFave & Scott 1986, §1.8, for a detailed discussion of the various standards of proof. Should the defendant fail to carry his burden, he will be placed in a mental treatment facility (18 U.S C. § 4241-4247).

Problems in Raising Psychiatric Defenses Based on Pathological Gambling

In most prosecutions for offenses other than that of gambling per se, counsel for a defendant who is a pathological gambler is generally reluctant to raise a claim of mental incompetency or severe mental disease or defect (as in insanity). There are several reasons for that reluctance. First, although pathological gambling has provided the basis for acquittals in isolated state and federal criminal prosecutions (McGarry 1983), it is difficult to satisfy the high standard of proof necessary today to establish such defenses. At the federal level, the term "severe mental disease or defect" is defined narrowly and does not include mere antisocial abnormalities or even the inability to conform one's behavior to legal requirements. The majority of states have also rejected the "irresistible impulse" and other volitional tests for insanity in favor of cognitive tests drafted along the lines of the 1984 federal legislation.

Second, a defendant in a federal case who is found incompetent or to be not guilty only by reason of a severe mental disease or defect will spend time confined in an institution for observation and may, in certain cases, be subject to involuntary commitment for treatment at a mental institution (18 U.S.C. § 4244). For a comprehensive review of this area in federal tax cases, see Ritholz & Fink 1970.

Psychiatric Evidence on the Issue of Willfulness

Rather than relying on a defense of insanity, defense counsel for a pathological gambler is more likely to attack the elements of the offense charged, arguing that the disease of pathological gambling rendered the defendant incapable of forming the specific intent requisite to the crime. Indeed, situations arise in which a defendant suffers from a mental disorder not amounting to a disease or defect that nevertheless may be highly relevant to the trier of fact. For example, in a case involving a tax offense—a not uncommon type of crime committed by pathological gamblers—defense counsel may contend that the defendant did not act "willfully" in filing an inaccurate tax return because his mental disorder prevented his forming a specific intent to violate the tax laws *(Wilson v. Commissioner* 1981). The question arises frequently as to whether the defense may introduce psychiatric testimony bearing on the issue of willfulness even though the threshold of an "insanity" or incompetency defense has not been met or even contended.

Some courts have adopted a position that psychiatric testimony should not be admitted on the issue of criminal intent unless an "insanity" defense is asserted *(Fisher v. United States* 1946; *United States v. Haseltine* 1970). The rationale of these decisions appears to be that to permit the use of psychiatric testimony merely on the issue of intent would effectively eliminate the carefully drawn judicial limitations on the mental disease or defect defense *(United States v. D'Anna* 1971). Moreover, it is argued that intent *is* the ultimate question of fact to be decided by the trier of fact and that about such question of fact an expert may not offer an opinion *(United States v. Bright* 1975).

Whereas psychiatric testimony may not be admissible on the ultimate question of intent, courts traditionally have permitted the introduction of evidence of a defendant's mental state as relevant to the issue of intent. For example, it is established that evidence of a defendant's educational background bearing on the issue of willfulness is admissible in a tax case *(Wallace v. United States* 1960). If the government can introduce evidence that a defendant took a course in accounting and is therefore capable of understanding books and financial records, it seems somewhat artificial to exclude expert testimony regarding other aspects of a defendant's life experience or personality.

Until recently, several courts had permitted the introduction of psychiatric testimony bearing on the issue of willfulness even where a defense of severe mental disease or defect had not been raised (see *United States v. Brawner* 1972; *United States v. Curren* 1961; *United States v. Popenas* 1985). A further liberalization in this area was suggested by the Second Circuit in *United States v. Busic* (1978). In *Busic*, the court excluded psychiatric testimony where the statute required only a general criminal intent. The court stated, however, that psychiatric testimony would be admissible in a case involving a statute requiring a *specific* criminal intent (p. 21). Accordingly, although *dicta, Busic* supported the admissibility of psychiatric testimony bearing on willfulness in a tax case. In *United States v. McBride* (1986), a specific intent case, the Second Circuit held that expert psychiatric testimony as to the defendant's ability to reach conclusions from known facts was relevant to the defendant's state of mind and could be admitted in a criminal prosecution despite the absence of an insanity defense. Similarly, in *United States v. Ericson* (1982) the district court permitted the introduction of expert medical testimony on the issue of the defendant's inability to form a specific intent even though the dsfense of mental incompetency was not asserted. The Tenth Circuit approved of the admission of the medical testimony for the limited purpose of determining the defendant's requisite specific intent to commit the alleged tax crimes.

In many cases, the defense may claim that preoccupation with family problems, addiction and problems arising therefrom, or other illness prevented the formation of a specific intent to violate the tax laws. In theory, a defendant's pathological gambling would seem to support such a claim. Under *United States v. Jalbert* (1974) that defense, if accepted by the trier of fact, is legally supportable. Defenses of this kind more often are raised in civil proceedings in justification of a failure to timely file a tax return, than in criminal prosecutions for a willful failure to timely file a tax return.

Psychiatric defenses are not often raised in criminal prosecutions for tax evasion. In the typical evasion case, it is rare that there are psychiatric explanations for the taxpayer's behavior. Rather, the predicate behavior is usually motivated by simple greed. Psychiatric defenses are much more common in prosecutions for willful failure to file tax returns (see *United States v. Haseltine* 1970; *United States v. Stern* 1975). Indeed, many defendants in such cases are psychological enigmas. Some legal practitioners have suggested that there is a "failure to file syndrome," in that persons who fail to file their tax returns are often the same persons who have a psychological inability to perform other routine, but somewhat unpleasant, tasks such as returning library books or paying bills. Others seemingly derive pleasure from such "knife-edging."

Upholding the validity of the traditional principles, some judges— unpersuaded by modern scientific knowledge in these matters—in exercising their broad discretion in evidentiary matters, effectively hold many persons liable, even though they are in fact afflicted with well-known diseases. The general failure of pathological gambling as a defense in most criminal prosecutions reflects precisely this process. Currently governing case law in most, but not all, jurisdictions is to be found in *United States v. Shorter* (1985: 1987), to which we now turn.

The Case of *United States v. Shorter*

In *United States v. Shorter* (1985) the defendant Shorter was charged with one count of tax evasion and six counts of willful failure to pay federal income taxes. Shorter contended that his history of pathological gambling was a *direct* cause of his failure to pay his taxes. The defense moved to introduce the testimony of three expert witnesses in pathological gambling—one psychiatrist and two psychologists—to prove that Shorter's gambling compulsion rendered him incapable of making the decision to pay his taxes, arguing that there was no willfulness in Shorter's avoidance of paying taxes. In a criminal tax case, willfulness means "a voluntary, intentional violation of a known legal duty" *United States v. Pomponio*, 1976, 23).

In ruling on this defense motion, the trial court judge used a three-part test to determine if expert testimony on the relationship between pathological gambling and failure to pay taxes was relevant to this case and should be admitted at the trial.

Based on standards established in *Frye v. United States* (1923), a case involving admission of polygraph evidence into trial proceedings, Judge Greene said testimony on pathological gambling would be admissible if the defense could prove "(1) that a disorder known as 'pathological gambling' is recognized by the relevant community of experts; (2) that experts generally accept a causal link between pathological gambling and the failure to pay taxes; and (3) that the facts are sufficient to create a jury question as to whether the particular defendant suffers from a pathological gambling disorder" (*United States v. Shorter* 1985, 257).

On the first issue, Judge Greene ruled that pathological gambling is a disorder recognized by the mental health community, which, following *United States v. Lewellyn* (1983), he held to be the relevant community of experts for pathological gambling. He based his ruling primarily on the inclusion of the condition in the American Psychiatric Association's *Diagnostic and Statistical Manual, Third Edition [DSM-III]* (1980). In a note in his opinion, he reasoned that

> Defendant appears to contend that the relevant scientific community is that of the limited number of psychologists and psychiatrists who specialize in pathological gambling disorders. That contention is clearly mistaken. It is, of course, always possible to locate a few experts in a field—such as the operation of polygraphs or the discovery of an exotic cure for cancer—who will be convinced of the efficacy of their particular methodology. But the *Frye* test demands an acceptance by a wider scientific community, precisely in order to eliminate those who are "experts" only in their own eyes and the eyes of a relatively small group of individuals with similar ideas. (*Shorter* 1985, 257, n. 4)

Under the second part of the *Frye* test, the pathological gambling disorder must be relevant to one or more elements of the charged offense. In this case, that element was the *willful* failure to pay taxes. Shorter contended that his compulsion to gamble negated the element of willfulness required to convict him for tax evasion or willful failure to pay. Regarding the causal link between the disorder and the failure to pay taxes, Judge Greene heard testimony from seven expert witnesses.

One defense expert said the pathological gambler "chooses not to" pay his taxes, hoping that the "big win" he knows is imminent will allow him to pay off his financial obligations. He did not maintain that these gamblers "are deprived of an ability to consciously choose between gambling and paying taxes." This expert was ultimately unable to offer a satisfactory explanation for evidence showing that during the period Shorter did not pay his taxes he had nonetheless managed a successful law practice and paid other bills related to his practice.

Two other witnesses appearing for the defense also testified that pathological gamblers make volitional choices not to pay taxes, although one also suggested that a pathological gambler lacks the specific intent to commit the tax offense because he is "irresistibly compelled" to gamble with most of his funds.

Each of the government's expert witnesses—three forensic psychiatrists and a forensic psychologist—rejected outright the contention that pathological gamblers are unable because of their disorder to pay their taxes. All stated that no link has been found between the disorder and a loss of will to meet tax obligations.

The Court noted that three Circuits had concluded that a link between pathological gambling and criminal intent is not sufficiently accepted by mental health professionals to sustain the relevance of the disorder with respect to an insanity defense for the crimes of robbery (*United States v. Gould* 1984, 52); embezzlement (*United States v. Lewellyn* 1983, 619); and interstate transportation of stolen goods (*United States v. Torniero* 1984, 732–734). Judge Greene agreed with the government's experts' assertion that, on the basis of current evidence, a causal link between pathological gambling and failure to pay taxes is not accepted in the mental health community. The court thus rejected the defense request that expert testimony be admitted during the trial since it failed to meet the second part of the *Frye* test.

The District Court was careful to note that its ruling on the inadmissibility of expert testimony should not be interpreted as precluding a defendant "through lay testimony, including his own, to seek to persuade the jury regarding his gambling propensities related to his inability to pay taxes when they were due" (*Shorter* 1985, 261, n. 16).

Shorter, a prominent trial attorney, was subsequently found guilty on all seven charges and was sentenced to forty months' incarceration and a fine of $10,000. The District Court's rulings on the issue of the introduction of expert testimony were upheld on appeal.

Judge McGowan, writing for the United States Court of Appeals, District of Columbia Circuit, relied upon *United States v. Torniero* (1984) in holding that unless the defendant could show that his insanity had a direct bearing on his commission of the act with which he is charged, any psychiatric evidence he might seek to introduce would have to be excluded as irrelevant (*United States v. Shorter* 1987, 59). The *Torniero* court had further limited the insanity defense to those instances in which a jury could find that the defendant's mind was "truly alienated from ordinary human experience at the time of the commission of the acts with which he is charged and where that mental condition had a direct bearing on the commission of those acts" (p. 734). As noted by Strassman (1987), "The link between compulsive gambling and a criminal offense is too tenuous to permit the court to find that the defendant lacks substantial capacity to conform his behavior to the requirements of the law as a result of his compulsive gambling disorder" (p. 201).

In his appeal, Shorter also advanced the closely related argument that the District Court erred in excluding the proffered expert testimony to explain that his cash lifestyle was characteristic of compulsive gamblers, and therefore was not, as alleged by the government, an affirmative act of tax evasion or indicative of a knowing and voluntary violation of tax laws. He reargued that the experts' familiarity with the personal habits of compulsive gamblers would help the trier of fact assess the government's claim that his lifestyle was evidence of an intent to willfully evade and willfully fail to pay taxes (*Shorter* 1985, 261, n. 14).

The appellate court affirmed the District Court's conclusion that there was no compelling indication that Shorter's gambling activities and their impact on his financial habits required the testimony of experts, as opposed to lay witnesses familiar with his activities (*Shorter* 1987, 61), citing an earlier case that held "[W]hen the specialized knowledge of an expert is unnecessary to a jury's assessment of the salient factual issues, expert testimony will normally be excluded" (*United States v. Navarro-Varelas* 1976, 1334). Citing *Spies v. United States* (1943), the appellate court commented that, in drafting the statute defining the crime of tax evasion, Congress had intended to provide that the act of willful evasion could be accomplished by any manner (p. 499). The appellate court also agreed that there was no clear agreement among the defense experts that a cash lifestyle, financial mismanagement, and the relinquishment of control over financial affairs are clinically accepted characteristics of compulsive gambling.

Although expert testimony is admissible under Rule 702 of the *Federal Rules of Evidence*, the issue of relevance is the preliminary question of law to be decided by the court (*United States v. Torniero* 1984, 730). A court has broad discretion when ruling on questions of relevance. Even though relevant, evidence may still be excluded by the trial court "if its probative value is substantially outweighed by the danger of unfair prejudice, confusion of issues, or misleading the jury, or by considerations of undue delay, waste of time, or needless presentation of cumulative evidence." *Federal Rules of Evidence*, Rule 403; *United States v. Roark* 1985, 994).

The Implications of *United States v. Shorter*

Addictive Processes and Intoxicated States

In his Memorandum Order in *Shorter* (1985) District Court Judge Greene wrote:

> If these experts are correct, it would be difficult, if not impossible, to establish a principled dividing line between a lawyer who evades his income taxes on account of his compulsive gambling, and an individual

who craves alcohol or drugs and commits robberies or other, similar offenses to obtain the funds to satisfy his needs. In both types of instances, there could be compelling forces which cause the individual to violate the law, and under the theory of the defendant here, both must be exonerated. That is not, and cannot be, the law. (p.261)

It may be that an alcoholic or an addict is entitled to consideration in terms of the availability of a lack of willfulness defense while in a state of intoxication or under the direct influence of the illegal substance. But such substance abusers are not regarded as deprived of free will for offenses committed during "lucid" intervals. The claim made on behalf of this defendant is that never, during a twelve-year period, was he sufficiently free from the pathological gambling disorder to pay his taxes (even though, among other things, he managed during this period to operate a busy and highly regarded litigation practice. (p. 261)

Judge Greene clearly views pathological gambling as an addictive disorder. He quite correctly identifies the serious conceptual problem that arises when the state of mind caused by such disorders exists over a long period, during which time the disordered person commits one or more crimes but otherwise manages to behave in a controlled and rational manner. This problem of temporal dysjunction is not unique to pathological gambling, however. As noted by Burglass (1985), this problem often arises in criminal cases involving cocaine and other psychostimulant intoxication. In such cases, as in those involving pathological gambling, the defense faces the daunting task of explaining to the judge or jury how certain behaviors can be the substantially involuntary products of the intoxication or disorder, yet other, relatively contemporaneous, behaviors need not be similarly affected. For this, there is no universal explanation. The elements of each offense must be analyzed in light of the associated fact-pattern. Such formulations are tenuous and, necessarily, case-specific.

Pathological Gambling, the Addictions, and Psychiatry

The *Shorter* decision (a) likened pathological gambling to an addiction, (b) recognized it as a psychiatric disorder, and (c) defined general (but not subspecialist!) psychiatrists and psychologists as its relevant experts. All three views would meet strong opposition from the fields of psychiatry, the addictions, and pathological gambling. These most fundamental points about pathological gambling, about which the numerous participating disciplines and the various concerned factions have been substantially unable to agree, the legal system apparently has decided! Clearly, if this one holding of *Shorter* were deemed authoritative for allocating resources and funds for research, training, public education, and treatment, the ensuing mayhem would make the recent controversies over controlled drinking and the disease model of alcoholism seem restrained. It would seem, however, that this startling development has largely escaped the notice of the fields potentially affected by it.

As a practicing forensic addictionologist, I can report that the point has not been lost on either prosecutors or defense attorneys. Indeed, since 1987, the conceptual points raised by the *Shorter* decision have been very much at issue in the courtroom. To date, however, no reviewed decision has superceded *Shorter*.

Pathological Gambling as a Mitigating Factor

A finding of severe mental disease, defect, or incompetence may result in public humiliation and the loss of professional licensure or privilege. Nonetheless, pathological gambling frequently has been successfully raised as either an explanation for exculpation or rationale for mitigation in professional licensure revocation proceedings before regulatory bodies. Such proceedings are, however, governed by different rules of evidence, procedure, and law.

In the ever-decreasing number of criminal cases where the judge retains discretion in imposing sentence, it is not unusual for defense counsel to introduce expert testimony on the nature, effects, and prognosis of pathological gambling at the sentencing hearing in support of mitigation. The success of this post-conviction tactic has varied widely at the federal and state levels.

Conclusion

It is impossible, and probably unwise, to predict the course of judicial thinking. However, given the composition of the present United States Supreme Court and the avowed commitment of the executive and legislative branches of government at all levels to affirmatively address the growing problem of crime, it would be unreasonable to expect any significant expansion or extension of the exculpatory doctrine in the immediate future. On the other hand, although vociferously intolerant of crime, and strident in its demands for a solution to the drug problem, society is beginning to demonstrate a growing, if reluctant, recognition that addiction is a complex, multidimensional problem for which there is no immediate solution. To what degree the rapidly evolving social attitudes toward addiction and addicts will interact with the more slowly changing legal rules governing responsibility and culpability remains to be seen.

References

American Law Institute. 1955. *Model Penal Code. Tentative Draft No. 4.* Washington, D.C.: Author.

American Psychiatric Association. 1980. *Diagnostic and statistical manual of disorders* (3rd ed.). Washington, D.C.: Author.

———. 1987. *Diagnostic and statistical manual of mental disorders* (3rd ed. revised). Washington, D.C.: Author.

Blume, S. B. 1988. Compulsive gambling and the medical model. *Journal of Gambling Behavior. 3,* 237–247.

Burglass, M. E. 1985. The role of the medical-psychiatric expert witness in drug-related cases. *Inside Drug Law,* 2(3), 1–6.

Burglass, M. E., & Shaffer, H. 1981. The natural history of ideas in the addictions. In H. Shaffer & M.E. Burglass (eds.) *Classic contributions in the addictions* (pp. xvii-xlii). New York: Brunner/Mazel.

———. 1984. Diagnosis in the additions I: Conceptual problems. *Advances in Alcohol and Substance Abuse,* 3(1&2), 19–34.

Carlton, P. L., & Manowitz, P. 1988. Physiological factors as determinants of pathological gambling. *Journal of Gambling Behavior, 3,* 274–285.

Cook, J. 1917. Act, intention, and motive in the criminal law. *Yale Law Journal,* 26, 645–658.

Custer, R. L. 1980. An overview of compulsive gambling. *Carrier Foundation Letter, 59*(2).

———. 1982. Gambling and addiction. In R. J. Craig & S. L. Baker (eds.) *Drug dependent patients* (367–381). Springfield, Illinois: Charles C. Thomas.

Durham v. United States, 214 F.2d. 862 (D.C. Cir. 1954).

Federal Criminal Code and Rules, 18 U.S.C. (1988).

Fisher v. United States, 328 US 463 (1946).

Frye v. United States, 293 F. 1013 (D.C. Cir. 1923).

Gambino, B., & Shaffer, H. 1979. The concept of paradigm and the treatment of addiction. *Professional Psychology, 10,* 207–233.

Goldstein, L. 1985. Differential EEG activation and pathological gambling. *Biological Psychiatry, 20,* 1232–1234.

Jellinek, E. M., & Jolliffe, S. 1940. Effects of alcohol on the individual: Review of the literature of 1939. *Quarterly Journal of Studies on Alcoholism, 1,* 110–153.

LaFave, W. R., & Scott, A. W. 1986. *Substantive criminal law.* St. Paul, Minnesota: West.

Leland v. Oregon, 343 US 790 (1952).

Lesieur, H. R. 1977. *The chase: Career of the compulsive gambler.* New York: Anchor Press/Doubleday.

McDonald v. United States, 312 F.2d. 847 (D.C. Cir. 1962).

McGarry, A. L. 1983. Pathological gambling: A new insanity defense. *Bulletin of the American Academy of Psychiatry and the Law, 11,* 301–308.

Milkman, H., & Sunderwirth, S. 1982. Addictive processes. *Journal of Psychoactive Drugs, 14*(3), 177–192.

M'Naghten's Case, 8 Eng. Rep. 718 (1843).

Moran, E. 1979. An assessment of the report of the royal commission on gambling 1976-1978. *British Journal of Addiction, 74,* 3–9.

Ritholz, J., & Fink, R. 1970. New developments and dangers in the psychiatric defense to tax fraud. *Journal of Taxation, 32,* 322–330.

Roy, A. 1988. Pathological gambling: A psychobiological study. *Archives of General Psychiatry, 45,* 369–373.

Scodel, A. 1964. Inspirational group therapy: A study of Gamblers Anonymous. *American Journal of Psychiatry, 18,* 115–125.

Shaffer, H. 1977. Theories of addiction: In search of a paradigm. In H. Shaffer (ed.) *Myths and realities: A book about drug users* (42–45). Boston: Zucker.

Shaffer, H., & Gambino, B. 1979. Addiction paradigms II: Theory, research and practice. *Journal of Psychedelic Drugs, 11,* 299–304.

Smith v. United States, 36 F.2d. 548. (D.C. Cir. 1929).

Spies v. United States, 317 U.S. 492, 499; 63 S. Ct. 364, 368 (1943).

Strassman, H. D. 1987. Forensic issues in pathological gambling. In T. Galski (ed.) *The handbook of pathological gambling* (195–204). Springfield, Illinois: Charles C. Thomas.

United States v. Addison, 498 F. 2d. 741, 744 (D.C. Cir. 1974).

United States v. Brawner, 471 F.2d. 969 (D.C. Cir. 1972).

United States v. Bright, 517 F.2d. 584 (2d Cir. 1975).

United States v. Busic, 592 F.2d. 13 (2d Cir. 1978).

United States v. Currens, 290 F.2d. 751 (3d Cir. 1961).

United States v. D'Anna, 450 F.2d. 1201 (2d Cir. 1971).

United States v. Drew, 25 Fed. Cas. No. 14,993 (C. C. D. Mass. 1828).

United States v. Ericson, 676 F.2d. 408 (10th Cir. 1982)

United States v. Freeman, 357 F.2d. 606 (2d Cir. 1966).

United States v. Gould, 741 F.2d 45, 52 (4th Cir. 1984).

United States v. Haseltine, 419 F.2d. 579 (9th Cir. 1970).

United States v. Jackson, 553 F.2d. 109 (D.C. Cir. 1976).

United States v. Jalbert, 504 F.2d. 892 (1st Cir. 1974).

United States v. Kohlman, 469 F.2d. 247 (2d Cir. 1972).

United States v. Lewellyn, 723 F.2d. 615, 619 (8th Cir. 1983).

United States v. McBride, 786 F.2d. 45 (2d Cir. 1986).

United States v. Moore, 486 F.2d. 1139, 1147 (D.C. Cir. 1972).

United States v. Navarro-Varelas, 541 F.2d. 1331, 1334 (9th Cir. 1976).

United States v. Pomponio, 429 U.S. 10 (1976).

United States v. Popenas, 780 F.2d. 545 (6th Cir. 1985).

United States v. Roark, 753 F.2d. 991, 994 (11th Cir. 1985).

United States v. Robertson, 507 F.2d. 1148 (D.C. Cir. 1974).

United States v. Sheller, F.2d. 293 (2d Cir. 1966).

United States v. Shorter, 608 F. Supp. 871 (D.D.C. 1985); *affd.,* 618 F. Supp. 255 (D.D.C. 1987).

United States v. Stern, 519 F.2d. 521 (9th Cir. 1975).

United States v. Torniero, 735 F.2d. 725, 730 (2d Cir. 1984).

Wallace v. United States, 281 F.2d. 657 (4th Cir 1960).

Wilson v. Commissioner, 76 TC 623 (1981).

Wray, I., & Dickerson, M. G. 1981. Cessation of high frequency gambling and "withdrawal" symptoms. *British Journal of Addiction, 76,* 401–405.

Part IV
Current Research on Compulsive Gambling

13
Current Research into Pathological Gambling and Gaps in the Literature

Henry R. Lesieur, Ph.D.

A review of the literature on pathological gambling was conducted with the view of examining the existing research and gaps in the literature on pathological gambling.

In 1974, 61 percent of the U.S. adult population gambled. At that time, $17.346 billion was wagered legally (Commission 1976, p. 64). According to *Gaming and Wagering Business Magazine* estimates, $166.47 billion was legally wagered in 1986 (Christiansen 1987a). This is a 960 percent increase. If we use "takeout" (industry win) as a measure of the change, the industry received $3.35 billion in 1974 (Commission 1976, p. 64), while in 1986 it was $16.9 billion (Christiansen, 1987b), a 500 percent increase. Gambling is now legal in some form in forty-six of the fifty states. Current estimates are that approximately 80 percent of the U.S. population gambles. However, other than polls of specific forms of gambling, no national survey of all gambling has been conducted since 1974.

One could hypothesize that there should be an increase in the number of individuals who are becoming pathological gamblers. Preliminary data seem to support this impression. A national survey in 1974 reported that 0.77 percent of the U.S. population were "probable compulsive gamblers" (Kallick et al. 1979). Polls done in Ohio, the Delaware Valley (parts of New Jersey and Pennsylvania) and New York State in 1984 and 1985 pointed to between 1.4 percent and 3.4 percent prevalence rates of "probable pathological gamblers" (Culleton & Lang 1984; Culleton 1985; Volberg & Steadman 1988). The national and state surveys used different

*This chapter is a revision of a presentation given at the Symposium on Compulsive Gambling, cosponsored by the Center for Addiction Studies, Harvard University, and the Massachusetts Council on Compulsive Gambling, June 1988.

Prepared as a chapter in Tom Cummings, Michael Furstenberg, Sharon Stein and Howard Shaffer (eds.), *Compulsive Gambling: Yesterday, Today, and Tomorrow*. Lexington Books.

measures of pathological gambling. Nadler (1985) has criticized the Gambling Commission survey, and Culleton (in press) has critiqued the Volberg & Steadman study. The consequence for research in the area is that there is no broadly accepted standard for epidemiological research into pathological gambling.

While there are contrasts in method, the surveys in New York and the Delaware Valley have found that males, people under age thirty-five, blacks and Hispanics, Catholics, and lower income individuals are over-represented among probable pathological gamblers in the population (Culleton & Lang 1985; Volberg & Steadman 1988). When we compare these samples with studies using Gamblers Anonymous and treatment populations (about 95 percent of what is written), we find that females, those under age thirty-five, blacks and Hispanics and lower income individuals are underrepresented in these populations. For example, the Custer & Custer profile (1978) (and the widely distributed chart of progression as well) was based on samples that were 98 percent male, while the epidemiological surveys show that one third of probable pathological gamblers are female. Clearly, there is a serious sampling bias in these studies. I wonder whether the "big ego," "high IQ," and other traits seemingly characteristic of compulsive gamblers (Custer & Custer 1981) are traits of those in the general population or just of those currently in treatment. The "big ego" and "high IQ" may be traits of middle class white males.

To counterbalance the white, middle class male treatment oriented samples that have generated current theories and data on compulsive gamblers (as well as the white, middle class female nature of their spouses), researchers need to investigate their theories on broader populations. Research is needed which focuses on female gamblers (I am writing up the results of one such study), young gamblers (an emphasis of Durand Jacobs), minorities (only one unpublished study by Rachel Volberg and Henry Steadman exists to my knowledge), and lower income individuals. In particular, we need *ethnographic research* that examines these groups in the process of gambling, negotiating with their spouses and children, dealing with employers and employees, and getting in gambling-related difficulties. The ethnographic research of these groups that does exist focuses on the social organization of gambling or the interaction between gambling and the wider society (Light 1977; Lesieur & Sheley 1987).

While those surveys are commendable for their groundbreaking nature, because the number of pathological gamblers found in them is small, gaps remain in our knowledge that might be addressed by future surveys. For example, some individuals have said lotteries are "less addicting" than casinos and race tracks. These observations are based on the rarity of lottery addicts in Gamblers Anonymous. However, in contrast with this, 17 percent of the 800-GAMBLER phone calls in New Jersey are from individuals who claim to be addicted to lottery gambling (Council on Compulsive Gambling of New Jersey 1986; 1987; 1988). Whether this would generalize to a wider population survey is unknown.

The question of higher rates of problem gambling among members of the lower class leads to questions which need answers. For example, the Rev. Bill Southrey of the Atlantic City Rescue Mission notes that 90 percent of their clients lose their money in the local casinos (Wagner 1988, p. 12D). Rather than relying on anecdotal evidence like this, we need to find out the extent to which pathological gamblers use social services like welfare, soup kitchens, missions, unemployment offices, and crisis centers. Not only would these answers be fruitful for theorizing, they would also help in determining where to provide services for pathological gamblers.

Theories of Pathological Gambling

An eclectic approach needs to be taken to the issue of pathological gambling. Quite probably, sociological, psychological, and biological processes are involved in an interactive and complex fashion in its etiology. In that vein, I see promise in each of these directions.

In a series of studies funded by the New Jersey Lottery Commission, Goldstein and colleagues (with surprisingly small samples given the amount of funding they received), studied eight male GA members and eight controls (Goldstein et al. 1985; Carlton & Goldstein 1987). They found that pathological gamblers showed lower levels of hemispheric differentiation than controls. The patterns were similar to those found in children with attention deficit disorder (ADD). Further support for this came from results of a questionnaire designed to show signs of ADD. The fourteen pathological gamblers had significantly higher scores than the sixteen controls (Carlton & Goldstein 1988; Carlton et al. 1987). Further research is needed to determine whether these results will generalize to larger samples.

Blaszczynski and colleagues have examined plasma endorphin levels (with inconclusive results) (1986) and Roy and colleagues found high levels of the neurotransmitter norepinephrine in pathological gamblers undergoing treatment (Roy et al. 1988). All these physiological studies have been done on small treatment samples. While they show some possible promise, there is a need to test the ideas on wider and larger samples.

Presence of high amounts of depression in pathological gamblers has been reported several ways. Virtually every study that could find depression has done so. However, there are still unanswered questions about the source of the depression. We confront a "chicken and egg" problem. Does depression cause pathological gambling or does pathological gambling cause depression? Evidence seems to be pointing in both directions at once. Gambling-related problems create tremendous stress, which increases as the pathological gambler becomes more involved in gambling and uses options for financing it (Lesieur 1979). Whitman-Raymond (1988) found evidence of loss in each of eight pathological gamblers he examined in detail. Coincident with this, Taber, McCormick & Ramirez (1987) found major traumatic events in histories of 23 percent of pathological gamblers seeking treatment. These authors focused on "the concept of learned dysthymia, a chronic state of negative affect related to cumulative life trauma and seemingly instrumental in potentiating addictive euphoria" (p. 71).

Recent evidence has revealed that pathological gambling overlaps with other psychiatric disorders. McCormick and colleagues examined rates of major affective disorders and schizophrenia among fifty inpatients at the Brecksville V.A. medical center (1984). Seventy-six percent of the subjects were diagnosed as having major depressive disorder and 38 percent as having hypomanic disorder [thirteen patients (26 percent) met the criteria for both major depression and hypomanic disorder]. Eight percent had manic disorder [three patients (6 percent) also met the criteria for major depressive disorder] and one patient (2 percent) had schizoaffective disorder, depressed type. Only four patients (8 percent) did not meet the criteria for another disorder.

In a study of twenty-five male Gamblers Anonymous members, Linden and colleagues used different methods but arrived at similar results (1986). Eighteen of their subjects (72 percent) had experienced at least one major depressive episode. Thirteen (52 percent) had recurrent major affective episodes. There was a high rate (20 percent) of panic disorders, also. In addition, twelve (52 percent) met the criteria for alcohol abuse or dependency.

Further evidence that depression is a major problem for pathological gamblers appears in each study which reports on suicide attempts. Moran found one in five of his sample of fifty pathological gamblers had attempted suicide (1970), and Livingston found eight attempted out of fifty-three questioned (1974). Custer & Custer in a survey of Veteran's Administration patients and Gamblers Anonymous members found 24 percent of the one hundred VA patients and 18 percent of the 150 GA members attempted suicide (1978). McCormick et al. studied fifty hospitalized pathological gamblers and found that 12 percent made a lethal attempt at suicide, another 12 percent made preparations for a serious attempt, 6 percent mentally rehearsed a specific plan or made a suicidal gesture, 18 percent thought of a specific method of suicide, 22 percent frequently thought of suicide but chose no method and 10 percent had occasional thoughts of wishing they were dead (1984: 217). Only 20 percent had no apparent suicidal tendency. To date, no study has examined the extent to which pathological gamblers call suicide hotlines.

The high rates of other psychiatric disorders in hospitalized and non-hospitalized male pathological gamblers indicates a possibility that some of these individuals have been treated for these disorders prior to the recognition that they had a problem with gambling. Some evidence for this comes from studies of Gamblers Anonymous members. Custer & Custer (1978) surveyed 150 members and revealed that 40 percent had seen mental health professionals prior to attending. In a study of 186 males and four female members, Nora (1984) found that 24 percent had been mental health professionals prior to GA. As part of intensive study of fifty female pathological gamblers I did for the New York State Office of Mental Health, I found that thirty-five (70 percent) had been treated by mental health professionals (Lesieur 1988a). Twenty-nine (58 percent) had been treated by these professionals before or at the time they entered GA. Twelve of the women (24 percent) mentioned that they had discussed their gambling with their therapist prior to entry into GA. The other seventeen (34 percent) went to therapists prior to GA *without* mentioning gambling at all. Of the fifty women, only four (8 percent) were referred to GA by a therapist.

Several conclusions can be drawn from that data. First, many pathological gamblers are receiving treatment for other disorders, but are not surfacing as pathological gamblers in diagnosis by health care providers. There is a need for screening of general psychiatric populations, particularly those with major affective disorders, for pathological gambling. Secondly, in spite of treatment, they are not being referred to Gamblers Anonymous. There is a need to educate mental health professionals about pathological gambling and Gamblers Anonymous.

Cognitive Social Learning (Behavioral) Theories

Learning theorists pose insightful and potentially useful information about problem gambling that connects it to broader patterns of gambling behavior. They start with the hypothesis that gambling is learned behavior. Mark Dickerson is one of the most convincing proponents of this point of view. He notes that there are multiple stimuli that can be perceived to be rewarding in gambling settings (1984). Events such as the pre-race and race sequence at the race track and OTB, the spinning wheel, the croupier's calls, placing bets, and other activities at roulette and other gambling-related activities can be reinforcing because they produce excitement, arousal, and tension. Through observations of last-second wagers at off-course betting shops Dickerson supported this hypothesis (1979). High-frequency bettors are more likely to place their bets in the last two minutes before the "off" than are low-frequency bettors. This has the effect of increasing the excitement and tension experienced by the players. Higher wagers by these players produce greater excitement. This interacts with the possibility of bigger wins to have a high reinforcing potential (Dickerson 1984). Dickerson explains continued wagering in spite of loss: Loss produces deprivation, which can be relieved by further gambling. Dickerson's ideas are useful because they have been developed in the field rather than with just patients in a treatment setting.

Other advocates of social learning (behavioral) theories of problematic gambling include Blaszczynski (1985), Brown (1987a), Walker & Trimboli (1985) and those who emphasize behavior modification techniques in treatment. Perhaps the chief distinction between learning theorists and others is the belief that since the pathology is learned, it can be unlearned. As it has produced controversy in alcoholism research and treatment, it will also do so in the area of compulsive gambling.

Psychologically Based Addiction Theories

Much recent theorizing about pathological gambling has come from the recognition that these gamblers have much in common with other addicted populations. Ramirez, McCormick, Russo, and Taber examined fifty-one consecutive compulsive-gambler admissions into a VA Medical Center using systematic screening procedures (1984). All patients were male veterans. Thirty-nine percent met the criteria for alcohol and/or substance abuse in the year prior to admission, while 47 percent met these criteria at some point in their life. Linden and colleagues studied twenty-five male Gamblers Anonymous members and found that 52 percent evidenced problems with alcohol and/or substance abuse (1986). Similarly, in a study of fifty female Gamblers Anonymous members, I found that 50 percent had abused alcohol and/or drugs at some point in their life (1988a).

Other addictions also intrude into the lives of pathological gamblers. Adkins, Rugle & Taber (1985) reported on one hundred consecutive admissions to the VA Medical Center in Cleveland. They found that 14 percent could be judged to have heterosexual addictive patterns following the criteria set forth by Carnes (1983). In the study of female pathological gamblers, I pointed out that 24 percent classified themselves as compulsive overspenders, 20 percent called themselves compulsive overeaters, and 12 percent were possibly sexually addicted (1988a).

Some research has been done on substance abusing populations to find out the extent to which those people have problems with pathological gambling. In a study of seventy alcoholics, Haberman found that 17 percent admitted to "gambling difficulties" (1969:164). According to treatment professionals at Danbury Federal Correctional Facility, eighteen out of the one hundred prisoners in their alcohol unit were directed to Gamblers Anonymous because of collateral gambling problems (personal communication with treatment team, 1984). A study of 458 alcoholism and drug dependency inpatients found forty (9 percent) were diagnosed as pathological gamblers and an additional forty-seven (10 percent) showed signs of problematic gambling (Lesieur, Blume & Zoppa 1985). They also found that 5 percent of patients abusing only alcohol, 12 percent of those with alcohol and another drug in combination, and 18 percent of those with other drug abuse problems without an alcohol component showed clear signs of pathological gambling.

To aid in the screening process, the South Oaks Gambling Screen was developed to help identify patients with a problem with gambling (Lesieur & Blume 1987). This screen is a valid, reliable instrument that has been found to be a useful adjunct in the assessment of alcohol and substance abusing patients. Using the South Oaks Gambling Screen (SOGS), one hundred multiple-substance-abusing residents of two interconnected therapeutic communities were screened for gambling-related problems by Lesieur and Heineman (1988). Out of eighty-six male and fourteen female residents tested, fourteen were diagnosed as pathological gamblers and an additional fourteen showed signs of problematic gambling. This screening devise is currently being used to assess alcohol and substance abusing patients at five pilot sites in New Jersey. To date, rates of pathological gambling ranging from 8 percent to 25 percent have been uncovered.

Further research is needed on the overlapping social worlds of the substance-abusing gambler and the gambling substance abuser. Current evidence suggests that multiple addiction may place pathological gamblers in greater risk of incarceration (Lesieur 1987a). In addition, substance-dependent patients who are also pathological gamblers have higher rates of stress-related diseases and serious psychiatric problems, including suicide attempts (Ciarrocchi 1987).

Recent research and theorizing has begun to concentrate on commonalities and overlaps among addictive disorders (Jacobs 1986; Levinson et al. 1983; Orford 1985; Peele 1985). Some researchers have found common personality traits (Blaszczynski et al. 1985) and criminal behavior patterns (Brown 1987b) that pathological gamblers and heroin addicts share. Others have conducted personality research on pathological gamblers and noted the similarities of their findings to those done with alcoholics and other substance abusers (Graham & Lowenfeld 1986; Taber et al. 1986).

In a promising view developed out of research on pathological gamblers, Durand Jacobs has hypothesized a general dissociative state common across addictions (1986). The four signs of dissociation Jacobs sees in compulsive gambling are: feeling like you are a different person, feeling like you have been in a trance, feeling like you are "outside yourself" watching yourself doing it, and experiencing a "memory blackout" for the period when gambling. These ideas have been tested using both treatment samples (Jacobs 1988a) and a sample obtained from newspaper ads and signs in cardrooms in California (Kuley and Jacobs 1988). In both instances the data supported the theoretical insights.

In another general addictions approach, Anderson & Brown developed a modification of arousal and reversal theory (1987). States of arousal and reversal occur in telic (goal-oriented) and paratelic (playful) states. The general idea behind this view is that pathological gamblers switch from highly aroused to highly anxious states during the course of play and vice versa. Anderson and Brown hypothesize:

> The pathological gambler who, having begun with high arousal in an unpleasant telic state, may continue to gamble in the face of the most distressing anxiety. This may be because he has learned to associate the high arousal in the telic state of losing with the anticipation of the subsequent powerful reward in pleasurable excitement when eventually that high arousal will be interpreted after a win and a reversal to the paratelic state (1987 p. 189).

This theory combines what is already known about the pathological gambler. He or she is concerned with both monetary gain and loss (the telic) as well as excitement (the paratelic). Consideration of both physiological (paratelic) and cognitive (telic) processes are essential to understanding pathological gambling.

Sociological Research

Sociological explanations of pathological gambling tend to recognize that rather than being a state, pathological gambling is the end on a continuum that includes social gamblers at one end and suicide attempters at the other. This approach is the logical consequence of doing research in gambling settings and through intensive interviews with gamblers of all types rather than focusing solely on those in treatment.

Oldman (who conducted research in a casino) notes that compulsive gambling is produced by a "defective relationship between a strategy of play on the one hand and a way of managing one's finances on the other"

(1978). Similarly, Hayano (who engaged in participant observation of card rooms) sees the pathological gambler as just one variety of loser. In his view, gamblers lose for one of three reasons: inexperience and imperceptive or bad play; erroneous ideas about cards, dice, and so forth; and inept money management (1982). My research with male compulsive gamblers led me to a similar conclusion. In *The Chase* I focused on inept money management, what gamblers call "chasing" (1984). Through the chase, compulsive gamblers become involved in a self-enclosed system that reinforces and creates further pressures to continue gambling despite heavy losses.

Rosecrance, in an article that critiques Custer (1982) and Moran's (1970) idea that a "big win" is the major impetus for pathological gambling, focuses on the "bad beat" as the catalyst for the development of problem gambling (1986). According to Rosecrance, a bad beat is "a significant monetary loss resulting from a seemingly inexplicable turn of events" (p. 463). This produces a disorienting state called being "on tilt." Most gamblers revive from this state as a product of having peer support and can continue gambling normally again.

Browne, in a participant observational study of card rooms, also comments on "going on tilt" (in press). It is his contention that this phenomenon is central to the career of the problematic gambler. Like Rosecrance, he sees that many individuals return to sensible gambling after having been on tilt. However, there are some individuals who, for whatever reason, are not able to handle the "emotion work" required to stay off tilt.

The sociological work points to a potential bridge between going on tilt and chasing. It is possible that going on tilt is but the first stage in the compulsive gambler's career. While on tilt, the gambler may then chase his or her losses to such an extent that it has devastating consequences.

Physiological, psychological, and sociological theories overlap in interesting ways. Those who are depressed or mentally ill may be less able to engage in the emotion work that Browne contends is necessary to stay off tilt. In addition, Rosecrance's bad beats may lead to an on-tilt state. Similarly, the on-tilt phenomenon is akin to Jacobs' dissociative state and Anderson and Brown's reversal. It is also possible that those with attention deficit disorders may be particularly at risk to going on tilt and ending up in a dissociative state. Once on tilt the gambler is susceptible to chasing losses. Should this occur often enough, the chasing may become an obsession. The most heartening aspect of these investigations is that they represent a convergence of Gamblers Anonymous, treatment, and ethnographic studies.

While providing an ethnographic base from which a biopsychosocial theory may be developed, the sociocultural orientation holds future promise. At present no studies compare the experiences of different ethnic groups with gambling and pathological gambling in particular. Folk wisdom has it that Chinese-Americans are heavy gamblers, yet there is no research on problem gambling among members of this ethnic group to my knowledge. While the survey data show that blacks and Hispanics are more likely to have gambling problems than other ethnic groups, there is no ethnographically based research here either. North American Indians were avid gamblers before the Europeans came. Did this already existing propensity insulate them or open them up to potential gambling problems? As a group, Jews also are overrepresented in Gamblers Anonymous meetings but do not seem to show up in epidemiological surveys of pathological gambling in the general population. Are they more adept at concealing their gambling problems from telephone interviewers? Are they more likely to refuse to be interviewed? Are they among those who are "not at home" when the interviewer calls? Or is there some other reason for their low rates of pathological gambling in the surveys?

Family Issues and Compulsive Gambling

Compulsive gambling creates serious problems for family members. Surprisingly, with some exceptions, not much research has been done on the impact on the family. What research there is tends to be based on questionnaires with attendees at Gam-Anon conclaves or with treatment samples.

Lorenz (1981; Lorenz & Shuttlesworth 1983) has conducted most of the research in this area. Most of her subjects have been wives of compulsive gamblers attending GA and Gam-Anon conclaves. Lorenz's data show signs of serious internal problems within the family, including harrassment by bill collectors, physical violence by the spouse against the gambler, and suicide attempts by the spouse. We cannot determine whether these are higher than in normal populations because Lorenz does not have controls built into her studies and does not compare the results with normed groups. One piece of data for which there are norms is the suicide attempt rate. The rates of 11 to 14 percent she has reported are three times higher than the rate of reported suicide attempts in the general population (Mintz 1970). One example of the limits of the data is the finding that 87 percent of the gamblers ridiculed, insulted, embarrassed, or belittled their wives in front of their children (1981). This percentage is high. Nevertheless, we cannot tell whether this is representative of all compulsive gambler-spouse interactions. For example, to what extent are spouses with this type of experience more likely to seek help and end up in Gam-Anon? In addition, it is quite possible that Lorenz' data are representative of female

Gam-Anon members without being representative of male spouses of compulsive gamblers or of spouses of problem gamblers in the general population. Only further research will help to fill this gap.

In more recent research, Lorenz and Yaffee have examined the psychosomatic, emotional, and marital difficulties of pathological gamblers and their spouses (1986; 1988). Five hundred questionnaires were filled out at GA and Gam-Anon conclaves. Of these, 215 were completed by spouses. They found very high incidence of the following illnesses when compared with studies of female hospital patients: chronic or severe headache, bowel problems (excessive constipation or diarrhea), asthma, depression, and suicide attempts. These data are outlined in table 13–1. Because there were few controls in their data, we do not know whether these troubled spouses have alcoholic husbands, are alcoholic themselves, or have other problems that might complicate the matter. In any case, they are worth following up with broader treatment groups and samples taken from the general population.

Some recent advances have been made in understanding relationships among family members. Both Sheila Wexler (1981) and Robert Custer (Custer & Milt 1985) recognize that the wife of the pathological gambler goes through definite stages: denial, stress, and exhaustion. Because female members of Gamblers Anonymous are more likely to be single, divorced, or separated than their male counterparts and married female pathological gamblers have different careers (Lesieur 1988a), validation with male spouses is needed.

Table 13–1
Lorenz and Yaffee Data Compared with Data on Hospitalized Females
(percent)

Illness or Problem	Hospitalized Females	Lorenz & Yaffee
chronic or severe headache	5	41
bowels problems	5	37
asthma	3	14
depression	8–20	47
suicidal	1–3	14
Problems where no comparative data are available		
feeling faint, dizzy, having cold clammy hands, excessive perspiring		27
hypertension, shortness of breath, rapid breathing, or other breathing problem		23
backaches		18

Source: Lorenz and Yaffee, 1988.

This research with spouses in treatment, while a good start, is limited in the extent to which it is generalizable. Like Lorenz's research, we need to examine this with broader populations and with some ethnographic data. Finally, what are the implications for the spouse when there are multiple addictions? Heineman has addressed this issue in treatment (1987) but more needs to be known concerning its impact on day-to-day living.

Children of Compulsive Gamblers

While there is a body of literature on pathological gambling itself, relatively little is known about the children of compulsive gamblers. What is known tends to point to serious levels of pathology in the children as well as their parents.

The children of compulsive gamblers are caught in a process that reflects extremes in behavior by their parents. At times the gambler dotes on them; at other times he ignores them. This seesaw relationship has been portrayed in the few accounts of the dynamics of the family of the pathological gambler (Custer & Milt 1985; Wanda G. 1971). The children respond by feeling angry, hurt, lonely, guilty, abandoned, and rejected. They experience troubled teen years and run away from home, use drugs, become depressed, and experience psychosomatic illnesses. Lorenz & Yaffee, in their study of the spouses of pathological gamblers, asked about the psychosomatic illnesses of the children (1988). They did not find any statistically significant differences between the rates of the children and that of the general juvenile population.

Some studies have obtained comparative data that support serious psychosocial maladjustment in the children of pathological gamblers. Jacobs, in a study of California high school students, found compulsive gambling in the parents of these students associated with abuse of stimulant drugs and overeating (1987). They were also more likely to report having an unhappy childhood, having a legal action pending, being depressed and suicidal, and showing other signs of psychosocial maladjustment than children without troubled parents (Jacobs 1987). In a different study, Lesieur & Klein (1987) found that high school students who reported that their parents had a gambling problem were more likely to have a gambling problem themselves than students who did not report having a parent with a gambling problem.

Lorenz, in a study of spouses of compulsive gamblers, asked these spouses some questions about their relationship with their children. She found that 8 percent of the gamblers and 37 percent of the spouses were physically abusive to the children (1981). Since those figures were not compared with national norms, there is no way at present of knowing whether children of compulsive gamblers are more or less likely to be abused than the rest of the population.

Both the Lorenz and Jacobs studies are in need of replication with samples of teenage children of compulsive gamblers. In spite of this, some *basic* research is needed to find out *from the child's point of view* what it is like growing up with a compulsive gambler.

While we have data on children of compulsive gamblers, there are no data at all on the impact of compulsive gambling on these children when they grow to be adults. Research is sorely needed in this area as well.

Gambling and Youth

Studies of high school and college students reveal that, in contrast with adult figures of between 1 and 3 percent prevalence rate for probable pathological gamblers, 3 to 5 percent of high school (Jacobs 1988b; Lesieur & Klein 1987; Ladouceur & Mireault 1988) and 6 to 8 percent of college students (Frank & Cashmere 1987; Lesieur 1988b) show signs of pathological gambling. I suspect that people experiment with gambling in their teens and early twenties. Most who have negative experiences quit as a product of those experiences; hence, the upward curve into the early twenties and then a decline. Longitudinal studies are needed to determine whether these data represent maturational difficulties, or experimentation with gambling, and whether gambling by youth poses potentially serious problems for the future.

The Workplace

Job disruptions produced by pathological gambling include exploitation of work time to gamble and handicap sporting and racing events, poor concentration on work, irritability, moodiness, and absenteeism (Lesieur 1984). Borrowing from work becomes more serious as the compulsive gambling progresses. It eventually includes employee theft and embezzlement. These findings are a product of my research with male Gamblers Anonymous members and have been repeated in the study of female GA members as well (Lesieur 1988a).

In spite of the problems it creates, very few compulsive gamblers are being referred for treatment by employee assistance programs (EAPs). A questionnaire study was conducted which found that only 1.4 percent of EAP referrals were compulsive gamblers (Lesieur 1987b). Many EAP clients are substance abusers. Given that 20-30 percent of substance abusers have gambling problems and half of these are probable pathological gamblers (Lesieur, Blume & Zoppa 1986; Lesieur & Heineman 1988), the identification and referral rate is probably quite low. Research is needed on supervisor identification and referral, co-worker involvement, and experiences of employees as well.

To date, only minimal mention is made by other researchers concerning the gambling-work nexus. The interaction of gambling and work is known, therefore, only from studies of Gamblers Anonymous members. Clearly, broader-based research is needed. The interaction of compulsive gamblers and their fellow employees, supervisors, and employers as well as the impact of compulsive gambling when the compulsive gambler is the employer needs greater attention.

Pathological Gamblers and Finances

Researchers have reported on different rates of indebtedness of pathological gamblers in treatment. The mean gambling-related debt (excluding auto loans, mortgages, and other "legitimate" debt) of individuals in treatment at the JFK treatment center in New Jersey had an average debt of $53,350 (Division of Alcoholism 1987). Individuals who entered the St. Vincent's treatment clinic in Staten Island, New York had an average debt of $54,662 (Blackman, Simone & Thoms 1986); that of another in the Baltimore, Maryland area was $92,000 (Politzer et al. 1985: 138). Female Gamblers Anonymous members have a lower level of debt, averaging $14,979 (Lesieur 1988a). This is only the debt that they accumulate and does not include the debt they pay off.

Based on a review of the available literature and discussions with members of Gamblers Anonymous, the following policies by gambling establishments appear to exacerbate the debt of pathological gamblers:

1. Ability to cash a check at the gambling facility.
2. Holding a check for months or allowing gamblers to "buy back" their checks at a later date rather than cashing them right away.
3. Cash machines at the gambling location or within easy walking distance from the casinos.
4. Credit in any form associated with gambling.
5. One-time credit checks on the gamblers rather than a periodic review of credit required.
6. Failure to totally review credit when a payment for a marker has "bounced" or is overdue.

7. Loan sharks operating in or near the gambling facility.
8. Drinking in association with gambling. This produces irrational play which increased debt.

Since those comments are based on overall assessments of debt related problems of GA members and those in treatment, a review of the interaction of these policies and the gambling patterns of the broader gambling public would prove useful in helping to guide public policy. For example, what percent of the gambling public uses check-cashing privileges? Economists might conduct more thorough analyses of microeconomic decision making to find out the personal impact of present policies. Finally, the above debt estimates are based on Gamblers Anonymous and treatment samples. There are no available estimates of total gambling-related debt in the wider population.

Pathological Gambling and Crime

Ultimately, pathological gambling results in crime. Approximately two-thirds of nonincarcerated and 97 percent of incarcerated pathological gamblers admit engaging in illegal behavior to finance gambling or pay gambling-related debts (Lesieur 1987a; Lesieur & Klein 1985). White-collar crimes predominate among treatment samples while street crimes and drug sales are more frequent among imprisoned compulsive gamblers. The total cost of this crime is unknown at present. An estimated 30 percent of prisoners are probable pathological gamblers. Most of them are also addicted to alcohol and other drugs. We need to find out what percent of their drug-related crimes are actually produced by their gambling in combination with drug use. Treatment programs that address multiple addictions are vitally needed in prisons and diversion programs, and halfway houses are needed for individuals on probation and parole.

Research by clinicians who have treated pathological gamblers typically glosses over crime and either tends to lump all crimes together or fails to differentiate or recognize the wide variety of crime categories implicated in the process. Most notable in this regard are studies by Custer & Custer (1978) and Politzer et al. (1985). Both uncovered arrests, prosecutions, and convictions of pathological gamblers for forgery, fraud, embezzlement, and income tax evasion. The image one gets from these two studies is of a middle class offender gone wrong.

Studies by Livingston (1974) and Lesieur (1984; 1988a) uncovered a wide variety of illegal behaviors among compulsive gamblers interviewed. Livingston found compulsive gamblers involved in check forgery, embezzlement and employee theft, larceny, armed robbery, bookmaking, hustling, con games, and fencing stolen goods. I uncovered these patterns as well and also found gamblers engaged in systematic loan fraud, tax evasion, burglary, pimping, prostitution, selling drugs, hustling at pool, golf, bowling, cards, and dice. From this research, I found that compulsive gamblers are engaged in a spiral of options and involvement wherein legal avenues for funding are used until they are closed off. As involvement in gambling intensifies, options for funding become closed. Dependent on personal value systems, legitimate and illegitimate opportunity, perceptions of risk, the existence of threats (for example, loan sharks) and chance, the gamblers became involved in more and more serious illegal activity (1984). For some, the amount of money runs into the millions of dollars.

In a study of pathological gambling among prisoners at Yardville and Clinton prisons in New Jersey, prisoners were given a questionnaire that asked them about the extent of their gambling and the nature of problems that might be associated with it (Lesieur & Klein 1985). Thirty percent of the prisoners who responded to the questionnaire (sixty-eight out of 230 at Yardville and thirty-six out of 118 at Clinton) showed clear signs of pathological gambling. Another striking finding from this study was the extent to which prisoners have multiple addictions. Fifty-five percent of the female and 50 percent of the male pathological gamblers said they were drug addicts. In addition, 58 percent of the female and 44 percent of the male pathological gamblers said they were alcoholics. Conversely, 40 percent of the female and 39 percent of the male drug addicts and 39 percent of the male and 63 percent of the female alcoholics showed signs of pathological gambling. Clearly, pathological gambling needs to be recognized and treated among the prison population. In particular, the extremely high rates of multiple addiction need to be addressed.

For the past few years, I have been trying to assess how frequent different forms of illegal behavior are among pathological gamblers. This has been done in concert with my contention that "arrest for forgery, fraud, embezzlement, and income tax evasion" (part of the old DSM-III criteria, see American Psychiatric Association 1980) is too narrow and middle class a focus to use. These offenses exclude larceny, burglary, and other "commonplace crimes" as options that pathological gamblers use in connection with their problems. It also ignored the presence of gambling-system-connected crimes such as bookmaking and various forms of hustling and cons gamblers use.

Studies of prisoners (Lesieur & Klein 1985), alcohol and drug abusing inpatients (Lesieur, Blume & Zoppa 1985), female members of Gamblers Anonymous (Lesieur 1988a), and a study of Veteran's Administration inpatients and Gamblers Anonymous members (Nora 1984) provide useful comparative information. In all four studies, the subjects were asked if they had engaged in a range of financially motivated crimes to gamble or to pay gambling debts. The specific offenses and the results of the four studies are listed in table 13–2.

One question that can be raised given the high level of property crime among pathological gamblers is, to what extent do they engage in violent behavior? In the only study to date that examines the hypothesis of nonviolence among pathological gamblers, Brown surveyed 107 Gamblers Anonymous members in England and Scotland and found that thirty-five of them (33 percent) had criminal convictions (1987b). He examined all these convictions to find out whether pathological gamblers had patterns

Table 13–2
Illegal Activities and Civil Fraud Engaged in by Pathological Gamblers to Gamble or Pay Gambling Debts Five Samples, 1984–1986

Type of Activity	Hospital Inpatients* n=40	VA & GA n=190	Male Prisoners n=68	Female Prisoners n=36	Female GA n=50
Loan Fraud (civil)	38%	41%	13%	8%	44%
White-Collar Crime					
Check forgery	30	33	28	56	40
Forgery	18	18	19	36	18
Embezzlement and Employee theft	28	38	13	22	24
Tax evasion	10	28	6	-	12
Tax fraud	13	18	1	3	4
Commonplace Crime					
Larceny	13	21	22	19	14
Burglary	13	15	47	31	2
Armed robbery	-	4	21	17	2
Pimping	-	2	19	11	0
Prostitution	5	-	3	39	10
Selling drugs	28	9	54	53	0
Fencing stolen goods	23	14	37	42	4
Gambling System Connected					
Bookmaking or working in an illegal game	18	23	13	25	26
Hustling at pool, golf, bowling, or other sport	23	19	51	50	10
Hustling at cards or dice	30	21	50	36	6
Running a "con game" Swindle suckers	18	9	50	31	12
Engaged in Any of the Illegal Activities Above	65%	n/a	97%	97%	68%

n/a = information not available

Sources: Hospital sample—research conducted for study of gambling among alcohol and drug inpatients (Lesieur, Blume & Zoppa 1986).

Veteran's Administration and Gamblers Anonymous sample (Nora 1984).

Prison samples of males and females (Lesieur & Klein 1985).

Female GA members (Lesieur 1988a).

of crime more similar to alcoholics (with a mix of violence and property offenses) or drug addicts (primarily property offenders). Theft and fraud offenses accounted for 94.3 percent of all criminal convictions these members sustained (p. 108). An additional 3.65 percent of convictions were for armed robbery. Fewer than 1 percent of convictions were for nonproperty violence offenses. Brown concluded that pathological gamblers are primarily nonviolent and their crime patterns are closer to those of heroin addicts than to alcoholics.

Given the multiply addicted nature of the prison population, along with the high percent of poor, black, and Hispanic prisoners, intensive interviews of prisoners may be a valuable source of information about pathological gambling among those groups that are most underrepresented in most studies of gambling to date. In addition, there is a need to find out how gambling and substance abuse interact. What alteration is there in criminal behavior when gambling dominates versus when substance abuse or alcohol use dominate? Do prisoners "switch addictions" from drugs to gambling and vice versa?

Research in the Future: What Next?

As an addendum, I would like to bring out four issues that will frame some of the future research. The first theme for the future is definitional and diagnostic issues researchers will have to grapple with. There are two camps in the field of compulsive gambling, as there are in alcoholism. They can roughly be called the problem-oriented and the disease-oriented camps. The problem-centered theorists include behavioral psychologists and most sociologists. These people view gamblers as lying on a continuum from problem-free to troubled. In addition, gambling problems are perceived to be socially learned maladaptive strategies that can conceivably be unlearned. The disease-oriented camp treats pathological gambling as an on/off switch that either exists or does not. If the switch is on, the obvious solution is to not gamble. I take a middle position (see Lesieur 1984). This is primarily because there are many gamblers who experience "roller coaster" careers without devestating results. On the other hand, there are those who experience devestation. At present, we have no way of determining who has gone "over the line" or even where the line is if there is one at all.

The second theme for the future represents the debate over whether the proper approach to studying pathological gambling is to focus primarily on pathological gamblers in treatment and to generalize from them or to focus on gambling itself and generalize to the problematic and compulsive gambler from there. In my view the first strategy is appropriate for initial knowledge but a deficient strategy in the end, because a distorted image of the world can be created by making it excessively pathological in orientation. The strategy of a focus on the gambler, however, can have potential long-run consequences but may be flawed if it omits the denial and stigma of the pathological gambler. There is too much tendency to view the gambling world as a confined social world that has minimal impact on the broader social worlds of family, work, and other social spheres. The only way to correct this view is to cross-check the gambler's image of the world with that of the spouse, children, fellow employees, creditors, and others. The irony is that some treatment professionals have a more detailed image of what family members think about problematic gambling than some field ethnographers. Research is needed on what family members, fellow workers, and friends of heavy gamblers think about gambling.

A third focus for the future will be determined by the theoretical strategy researchers wish to take: deduction versus induction. A deductive strategy starts out with a theory that is then tested using laboratory or field experiment, survey, or some other method. This strategy has its drawbacks and benefits. Its drawback is that there are far too many theories created from impressionistic and anecdotal data. Additionally, people come to invest in these theories. Its major benefit is that it can examine cherished ideas to see if they square with reality. For example, Freud and Bergler's idea that compulsive gamblers gamble to lose (as a way of expiating guilt through self-punishment) has been examined and found wanting, primarily because of early winning histories of (primarily male) compulsive gamblers. The second strategy (induction) has the most potential benefit because it is based in grounded research. The ideas of the "bad beat," "chasing," and "on tilt" gambling are all inductively grounded. It is my view that these ideas will last and stand the test of time. This is not to say that some views deduced from more general theories, say in addictions, will not prove valid, but at this stage we need to keep to basics and continue the process of discovery.

The fourth and final issue I would like to pose is a question: Why do we do research? There are many reasons, but I would contend that in this field there are primarily two: personal aggrandizement and helping the pathological gambler. It is my belief that we can continue to test our own theories without regard to whether it will help those who suffer in the end. We can continue to "publish or perish" in academia. We can publish to get our names in print. Or, we can publish as an end product of consulting that we do. On the other hand, we can do the type of research that will help the compulsive gambler in the end. Personally, I have done all the above but have tried to keep the last goal in mind at all times. For example, my consulting work has been directed toward creating an instrument to screen individuals for a problem with pathological gambling (Lesieur & Blume 1987), finding out whether it is feasible to screen alcohol and substance abusers in treatment for pathological gambling (Lesieur, Blume & Zoppa 1986; Lesieur & Heineman 1988) and trying to redress male bias in views of pathological gamblers (Lesieur 1988a).

In my view the challenge for the future lies in addressing the types of questions that may help problem gamblers and increase funding for organizations like the National Council on Compulsive Gambling and its affiliates. I challenge researchers to ask questions like: What percentage of welfare recipients have gambling problems? Do people "gamble away their welfare check" or is this a myth? What is the gambling culture of Native Americans? Does this culture insulate its members from compulsive gambling or does it exacerbate the problems? These questions demonstrate a value bias but require value-free answers. If, for example, welfare recipients are no more likely to have gambling problems than middle class gamblers then we should say so and not leave the question unasked. Many gaps exist in the literature on pathological gambling. I invite the reader to help fill in a few.

References

Adkins, B. J., Rugle, L. J., & Taber, J. I. 1985. *A note on sexual addiction among compulsive gamblers.* Paper presented at the First National Conference on Gambling Behavior of the National Council on Compulsive Gambling, New York (November).

American Psychiatric Association. 1980. *Diagnostic and statistical manual, third edition.* Washington, D.C.: Author.

Anderson, G., & Brown, R. I. F. 1987. Some applications of reversal theory to the explanations of gambling and gambling addictions. *Journal of Gambling Behavior, 3,* 179–189.

Blackman, S., Simone, R., & Thoms, D. 1986. Letter to the editor: Treatment of gamblers. *Hospital and Community Psychiatry, 37,* 404.

Blaszczynski, A. P. 1985. Pathological gambling: An illness or myth. In J. McMillen (ed.) *Gambling in the 80s.* Proceedings of the inaugural conference of the National Association for Gambling Studies (NAGS), Brisbane.

Blaszczynski, A. P., Buhrich, N., & McConaghy, N. 1985. Pathological gamblers, heroin addicts, and controls compared on the E.P.Q. 'addiction scale.' *British Journal of Addiction, 80,* 315–319.

Blaszczynski, A. P., Winter, S. W., & McConaghy, N. 1986. Plasma endorphin levels in pathological gambling. *Journal of Gambling Behavior, 2,* 3–14.

Brown, R. I. F. 1987[a]. Models of gambling and gambling addiction as perceptual filters. *Journal of Gambling Behavior, 3,* 224–236.

———. 1987[b]. Pathological gambling and associated patterns of crime: Comparisons with alcohol and other drug addictions. *Journal of Gambling Behavior, 3,* 98–114.

Browne, B. 1987. *Going on tilt: Frequent poker players and control.* Paper presented at the Seventh International Conference on Gambling and Risk Taking, Reno, Nevada (August).

Carlton, P. L., & Goldstein, L. 1987. Physiological determinants of pathological gambling. In T. Galski (ed.) *Handbook on pathological gambling.* (111–122). Springfield, Illinois: Charles C. Thomas.

———. 1988. Physiological factors as determinants of pathological gambling. *Journal of Gambling Behavior, 3,* 274–285.

Carlton, P. L., Manowitz, P., McBride, H., Nora, R., Swartzburg, M., & Goldstein, L. 1987. Attention deficit disorder and pathological gambling. *Journal of Clinical Psychiatry, 48,* 487–488.

Carnes, P. 1983. *The sexual addiction.* Minneapolis: Comp Care.

Christiansen, E. M. 1987a. The 1986 U.S. gross annual wager. *Gaming & Wagering Business, 8,* July 15, 7–10.

Christiansen E. M. 1987b. U.S. gaming revenue tops $22 billion in '86; up 8%. *Gaming & Wagering Business, 8,* July 15, 7–10.

Ciarrocchi, J. 1987. Severity of impairment in dually addicted gamblers. *Journal of Gambling Behavior, 3,* 16–26.

Commission on the Review of the National Policy toward Gambling. (1976). *Gambling in america.* Washington, D.C.: U.S. Government Printing Office.

Council on Compulsive Gambling of New Jersey. 1988. *1987—Monthly activity report.* Trenton, New Jersey: Author.

———. 1987. *1986—Monthly activity report.* Trenton, New Jersey: Author.

———. 1986. *1985—Monthly activity report.* Trenton, New Jersey: Author.

Culleton, R. P. 1985. *A survey of pathological gamblers in the State of Ohio.* Philadelphia: Transition Planning Associates.

———. In press. The prevalence rates of pathological gambling: A look at methods. *Journal of Gambling Behavior, 5.*

Culleton R. P., & Lang, M. H. 1985 *Supplementary report on the prevalence rate of pathological gambling in the Delaware Valley in 1984.* Camden, New Jersey: Rutgers/Camden Forum for Policy Research and Public Service.

———. 1984. *The prevalence rate of pathological gambling in the Delaware Valley in 1984.* Camden, New Jersey: Rutgers/Camden Forum for Policy Research and Public Service.

Custer, R. L. 1982. An overview of compulsive gambling. In P. A. Carone, S. F. Yoles, S. N. Kiefer, & L. Krinsky (eds.) *Addictive disorders update: Alcoholism, drug abuse, gambling.* New York: Human Sciences Press.

Custer, R. L., & Custer, L. F. 1981, October. *Soft signs of pathological gambling.* Paper presented at the Fifth National Conference on Gambling, University of Nevada, Reno.

———. 1978. *Characteristics of the recovering compulsive gambler: A survey of 150 members of Gamblers Anonymous.* Paper presented at the Fourth Annual Conference on Gambling, Reno, Nevada (December).

Custer, R. L., with Milt, H. 1985. *When luck runs out.* New York: Facts on File Publications.

Dickerson, M. G. 1979. FI schedules and persistence at gambling in the UK betting office. *Journal of Applied Behavioral Analysis, 12,* 315–323.

———. 1984. *Compulsive gamblers.* London: Longman.

Division of Alcoholism. 1987. *Admissions on compulsive gamblers—JFK hospital.* Trenton, New Jersey: MIS Unit.

Frank, M. L., & Cashmere, C. 1987. *Youth: Casino gambling and college students.* Paper presented at the Fifth Annual Statewide Conference on Compulsive Gambling of the Council on Compulsive Gambling of New Jersey, Asbury Park, New Jersey, (September).

Goldstein, L., Manowitz, P, Nora, R., Swartzburg, M., & Carlton, P. L. 1985. Differential EEG activation and pathological gambling. *Biological Psychiatry,* 20, 1232–1234.

Graham, J. R., & Lowenfeld, B. H. 1986. Personality dimensions of the pathological gambler. *Journal of Gambling Behavior,* 2, 58–66.

Haberman, P. W. 1969. Drinking and other self-indulgences: Complements or counter-attractions? *The International Journal of the Addictions,* 4, 157–167.

Hayano, D. 1982. *Poker faces: The life and work of professional card players.* Berkeley: University of California Press.

Heineman, M. 1987. A comparison: The treatment of wives of alcoholics with the treatment of wives of pathological gamblers. *Journal of Gambling Behavior,* 3, 27–40.

Jacobs, D. F. 1988a. Behavioral aspects of gambling: Evidence for a common dissociative-like reaction among addicts. *Journal of Gambling Behavior,* 4, (in press).

———. 1988b, May. *A survey of drinking, drug use, overeating, and gambling behavior among high school students in Riverside County, California.* Paper presented at the Third National Conference on Gambling, National Council on Compulsive Gambling, New York.

———. 1987. *Effects on children of parental excesses in gambling.* Paper presented at the seventh International Conference on Gambling and Risk Taking, Reno, Nevada, August.

———. 1986. A general theory of addictions: A new theoretical model. *Journal of Gambling Behavior,* 2, 15–31.

Kallick, M., Suits, D., Dielman, T., & Hybels, J. 1979. *A survey of gambling attitudes and behavior.* Ann Arbor, Missouri: Institute for Social Research.

Kuley, N. B., & Jacobs, D. F. 1988. The relationship between dissociative-like experiences and sensation seeking among social and problem gamblers. *Journal of Gambling Behavior,* 4, 197–207.

Ladouceur, R., & Mireault, C. 1988. Gambling behaviors among high school students in the Quebec area. *Journal of Gambling Behavior,* 4, 3–12.

Lesieur, H. R. 1988a. The female pathological gambler. In W. R. Eadington (ed.) *Gambling research: Proceedings of the seventh international conference on gambling and risk taking.* Reno, Nevada: Bureau of Business and Economic Research, University of Nevada, Reno.

———. 1988b. Altering the DSM-III criteria for pathological gambling. *Journal of Gambling Behavior,* 4, (in press).

———. 1987a. Gambling, pathological gambling, and crime. In T. Galski (ed.) *Handbook on pathological gambling.* (89–110). Springfield, Illinois: Charles C. Thomas.

———. 1987b. Experiences of employee assistance programs with compulsive gamblers. *Research presentations: 16th ALMACA annual meetings.* Arlington, Virginia: Association of Labor-Management Administrators and Consultants on Alcoholism.

———. 1984. *The chase: Career of the compulsive gambler.* Cambridge, Massachusetts: Schenkman Books.

———. 1979. The compulsive gambler's spiral of options and involvement. *Psychiatry: Journal for the Study of Interpersonal Processes, 42,* 79–87.

Lesieur, H. R. & Blume, S. 1987. The South Oaks Gambling Screen (SOGS): A new instrument for the identification of pathological gamblers. *American Journal of Psychiatry 144,* 1184–1188.

Lesieur, H. R., Blume, S. B., & Zoppa, R. M. 1985. Alcoholism, drug abuse, and gambling. *Alcoholism: Clinical and Experimental Research, 10,* 33–38.

Lesieur, H. R., & Klein, R. 1987. Pathological gambling among high school students. *Addictive Behaviors, 12,* 129–135.

———. 1985 *Prisoners, gambling, and crime.* Paper presented at the Annual Meetings of the Academy of Criminal Justice Sciences, Las Vegas, Nevada (April).

Lesieur, H. R., & Heineman, M. 1988. Pathological gambling among youthful multiple substance abusers in a therapeutic community. *British Journal of Addiction,* (in press).

Lesieur, H. R., & Sheley, J. F. 1987. Illegal appended enterprises: Selling the lines. *Social Problems, 34,* 249–260.

Levinson, P. K., Gernstein D. R., & Maloff D. R. (eds.). 1983. *Commonalities in substance abuse and habitual behaviors.* Lexington, Massachusetts: Lexington Books.

Light, I. 1977. Numbers gambling among blacks: A financial institution. *American Sociological Review, 42,* 892–904.

Linden, R. D., Pope, H. G., & Jonas, J. M. 1986. Pathological gambling and major affective disorder: Preliminary findings. *Journal of Clinical Psychiatry, 47,* 201–203.

Livingston, J. 1974. *Compulsive gamblers: Observations on action and abstinence.* New York: Harper Torchbooks.

Lorenz, V. 1981. *Differences found among Catholic, Protestant and Jewish families of pathological gamblers.* Paper presented at the Fifth National Conference on Gambling and Risk Taking, Lake Tahoe, Nevada, (October).

Lorenz, V., & Shuttlesworth, D.E. 1983. The impact of pathological gambling on the spouse of the gambler. *Journal of Community Psychology, 11,* 67–76.

Lorenz, V. C., & Yaffee, R. A. 1986. Pathological gambling: Psychosomatic, emotional, and marital difficulties as reported by the gambler. *Journal of Gambling Behavior, 2,* 40–49.

———. 1988. Pathological gambling: Psychosomatic, emotional, and marital difficulties as reported by the spouse. *Journal of Gambling Behavior, 4,* 13–26.

McCormick, R. A., Russo, A. M., Ramirez, L. F., & Taber, J. I. 1984. Affective disorders among pathological gamblers seeking treatment. *American Journal of Psychiatry, 141,* 215–218.

Mintz, R. S. 1970. Prevalence of persons in the city of Los Angeles who have attempted suicide. *Bulletin of Suicidology, 7,* 9–16.

Moran, E. 1969. Taking the final risk. *Mental Health, (London)*, 21–22.

――――. 1970. Gambling as a form of dependence. *British Journal of Addictions*, 64, 419–428.

Nadler, L. 1985. The epidemiology of pathological gambling: Critique of existing research and alternative strategies. *Journal of Gambling Behavior*, 1, 35–50.

Nora, R. 1984. *Profile survey on pathological gamblers*. Paper presented at the Sixth National Conference on Gambling and Risk Taking, Atlantic City, N.J. (December).

Oldman, D. 1978. Compulsive gamblers. *Sociological Review*, 26, 349–371.

Orford, J. 1985. *Excessive appetites: A psychological view of addictions*. Chichester: Wiley & Sons.

Peele, S. 1985. *The meaning of addiction: Compulsive experience and its interpretation*. Lexington, Massachusetts: Lexington Books.

Politzer, R. M., Morrow, J. S., & Leavey, S. B. 1985. Report on the cost-benefit/ effectiveness of treatment at the Johns Hopkins Center for Pathological Gambling. *Journal of Gambling Behavior*, 1, 119–130.

Ramirez, L. F., McCormick, R. A., Russo, A. M., & Taber, J. I. 1984. Patterns of substance abuse in pathological gamblers undergoing treatment. *Addictive Behaviors*, 8, 425–428.

Rosecrance, J. 1986. Attributions and the origins of problem gambling. *The Sociological Quarterly*, 27, 463–477.

Taber, J. I., McCormick, R. A., & Ramirez, L. F. 1987. The prevalence and impact of major life stressors among pathological gamblers. *The International Journal of the Addictions*, 22, 71–79.

Taber, J. I., Russo, A. M., Adkins, B. J., & McCormick, R. A. 1986. Ego strength and achievement motivation in pathological gamblers. *Journal of Gambling Behavior*, 2, 69–80.

Volberg, R., & Steadman, H. 1988. Refining prevalence estimates of pathological gambling. *American Journal of Psychiatry*, 145, 502–505.

Wagner, M. G. 1988. Crime, poverty, the mob—it's just not worth the risk. *The Detroit Free Press*, May 18, 1D & 12D.

Walker, M., & Trimboli, L. 1985. An analysis of heavy gambling as an addiction. In J. McMillen (ed.) *Gambling in the 80s*. Proceedings of the inaugural conference of the National Association for Gambling Studies (NAGS), Brisbane.

Wanda G., & Foxman J. 1971. *Games compulsive gamblers, wives, and families play*. Downey, California: Gam-Anon, Inc.

Wexler, S. 1981. *A chart on the effects of compulsive gambling on the wife*. Parlin, New Jersey: Author.

Whitman-Raymond, R. G. 1988. Pathological gambling as a defense against loss. *Journal of Gambling Behavior*, 4, (in press).

14

Illegal and Undocumented: A Review of Teenage Gambling and the Plight of Children of Problem Gamblers in America

Durand F. Jacobs, Ph.D.

Overview

This chapter presents some new and provocative information about teenage gambling and about the vulnerabilities revealed by children of problem gamblers.

The chapter is divided into two main sections. Part I is a review of the extent, types, and consequences associated with gambling among underage high school students from several locales across the United States. Part II offers the first published estimates of the prevalence of both adult and juvenile children of problem gamblers in the United States.

A distillation of the literature is presented on how parental excesses in alcohol and other potentially addictive substances and activities have affected their children. From these studies the author abstracts a set of expectations about the vulnerabilities and risks of unfavorable outcomes that may be anticipated among children of problem gamblers. These *a priori* surmises are then compared to findings from the first study yet reported on the intergenerational effects of excessive parental gambling on their children.

Recommendations are made for further research and prompt social action.

Part I

A Review of Teenage Gambling in America

Many legally underage adolescents in today's society gamble. Yet, there seems to be little public recognition of or concern with teenage gambling. To paraphrase Milgram (1982), the apparent unwillingness of adults in society to acknowledge gambling behaviors in their adolescents may reside in their belief that legal sanctions will discourage any "really serious" gambling among those under eighteen years of age—so, not to worry. Or perhaps it reflects the hesitancy of adult society to face up to its own role in fostering childhood and teenage gambling, since the overwhelming majority of young people who gamble were introduced to this recreational diversion by their parents and relatives. Could it be that underage gambling simply is dismissed as "harmless fun and games?" Or is it a delayed awareness on the part of adults, including school authorities, about this component of the current adolescent experience? And finally, how big a problem can it be? In the materials to follow I will present my reasons for believing that in 1988 as many as 7 million juveniles were gambling for money with or without adult awareness or approval, and more than 1 million of these were experiencing serious gambling-related problems (see tables 14–3 and 14–4).

Several independent studies have been conducted surveying the prevalence of gambling among high school age youth as shown in table 14–1.

The results of these studies conducted in several states spanning our country suggest that 40 percent to 86 percent (varying somewhat from locale to locale) have gambled for money in the past twelve months (table 14–2).

Eighty-five to 90 percent of these high school youth are under eighteen years of age. Therefore, they have been gambling illegally, according to the statutory age limit established in their respective states of residence.

Quoting results of a survey of more than one thousand high school students in an Atlantic City high school, Arcuri et al. (1985) report that 42 percent of the fourteen-years-olds, 49 percent of the fifteen-year-olds, 63 percent of the sixteen-year-olds, 71 percent of the seventeen-year-olds, 76 percent of the eighteen-year-olds, and 88 percent of the nineteen-year-olds had gambled at some time. These rates mirror the 86 percent rate of gambling in the previous twelve months reported by Lesieur and Klein (1987) among students at four different high schools in New Jersey (table 14–2).

As seen in table 14–2, adolescents from locales across the United States show an age of onset for gambling long before entering high school. More than a third report their first experience with gambling for money before they were eleven years of age, and 70 percent to 88 percent say they first gambled before they were fifteen years old. The paradoxical fact is that the overwhelming majority of teenagers who ever gambled were doing so long before they reached the legal age of permission established by society. As is the case with adolescent drinking, society's adults generally appear to forget their role as accessory-before-the-fact, and seem to imply that teenagers invented gambling rather than learned it from them (Milgram 1982, 304).

Table 14–1
A Profile of the Five High School Populations Surveyed between 1984 and 1988

Investigators	Lesieur & Klein[a]	Jacobs et al.[b]	Jacobs et al.[c]	Jacobs & Kuley[d]	Steinberg[e]
Year survey completed	1987	1985	1987	1987	1988
Location	North, Central South New Jersey	Inland Empire, California	Inland Empire, California	Upper Virginia	East and West Connecticut
Number of high schools surveyed	N=4	N=4	N=2	N=2	N=2
Total students responding*	N=892	N=843	N=257	N=212	N=573
Grades represented	11th–12th	9th–12th	9th–12th	9th–12th	9th–12

*all self-administered
all anonymous

[a]Lesieur, H.R. & Klein, R. (1987). Pathological gambling among high school students. *Addictive Behaviors*, 12, 129-135.
[b&c]Jacobs, D.F., Marston, A.R., Singer, R.D., Widaman, K. & Little, T. (1985, 1987). Unpublished research reports. Jerry L. Pettis Memorial Veterans Hospital, Loma Linda, California.
[d]Jacobs, D.F. & Kuley, N. (1987). Unpublished research report. Jerry L. Pettis Memorial Veterans Hospital, Loma Linda, California.
[e]Steinberg, M.A. (1988). Unpublished research report. Connecticut Council on Compulsive Gambling, Hamden, Connecticut.

Table 14–2
Extent and Types of Gambling Reported by High School Age Youth in the United States 1984–1988

Investigators Year survey' completed	Lesieur & Klein 1984	Jacobs et al[a] 1985	Jacobs et al[b] 1987	Jacobs & Kuley 1987	Steinberg 1988	Median Prevalence Level
Age at onset of gambling						
–before 11 years		41%	30%	39%	27%	36%
–11–15 years		40	58	48	43	46
–after 15 years		19	12	13	31	18
Gambled for money in past twelve months	86	20	45	40	60[c]	45
Types of gambling activities in the past twelve months[a]						
–cards with family or friends	49		40	36	66	45
–state lottery	45		40	27[b]	51	43
–bowled, shot pool or other game of skill	42		33	30	34	34
–sports betting, football pools, OTB	45		34	24	26	30
–bingo	18		13	24	66	22
–shot dice (outside casinos)	18		9	13	23	16
–horse or dog races	29		14	12	6	13
–casinos	46		7	5	11	8
–illegal numbers with a bookie	*		8	9	14	9
–jai alai	**		2	2	14	2
–commercial card parlors			3	5		4

*Included with lottery
**Included with sports betting
[a]Jacobs et al., 1985, did not include a listing of types of gambling in this survey.
[b]The Virginia State Lottery was not approved until November 1987. These students had purchased lottery tickets in other states or the District of Columbia.
[c]Dr. Steinberg did not ask explicitly about the extent that students had gambled on such activity "over the past 12 months." All data in this column reflect students' responses to the question "Have you bet. . ." This leaves the question open as to whether the students' responses reflected "ever bet" or "currently bet." Consequently, a conservative estimate is made regarding the percent of students who had gambled in the past 12 months.

Further evidence that underage gamblers follow the model of their parents and other adults is seen in the types of wagering that high school students pursue. Again referring to table 14–2, these appear to be strikingly similar among teenagers residing in different states. No systematic data had been available on the types of gambling in which teenagers were involved until Lesieur & Klein, and Jacobs et al. conducted the first studies of this behavior in the mid-1980s (table 14–2). However, since 1984 it is quite clear that the four favorite games that teenagers play for money are (in rough order of preference): cards with friends and family (approximately 45 percent), the lottery in the growing number of states where it is available and in neighboring states where it is not (approximately 43 percent), games of skill, such as golf, bowling, and pool played with friends and associates (approximately 34 percent), and sports betting on football and baseball pools, offtrack betting, etc. (approximately 30 percent), even though most sports betting is illegally pursued with a bookie. Following in preference behind the top four are playing bingo, shooting dice, and betting at race tracks.

In locales easily accessible to casinos, such as in Nevada and in the Eastern Seaboard states, these glitter palaces seem to have an irresistible lure for underage high school students that tends to preempt their gambling time and dollars. Casino gambling made its debut in Atlantic City in 1978 with great fanfare. In 1985 one Atlantic City high school newspaper surveyed 1,120 ninth- to twelfth-grade students, and determined that 64 percent of these legally underage students had gambled at the casinos and that 9 percent of them had gambled at least once a week during the preceding month. Most of the casino betting (66 percent) was reported to be at the slot machines, but about one quarter of those surveyed had played blackjack and 25 percent of these students had been given free drinks (Arcuri et al. 1985). Once again, the paradox of ambivalent parent attitudes is encountered: 79 percent of these students said their parents knew they gambled. Apparently the casinos knew, too.

In a recent report specifically targeting casino gambling among legally underage college students, Frank (1988) surveyed two hundred students in an undergraduate college about fifteen minutes driving time from Atlantic City casinos. Sixty-six percent of the students who gambled at the casinos were under New Jersey's minimum legal gambling age of twenty-one. Sixty-four percent of Frank's subjects reported the slots as their favorite game, while 24 percent preferred blackjack and 6 percent roulette. Frank reports that this order of college student preference for casino games has remained relatively stable over the past three years of his successive surveys. Consistent with the wide range of gambling activities for high school students reflected in table 14–2, Frank found that underage students who gamble in casinos typically engage in other sorts of gambling activities as well, legal and illegal. Almost 75 percent of Frank's subjects who gambled in a casino in the previous year also had played the state lottery. This was considerably higher than the 59 percent of all students at this college who had played the lottery. Frank found that his group of underage casino gamblers also admitted to sports betting (most of which is illegal in New Jersey) and betting on horses at the racetrack. Further evidence that even younger juveniles have been gambling in casinos for some years past is offered by Lesieur & Klein (1987). They report that, as early as 1983-84, 46 percent of their large sample of legally underage students from high schools throughout New Jersey had bet at Atlantic City casinos during the previous twelve months (table 14–2).

It is clear from the data portrayed in table 14–2 that statutory age controls on gambling simply are not being observed or enforced. This is particularly evident in sales of state lottery tickets, as well as at other state-licensed gambling establishments such as betting counters at horse and dog tracks and in gaming areas of casinos. To its credit, in 1987 the New Jersey Casino Control Commission reported that 197,842 underage persons were prevented from entering the gaming areas in the twelve Atlantic City casinos, and that 34,018 persons were escorted from the casino floor because they were under twenty-one years of age. Obviously, these figures represent an unknown fraction of the underage gamblers who continued to play undisturbed at the casinos.

The only other study known to me that included high school students who lived in a casino gambling city was completed by Wittman et al. (1988) in Reno, Nevada. They sampled 119 ninth-graders, equally divided among boys and girls. The average age of the group was 14.6 years. They found that 58 percent of the boys and 15 percent of the girls had gambled for money. This study gathered no further information on the nature of their gambling behavior.

Canadian high school students also appear to be active gamblers. Ladouceur & Mireault (1988) report a study involving 1,612 students from nine high schools in the region of Quebec City. These students completed the same questionnaire developed by Lesieur & Klein (1987). Seventy-six percent had gambled once in their lifetime, 65 percent had placed a bet in the previous year, and 24 percent gambled at least once a week. The three most popular games for these ninth- to twelfth-grade students were the lottery (60 percent), sports betting (45 percent), and card games with family and friends (36 percent). Results from this study reveal that 90 percent of the parents knew their children gambled, and 84 percent did not object. Indeed, 61 percent of the adolescents said they wagered in the company of their parents, 57 percent wagered with their brothers and sisters, and 15 percent with other members of the family. More than 25 percent of these students reported they had borrowed money from parents or other relatives, either to bet or to pay their gambling debts. Ten percent reported that gambling had created family problems.

Reports of youthful gambling are not restricted to the North American continent. Ide-Smith and Lea (1988) surveyed fifty-one students from a comprehensive high school in Exeter, Devon, England. There were thirty-one male and twenty female pupils in the sample. Their mean age was 13.7 years. This high school was said to be representative of those throughout the city. The authors note that Exeter has easy access to nearby seaside towns where children can enjoy unrestricted play on slot machines. These subjects reported their average age at onset of gambling at between eight and nine years (much earlier than reported in table 14–2 for American youth). Eighty-nine percent of this sample claimed to have gambled in some way. The most common form of gambling was slot machines (81 percent), followed by card games with family and friends (53 percent), wagers on local events and activities involving personal skills (51 percent), and coin games such as those found in amusement arcades (26 percent). A few of these children admitted wagering at a betting shop and greyhound races, as well as participating in football pools—all of which would require adult cooperation. Ide-Smith & Lea determined that the major locus for gambling was in the home, followed by activities at school where, despite school rules forbidding all games of chance, wagering of many kinds, including throwing pennies against a wall, were prevalent. The authors note that "it was only in relation to slot machines that the children came forward with anecdotes of anything like compulsive behavior" (p. 116).

For the most part, teenagers, like adults, gamble socially and recreationally without encountering serious problems. However, for a minority of youngsters gambling is no longer fun. An array of gambling related problems encountered by high school students across the United States is portrayed in table 14–3.

Lesieur & Klein's sample included primarily middle class high schools throughout New Jersey. Of the four high schools surveyed, two were chosen because of their proximity to Atlantic City casinos. Unique, but unexplained in their results, is the extremely high rate of weekly gambling reported by their sample of students. Surveys of students in California (Jacobs et al. 1985, 1987) and Virginia (Jacobs & Kuley 1987) show a much lower order of frequent gambling. Unfortunately, Steinberg (1988) did not ask about *current levels* of gambling among students in Connecticut where many different forms of legalized gambling are very prevalent. Much more research will be required to identify factors that tend to elevate frequency and intensity of gambling activities among high school students.

Yet, two trends are discernable from the data in table 14–3 regarding the rate and intensity of gambling among underage high school students. Not surprisingly, the first appears to be associated with more favored forms of gambling, particularly when these are readily accessible to these young students. The second is less self-evident. More careful investigation is needed to determine how to weigh heavy and frequent gambling before age eighteen as a "soft sign" for present or later "pathological gambling."

Much more definitive indications of current and serious problems related to gambling are seen in the remaining items listed in table 14–3. The most authoritative basis for identifying a person as a "pathological gambler" is the diagnostic criteria in the Diagnostic and Statistical Manual

Table 14–3
Prevalence of Gambling Problems among High School Youth in the United States 1984–1988

Investigators Year survey completed	Lesieur & Klein 1987	Jacobs et al 1985	Jacobs et al 1987	Jacobs & Kuley 1987	Steinberg 1988	Median Prevalence Level
One or both parents described as problem gamblers	5%	6%	9%	7%	13%	7%
Gambling weekly or more often, (or) moderate to heavy involvement	32	4	6	10		8
Gambling has harmed relationships with family	11				7	9
Would like to stop gambling, but could not (or) believed gambling out of control	5	4	4	12	15	5
Committed illegal acts to get gambling money or to pay gambling debts	10				9	9
Revealed signs of "compulsive/pathological" gambling: —met or exceeded GA Twenty Questions criteria		4	4			4
—met or exceeded DSM-III criteria	6				5	5
—sought organized program or professional help to stop gambling		1	1	1	7	1

(DSM-III), published by the American Psychiatric Association (1980). These are:

A. The individual is chronically and progressively unable to resist impulses to gamble.

B. Gambling compromises, disrupts, or damages family, personal, and vocational pursuits, as indicated by at least three of the following:

(1) Arrest for forgery, fraud, embezzlement, or income tax evasion because of attempts to obtain money for gambling.

(2) Default on debts or other financial responsibilities.

(3) Disruption of family or spouse relationships because of gambling.

(4) Borrowing of money from illegal sources (loan sharks).

(5) Inability to account for loss of money or to produce evidence of winning money, if this is claimed.

(6) Loss of work caused by absenteeism to pursue gambling activity.

(7) Necessity for another person to provide money to relieve a desperate financial situation.

C. The gambling is not due to Antisocial Personality Disorder (p. 292–293).

Obviously, these criteria were developed to identify adult problem gamblers. Their application to juvenile gamblers remains an open issue. Only Lesieur & Klein and Steinberg, imbedded questions reflecting these DSM-III criteria in their surveys of American high school students. As seen in table 14–3, 6 percent of the New Jersey sample and 5 percent of the Connecticut sample met the DSM-III criteria for pathological gambling. Ladouceur & Mireault (1988) in Quebec found that just under 2 percent of their sample could be diagnosed as pathological gamblers according to DSM-III criteria. Frank (1988) found that 5 percent of his underage college students met or exceeded the cutting score on the South Oaks Gambling Screen (Lesieur & Blume 1987), which is based largely on the DSM-III criteria. In the surveys conducted by Jacobs et al. in 1985 and 1987, approximately one-third of the students surveyed were asked to complete the Gamblers Anonymous Twenty Questions (see Stein, this volume). Many of these questions are incorporated in the DSM-III criteria for "pathological gambler". In both these samples of California high school students (N = 844 and N = 257), 4 percent responded in the affirmative to seven or more of these questions, which would classify them as "compulsive gamblers," according to the Gamblers Anonymous guidelines.

Perhaps the most ominous sign among these high school students is their admission that they would like to stop gambling but could not, or that they believed their gambling was "out of control" (see DSM-III criterion A). Between 4 and 15 percent of the high school students surveyed between 1984 and 1988 reported this to be the case. Data presented in table 14–3 also suggest that the proportion of student gamblers who experience these problems has progressively increased over that four-year period.

While assessed in only two surveys noted in table 14–3, the fact that gambling has "harmed relationships with the family" appears to be another serious sign of present and potential troubles for these underage high school students (see DSM-III criterion B). Eleven percent of Lesieur & Klein's sample reported this to be so, as did 7 percent of Steinberg's sample.

Disruption of school or work activities (see DSM-III criterion B) is reported in 5 percent of Lesieur & Klein's sample, in 6 percent of Steinberg's sample, and in 6 percent of Ladouceur & Mireault's sample of Canadian students (1988). Steinberg reported additionally that 20 percent of the students in his sample admitted to cutting classes to gamble (see DSM-III criterion B). As early as 1981, Schwaneberg reported similar school problems among high school students in Atlantic City who gambled regularly.

Committing illegal acts to get gambling money or to pay gambling debts is another DSM-III "hard sign" of pathological involvement in gambling activities. Berger (1987), working with a group of thirteen- to eighteen-year-old adolescents (N = 27) in a chemical dependency unit in Council Bluffs, Iowa, reports that 70 percent of his sample had gambled during the past year. Sixty-five percent had purchased lottery tickets, 40 percent had bet at dog tracks, and 33 percent had engaged in sports betting with a bookie. No other details were available, except that many of these adolescents had obtained their gambling money from dealing in drugs. Lesieur & Klein (1987), as well as Ladouceur & Mireault (1988), also indicate that dealing in drugs, working for a bookmaker, selling sports cards, and shoplifting are among the more frequent illegal means used by high school students for obtaining money to gamble or to pay gambling debts. Steinberg reports that as many as 8 percent of the students in his sample have sold drugs to obtain money to gamble or to pay gambling debts. Just under 6 percent of Steinberg's sample admit to having been arrested for illegal acts stemming from their attempts to obtain money for gambling. Lesieur & Klein report that 10 percent of the high school students in their New Jersey sample admitted to this activity, as did 9 percent of students in the Connecticut sample (table 14–3). Ladouceur & Mireault (1988) also found 10 percent of their sample admitted to illegal activities to get gambling money.

In the surveys of U.S. high school students reviewed in table 14–3, all but Lesieur & Klein asked each respondent if he or she had sought an organized program or professional assistance to stop gambling. One percent of each of the high school samples from California and 1 percent of the Virginia sample reported taking this action to deal with their gambling problems. Seven percent of the Connecticut group reported they had sought professional help about gambling-related problems.

The data portrayed in table 14–3 represents responses of the *entire* population of high school students surveyed, whether or not they admitted to gambling. Table 14–4 sets forth the responses of only those students who had admitted to gambling in the previous twelve months.

When focusing exclusively on those students who were gambling actively, one obtains an even more troubling impression of the consequences of problem gambling among the high school age population. Table 14–4 reveals that, among high school students who gamble, one in five on the average tends to gamble at least weekly or more often. On the average approximately 20 percent of the gambling students reported they either would like to stop gambling but could not, or that their gambling was "out of control." A more optimistic note is struck by the numbers of high school gamblers who have sought self-help groups (such as Gamblers Anonymous) or professional assistance because of problems associated with their gambling behavior. Proportions of students who have done so range from 2 to 5 percent in Virginia and California to as much as 12 percent in the most recent Connecticut sample (table 14–4).

One factor that has all but become a national secret is the number of

Table 14–4
Gambling-Related Problems Reported by High School Age Gamblers in the United States (1984–1988)

Investigators Year survey completed	Lesieur & Klein 1987	Jacobs et al[a] 1985	Jacobs et al[b] 1987	Jacobs & Kuley 1987	Steinberg 1988	Median Prevalence Level
Among those who gambled:	N = 767	N = 169	N = 116	N = 85	N = 344	
Gambling weekly or more often, (or) moderate to heavy involvement	37%	20%	13%	25%		22%
Gambling has harmed relationships with family	13				12%	12
Would like to stop gambling, but could not (or) believed gambling out of control	6	20	9	29	25	20
Committed illegal acts to get gambling money or to pay gambling debts	12				15	13
Revealed signs of "compulsive/pathological" gambling:						
—met or exceeded GA Twenty Questions criteria		20	9			14
—met or exceeded DSM-III criteria	7				8	7
—sought organized program or professional help to stop gambling		5	3	2	12	4

high school students who describe their parents as problem gamblers. Within the studies summarized in table 14–3, reports of parental problem gambling range from as low as 5 percent in 1984 to as much as 13 percent in 1988. Ladouceur & Mireault's Canadian high school students reported that 8 percent of their parents "gambled too much." As will be discussed at length, this circumstance does more than provide an adult role model, companion, and/or mentor in gambling activities for the maturing child. The presence of a parent excessively involved with a substance or pursuit of a potentially-addictive activity has been shown to have a pervasive and destructive influence on the child rearing environment. Zucker & Linsansky Gomberg (1986) reviewed all studies originating in childhood and adolescence that followed respondents into adulthood and established an adult diagnosis of either alcoholism or problem drinking. In addition to the greater loading of alcoholic relatives in the family background of these alcoholic individuals, they found significant family problems, including heightened marital conflicts, inadequate parenting, and inadequate parental role modeling among the potent environmental factors that predated the alcoholic adaptation. Results of the first study that has evaluated the extent to which excessive parental gambling impacts children raised in the home of a problem gambler will be discussed later in this chapter. Prior to examining the plight of children of problem gamblers, it is necessary (and politically prudent) to establish some estimate of how many persons in the United States have been and are currently being affected by this problem. The scope of this problem will be determined by interfacing several interrelated factors: the prevalence of adult problem gamblers in the United States, and the proportions of adults and children who describe one or both of their parents as a problem gambler (to be defined). These matters are addressed in turn in the sections that follow.

Part II

Prevalence of Adult Problem Gamblers in the United States: Approximately 7 Million

I have based my estimate of approximately 7 million adult problem gamblers in the United States on partial findings that have emerged from a national NIMH-sponsored study on gambling currently being conducted by Volberg & Steadman (1988b). To date these investigators have amassed responses from a randomly selected stratified sampling of approximately 2,700 men and women eighteen years of age and older from New York, New Jersey, and Maryland. They have operationally defined the term "problem gambler" to represent the *combined* group of respondents who scored five or more on the South Oaks Gambling Screen (SOGS)—that is, "probable pathological gamblers," and those who scored three or four on this instrument—"potential pathological gamblers" (Lesieur & Blume 1987).

Based on results available from the first three states in what will be a six-state national sampling, Volberg & Steadman (1988b) estimate (provisionally) that 4.1 percent of the adult U.S. population may be classified as "problem gamblers." When multiplying this percentage by the approximately 174,561,000 adults reported in the 1985 U.S. Census (Statistical Abstract of the U.S. 1987) I arrived at the estimate of approximately 7 million adult problem gamblers in the United States.

Prevalence of Adult Children of Problem Gamblers in the United States: Between 5.2 Million and 9.6 Million

Volberg & Steadman (1988b) found that 82 percent of their current three-state sample of adults (that is, those eighteen years of age and older) had gambled at some time in their lives. Only those who reported they had ever gambled were asked, "Did either of your parents ever have a gambling problem?" Three percent responded "yes". There is no way for determining the extent of parental gambling problems among the remainder of the sample (18 percent) who were not asked the question. However, as is seen in table 14–5, those adults whose SOGS scores revealed a gambling problem of their own reported gambling problems among their parents at a rate over four times that of those whose SOGS scores reflected no gambling problem (11.6 percent vs. 2.7 percent). Further evidence documenting the vulnerability of juvenile children of problem gamblers will be discussed at length later in this chapter.

By extrapolating the 3 percent of adults who reported a parental gambling problem (table 14–5) to the general adult population, I projected an estimate of slightly over 5,200,000 persons in the United States who are adult children of a problem gambler. Because of the controlled sampling procedures used by Volberg & Steadman, this estimate represents what must be considered the most reliable set of data yet available on this topic. However, this estimate also must be recognized as a very conservative one, since Volberg & Steadman's data has deleted input from the 18 percent of their sample who have never gambled themselves, but who may have had a parent who was a problem gambler. Moreover, I based my estimate on 1985 Census figures, which do not take into account the adult population increases between 1985 and 1988. On the other hand, one could argue that in 1985 the prevalence of adult problem gamblers may have been less than the 4.1 percent estimated for 1988. We have no way for determining if this were so. However, Volberg & Stead-

Table 14–5
Prevalence of Parental Problem Gambling Reported by a Stratified Random Sample of Adults Who Had Ever Gambled from New York, New Jersey and Maryland (1988)

	(N = 2262)					
	Responses to South Oaks Gambling Screen (SOGS)					
Parental gambling problem reported	SOGS scores reflect no gambling problem		SOGS scores reflect gambling problem		TOTALS	
	N	%	N	%	N	%
No	2091	97.3	100	88.4	2191	97
Yes	58	2.7	13	11.6	71	3
	2149	100%	113	100%	2262	100%

From Volberg, R. A., and Steadman, H. J. (1988b). Personal communication.

man (1988a) had reported a 4.2 percent prevalence rate for problem gamblers in New York State when they completed their initial survey in 1986.

An alternate, but even less defensible, basis for estimating the number of adult children of problem gamblers in the United States is provided by data collected by Jacobs et al. (1985) from two uncontrolled samples of adults. The first was a sample of freshmen and sophomore college students (N = 281) from two Southern California universities. Twenty-five percent of the total group admitted to gambling in the twelve months preceding completion of a Health Survey. Six percent of this group of equally represented males and females reported that one or both of their parents had a problem with "compulsive gambling." A second sample (N = 168) was obtained from an older group of adults (median age sixty-three years) with a median educational level of thirteen years. These subjects (83 percent male) were drawn from members of a veterans and a civilian service club also located in Southern California. Fifty-one percent of these subjects admitted to gambling in the twelve months preceding completion of the same Health Survey. Five percent reported that one or both of their parents had a problem with "compulsive gambling." Multiplying the 5.5 percent of adults who described a parent as a problem gambler times the adult population reported in the 1985 U.S. Census yields a rough estimate of the prevalence of adult children of problem gamblers in the U.S. population at that time. This amounts to approximately 9,600,000. This represents my possible upper range of the prevalence rate for adult children of problem gamblers.

Prevalence of Youth Under Eighteen Years of Age
Who Are Children of Problem Gamblers: Between 2.5
Million and 3.4 Million.

> "As in many life areas, we teach our children
> as we have been taught."
> —Milgram 1982 (p. 289)

There is justification from several quarters to assume that the prevalence of gambling—and particularly problem gambling—among adults in America has been increasing steadily over the past decade and a half. By the same token, it is idle to assume that gambling and problem gambling, as well, have no life of their own until age eighteen or after.

The first national Survey of Gambling in America (Commission on the

Review of the National Policy toward Gambling, 1976) completed in 1975, estimated that .77 percent of the adult population were "probable compulsive gamblers", with an additional 2.22 percent classified as "potential compulsive gamblers." Projecting Volberg & Steadman's (1988b) current findings against the 1985 Census reports indicates that the current rate of "probable pathological gamblers" (1.4 percent) has almost doubled between 1975 and 1985, while the rate of "potential pathological gamblers" (2.7 percent) has risen about 23 percent. Whether the magnitude of these trends increase or decrease as a result of Volberg & Steadman's upcoming studies in Massachusetts, Iowa, and California remains to be seen. Still, the 37 percent overall rate of increase in the prevalence of "problem gamblers" among American adults between 1975 and 1988 is not only striking, but also likely underestimated. This is because the criteria defining the composite category of "problem gambling" in the ongoing NIMH-supported studies are much more stringent than those used in the 1974 survey.

While the possibility exists that the 1974 survey may have underestimated the prevalence of problem gambling in the United States (Nadler 1985), few would argue with the conclusion that the extent of both recreational and of problem gambling among U.S. adults truly has increased from the mid-1970s to the late 1980s (Anson 1981; Eadington 1988). This is attributed to the unprecedented growth of the legalized gambling industry in America. This burgeoning set of diversified activities include expansion of casino gambling from Las Vegas to many other Nevada locations and more recently to Atlantic City, an increase of horse and dog tracks throughout the country, rapid proliferation of card and bingo parlors, including high stakes "Indian Bingo," increased off-track betting on animal races and sports events, not to mention thirty states and the District of Columbia actively promoting lotteries in 1988, and more in the wings (*Gaming and Wagering Business Magazine* 1988).

No benchmark for estimating the prevalence of gambling among *legally underage youth* in the United States had been available until the studies by Jacobs et al. and Lesieur & Klein (1987) were completed in the mid-1980s (table 14–2). Consequently, no early data set was available from which to project trends in teenage gambling since 1975 that might be compared to the rise in adult gambling over that same period.

Indeed, teenage gambling was not yet conceptualized as an issue fifteen years ago, even though teenage involvement with potentially addictive substances such as alcohol, prescription, and illicit drugs were matters of serious concern and have remained the subject of systematic nationwide evaluation since 1975 (Johnston et al., 1980). Potentially harmful effects of teenage gambling simply had not been a matter for professional, scientific, governmental, or lay scrutiny, as attested to by the virtually silent literature on this topic before 1980. In fact, it was not until the early 1980s that the first reports of youthful gambling were presented at national and international meetings and subsequently published in journals. The numbers of national and international professional and scientific conferences that included reports of teenage gambling, as well as published articles and books on this topic, have increased markedly since 1985. However, it was not until the latter months of 1988 that the issue of teenage gambling, its extent, content, and risks first crossed the threshold of general public awareness. This was caused by a flurry of research reports and interviews with knowledgeable professionals that appeared in newspapers and magazines throughout the country and were highlighted in radio talk shows and in national TV news and dramatic programs. Ironically, it was due mainly to the publicity surrounding the largest-ever $60 million California lottery prize that led to "the dark side of underage gambling" being illuminated by the national media. Adding further impetus and substance to the unprecedented media coverage about "the biggest prize" was information released at a news conference held a month earlier at the Los Angeles Press Club on September 28, 1988, by the California Council on Compulsive Gambling. The purpose of the news conference (scheduled on the eve of the California lottery's third anniversary) was to air the council's concerns that the substantial increase in gambling by legally underage California high school students between the spring of 1985 and the spring of 1987 (see table 14–2) was linked to the initiation of the California State Lottery in October 1985, and its spirited promotion since that time. The fact that the lottery was shown to be a favorite bet of these underage adolescents added substance to the Council's allegation and provided a target for continuing investigation by reporters of controls exercised by the Lottery Commission to discourage underage players. As a result of this combination of events, illegal underage gambling and the special vulnerability of children of parents who gamble excessively may have found a place on the public's agenda of health, social, law enforcement, and legislative issues to be addressed in the late 1980s and into the 1990s.

Clinicians who have treated adult compulsive gamblers and their families may assert it's well about time that the public recognize the potent intergenerational effects that parents with gambling problems visit on their children. On the other hand, it was only in 1980 that "pathological gambling" first gained authoritative recognition as a diagnostic entity and as a treatable illness (American Psychiatric Association 1980). In this light the newly emerging public awareness of the problems that may confront gamblers of all ages, and especially the children of problem gamblers, does not appear quite so tardy. Still, it is most welcome!

A much more pressing matter is how to maintain public interest and build upon it in the future. This will require prompt, systematic, and continuous accumulation of a scientifically defensible body of research findings that will confirm or disconfirm and greatly extend the preliminary, exploratory, "catch-as-catch-can" studies of adolescent gambling reported in this chapter. It is very important that future studies go beyond merely documenting the extent and nature of gambling, and the consequences of problem gambling among youth. They also must examine carefully the reciprocal interactions between parental and offspring gambling. Optimally, a program of international research will be undertaken (Jacobs 1988) to look in depth at different ethnic subcultures in America and abroad, and examine similarities and differences in the health, social, legal, occupational, and financial risks encountered by gamblers, as well as the negative consequences experienced by their respective families and associates.

My concern extends far beyond the possibility that some children of problem gamblers will in turn become problem gamblers, themselves. There already is evidence that this, indeed, is a highly probable risk for some such children (Custer 1982; Jacobs et al. 1985). However, the literature also reminds us that the majority of persons presenting themselves for treatment of gambling-related problems (or similarly for treatment of alcohol, or drug, or eating, or sex-related problems) have *not* come from homes where a parent had the same problem (McCormick et al. 1984). A fact more often apparent in the histories of children, youth, and adults with adjustment problems is that the majority have come from child rearing settings that were rendered dysfunctional because of a variety of parental problems that had the common effect of undermining or further limiting the parenting capabilities of the householder(s) (Zucker & Linsansky Gomberg 1986).

It often has been advanced that problem drinking is a "family disease." As will be substantiated later in this chapter, precisely the same may be said for problem gambling. When considering any subgroup of potentially vulnerable children, a basic requirement is to determine the manifold ways they may be affected by a home environment in which one or both parents are so deeply enmeshed in dealing with their own stressors that they have little interest, or energy, or time to devote to child rearing. One also must consider the long-term implications of the flawed role models that such parents present to their often confused, frightened, abused, rejected, and neglected offspring. Finally, one must be sensitive to how children trapped in that kind of family setting may, themselves, begin to assume similar, reciprocal, or still other types of dysfunctional roles and health-threatening behaviors.

An extensive literature has accumulated around the potential vulnerabilities and risks of children raised by an alcoholic parent (see an excellent review by Russell et al. 1985). No comparable literature yet exists about children who have been raised in homes in which one or both parents are described as problem gamblers. Retrospective reports obtained from adult problem gamblers who had entered treatment or were members of Gamblers Anonymous indicate that the extent of problem gambling in their parents ranged from 25 percent to 40 percent (Custer 1982; Custer et al. 1975; Jacobs et al. 1985; Taber 1982). However, such reports also reveal comparable prevalence levels of parental problem drinking (Jacobs et al. 1985). Thus, it appears that parental dysfunction, per se, rather than explicit modeling of a particular problem behavior, is the dominant factor contributing to a child's level of vulnerability and risk. However, even this does not alone predict a child's later involvement in one or another form of addictive behavior, if and when this materializes. Relevant here are studies reporting "resistive" (Rutter 1979; Werner 1986) or "invulnerable" children (Werner & Smith 1982; Garmezy & Nuechterlein 1972) who, although raised by problem parents, do not, as youth or young adults, succumb to the particular problem behavior shown by a parent or even to some other type of maladjustment (Garmezy & Rutter 1983).

Single-track attempts to designate risk values for children, based primarily on whether such children later show addictive behaviors corresponding to those of their parents, fail to assign proper weight to a much more complex, but far more potent, variable: namely, the general climate of the child rearing environment. Herein the personal strengths and limitations of parents (influenced in part by their own childhood experiences), their continuing presence in the home, the extent of their involvement with potentially addictive substances and activities, the nature of interactions between them, together exert tremendous potential influence for good or ill throughout the formative years of children raised in that home (Zucker & Linsansky 1986).

An example of the influence of the general child rearing environment on children's functioning may be drawn from a recent report comparing the lifestyles of two groups of ninth- to twelfth-graders (N=844) from four Southern California high schools. The report was titled, "Adolescents apparently invulnerable to drug, alcohol, and nicotine use" (Marston, Jacobs, Singer et al. in press). Based on anonymous responses to an extensive Health Survey, these investigators identified a cohort of students (N=77) who claimed they had never used tobacco, alcohol, or any one of a listing of illicit and prescription psychoactive drugs. Responses given by these "pristine youth" to items in the Health Survey were then compared with those of their classmates (N=767) who had admitted using one or more of these products. Out of 150 T-tests, the nonusers were found to be significantly different ($p. < .05$) from users on twenty-four comparisons—over three times the number that would be expected by chance. Some of the items that differentiated these two groups included self-reports of better general health, sleep quality, and state of mind, less extreme emotional states, higher ratings of happiness during childhood and adolescence, better overall quality of life, better social relations with people in general and with the person closest to them, and better school performance.

Of special relevance to the topic covered in this chapter was the finding that children who were users described a significantly greater array of parental problems than did those who were nonusers. These problems, attributed by these students to one or both parents, were described as excessive use or involvement with each of the following substances or activities: alcohol, uppers, downers, other drugs, overeating, and "compulsive gambling." The vital importance of this finding as it relates to the lifestyles of children of problem gamblers will be elaborated in a later section of this chapter.

The first national scientifically controlled study of the prevalence and problems attending gambling among U.S. youth under eighteen years of age has yet to be designed and implemented. When that happens, the study protocol undoubtedly will include an inquiry such as, "Did either (or both) of your parents ever have a gambling problem?" Meanwhile, we need not wait for completion of that great future project to ponder some preliminary answers to this question that a set of more modest recent studies have provided.

Since the mid-1980s, five independent studies on gambling among fairly large samples of high school age students in the United States have been completed. Results of a cross comparison of the major findings from each of these studies were reviewed earlier in this chapter. Although the wording of the question varied somewhat from study to study, each investigator asked his or her respective respondents whether either or both of their parents had a gambling problem. As seen in table 14–3, the results of these separate investigations revealed a remarkable degree of consistency in the percent of affirmative answers obtained from students residing in different parts of the country during comparable time periods. For instance, in the two surveys completed in 1984 and 1985, 5 percent of high school students in New Jersey reported one or both of their parents "gambled too much," while 6 percent of the high school students in California described their parent(s) as having a "problem with compulsive gambling." Two more studies were completed in 1987. Both of these used the same Health Survey questionnaire developed for Jacobs' 1984-1985 survey of high school students in California. In 1987 9 percent of the students from two of the four California high schools surveyed in 1985 described their parent(s) as having a "problem with compulsive gambling," while 7 percent of students from high schools in Virginia similarly described their parent(s). The only study known to have been completed in 1988 found that 13 percent of Connecticut high school students reported one or both of their parents "gamble too much" (table 14–3).

The similarity of independently acquired findings, obtained during given time periods from adolescents living in widely separated states, provides a measure of confidence in the stability and probable accuracy of the obtained results. The combined data from the five studies also indicate that since 1984 the proportions of children who described their parents as problem gamblers have progressively increased at what appears to be an exponential rate.

Short of a future national study, is there any way we can estimate the current prevalence of youth under eighteen years of age in the general population of the United States who are children of problem gamblers? There is a historical precedent for answering this very question. When seeking to formulate an early estimate of the number of children of alcoholics in America, The Children of Alcoholics Foundation, Inc. used a statistical method suggested by Booz-Allen & Hamilton (1974). This involved extrapolating findings from a national survey on problem drinking to the U.S. population and multiplying the resulting estimate of adult problem drinkers by the ratio of adults to children in the general population. This approach was premised on two assumptions: (1) that adult problem drinkers were randomly dispersed throughout the population, and (2) that the ratio between adult problem drinkers and children of problem drinkers was the same as the ratio of adults to children in the general population. Applying data from the 1979 National Drinking Practices Survey, which projected a 10 percent rate of adult problem drinkers (Clark & Midanik 1982) and from the 1980 Census (U.S. Department of Commerce 1983), it was estimated that there were approximately 6,600,000 children of problem drinkers under the age of eighteen years in the United States (Russell, Henderson & Blume 1985).

A similar method was applied to obtain an estimate of the numbers of adult children (18 years and older) of problem drinkers. Included in the Drinking Practices Survey was a question asking whether in the respondent's judgment his or her father, mother, sisters, or brothers had been alcoholics or problem drinkers at any time in their lives. Parental alcoholism/problem drinking was reported by 11 percent of the males and by 16 percent of the females. Applying these rates to the 1980 Census data yielded an estimate of approximately 22 million children of alcoholics, *age eighteen or older* (Midanik 1983). Midanik (1983) hastened to observe that reports of alcoholism/problem drinking in parents reflected the perceptions of the respondents only and were not validated by an independent measure. With this caveat acknowledged, Russell et al. (1985) proceeded to add the 22 million adults (aged eighteen and over) to the 6.6

million children under eighteen years of age, and arrived at an overall estimate of 28.6 million Americans who were children of problem drinkers. In 1980 this amounted to one out of every eight persons living in the United States! Russell et al. (1985) capitalized on these projections in what has proven to be a highly successful campaign to draw public interest and attract considerable government and private funding to reinforce their conclusion that, "It is, therefore, a matter of great interest and importance to our society to learn more about how parental alcoholism influences children" (p. 2). I believe precisely the same argument can be developed for marshalling interest in how parental gambling influences children.

Following the approach suggested by Booz-Allen & Hamilton (1974), I have projected what I believe represents the first, most reliable, but also the most conservative, estimate of the prevalence of youth in American under eighteen years of age who are children of problem gamblers. This computes to be approximately 2.5 million children. This estimate was developed by multiplying the 7 million adult problem gamblers in American (derived from my projection of Volberg & Steadman's data estimating that 4.1 percent of the adult population are problem gamblers) times the ratio of adults to children under eighteen years of age reported by the 1985 U.S. Census that is, 174,561,000 over 62,475,000).

An alternate, but less defensible, basis for estimating the prevalence of U.S. youth under eighteen years of age who are children of problem gamblers is provided in table 14–3 by data from Lesieur & Klein's (1987) and Jacobs' et al. (1985) independent surveys of high school students in New Jersey and California. Table 14–3 shows that 5.5 percent of this combined sample of high school students reported that one or both parents were problem gamblers. According to U.S. Census reports, in 1985 there were over 31,112,000 family households, including over 62,475,000 children under eighteen years of age (Statistical Abstract of the United States 1987). The average number of children under eighteen years per household was 2.01. (A married couple was present in 78 percent of these family households, a sole female householder in 19 percent, and a sole male householder in 3 percent). To the extent that the sample of high school students noted above came from homes representative of the 31 million plus households in America in 1985, one can hazard a projection of approximately 3.4 million youth under eighteen years of age who were children of problem gamblers in 1985.

This estimate is presented with several accompanying caveats. The first, of course, is that I can offer no evidence that the youngsters surveyed were truly representative of high school students throughout the United States, much less that they came from households representative of those occupied by 62 million plus children at large who were under eighteen years of age in 1985. The second concern is that the reports of their parents having a gambling problem reflected only the perceptions of these students. These subjective reports were not verified by any independent source. (It is recalled that the authors of the National Drinking Practices Survey previously had recognized the same kind of limitation in data obtained from their respondents). However, a study by Stacey et al. (1985) does support the reliability of anonymous reports from samples of students who revealed sensitive information about their lives. The third major potential flaw is that, given the above and other unknown sources of possible error, the estimate may still be too conservative when applied to the current U.S. population of children under eighteen years of age who may be living with a parent who is a problem gambler. The reader's attention is again directed to table 14–3. Here it is seen that the proportion of high school students describing one or both parents as a problem gambler has increased by over 45 percent between surveys completed in 1985 and 1987. Moreover, the 1988 survey of high school students in Connecticut reveals more than a 60 percent increase over the 1987 figures. Clearly, flawed as they may be, what reports are available from these youngsters indicate a rapidly rising trend in the prevalence of problem gambling among their parents. How problem gambling among parents may affect their children is addressed in the section that follows.

To the best of my knowledge, nothing yet has been published about the kinds of vulnerabilities that children of problem gamblers may be heir to, or the risks of unfavorable outcomes they may later encounter as adolescents and young adults. Because of this, we are doubly grateful to Russell et al. (1985) who have provided an extensive review of the literature spanning the past forty years that deals with problems encountered by children of alcoholics. Results of these studies serve to alert us about what may be expected when the parental problem is excessive gambling.

Many reports, dating back to Rowe's pioneering study in 1945, emphasize the importance of the family constellation in the later adjustment of children. These writings reinforce my position that, when one or both parents are involved in some form of excessive behavior, the home setting is so upset that children are more likely to develop poor interpersonal relations and themselves become higher risks for acquiring one or another health threatening behavior. (Also see Adler & Raphael 1983). Moreover, children raised in such settings may demonstrate a greatly inflated divorce rate as adults (Goodwin et al. 1973) and also reveal themselves in turn to be poor parents, thereby contributing to a progressive intergenerational cycle of dysfunctional behavior (Hall et al. 1983a, 1983b; Jacob et al. 1978).

The impact of parental excessive behaviors on children in the home has been poignantly described in literature distributed by the Children of

Alcoholics Foundation, Inc. (1985). These handouts contain the following sets of statements:

How do children of alcoholics feel?

—Guilty and responsible for parental drinking
—Invisible and unloved since the household revolves totally around the alcoholic parent
—Insecure because of inconsistencies in parental behavior, attitudes, and rules
—Fearful that the alcoholic parent will become ill, have an accident, or die
—Embarrassed by the public behavior of alcoholic parents
—Ashamed because of the stigma society attaches to alcoholism and the need to keep it a family secret
—Frightened by family violence and abuse

How do children of alcoholics react?

As youngsters, the children of alcoholic parents:
—May do poorly in school
—Have few friends
—Are frequently truant or delinquent
—May use alcohol or other drugs

What happens to adult children of alcoholics?

Some children of alcoholics are superstars, highly successful in adolescence, but develop serious problems later on. As adults, children of alcoholics may be alcoholic, suicidal, physically or mentally ill, or rigidly controlled overachievers who become depressed in midlife (Russell et al. 1985).

It is obvious that parental excesses do not occur in a vacuum. For instance, in addition to experiencing the stressor of parental alcoholism, children were found to be more likely to have experienced a variety of other family problems, ranging from economic, to parental arrests and incarceration, to a high incidence of separation and divorce (Miller & Jang 1977). In addition, children of alcoholics were significantly less likely to graduate from high school, more likely to receive counseling in school for psychological or discipline problems, and were more than three times as likely to have been expelled from school than children of nonalcoholic parents (Miller & Jang 1977). Rutter (1979) emphasizes that a combination of several stressors within a family may potentiate each other, resulting in more risk of impairment than would be expected from the simple summation of the effects of separate stressors.

West & Prinz (1987) in their extensive review point out that most of those studies failed to assess family stressors other than parental alcoholism, which may have accounted for some of the variants in children's health status. They note that consistent reports from ten of eleven investigations showed a positive association between parental alcoholism and impaired emotional functioning of offspring. When comparing school-age children from homes of alcoholics and those from normal families, Moos & Billings (1982) found more than twice the rate of emotional disturbances in alcoholic families where anxiety and depression was particularly evident among the children. Similar findings of emotional distress, including significantly lower self-esteem and more extreme mood states, were found by Hughes (1977) when comparing children from alcoholic homes with children from nonalcoholic families.

While consistent in their findings, all those studies may be flawed by uncorroborated self-report measures and less-than-objective or consistent descriptions of the nature and extent of parent alcoholism and child adjustment. Nonetheless, the sheer volume and consistency of their findings are undeniable. West & Prinz (1987) conclude their extensive review by stating, "Findings taken as a whole support the contention that parental alcoholism is associated with a heightened incidence or child symptomology" (p. 214). However, they hasten to point out that "neither all nor a major portion of the population of children of alcoholic homes are inevitably doomed to psychological disorder" (p. 214). This again highlights the matter of so-called "invulnerable" or "resilient" children that had been discussed earlier in this section.

It is idle to speculate whether parental alcoholism alone produces a higher incidence of childhood drinking and/or childhood symptomatology. A more logical approach supported by the literature is that the presence of an alcoholic parent severely disrupts family interaction and equilibrium. This in turn may lead in ways not fully understood to the child, adolescent, or young adult raised in that home to be placed at greater risk for developing some form of psychopathology or maladaptive behaviors (including alcoholism). This paradigm for parental problems and increased child vulnerability and risk has been well established in the field of alcohol studies. Let us now replace the former principal actor in the paradigm with a parent who is a problem gambler.

What do we know about children raised in homes where a parent was a problem gambler? As noted earlier, no literature has yet focused on this topic. Nonetheless, from what we have come to realize from clinical histories describing the home life of problem gamblers, there is ample reason to expect that each of the experiences attributed to children of alcoholic parents also, and in very similar ways, affect the lives of children raised by parents who are problem gamblers.

The family life of the problem gambler often is complicated by financial crises associated with the gambler's attempts to funnel more and more dollars into an increasingly costly activity (Lesieur 1979; Lesieur 1984;

Custer & Milt 1985). Typically, excessive parental gambling exposes children to frequent parental arguments, a pattern of lies and deception, a repeated victimizing of spouse and children by the gambler, and all this often accompanied by a disruptive series of separations and reconciliations and threats of divorce (Wanda G. 1971; Lorenz & Shuttlesworth 1983; Lesieur 1984; Heineman 1987; Lesieur & Heineman 1988; Lorenz & Yaffee 1988). Children of problem gamblers are portrayed as being caught up in a seesaw relationship with the affected parent(s), who at one time lavishes them with gifts and attention and at other times ignores them (also see Nardi 1981). The children are said to respond by feeling hurt, angry, confused, guilty, and rejected. To complicate family matters even further, Ramirez et al. (1984) and Jacobs (1984) report that many problem gamblers tend to indulge excessively in alcohol, food, and/or drugs. All these reports have been gleaned from problem gamblers or their spouses. To date only one study has explored the effect of living with a gambling parent from the perspective of the affected child (Jacobs 1986). Results of that study are summarized next.

The Plight of Children of Problem Gamblers

Background

A substantial but narrowly targeted literature has accumulated in recent years describing the kinds of health and behavior problems that threaten children of alcoholic parents. No systematic information, however, has been gathered on the vulnerability and risks of youth who describe their parent as a compulsive or problem gambler. This study is the first to be completed on a self-identified, but anonymous, group of adolescents in a high school setting who described themselves as children of problem gamblers.

An anonymous thirty-seven-item Health Survey was administered to 844 randomly selected ninth- to twelfth-grade students in four Southern California public high schools. Systematic information was gathered about their general health, quality of life, school and work adjustment, involvement with a range of potentially addictive substances and activities, and indications of psychosocial maladjustment, including difficulties with the law and suicide attempts (Jacobs 1986a).

Of the 844 students, 45 percent (N = 384) reported they believed that one or both of their parents exhibited one or more of the following problems: 26 percent of the students (N = 218) characterized their parent(s) as "overeaters;" 23 percent (N = 196) described one or both as having a problem with "alcoholism;" 18 percent (N = 148) said one or both engaged in "excessive drug use;" and 6 percent (N=52) described one or both parents as having a problem with "compulsive gambling." It is immediately apparent that a considerable overlap exists among this listing of parental problems.

In this study parents who were described by their offspring as having a problem with compulsive gambling also were described as having a number of companion problems. Contrasted below in table 14–6 is the relative incidence of each of these parental problems as reported by children of problem gamblers and by the control group who denied that their parent(s) had a gambling problem.

Obviously, a substantial number of these problem gamblers also showed evidence to their children that they had additional problems. These, undoubtedly, further raised the stress levels within the family constellation. The incidence of these companion problems among problem gamblers ranged between one-and-a-half and four times those reported for parents without a gambling problem. These reports by children of problem gamblers that describe multiple involvements of their parents with other potentially addictive substances and activities are highly consistent with clinical reports of comorbidities obtained directly from pathological gamblers in treatment settings (Ramirez et al. 1983).

The specific nature and relative extent of the negative effects reported by adolescents who described one or both parents as having a "compulsive gambling" problem (that is, being a "problem gambler") is presented next.

Method

Self-rating of students who characterized one or both of their parents as "problem gamblers" (N=52) were compared with those of their classmates who had reported no gambling problem among their parents (N=792). Henceforth, this control group will be referred to as children with "average parents."

Findings have been grouped into three major areas:

Table 14–6
Parental Problems

	Compulsive Gambling	Alcoholism	Excessive Drug Use			Overeating
			Uppers	Downers	Others	
Children of problem gamblers (N=52)	100%	54%	19%	12%	17%	40%
Children of parents without a gambling problem (N=792)	0%	21%	5%	4%	6%	25%

1. *Comparative levels and reported effects of involvement with health-threatening behaviors* (that is, smoking, drinking, drug use, overeating, and gambling).

2. *Comparative incidence of psychosocial risk indicators* (that is, loss of a parent from the home before age fifteen, unhappy childhood, unhappy teens, perceives self as "fat," legal action pending, overall quality of youth rated as "poor").

3. *Comparative incidence of dysphoria, performance problems and suicidal risk* (that is, more insecure than peers, greater need for success than peers, poorer mental state than peers, school and job adjustment, emotional state "down," suicide attempts).

Results

Levels of Involvement with Health-Threatening Behaviors. Without exception, children of parents described as "problem gamblers" showed higher levels of use for tobacco, alcohol, and drug products during the previous twelve months than did their classroom peers with "average parents." Comparative percentages for cigarette use were 37 to 23 percent; snuff and chewing tobacco, including "dipping"(15 to 10 percent). Overall, children of gambler parents showed a greater preference for stimulant-type drugs than did their peers. "Moderate to heavy" cocaine use showed comparative percentages of 10 to 5 percent, while moderate to heavy use of other drugs classed as "uppers" showed a 25 to 11 percent difference in use patterns. Children of problem gamblers also showed greater use of prescription antidepressants (5 to 2 percent). Use of marijuana was the same (18 to 18 percent). "Moderate to heavy" use of alcohol was disturbingly high for both groups, but slightly more for those with gambler parents (40 to 37 percent). Use of "downer" drugs was also greater for those who described their parent(s) as a problem gambler (4 to 1 percent), as was their use of "other" drugs (8 to 6 percent).

Compared to their peers, a greater proportion of children with gambler parents showed more "moderate to heavy" levels of involvement with overeating (35 to 17 percent). Children with gambler parents also were involved in more "moderate to heavy" gambling (8 to 4 percent). In addition, more children with gambler parents reported having "ever gambled" (85 to 72 percent). Most striking was the finding that 75 percent of those whose parents were problem gamblers reported an age of onset for gambling before eleven years of age, compared to 34 percent of their classmates with average parents. Although differences between the two groups were not as dramatic, children of problem gamblers also showed earlier average age of onset for gorging food, use of upper and downer drugs, and smoking cigarettes. Children of average parents showed a slightly earlier age of onset for alcohol use.

Children of problem gamblers showed what may be inferred to be a greater drive state to escape reality and a greater propensity for seeking mood-elevating substances and stimulating experiences than did their peers with average parents. This possibility has important theoretical, as well as clinical, implications (see Jacobs' chapter in this volume titled "A General Theory of Addictions . . ."). Support for this position is suggested by the manner in which the two groups recalled their first experiences with a variety of potentially addictive substances and activities. Most striking was the consistently greater proportion of children of problem gamblers who remembered "with great clarity and completeness, like it was yesterday" their first experiences with alcohol (25 to 19 percent), cocaine (15 to 9 percent), marijuana (19 to 18 percent), overeating (27 to 7 percent), and gambling (13 to 5 percent). This level of vivid recollection was associated much less frequently with their first use of other substances, where it was essentially of the same order as reported by their peers.

When asked to check off their primary goal when indulging in each of a list of potentially addictive substances and activities, all these high school students were very much alike in ranking either "stimulation" or "relaxation" as their primary objective. However, an alternative choice was a set of items related to "escape:" escape from "emotional tension," from "an unhappy home," or from "a humdrum life." Children of problem gamblers selected this set of items as their primary goal for indulging 20 percent more often than did their peers with average parents.

Studies (Jacobs et al. 1985); Jacobs 1988a; Kuley & Jacobs 1988) have shown conclusively that dissociative-like reactions while indulging are pathognomic among addicts of various types. These reactions take one or more of the following forms: feeling "like you've been in a trance," feeling "like you are a different person," an out-of-body experience of feeling like you are "outside yourself—watching yourself behave," and a "memory blackout" for periods when you had been indulging. When compared to their classmates with average parents, children of problem gamblers reported these experiences 17 percent more often when drinking and when taking drugs, 49 percent more often when overeating, and 18 percent more often when gambling. The consistently higher frequencies of these unusual dissociative-like reactions are a somber indication that children of problem gamblers not only indulge more frequently and more heavily in potentially addictive substances and activities, but also that they appear to be at much greater risk for developing a frank addictive pattern of behavior.

Incidence of Psychosocial Risk Indicators. Across the entire range of these factors, children of problem gamblers appeared to be at much greater risk than their classmates.

Children with gambler parents experienced almost twice the incidence of broken homes caused by separation, divorce, or the death of a parent before they had reached the age of fifteen (37 to 20 percent). While the number reporting "unhappy" early childhood years was somewhat less than their peers (8 to 11 percent), children of gambler parents reported a much higher incidence of unhappy teen years (25 to 14 percent). Possibly contributing to the latter findings was the somewhat higher proportion of the gambler parent group who perceived themselves as "fat" (23 to 18 percent). Children of problem gamblers listed their "most typical reaction to rejection by important adults in your life" to be "pretend I didn't care" (34 to 24 percent), in marked contrast to their peers with average parents, whose most prevalent response was "try to do things that would please them" (34 to 29 percent). Twice the proportion of the gambler parent group had some kind of legal action pending (such as a court date, an outstanding summons, and so on) at the time of the survey (10 percent to 5 percent).

Perhaps the most telling of all this array of risk indicators is that almost half the children of gambler parents (42 percent) rated their overall quality of youth as "poorer than most" in sharp contrast to 27 percent of their classmates who had admitted to no problems of gambling among their parents. (From a broad societal perspective it is highly disconcerting that more than one out of every four high school age youth in this sample (N = 844) have such a negative perception of the overall quality of their adolescent years.)

Children of problem gamblers admitted being more preoccupied than their peers with a combination of "thinking" and "dreaming about" and "constantly resisting a strong impulse to" drink (31 to 24 percent), use drugs (37 to 24 percent), and to eat (46 to 23 percent). Preoccupation with gambling was much less frequent for both groups (6 to 6 percent).

Consistent with what may be inferred as their relatively greater levels of involvement with each of the above substances and activities, children of problem gamblers reported twice the number of initiatives to actually "join an organized program to help me avoid" one or more of these behaviors (2 to 1 percent). Children of problem gamblers also showed a consistently greater readiness than their classroom peers to "go for a month of in-hospital treatment," *if* they had a drinking problem (79 to 69 percent), a drug problem (81 to 71 percent), an overeating problem (67 to 59 percent), or a gambling problem (54 to 48 percent). For both groups of students this set of items may reflect a measure of insight into the possible consequences of their own excessive behaviors. One certainly would hope this is the case in view of the fact that more than two out of every ten high school students in this large sample (total N = 844) admit to being obsessively preoccupied with pursuing one or another potentially addictive means for escaping their present realities.

Incidence of Dysphoria and Suicide Risks. Without exception, children who described one or both parents as problem gamblers reported a greater incidence of factors reflecting anxiety and depressive mood. They consistently rated themselves as much more insecure than their peers (38 to 20 percent); feeling a greater need for success (25 to 20 percent); more often reported "poor mental state" (21 to 13 percent); and more stated that they felt emotionally "down" and "unhappy with life and myself" (25 to 11 percent). Consistent with the these indices of compromised mental health was the somewhat poorer levels of performance reported by children of gambler parents in their school (13 to 11 percent) and successful employment (21 to 27 percent) endeavors.

Dramatically underscoring the greater pervasiveness and seriousness of the combined family, health, and personal adjustment problems faced by children of parents described as problem gamblers is the finding that their level of acknowledged attempts to commit suicide is twice that of their classmates who attributed no problems with gambling to their parents (12 to 6 percent).

Discussion of Results

The results reflect a definite link between parental problem gamblers and elevated risks for dysfunctional behaviors among offspring raised in what may be termed "pathologenic families." In this study, such families may be characterized by the presence of one or both parents who are so unable to deal with their own problems that they have turned to gambling (among other potentially addictive behaviors) to "self-treat" their own chronic stress conditions. The finding that such marriages show a very high incidence of separation, divorce, and even death of a parent before the children are fifteen years of age, underscores the instability of this child rearing environment.

What is suggested by these results are intergenerational effects wrought by highly stressed, preoccupied, inconsistent, and often absent parents who have provided seriously flawed parenting, sex, social, and occupational role models for their children. The results of this study indicate that deficiencies in the home life of children who describe one or both parents as having a problem with "compulsive gambling" become evident among such youth by their greater involvement in a number of potentially addictive health-threatening behaviors, coupled with a consistent pattern of inadequate stress management and inferior coping skills. Similar findings regarding the association of parental alcoholism and childhood psychopathology have been reported by others (West & Prinz 1987; Nardi 1981; Capuzzi & LeCoq 1983; Lund & Landesman-Dwyer 1979; Moos & Billings 1982; Tharinger & Koranek 1988; Adler & Raphael 1983).

One cannot resist the conclusion that without early and competent intervention, children of problem gamblers a) will be seriously disadvantaged when attempting to solve their present and future problems of living, and b) as a consequence are, themselves, high-risk candidates for developing one or another form of dysfunctional behavior, including an addictive pattern of behavior.

Conclusions

Family instability appears to have its greatest effect on the more vulnerable child and junior high school student (Anhalt & Klein 1976). In their longitudinal studies of adolescents and young adults Kandel (1973) and Yamaguchi and Kandel (1984) project five sequential stages of initiation and use of substances. They identify parental modeling as the primary influence on early beer and wine (Stage 1) and cigarettes or hard liquor (Stage 2) involvements of young adolescents. Peer usage is identified as the primary influence during somewhat later Stage 3 activities, when marijuana use predominates. In mid to late adolescence, where other illicit drugs tend to be initiated, poor family relationships are listed as the primary influence (Stage 4). Stage 5, involving prescribed psychoactive drugs, applies predominantly to young adults with no primary family or peer influence noted. Studies of high school age youth by Jacobs et al. (1985a, unpublished) showed that, developmentally, the age of gambling onset typically occurred somewhere between use of cigarettes and hard liquor and initiation of marijuana. This would lead us to suggest (when extrapolating from Kandel's data) that the primary correlates of early gambling among youth are parental modeling, compounded by poor family relationships between parents and children. These influences interact to produce dysphoria and efforts to escape through activities that are mood-elevating and distracting from the unhappy family situation. The studies of drug abuse in junior high school populations by Anhalt & Klein (1976) tend to support this general thesis. These workers also conclude that the major influence on drug abuse is family instability. Repeated findings of the close association of family dysfunction and increased involvement of children from such homes in health-threatening activities have given rise to the notion of "self-medication" (Jacobs 1986b; Blum 1987) as a mechanism for dealing with stress among dysfunctional youth.

Longitudinal studies by Kandel (1975) and Kandel et al. (1984) have shown that use of most drugs such as alcohol, cigarettes, marijuana, psychedelics, and cocaine peak between sixteen and eighteen years of age, with highest incidence of use between eighteen and twenty-two years of age, after which there is marked diminution of use. Blum (1987) suggests that the temporal process of "buying into" drug use during early to late adolescence is part of the developmental task of growing up. His position is that those who demonstrate high levels of alcohol or drug use during adolescence are not necessarily going to demonstrate the same behaviors as adults. Blum and others (Donovan et al. 1983) propose a high likelihood for a "maturing out" process during the mid-twenties. Consequently, Blum (1987), like others, (Offer et al. 1981) has cautioned that professionals run the risk of overdiagnosing psychopathology "even among a random sample of functionally normal teenagers" (p. 527). A point well taken. However, at the present time there is no evidence, pro or con, to demonstrate that teenage gambling behaviors might follow the same "maturing out" sequence observed for drug use. Kallick et al. (1976) observes that, among adults, participation in gambling peaks in the age range of eighteen to twenty-four years, and then declines. They also note that increased exposure and accessibility to gambling and to varied forms of gambling produces new gamblers. They conclude:

"Gambling is a young person's pursuit . . . making it probable that subsequent generations which are exposed to gambling early and start early may not have a rate of decline as steep as we observe now." (p. 7)

The limited evidence in the field of adolescent gambling would lead me to challenge any *a priori* expectation that juvenile gamblers who already show serious gambling-related problems (table 14–4) will somehow "mature out" of it. This question must await results from a series of longitudinal research studies for a definitive answer.

Meanwhile, as clinicians, we cannot wait and see; we must treat youthful gamblers when and where they present themselves. For example, Lesieur & Heineman (1988) reported a 13 percent prevalence rate for pathological gambling among one hundred thirteen- to thirty-year-old multiple substance abusers who had been patients in a residential treatment center. They found that among residents aged eighteen years or younger, 8 percent showed clear signs of pathological gambling on the South Oaks Gambling Screen. Ten percent of the total sample said one or both parents had a gambling problem, and 50 percent of the residents who said their parents had a gambling problem showed signs of pathological gambling themselves. They also found that the pathological gamblers within this sample (N = 13) were significantly more likely to mix alcohol and drugs with their gambling activities than the nonpathological gamblers. Pathological gamblers in this study tended to be somewhat older than nonpathological gamblers. Noted by Lesieur & Heineman, and found consistently across all studies of youth and adults, is the higher incidence of pathological gambling among males than females.

Reports of the prevalence of "compulsive/pathological gambling" among nonclinical samples of functionally normal high school students who also gamble are summarized in table 14–4. Even after discounting the tendency among indulging teenagers to exaggerate accounts of their involvement in what they perceive as socially disapproved activities, there is no denying that the behavioral signs of "compulsive/pathological" gambling a minority of these youth ascribe to themselves are most disturbing. Indeed, as seen in table 14–3, the prevalence of self-described indicators of "*probable* compulsive/pathological gambling" among all the high school samples (including both gamblers and nongamblers) is between 4 and 6 percent. This is more than three times that currently reported for the adult population in the United States! Two controlled studies have purported to establish the prevalence of "probable compulsive or pathological gamblers" among adults in the general U.S. population (Kallick et al. 1979; Volberg & Steadman 1988b). These prevalence rates for adults ranged from 0.77 percent (Kallick et al. 1979) to 1.4 percent (Volberg & Steadman 1988b).

According to prevalence rates I developed earlier in this chapter, the numbers of juvenile plus adult children of problem gamblers could be as many as one in every twenty-five Americans. To paraphrase Russell et al. (1985):

> It therefore must become a matter of great interest and importance to our society to learn more about how parental problem gambling influences children.

The collective reports of the prevalence of problem gamblers among juvenile and adult populations should send a clear message to all levels of American society that the serious consequences of excessive gambling must be recognized, and plans for remedial and preventive programs must be included in any future agendas addressing health, education, social, economic, and law enforcement issues.

Closing remarks

Some day we may have answers to how teenage gambling has continued so long without arousing the attention and concern of the general public.

It boggles the mind to understand how a phenomenon so pervasive, openly practiced, and patently illegal could continue during every week in virtually every state across the United States without drawing the attention of the media, much less the authorities. Even more confounding is the possibility that millions of legally underage high school students could be buying lottery tickets at stores in their own neighborhoods from hundreds of thousands of state-employed lottery vendors, placing bets at scores of state-licensed horse and dog tracks, playing at municipally registered bingo games and (to a lesser extent) wagering at casinos, commercial card parlors, Jai Alai games, and legal offtrack betting emporia, without being challenged ("carded"), and unceremoniously ejected.

The current projections that 4-6 percent of high school students across America could already be problem gamblers are very provocative (table 14–3). For the moment, results from the studies reviewed in this chapter stand as the only available estimates of the possible scope and nature of this problem. Critics may justifiably question the validity, even the temerity, of projections based on the five surveys of American high school students reviewed in this chapter. They may label the collective results as no more than "straws in the wind." This, too, may later prove to be so, as new information is assembled. Meanwhile, it is noteworthy that all the "straws" appear to be blowing in the same direction, and they bear essentially the same message: there is reason enough to acknowledge that gambling is well established among American high school age youth and that a minority of them already are in serious straits, and probably are at considerable risk of experiencing future mental, physical, and social dysfunctional consequences of the their gambling-related activities. Likely, these revelations will be met by a combination of fear and denial that typically constitutes the public response to alleged problems among youth. In the best case this will stimulate a series of research projects that will scientifically verify or disconfirm the proported prevalence rates of juvenile gambling in America, as well as the extent and nature of gambling-related problems among these youth. I hope the findings reported here will spur initiation of even more ambitious longitudinal studies aimed at identifying those sets of familial and environmental circumstances that presage risk or resistiveness among as many as 10 million adult and juvenile children of problem gamblers.

Over the past decade the social zeitgeist in America has changed radically because of to the greatly increased availability, promotion, and glamorization, not to mention the inflated payoffs, associated with commercial gambling. *Gaming and Wagering Business Magazine* (October 1988) notes that, "the twenty-seven U. S. lotteries operating in fiscal '88 grossed $14.8 billion, a 19.27 percent leap over the previous year. Net revenues accruing to state governments are estimated at $5.6 billion, up

14.7 percent over fiscal 1987" (p. 30). In November 1988, four more states entered the lottery business. Eadington (1988) reports that by the close of 1987, the casinos of Las Vegas and Atlantic City each generated annual gross winnings in excess of $2.5 billion per year. Total casino winnings in Nevada alone exceeded $3.5 billion. Comparable statistics from the revenues of race tracks and card parlors were not available at the time of this writing. I share Eadington's opinion that, ". . . the gaming industries in the United States have been relatively insensitive to the existence of problem or pathological gambling, choosing to ignore it rather than trying to deal with it in any constructive mitigating way. Unless and until this issue is adequately addressed by the commercial gambling industries or the appropriate regulatory bodies, commercial gambling will not be able to achieve a level of acceptance and legitimacy comparable to other industries. However, given the general direction of the evolution of commercial gambling in the United States and in many foreign jurisdictions, it is likely the industry itself, or the regulatory body governing it, will realize the enlightened self-interest involved in adequately dealing with this issue" (1988, p. vii).

After a decade of unbridled growth, it may well be time for American society to reexamine the long-range consequences of its love affair with legalized gambling. Public understanding of gambling problems is where our understanding of alcoholism was some forty or fifty years ago. Public education is the prime vehicle for generating widespread consciousness of the extent and potential negative consequences of juvenile gambling. It also may motivate involved youth to critically evaluate their own behavior. Greater awareness at governmental levels regarding the large numbers of underage youth who gamble and the potential harm associated with their gambling may lead to firmer enforcement of existing laws that set statutory age limits for gambling and, thereby, reduce the accessibility of this activity to those who are more vulnerable to its impact. The gambling industry itself may generate more vigorous and effective methods for discouraging play by underage youth.

Long past due are periodic, state-funded independent social impact studies to identify the extent to which new and changing forms of legalized gambling contribute to gambling rates and, particularly, to rates of problem gambling among potentially vulnerable groups such as juveniles, females, and minorities. The scientific literature consistently indicates that adolescents are most at risk for developing addictive patterns of behavior, including pathological gambling (Kallick et al. 1976; Nadler & Meeland 1982). The already high rates of tenuously controlled problem gambling behaviors among high school students reported in this chapter accentuate the need for early identification and enhanced educational, counseling, and preventive interventions for this high-risk group of young Americans.

There is no consensus on how, if at all, youngsters should be prepared for participation in a society where most adults gamble. Results from the ongoing scientific study of gambling in America (Volberg & Steadman 1988b) reveal that more than 80 percent of American adults have gambled at some time in their lives. Best estimates available for gambling by adolescents under eighteen years of age indicate that since 1987 more than 40 percent have gambled within the previous twelve months (table 14–2). The finding that 4 to 6 percent of the high school students reviewed in this chapter already show serious gambling-related problems must be made known when educating sixth- to twelfth-grade students, as well as their parents and teachers, to the possible problems that may attend excessive gambling. Materials carrying this message could be included with ongoing educational programs about tobacco, alcohol, and drug use, since all of these behaviors appear to be fellow travelers among adolescents. The data discussed in this chapter about the surprisingly early age of onset of gambling make it imperative that educational programs be introduced at or before entry into junior high school. Indeed, there is good justification for beginning early prevention efforts at the primary school level where preadolescents may be taught social skills of communication, stress management, and various coping skills and problem-solving strategies that will anticipate and put them in better stead to deal with the physical, psychological, and social stresses that characterize the adolescent years. Meanwhile, prompt availability of treatment must be organized for adolescents who already show serious problems related to their gambling behavior. This resource could rather easily and economically be integrated into existing adolescent drug, alcohol, and overeating programs already functioning in hospital and outpatient settings.

Lying somewhere between treatment and prevention is a special need for programs directed to that forgotten population who are the children of problem gamblers. Virtually nonexistent for them are support groups like those established for children of other addicts, such as Al-Ateen. Meeting this need would require revitalizing and rapidly expanding the nascent Gam-Ateen movement in America. Our enthusiasm to identify and assist these youth must be tempered by care that such efforts avoid violating child and parent rights to privacy, and not create self-fulfilling prophesies by polarizing the expectations of parents, teachers, and peers, and thereby stigmatize the child. The willingness of gambler parents to cooperate in family interventions is another problem inviting future attention. In all these considerations, fruitful methods can be borrowed and progress can be accelerated by drawing on the examples and expertise provided by those who have long been active in programs for children of alcoholics.

Since 1975, the University of Michigan Survey Research Center has been conducting a series of longitudinal "Monitoring the Future" studies of drug use among high school seniors (Johnston et al. 1980). Results of the 1986 survey indicate that the downward trend noted since 1980 in the use of all illicit drugs continues, except for cocaine, which remains a serious problem among high school youth. Reports from the U.S. Surgeon General indicate declining rates of cigarette smoking among high school youth. The cocaine problem is being attacked on an international front, and the use of alcohol by teenagers is also under fire. As a result of the AIDS epidemic, sex is seen to have its perils among experimenting adolescents. Soon people will wonder, "What's left that will provide recreation, relieve boredom and stress, and add excitement in people's lives?" I predict that the 1990s will mark the historic heyday of legalized gambling throughout the world. How we plan to meet this eventuality will determine the extent to which future generations of youth will be placed at risk.

References

Adler, R., & Raphael, B. 1983. Children of alcoholics. *Australian and New Zealand Journal of Psychiatry*, 17, 3–8.

American Psychiatric Association. 1980 . *Diagnostic and statistical manual: Third edition (DSM-III)*. Washington, D.C.: Author.

Anhalt, H., & Klein, M. 1976. Drug abuse in junior high school populations. *American Journal of Drug and Alcohol Abuse*, 3(4), 589–63.

Anson, R. S. 1981. Land of the big casino. *NEXT*, January, February.

Arcuri, A. F., Lester, D., & Franklin, O. Smith. 1985. *Adolescence*, Vol. XX (80), 935–938.

Bachman, J., O'Malley, P., & Johnston, L. 1984. Drug use among young adults: The impacts of role status and social environment. *Journal of Personality and Social Psychology*, 47, 629–654.

Berger, H. 1987. Personal communication.

Biddle, B., Bank, B., & Marlin, M. 1980. Social determinants of adolescent drinking.

Black, C. 1979. Children of alcoholics. *Alcohol, Health, and Research World*, 4, 23–27.

———. 1981. *It will never happen to me*. Denver, Colorado: M.A.C. Printing & Publications Division.

Blane, H. T., Hill, M. J., & Brown, E. 1968. Alienation, self-esteem, and attitudes toward drinking in high school students. *Quarterly Journal of Studies on Alcohol*, 29.

Blum, R. 1987. Adolescent substance abuse: Diagnostic and treatment issues. *Pediatric Clinics of North America*, 34, 2, 523–537.

Booz-Allen & Hamilton, Inc. 1974. *An assessment of the needs of and resources for children of alcoholic parents*. Prepared for the National Institute of Alcohol Abuse and Alcoholism. Springfield, Virginia: National Technical Information Service.

Capuzzi, D., & LeCoq, L. 1983. Social and personal determinants of adolescent use and abuse of alcohol and marijuana. *The Personnel and Guidance Journal*, December, 199–205.

Ciarrocchi, J. 1987. Severity of impairment in dually addicted gamblers. *Journal of Gambling Behavior*, 3, 16–26.

Clark, W., & Midanik, L. 1982. Alcohol use and alcohol problems among U. S. adults: Results of the 1979 National Survey. In *U. S. Department of Health and Human Services Alcohol and Health Monograph No. 1: Alcohol Consumption and Related Problems*, 3–52.

Commission on the review of the national policy toward gambling. 1976. *Gambling in America*. Washington, D.C.: U.S. Government Printing Office.

Cooperative Commission on the Study of Alcoholism. 1967. *Alcohol Problems: A Report to the Nation*. Prepared by Thomas F. A. Plaut, Oxford University Press, New York.

Culleton, R. 1985a. *A survey of pathological gambling in the state of Ohio*. Philadelphia: Transition Planning Associates.

———. 1985b. *The prevalence rate of pathological gambling in the Delaware Valley in 1984*. Camden, New Jersey: Forum for Policy Research and Public Service, Rutgers University.

Custer, R. 1982. An overview of compulsive gambling. In P.A. Carone, S. F. Yoles, S. N. Kieffer, & L. Krinsky (eds.) *Addictive Disorders Update: Alcoholism, Drug Abuse, Gambling*, 107–124. New York: Human Sciences Press.

Custer, R., & Milt, H. C. 1985. *When Luck Runs Out*. New York: Facts on File Publications.

Donovan, J., Jessor, R., & Jessor, L. 1983. Problem drinking in adolescence and young adulthood: A followup study. *Journal of Studies on Alcohol* 44, 109–137.

Eadington, W. R. 1988. Preface. In William R. Eadington (ed.) *Gambling Research: Proceedings of the Seventh International Conference on Gambling and Risk Taking*. Reno, Nevada: University of Nevada-Reno.

El-Guebaly, N., & Offord, D. 1977. The offspring of alcoholics: A critical review. *American Journal of Psychiatry*, 134, 357–365.

———. 1979. On being the offspring of an alcoholic: An update. *Alcoholism: Clinical and Experimental Research*, 3, 148–157.

Frank, M. L. 1988. Casino gambling and college students: Three sequential years of data. Presented at the Third National Conference on Gambling Behavior, May 19–20, New York City, New York.

Gaming and Wagering Business Magazine. 1988. Personal Communication.

Garmezy, N. 1983. Stressors of childhood. In N. Garmezy & M. Rutter (eds.) *Stress, coping and development in children*, 43–84. New York: McGraw-Hill.

Garmezy, N., & Nuechterlein, K. 1972. Invulnerable children: The fact and fiction of competence and disadvantage. *American Journal of Orthopsychiatry*, 42, 328–329.

Garmezy, N., & Rutter, M. 1983. (eds.) *Stress, Coping and Development in Children*. New York: McGraw-Hill.

Garmezy, N., Masten, A., & Tellegen, A. 1984. The study of stress and competence in children: A building block for developmental psychopathology. *Child Development*, 55, 97–111.

Glen, A., Custer, R. L., & Burns, R. 1976. *The inpatient treatment of gambling.* Paper presented at the 84th Annual Convention of the American Psychological Association, Washington, D.C.

Goodwin, D. W., Schulsinger, F., Hermansen, L., Guze, S. B., & Winokur, G. 1973. Alcohol problems in adoptees raised apart from alcoholic biological parents. *Archives of General Psychiatry*, 28, 238–243.

Gorsuch, R. L., & Butler, M. 1976. Initial drug abuse: A review of predisposing social and psychological factors. *Psychological Bulletin*, 33, 120–137.

Hall, R., Hesselbrock, V., & Stabenau, J. 1983a. Familial distribution of alcohol use: I. Assortative mating in the parents of alcoholics. *Behavior Genetics*, 13, 361–373.

———. 1983b. Familial distribution of alcohol use: II. Assortative mating of alcoholic probands. *Behavior Genetics*, 13, 373–382.

Heineman, M. 1987. A comparison: The treatment of wives of alcoholics with the treatment of wives of pathological gamblers. *Journal of Gambling Behavior*, 3, 27–40.

Hughes, J. 1977. Adolescent children of alcoholic parents and the relationship of Alateen to these children. *Journal of Consulting and Clinical Psychology*, 45, 946–947.

Ide-Smith, S. G., & Lea, S. E. G. 1988. Gambling in young adolescents. *Journal of Gambling Behavior*, 4(2), 110–118.

Jacob, T. 1978. Family interaction in disturbed and normal families: A methodological and substantive review. *Psychological Bulletin*, 82, 33–65.

Jacob, T., Favorini, A., Meisel, S., & Anderson, C. 1978. The alcoholic's spouse, children and family interactions. *Journal of Studies on Alcohol*, 39, 1231–1251.

Jacob, T., & Leonard, K. 1986. Psychosocial functioning in children of alcoholic fathers, depressed fathers, and control fathers. *Journal of Studies on Alcohol*, 47, 373–380.

Jacobs, D. 1982. The Addictive Personality Syndrome (APS): A new theoretical model for understanding and treating addictions. In W. R. Eadington (ed.) *The Gambling Papers Vol. II: Pathological gambling, theory and practice.* Reno, Nevada: University of Nevada.

———. 1984. Factors alleged as predisposing to compulsive gambling. *In Sharing Recovery through Gamblers Anonymous.* Los Angeles: Gamblers Anonymous Publishing Company.

———. 1986a. *Early identification and prevention of health-threatening behaviors in adolescents.* Paper presented at the twenty-first International Congress of Applied Psychology, Jerusalem, Israel.

———. 1986b. Application of a general theory of addictions to treatment and rehabilitation planning for pathological gamblers. In T. Galski (ed.) *Handbook of Pathological Gambling.* Detroit, Michigan: Thomas Press.

———. 1986. *High risk youth: Children of Compulsive Gamblers.* Invited address presented at the Western Conclave of GA/Gam-Anon. Palm Springs, California.

———. 1987. *Effects on children of parental excesses in gambling.* Paper presented at the Seventh International Conference on Gambling and Risk Taking, Reno, Nevada.

———. 1988a. Behavioral aspects of gambling: Evidence for a common dissociative reaction among addicts. *Journal of Gambling Behavior*, 4(1), 27–37.

———. 1988. Planning for a uniform epidemiological survey of problem gambling on four continents. In William R. Eadington (ed.) *Gambling research: Proceedings of the Seventh International Conference on Gambling and Risk Taking*. Reno, Nevada: University of Nevada.

———. 1988b. *Gambling behaviors of high school students: Implications for government-supported gambling*. National Policy Symposium on Lotteries and Gambling. Vancouver, British Columbia.

Jacobs D. & Kuley N. 1987. Unpublished research report. Jerry L. Pettis Memorial Veterans Hospital, Loma Linda, CA.

Jacobs, D., & Wright, E. 1980. *A program of research on the causes and treatment of addictive disorders: Using the compulsive gambler as the prototype subject*. Unpublished research proposal. Jerry L. Pettis Memorial Veterans Hospital, Loma Linda, California.

Jacobs, D., Marston, A., & Singer, R. 1985. Testing a general theory of addiction: Similarities and differences among alcoholics, pathological gamblers, and overeaters. In J. J. Sanchez-Soza (ed.) *Health and Clinical Psychology* (Vol. 4). Netherlands: Elsevier Science.

Jacobs, D., Marston, A., Singer, R., Widaman, K., & Little T. 1985c. Unpublished research study. Jerry L. Pettis Memorial Veterans Hospital, Loma Linda, California.

Jessor, R., & Jessor, S. 1978. *Theory testing in longitudinal research on drug use: Empiral findings and methodological issues*. Washington, D.C.: Hemisphere-Wiley.

———. 1975. Adolescent development and the onset of drinking. *Journal of Studies on Alcohol*, 36(1):27–51.

Johnston, L., Bachman, J., & O'Malley, P. 1979. *1979 Highlights: Drugs and the nation's high school students—five year national trends*. National Institute of Drug Abuse, Rockville, Maryland.

———. 1980. *Monitoring the future: Questionnaired responses from the National High School Seniors, 1979*. Ann Arbor, Michigan: Survey Research Center, University of Michigan.

———. 1982. *Student drug use, attitudes, and beliefs: National trends, 1975–1982*. National Institute on Drug Abuse, Rockville, Maryland.

Kallick, M., Suits, D., Dielman, T., & Hybels, J. 1976. *Survey of American gambling attitudes and behavior, Appendix 2*. Washington, D.C.: U. S. Government Printing Office.

———. 1979. *A survey of gambling attitudes and behavior*. Survey Research Center, Institute for Social Research. The University of Michigan.

Kandel, D. 1973. Adolescent marijuana use: Role of parents and peers. *Science*, 181, 1067–1070.

———. 1980. Stages in adolescent involvement in drug use. *Science*, 190:912–914.

Kandel D. & Logan J. 1984. Patterns of drug use from adolescence to young adulthood: I. Periods of risk for initiation, continued use, and discontinuation. *American Journal of Public Health*, 74(7): 660–667.

Kandel, D., Kessler, R., & Margulies, R. 1978 Antecedents of adolescent initiation into stages of drug use: A developmental analysis. In D. B. Kandel (ed.) *Longitudinal research on drug use: Empirical findings and methodological issues.* Washington, D.C.: Hemisphere.

Kandel, D., & Yamaguchi, K. 1985. *Developmental patterns of the use of legal, illegal, and medically prescribed psychotropic drugs from adolescence to young adulthood.* (Research Monograph 56). Washington, D.C.: U. S. Government Printing Office.

Kaplan. H. 1977. Antecedents of deviant responses: Predicting from a general theory of deviant behavior. *Journal of Youth and Adolescence,* 7, 253–277.

Kuley, N., & Jacobs, D. 1988. The relationship between dissociative-like experiences and sensation seeking among social and problem gamblers. *Journal of Gambling Behavior,* Vol. 4(3).

Ladouceur, R., & Mireault, C. 1988. Gambling behaviors among high school students in the Quebec area. *Journal of Gambling Behavior,* 4(1), 3–11.

Lesieur, H. 1979. The compulsive gambler's spiral of options and involvement. *Psychiatry,* 42, 79–87.

———. 1984. *The Chase: Career of the Compulsive Gambler.* Cambridge, Massachusetts: Schenkman Publishing Company.

———. 1985. Screening and treatment of the dually addicted patient. *National Council on Compulsive Gambling Newsletter,* 1,:1, 3.

Lesieur, H., Blume, S., & Zoppa, R. 1986. Alcoholism, drug abuse, and gambling. *Alcoholism: Clinical and Experimental Research,* 10, 33–38.

Lesieur, H. 1988. The female pathological gambler. In William R. Eadington (ed.) *Gambling Research: Proceedings of the Seventh International Conference on Gambling and Risk Taking.* Reno, Nevada: University of Nevada-Reno, p. 230–258.

Lesieur, H., & Blume, S. 1987. The South Oaks Gambling Screen (SOGS): A new instrument for the identification of pathological gamblers. *American Journal of Psychiatry,* 144, 1184–1188.

Lesieur, H., & Heineman, M. 1988. Pathological gambling among youthful multiple substance abusers in a therapeutic community. In William R. Eadington (ed.) *Gambling Research: Proceedings of the Seventh International Conference on Gambling and Risk Taking.* Reno, Nevada: University of Nevada-Reno, 259–275.

Lesieur, H., & Klein, R. 1987. Pathological gambling among high school students. *Addictive Behaviors,* 12, 129–135.

Lorenz, V. C. 1987. Family dynamics of pathological gamblers. In Thomas Galski (ed.) *The Handbook of Pathological Gambling.* Springfield, Illinois: Thomas.

Lorenz, V. C., & Shuttlesworth, D. E. 1983. The impact of pathological gambling on the spouse of the gambler. *Journal of Community Psychology,* 11, 67–76.

Lorenz, V. C., & Yaffee, R. A. 1988. Compulsive gamblers and their spouses: A profile of interaction. In William R. Eadington (ed.) *Gambling Research: Proceedings of the Seventh International Conference on Gambling and Risk Taking.* Reno, Nevada: University of Nevada-Reno, p. 276–292.

———. 1988. Pathological gambling: Psychosomatic, emotional, and marital difficulties as reported by the spouse. *Journal of Gambling Behavior,* 4.

Lund, C., & Landesman-Dwyer, S. 1979. Pre-delinquent and disturbed adolescent: The role of parental alcoholism. *Currents in alcoholism*, 5, 339–348. New York: Grune & Stratton.

Marston, A., Jacobs, D., Singer, R., Widaman, K., & Little, T. In press. Adolescents apparently invulnerable to drug, alcohol, and nicotine use. *Adolescence*.

McCormick, R., Russo, A., Ramirez, L., & Taber, J. 1984. Affective disorders among pathological gamblers seeking treatment. *American Journal of Psychiatry*, 141, 215–218.

Midanik, L. 1983. Familial alcoholism and problem drinking in a national drinking practices survey. *Addictive Behaviors*, 8, 133–41.

Milgram, G. G. 1982. Youthful drinking: Past and present. *Journal of Drug Education*, 12 (4), 289–308. *Statistical Abstract of the United States*. 1987. U. S. Department of Commerce, Bureau of the Census, Washington, D.C.

Miller, D., & Jang, M. 1977. Children of alcoholics: A twenty-year longitudinal study. *Social Work Research and Abstracts*, 13, 23–29.

Moos, R., & Billings, A. 1982. Children of alcoholics during the recovery process. *Addictive Behaviors*, 7, 155–163.

Murray, D., & Perry, C. 1985. The prevention of adolescent drug abuse: Implications of etiologic, developmental, behavioral, and environmental models. In D. Jones, R. Battjes (eds.) *Etiology of drug abuse: Implications for prevention*. NIDA Research Monograph #56, Washington, D.C.

Nadler, L. 1981. The conduct of pathological gambling research: Covering all bets. In W. Eadington (ed.) *The Gambling Papers: Proceedings of the Fifth Annual Conference on Gambling Behavior*. Reno, Nevada: University of Nevada.

Nadler, L. B., & Meeland, T. 1982. *Pathological gambling and American youth*. National Foundation for Study & Treatment of Pathological Gambling, Washington, D.C.

Nadler, L. B. 1985. The epidemiology of pathological gambling: Critique of existing research and alternative strategies. *Journal of Gambling Behavior*, 1(1), 35–50.

Nardi P. 1981. Children of alcoholics: A role-theoretical perspective. *Journal of Social Psychology*, 115, 237–245.

National household survey on drug abuse. 1985. Rockville, Maryland: NIDA.

Newcomb, M., Huba, G., & Bentler, P. 1983. Mothers' influence on the drug use of their children: Confirmatory tests of direct modeling and mediational theories. *Developmental Psychology*, 19, 714–726.

Offer, D., Ostrov, E., & Howard, K. 1981. The mental health professional's concept of the normal adolescent. *Archives of General Psychiatry*, 38(2):149–152.

———. 1981. *The Adolescent: A Psychological Self-Portrait*. New York: Basic Books.

Ramirez, L., McCormick, R., Russo, A., & Taber, J. 1984. Patterns of substance abuse in pathological gamblers undergoing treatment. *Addictive Behaviors*, 8, 425–428.

Rowe, A. 1945. The adult adjustment of children of alcoholic parents raised in foster homes. *Quarterly Journal of Studies on Alcohol*, 5, 378–393.

Russell, M., Henderson, C., & Blume, S. B. 1985. *Children of alcoholics: A review of the literature.* New York: Children of Alcoholics Foundation, Inc.

Rutter, M. 1979. Protective factors in children's responses to stress and disadvantage. In M. W. Kent & J. E. Rolf (eds.) *Social competence in children,* 49–74. Hanover, New Hampshire: University Press of New England.

Schwaneberg, R. 1981, April. Resort aide tells of casino lure for underage teens. *The Star Ledger,* 4.

Stacy, A., Widaman, K., Hays, R., & DiMatteo, M. 1985. Validity of self-reports of alcohol and other drug use: A multitrait-multimethod assessment. *Journal of Personality and Social Psychology,* 49, 219–232.

Straus, M., Gelles, R., & Steinmetz, S. 1980. *Behind closed doors: Violence in the American family.* Garden City: Anchor Books.

Steinberg, M. (1988) Gambling Behavior among high school students in Connecticut. Paper presented at Third National Conference on Gambling, May 1988.

Taber, J. I. 1982. Group psychotherapy with pathological gamblers. In W. R. Eadington (ed.) *The Gambling Papers: Proceedings of the Fifth National Conference on Gambling and Risk Taking.* Reno, Nevada: University of Nevada.

Tharinger, D., & Koranek, M. 1988. Children of alcoholics—at risk and unserved: A review of research and service roles for school psychologists. *School Psychology Review,* 17(1), 166–191.

U. S. Department of Commerce. 1983. *1980 Census of Population: General Population Characteristics, U.S. Summary.* Washington, D.C.: U.S. Government Printing Office.

Volberg, R. A., & Steadman, H. J. 1988a. Refining prevalence estimates of pathological gambling. *American Journal of Psychiatry,* 145 (4), 502–505.

———. 1988b. Personal communication.

Wanda G. (anonymous), & Foxman, J. 1971. *Games compulsive gamblers, wives, and families play.* New York: Gam-Anon National Services Offices.

Warner, R., & Rosett H. 1975. The effects of drinking on offspring. *Journal of Studies on Alcohol,* 36, 1395–1420.

Werner, E., & Smith, R. 1982. *Vulnerable but invincible.* New York: McGraw-Hill.

Werner, E. 1984. Resilient children. *Young Children,* 40, 68–72.

———. 1986. Resilient offspring of alcoholics: A longitudinal study from birth to age eighteen. *Journal of Studies on Alcohol,* 47, 34–40.

West, M. O., & Prinz, R. J. 1987. Parental alcoholism and Childhood Psychopathology. *Psychological Bulletin,* Vol. 102 No. 2, 204–218.

Wittman, G. W., Fuller, N. P., Taber, J. I. 1988. Patterns of polyaddiction in alcoholic patients and high school students. In William R. Eadington (ed.) *Gambling Research: Proceedings of the Seventh International Conference on Gambling and Risk Taking.* Reno, Nevada: University of Nevada-Reno, 293–305.

Yamaguchi, K., & Kandel, D. 1984. Patterns of drug use from adolescence to young adulthood. II. Sequences of progression. *American Journal of Public Health,* 74(7), 668–672.

———. 1984. Patterns of drug use from adolescence to young adulthood. III.

Predictors of progression. *American Journal of Public Health*, 74(7), 673–681.

Zucker, R., & Lisansky Gomberg, E. 1986. Etiology of alcoholism reconsidered: The case for a biopsychosocial process. *American Psychologist*, 41, 783–793.

Acknowledgments

Gratefully acknowledged is the valuable assistance received from Albert R. Marston, Ph.D., professor of psychology, University of Southern California, and Robert D. Singer, Ph.D., professor of psychology, University of California at Riverside, for their consultation during development of the Health Survey and in obtaining entry to respondents in some high school and college settings involved in this research.

Also acknowledged is the valuable consultation provided by Keith Widaman, Ph.D., associate professor of psychology, University of California at Riverside; and UCR psychology graduate assistants Mr. Todd Little and Ms. Jeannette Veizades for their contributions to the statistical design and implementation of data analysis for this series of studies.

15
The Search for
Prescriptive Interventions

Blase Gambino, Ph.D.

Introduction

At present clinicians lack a sound theoretical frame upon which to base an eclectic, prescriptive clinical practice (Shaffer 1986). A large body of research has been generated on the treatment of mental illnesses and the addictive disorders. Yet the practitioner has not benefited greatly from this work (Shaffer & Gambino 1984). A similar situation holds for the future of the treatment of compulsive gambling (Taber 1987). Treatment researchers need to turn away from the search for the causes of compulsive gambling or any other addiction. That is the province of the prevention researcher and the clinical theorist. They need to turn to a focus on the causes and determinants of treatment outcomes. That is the province of the treatment researcher. It is in this area that the treatment researcher can best advise the practitioner and demonstrate that research is relevant to the needs of the patient.

We propose an "epidemiology of treatment outcome" be developed. We shall argue that an epidemiologic model for research on the treatment of compulsive gambling (or any other treatable addiction) should be a major tool to develop treatment interventions beneficial to patients and clients. We present these views to stimulate the interest of clinicians to become more involved in research. We also expect the approach we describe will provide more immediate relevance to the questions the researcher seeks to answer, and thus more inherent satisfaction with the task addressed. The epidemiological model we advocate is one which emphasizes the search for "occurrence relationships" (Miettinen 1985) between key indicator variables and clinically significant outcomes. The

Thanks are extended to Howard Shaffer and Sharon Stein for their helpful input and comments on earlier drafts of this chapter.

paradigm of occurrence research has been defined rigorously by Miettinen (1985) within the domain of medical epidemiology.

In this chapter we will outline a view of clinical research that focuses on the search for key indicators. This focus will provide the necessary direction for the establishment of prescriptive interventions. A search whose goal is the discovery of the parameters that define the boundaries of our capacity to provide effective treatment. We propose a perspective and emphasis we believe will help identify the relevant questions for treatment research, and generate new possibilities for treatment intervention. Answers to these questions require cooperation between the researcher and the practitioner. We will begin with a discussion of why the current etiologic emphasis in our research may be inappropriate.

Etiology and Determinants of Risk

Most practitioners and researchers in the field of compulsive gambling would probably agree that the major and primary concern must be the study of the personal (biological, psychological, behavioral) and environmental (social, cultural, economic, organizational, physical, chemical) determinants of the disorder referred to as compulsive AKA pathological gambling (our arguments apply equally to the more general case of addictive behavior). Identification of these determinants, it is presumed, will provide the necessary evidence for needed insights into strategies for treatment intervention.

At first glance this appears to direct attention to the causes of compulsive gambling. Such an emphasis is inappropriate if the primary concern is the effectiveness of treatment. The first order of business is the identification of those variables for which the evidence indicates a correspondence (association) with treatment outcomes. Treatment outcomes are those events or states that hold clinical significance as evidence for defining the achievement of treatment and extratreatment benefits (our use of the term benefits is deliberate; it stresses the distinction between goal attainment and the relevance of the attained goals to meeting the needs of the patient, a distinction too often ignored by treatment planners and evaluators) and adverse consequences that define the risks of treatment (attention to risks reflects the need to identify our failures of treatment interventions and/or those cases in which harm accrues to the patient through treatment efforts).

This is not to claim that the search for the causes of illnesses such as compulsive gambling is unimportant. We suggest rather, that it is typically unproductive in that it may have little to do with treatment intervention (see special issue of *Journal of Gambling Behavior,* 1987, on relevant models of compulsive gambling). This is particularly the case if the factor is not amenable to change; for example, knowing the age at which the compulsive gambler began to gamble may or may not be helpful in designing a treatment program. It may of course say a great deal about the age at which preventive education should begin.

Theories that purport to deal with putative causes of problems will contribute to the solutions of those problems only when their implications for practice are made explicit. To understand the etiology of a client's problem is not equivalent to understanding how to help the client; although it may provide important insights to the creative practitioner (Gambino & Shaffer 1979). We suggest that an emphasis on the etiology of compulsive gambling (or any addictive disorder) is inappropriate at present in that such research is unlikely to provide the means to effective treatment.

The objective of studies that address the etiology of a disorder is to establish firmly a causal relation between a presumed cause and the adverse status of the patient. It is rare, however, to find strong evidence for causal relations, mostly because of the lengthy induction period characteristic of chronic disorders. Induction period refers to the time between instigation of the effects of each causal component and onset of the disease (Rothman 1986). This period is rarely measurable and is usually lengthy (except the last, for which the induction period is zero). In the typical case, we are left with measurement of the time of detection of the disease rather than onset (although in theory this interval may be eliminated). The identification of any single component of a sufficient cause, however, may be extremely valuable for the purposes of early detection. In similar fashion, such identification may have great value for efforts at prevention even in those cases in which the identified variable cannot be manipulated or changed (such as gender or age). As we will show, early detection and prevention have their counterparts in the treatment setting— for example, in the identification of factors associated with relapse.

We need to adopt a "creative research methodology" that will provide the practitioner with the means to identify clinical hypotheses about significant treatment relationships supported by our data. Relationships that can be explored by the clinician in depth with those patients to which the relationship applies. This is the first step in developing a testable clinical hypothesis about the causal relationships in the treatment of compulsive gambling to which the power of our confirmatory procedures can be applied.

Causal Thinking and Epidemiologic Models

Many argue that the search for etiologic factors in disease and the distribution of such factors among populations should take precedence in epidemiologic research. Similar arguments pervade our views of treatment evaluation (Maisto & Conners 1988; Franklin & Richardson 1988; Abt 1987). A careful study of the results of epidemiological research reveals that it is rare that we can confirm the existence of specific cause-effect relationships and this is particularly the case for chronic disease. While many epidemiologists have been reluctant to accept this evidence (Rothman 1986; Kleinbaum, Kupper & Morgenstern 1982), and give up the classical model of causality, few treatment researchers in the addictions have even begun to consider the obvious implication. It will be more profitable to turn our attention from the etiology of the process and direct our focus to the etiology of treatment outcome—where we want to go.

Whether a determinant is causal is important only if this knowledge is useful for intervention to promote health or prevent disease (Miettinen 1985). In this light, the epidemiological model we advocate does not presume the primary goal to be the search for etiological factors responsible for pathological gambling. Instead we direct the search at treatment outcomes, positive or negative consequences during and after treatment; for example the likelihood of relapse. The discipline of treatment research must be focused on the search for determinants, causal or conditional, of treatment outcomes and how these are distributed in clinical populations.

In many, if not all, cases involving the disorders we treat, the causal process cannot be described in terms of specific linkages. Adherents of such a model of causation "risk instant obsolescence [and] . . . chance . . . harm [to] others with legitimate interests and problems" (Taber 1987 p. 221). The classical model of disease causation is that in which a single cause, such as a germ, leads to a single effect, such as a specific disease. We are learning that it is unlikely we will find any direct relationship between exposure to a single determinant, such as parent was a compulsive gambler, and the etiology of compulsive gambling. It is more likely that several variables must come together to complete the causal link—that is, establish a sufficient cause. Single causality is also reflected in models that appear to address the multicausal aspects of the disorders we treat but are limited in fact to a single dimension or set of processes. We are learning that multicausality and multispecificity of relationships is probably the rule rather than the exception (Shaffer 1986; Shaffer & Neuhaus 1985; Donovan 1988; Maisto & Connors 1988). Multispecificity refers to the fact that our treatment interventions will have more than one outcome. An example from the treatment of compulsive gambling is helpful. An intervention designed to produce abstinence from gambling may also result in a concomitant increase in the severity of other behaviors, such as problem drinking. Similar results have been found in the treatment of substance abuse (Tims & Ludford 1984).

The need to shift away from the classical model of causality may be found in the following (cf, Kleinbaum, Kupper & Morgenstern 1982):

1. The evidence for multifactorial etiology is mounting and beginning to be accepted as the rule rather than the exception. "Consequently, in any particular instance, we must challenge either the necessary or the sufficient condition for identifying a causal relationship. Regarding noninfectious chronic disease, there is no factor known to be present in every case. Also if we recognize that certain causes of disease may not be physical agents, the classical model of causality does not enable us to consider chains of two or more factors that eventually result in the disease (Kleinbaum et al. 1982).

2. There is also growing evidence of multiplicity of effects. For example, smoking appears to be involved in the etiology of many diseases. We can expect similar relationships to hold for many other nonbiologic variables, such as poverty and overcrowding, especially those associated with chronic stress (cf, Cooper 1987). We should not be surprised to find that the increased risk of compulsive gambling associated with having a parent who was a compulsive gambler may have a similar association with other outcomes, such as a higher risk of being a problem drinker.

3. The popular model of causality has been shown to provide a limited conceptualization of reputed causal factors. The classic definition requires that the effect be tied to a *change* in the causal factor. This makes it difficult to account for sex, race, genetic predispositions, etc. and other fixed characteristics. Second, the pure deterministic model does not allow a clear role for causal factors that are continuous, such as age, blood pressure, obesity, and so on. There are no uniform cutoff values (thresholds) above which the effect occurs and below which no effect occurs (Kleinbaum et al. 1982). In compulsive gambling, clinicians rarely collect data on levels and patterns of gambling conditional on life intervals, such as first year of gambling versus last five years. Such information may be crucial in determining levels of risk for relapse, or responsiveness to treatment. The obvious relationship of such historical data and the need to evaluate concepts such as progressivity of the disorder are typically ignored.

The important implication of this finding is that such ill-defined and incompletely specified [multifactorial] causal sets cannot be subjected to the usual confirmatory tests. We need to resort to a different conceptual schema to guide our interventions. Fortunately one exists. We require three elements. The first is a methodology that will enable us to identify those risk factors associated with treatment outcomes. The second is a process whereby those variables identified as key indicators of risk may be clinically validated for designing appropriate treatment interventions. The final element is the rigorous evaluation of our clinical intervention to assess its effectiveness. We begin our discussion with a description and demonstration of risk factor methodology.

In the next section we will describe two measures: (1) relative risk, and (2) attributable risk, unfamiliar to most practitioners. These measures are also little known or vastly underused among clinical researchers who are not expressly interested in epidemiology. More recently these measures have been applied to the analysis of life-event research by psychiatric epidemiologists (Cooke 1987). While it is possible to argue the validity of their usage as described later, that is beyond the scope of this chapter. We have presented our views on the value of a creative use of research methodology for the purposes of exploration and development of testable causal propositions. We refer the interested reader to other sources we believe justify this approach. These include Miettinen (1985), Rothman (1986), Kleinbaum et al. (1982), Kahn (1983), and Cooke (1987), among others.

Relative Risk and Attributable Risk

In this section we present two concepts drawn from the field of epidemiology-relative risk and attributable risk; the latter is sometimes referred to as the etiologic fraction (Miettinen 1985). We will show that these concepts are easy to apply, and have natural interpretations in everyday as well as clinical language. We will demonstrate the heuristic value of the use of these concepts in identifying clinical hypotheses that may provide insight into developing appropriate interventions with selected clinical populations defined by identified risk factors. First we will define the concept of risk.

Risk is the probability of an individual's developing a specific disorder, exhibiting a particular behavior, or experiencing a change in status in health during a defined period of time. The risk or likelihood is expressed as a probability value that can vary from zero to one. Risk requires a specific period reference to be understood, such as the risk of becoming a compulsive gambler in the year following introduction of a state lottery.

The concept of relative risk is intuitively easy to grasp. It is simply the ratio of two risks such that a value of 1.0 signifies equal risk. The value of relative risk for the clinical researcher stems from the demonstration by Cornfield (1951) that under suitable conditions retrospective studies can provide estimates of relative risk equivalent to that obtained in prospective studies. The particular form we have adopted is called the odds ratio. (Technically there is a distinction between risk and odds; for our purposes they are interchangeable. We refer the interested reader to Kahn 1983.) The use of relative risk has since been advocated by Paykel (1978) as a valuable measure in life event research. Its versatility, along with that of the related measure population attributable risk, has been demonstrated by Cooke (1987). Cooke showed its value in demonstrating the association of a variety of physical and psychological disorders to a range of life events. Cooke demonstrated that it could be defined as the ratio of the rate of illness among those who have experienced defined events, such as father was a compulsive gambler, to the rate among those who have not experienced such events (Cooke & Hole 1983). Cooke showed that it could be calculated simply as described in table 15–1 (the calculations are based on formulas given in Lilienfeld & Lilienfeld 1980).

The concept of relative risk may be demonstrated with an example taken from an analysis of a cohort of forty-five patients enrolled in a program of treatment for problem gambling. Twenty-one (46.7 percent) of these patients reported severe to extremely severe problems with their family of origin; 26 (57.8 percent) reported they had endured an extended period of inactivity (from work) in the year before entering treatment. Table 15–2 presents the rest of the data.

Using the formula in table 15–1 we find that relative risk = (17)(15)/ (9)(4) = 255/36 = 7.08:1. In other words, reported severity of family problems is seven times higher among those who suffered a long period of inactivity in the year before entry into treatment than for those who did not experience any extended inactivity during that time. A high relative risk indicates a strong association between the determinant (long layoff) and the outcome (family problems). This increases the plausibility of a causal relationship. It must be kept in mind that consideration of a causal

Table 15–1
Mapping of Relationship of Diagnosis to Determinant

C = case of interest, such as compulsive gambler

NC = non case, such as social gambler

D = determinant (sometimes called the exposure variable or risk factor)

ND = the absence of the determinant

Presence and Absence of Diagnosis of Case:	Presence and Absence of Determinant		
	D	ND	Total
C	a	c	a + c
NC	b	d	b + d
Total	a + b	c + d	(a+b+c+d)

Relative risk = ad/bc [comparative odds or risk]

Table 15–2
Relationship of Prior Inactivity to Severe Family Problems upon Entry to Treatment

	Severe	Nonsevere	Total	Percent
Inactive	17	9	26	57.8%
Working	4	15	19	42.2%
Total	21	24	45	
Percent	46.7%	53.3%		

relationship requires a clinical causal hypothesis. Otherwise the relationship has no inherent clinical meaning.

For the clinician to decide that the strength of the relationship is important enough to take action, a second measure is usually required. The measure of choice is that of attributable risk. This measure provides the clinician with an intuitively congruent measure of the power of an effect—that is, what is "a *big* relative risk" (Cooke 1987 p. 71). As Cooke notes, [Big] "depends upon the disorder being studied and the base risk [prevalence] of the disorder" (p. 71). It may be defined as the maximum percentage of cases of a disorder or behavior that can be directly attributed to the experience of the determinant. It is calculated as follows (Cooke 1987):

$$\text{Attributable risk} = \text{AR}(\%)$$
$$\text{AR}(\%) = (ad - bc)/(ad + cd) \times 100$$
$$= (ad - bc)/[(a + c)d] \times 100$$

where % = percent attributable to determinant.
In the above example the attributable risk is calculated as:

$$\text{AR} = [(17)(15) - (4)(9)]/[(17)(15) + (4)(15)] \times 100$$
$$= 219/315 = 69.5\%$$

If long periods of layoff were the principal causal factor in the creation of problems between the compulsive gambler and their family, then it would follow that a program of intervention designed to resolve this situation would reduce the prevalence of such problems by approximately 69.5 percent.

Naturally there are cautions to be observed in making too liberal an interpretation of concepts such as relative and attributable risk for the purposes of taking action. In the example, an intervention designed to deal with the effects of a long layoff would, if effective, reduce the number of cases of family problems by (.695) x (21 cases) = approximately fifteen cases. Whether such a reduction among the clinical population to be treated is considered valuable is an extrastatistical determination—a clinical or administrative one that involves clinical importance independent of numbers, such as in the reduction of suicides, or is deemed cost-effective despite numbers, such as because it relates to other problem areas.

We will now provide some further examples to demonstrate the value and versatility of these measures. We will also demonstrate the need for the clinician to become involved in the validation process. The clinician's task is twofold: first, to determine if the problem is important enough to require action, and second, to determine the existence of relationships that may be amenable to intervention. For these purposes we present some data obtained from analysis of the pretreatment intake assessment of the forty-five patients cited earlier. For those interested in a more detailed explanation of these concepts we recommend Kahn's (1983) introductory book. It bears repeating that the importance of any data requires more than just having enough cases upon which to base the analysis. We must use our knowledge and experience to decide which effects are real and important. In other words, the defining criteria must always be clinical significance and not statistical significance. This is true whether we employ descriptive procedures as we do here, or confirmatory analyses in which we test statistical hypotheses (we add the obvious, that if we are interested in statistical significance such tests are available, cf, Miettinen 1985, this includes tables and formulas to assist the clinical researcher in making decisions about sample size, Rothman 1986).

Our first set of results is shown in table 15–3, which provides the relative risk for selected behaviors by patients who indicated that one or more of their parents were compulsive gamblers. The values shown in the relative risk column give the odds that such behavior will be engaged in by a patient with a compulsive gambler as parent relative to a patient whose parents were not reported to have problems with gambling. Each of the behaviors listed in the at-risk column were obtained from self-reports of patients at intake. The first four behaviors were part of a set of gambling-related behaviors drawn from the New York State evaluation intake form supplied to us by their office. The last three behaviors were taken from the list of problem areas patients were questioned about at intake in terms of problem severity and need for treatment. In the discussion to follow we will refer to the parental gambler as the patient who indicated that one or both parents were problem gamblers. Because it is our purpose to demonstrate the value of the use of relative risk and attributable risk measures, we will concentrate on those results that represent the largest effects.

Table 15–3
Parental Problem Gambling as a Determinant

Behavior at Risk	Relative Risk	Attributable Risk Percent
Gambling alone	3.7	25%
Memory lapses	8.0	44%
Quarrels with strangers	5.2	48%
Physical violence	35.5	88%
Severe sleeping problem	3.9	37%
Severe drinking problem	4.8	45%
Severe gambling problem	3.1	21%

The first thing the data compel us to note is that the parental gambler is eight times as likely to have experienced blackouts for events unrelated to gambling. An interesting clinical hypothesis that immediately jumps to mind is whether a genetic factor is involved. The attributable risk of 48 percent is relatively high and supports a causal hypothesis. Given the preliminary nature of this data, we look for additional links that are interpretable as genetic. One such link may be reflected in the higher odds associated with having a drinking problem, almost five times as likely as the nonparental gambler. The attributable risk percent is again close to 50 percent. Since there is evidence that drinking has a genetic component, we might ask whether multiple addictions are also genetically transmitted. Finally, we note the large odds associated with engaging in physical violence. It is an accepted interpretation that physical violence is not an attribute of the compulsive gambler (Brown 1987). These data demonstrate clearly the value of these measures, since they are sensitive to rare behavior and yet are capable of indicating a possible major causal link. In this case, attributable risk suggests that parental factors may be responsible for almost all the observed physical violence in this group of patients (88 percent).

To demonstrate that the technique is sensitive to the number of cases, consider the relationship between whether the patient at entry will report severe marital problems conditional on whether the patient admitted to being physically abused in childhood. Only four patients out of forty-five reported themselves victims of physical abuse. These patients, however, were eight times as likely to admit to having severe marital problems as those patients who had not been so abused. When we examine this relationship in terms of attributable risk, however, we find that it accounts for only 18 percent, not a very strong indication of a risk factor of clinical importance in the resolution of such problems. Consider, however, the interpretation if the occurrence relationship was between physical abuse and physical violence. In this case, any clinical hypothesis about an intervention that would prevent future occurrences of patient violence would have high value.

As another example, these same four individuals are twenty-eight times more likely to admit to a severe drinking problem than other patients. In this case, attributable risk suggests that if the therapist can resolve this problem because it is related to physical abuse, it would reduce the problem among patients by 41 percent, as measured by attributable risk. Again, we remind the reader that this is an oversimplification and a liberal interpretation of the data supplied by these measures. It is clear, however, that by engaging the clinician in the research process, the clinical importance of these relationships may be determined. The clinicians' mastery of the clinical interview allows them to contribute to the interactive process that should characterize the relationship between research and practice (Shaffer & Gambino 1984).

We turn next to additional data on the relationship of several background variables and the occurrence of selected behaviors. The background variables include (a) whether the patient had previously been in treatment for gambling associated problems, (b) whether the patient's father had a drinking problem, and (c) whether the patient had gone through a major job or career change in the year before treatment. In selected cases the values are marked by an asterisk to signify that the risk factor or determinant acted as a preventive in that case—that is, 59 percent* would imply that 59 percent of all patients with that attribute would not exhibit the behavior of interest. The relative risk or odds ratio would be the odds that the individual without the exposure would exhibit the behavior. When a determinant serves to indicate a relative reduction in disease or problem behavior, the measure is referred to as the preventive fraction (Miettinen 1985). These results are presented in table 15–4.

The first striking result in table 15–4 occurs in part a. Here we find dramatic indications that previous treatment for gambling has resulted in almost a 60 percent reduction in the number of patients who reported instances of solitary gambling. This demonstrates that solid evidence may be obtained from the use of these measures of the value of the treatment of gambling for those who must repeat the process. This result is not surprising in light of similar data from the evaluation of treatment in the field of drug abuse (Simpson 1984).

The second notable results in table 15–4 are to be found in section b. Here we find that the father's drinking problem strongly increases the likelihood that the patient will have a drinking problem, but not so if the

Table 15-4
Relative Risk (RR) and Attributable Risk (AR) Associated with:

a. Prior treatment for gambling problems

Problem area	RR	AR(%)
Solitary gambling	6.9*	59*
Memory lapses	3.0	37
Loneliness	2.0	33
Quarrels with strangers	7.4	69
Sexual problems	7.4	69

b. Father had serious drinking problem

Problem area	RR	AR(%)
Solitary gambling	2.7	24
Memory lapses	4.4	39
Quarrels with spouse	2.5	24
Quarrels with employer	14.5	72
Drinking problem	7.8	62
Drinking problem (mother)	2.6	18

c. Career Change in Past Twelve Months

Problem area	RR*	AR(%)*
Financial problems	3.7	40
Social/interpersonal problems	4.9	58
Leisure time activities	3.3	45
Reported physical problems	6.2	65
Problems with sleeping	7.7	70
Eating problems	3.1	46
Sexual problems	6.0	67
Drinking problems	3.8	53
Gambling problems at entry	23.6	94

*reverse scored in this case the percent is known as the preventive fraction rather than the etiologic fraction. It represents the percent of cases in which the exposure variable, such as prior treatment for gambling, acts as a preventive.

patient's mother had the problem. This suggests an interpretation in terms of social learning or modeling theory. Third, we note the major relationship between the father's drinking and the likelihood the patient will engage in quarrels with their employer. We will leave interpretation of that relationship to someone more qualified and creative. We again remind the reader that such a relationship may not be clinically important in terms of numbers. Thus, the clinician may use this relationship to explore the issue with those few patients whose fathers had drinking problems, but may not consider it worth the development of a programmatic intervention.

Finally, we invite the reader to examine the results of section c, which reports a set of behaviors associated with a career change in the last twelve months. Our initial expectation in constructing the list of events that might be significant, such as death of a loved one, was to identify stressors related to the problems brought into treatment. In this instance, the event (and we do not rule it out as a stressor, since there are positive stressors) served as a positive force. For each of the behaviors listed in section c, the individual patients were much better off than their counterparts who did not experience a career change. This will have to be followed up through the interview process to extract its full meaning. We can, however, offer some speculation. If theory and wisdom is correct (Custer & Custer 1978), these gamblers may have bottomed out just before this situation. Obtaining a job, any job, may have been a positive event relative to what had preceded. This may have allowed the compulsive gamblers the time to gather their resources and to decide to seek formal treatment so that any gains could be maintained.

The next data presented in this section are obtained by considering age as the background determinant. Specifically, a median split was conducted on reported age at which gambling began. The assumption in the literature is that the compulsive gambler starts their addictive career at a relatively young age. Relative risk and attributable risk refer to the younger 50 percent of the clients. These results are presented in table 15–5.

As would be expected by theory, for the problem areas reported, the patients who began their gambling careers at a younger age were much more likely to be troubled by memory lapses, sexual problems, drinking problems, and physical violence. Since there were only four reported cases of physical violence, this finding deserves further inquiry. It is also of interest to consider why those who began gambling at a younger age are almost eight times more likely to admit to having a severe gambling problem at entry into treatment. We admit to no ready answer. The final result we report is the finding that those who began at a younger age are

Table 15–5
Relative Risk (RR) and Attributable Risk (AR) with Age at Which First Gambled as Background or Exposure Variable (Median Split-Younger v. Older)

Problem Area	RR	AR(%)
Quarrels with children	2.3*	31*
Memory lapses	4.0	50
Physical violence	3.8	55
Sexual problems	5.8	66
Drinking problem	3.7	52
Admits to severe gambling problem at entry	7.8	46

*reverse scored in this case the percent is known as the preventive fraction rather than the etiologic fraction. It represents the percent of cases in which the exposure variable, such as started gambling at early age, acts as a preventive.

moderately less likely to engage in unseemly disputes with their children. Although the finding does not seem to hold much clinical importance at least by these measures, the finding should be kept in mind. It is almost assuredly not a case of accidental happening.

We will close this section by noting that our primary interests in the concepts of relative and attributable risk are in the examination of life events on the course and development of compulsive gambling and their implications for treatment. We have taken our lead from several sources. The first of these is the accumulation of important findings on the relationship of such events to psychiatric disorders and physical illness, especially affective disorders (Cooke 1987; Harris 1987; Dohrenwend, Link, Kern, Shrout & Markowitz 1987). The second is the emphasis placed by the American Psychiatric Association in DSM-III-R on Axis IV, the importance of psychosocial stressors. We are also encouraged by the recognition of Taber and his associates of the importance of such events for the etiology of the compulsive gambler (Taber, McCormick & Ramirez 1987). Taber (unpublished manuscript) has formulated a general model of addictive behavior on this basis. It conceptualizes the development of addiction in terms of significant life events and individual vulnerabilities. Taber's theory is ideally suited for testing through the identification of risk factors. The use of measures such as relative risk and attributable risk are especially congruent with Taber's thesis. These measures can provide a powerful test of the strength of the causal relationships described by the model. The heuristic value of Taber's theory rests in great part on its richness of empirical content. It tells us where to look for the evidence, an important characteristic of good theory (Rothman 1986).

Clinical Validation of Identified Risk Indicators

In this section, we would like to discuss the means of getting clinicians more involved in research into matters that bear upon our understanding of the distribution of important traits related to compulsive gambling and the identification of those variables that are the principal determinants of treatment outcome. This is the epidemiological model of research we advocate clinicians to follow. We will define the major role of the clinician in making the research-practice interaction a productive one.

The primary interest of the clinician in the field of pathological or compulsive gambling is the care of the patient. This presumably leads to a focus on collecting information relevant to diagnosis, assessment, and treatment planning. Epidemiological concerns would appear to be of little or no interest in this schema. Clinicians may or may not develop a systematic method to describe cases. Some clinicians will try to search for commonalities among patient types, but again this is rarely done. This focus on individual patients discourages any interest in how the problems they confront reflect outcomes applicable to the general clinical population, or how the knowledge clinicians acquire from solutions may be articulated into general principles of a theory of practice (Shaffer & Gambino 1979).

Shepherd (1978) has pointed out the clinician often does not realize that in many instances they are talking epidemiology. An example of the direct relevance of epidemiology for psychiatric practice is the observation by Cooper and Morgan (1973) that every diagnosis depends on actuarial data, since it consists in essence of a probability statement about the etiology, pathology, course, and response to treatment of a given disease. They also note that in seeking the origin and mode of transmission of a disease among their patients, clinicians use a basically epidemiological approach.

Weissman and Klerman (1978) recognized that epidemiological research rarely establishes etiology by its findings alone. They note that discovery of risk factors generates causal hypotheses, whose testing then usually requires other methods, such as animal and lab research experiments. They concluded that recent advances in psychiatric research had reestablished the importance of specific diagnostic groupings, and predicted that the future of psychiatric epidemiology would produce: (1) rates for discrete mental disorders, (2) a greater separation of the independent variables (risk factors) from the dependent variables (discrete psychiatric disorders), and (3) a greater exploration of causal relationships, whether necessary, sufficient, or multifactorial.

These observations apply to an epidemiology of treatment outcome as well. The process of treatment may be given the same logical status as the process of disease. This is particularly obvious in the case of instances of relapse. Whether we describe these processes as stochastic (to reflect chance), or deterministic (cf, Rothman, 1986 for a discussion of the equivalence of these approaches and the benefit of assuming a deterministic process), we are interested in the occurrence of relationships between critical events or states (outcomes) and those variables that hold a strong association with these outcomes (whether labeled determinants, risk factors, independent variables, or other). We have already noted that the focus presented by Weissman and Klerman (1978) is more productive for preventive aims than treatment intervention when the focus is on a chronic disorder. For treatment we would revise their conclusions as follows: (1) more specific identification of risk and benefit indicators and the outcome states for which the identified determinants are the primary, or at least important, contributors, (2) the identification of the rates (incidence and prevalence) of clinical criteria for treatment progress (evaluation of process) and adverse and beneficial states (evaluation of outcome), and (3) more rigorous testing of clinical hypotheses about the causal relationships in treatment.

Most clinicians would find such aims relevant to their own concerns. Yet clinicians do not play a major role in research. This is of great concern if we are to advance as a clinical science. The clinician is needed for the conduct of studies that identify important risk factors in treatment. Just as the clinician is necessary for the conduct of more customary epidemiological research. Only clinicians have the knowledge to establish the validity of diagnostic decisions or to develop clearer diagnostic guidelines for epidemiologic research (Sadoun 1987). In like manner, we need the clinician to contribute substantially to the development of instruments for the collection and classification of clinical data that will be relevant to an epidemiology of meaningful treatment outcomes. This is never more true than in the developmental stage of a field such as compulsive gambling.

There is a second essential contribution that only the clinician can make. The clinician must apply his or her skills to systematically "harvest" (Miettinen 1985) the information of the clinical experience. In this endeavor, the clinician learns whether the risk factors identified by our research are part of occurrence relationships amenable to intervention. This is the vital information the researcher needs to conduct proper outcome studies. It is equally important that the clinician learn to present this information in the form of a clinical hypothesis. At this point the researcher can apply his or her skills to develop an appropriate test of the clinical hypothesis with scientific methods. It then remains for the clinician to conduct the field studies or clinical trials to assess the results of therapy. The noted psychiatric epidemiologist Lee Robins (1978) has stated that this is the future priority area of substantive clinical research.

If research is to inform the practicing clinician, the practitioner must learn to contribute his or her store of knowledge to research for further refinement and verification. The clinician must become more involved in the understanding and conduct of research (Shaffer & Gambino 1984). If the clinician is to take a more active role in population based research, he or she will have to become better acquainted with the epidemiologist's way of thinking and his or her methodological expertise (Sainsbury & Kreitmena 1975). Epidemiologists and researchers also need to get closer to the realities of the clinical situation to develop viable hypotheses that typically are generated only by contact with patients. This requires a more constructive alliance between the treatment provider and the treatment researcher than exists now.

Evaluation of Treatment Outcome

Maisto & Conners (1988) present a framework to evaluate models of treatment in the addictions and to describe the strength and weaknesses of treatment evaluation research. These authors also conclude that there is a need for clinicians to become more involved in the generation and use of research than they do now. While we agree that clinicians need to become more involved in evaluative research, we cannot help but note that the Boulder model to which they refer has not worked. We do not believe the clinician can operate effectively as a scientist-practitioner. By temperament and by training, clinicians in most of the helping professions are unsuited to the role envisioned under that model (Shaffer & Gambino 1984).

As an alternative, we would argue that the clinician can become interested in serving as an integral part of research that is tied to improvement of the outcomes of our treatment strategies. When research is made relevant, the practitioner is more, not less, likely to use it and to get involved. The failure of clinicians in practice to adhere to our models is caused by a recognition on their part that such models have little relevance to practice in their present form. This is the primary reason that clinicians make little use of our research, although there are many other reasons as well (cf, Gambino & Shaffer 1979; Shaffer & Gambino 1984). As clinical scientists we often forget that science must be relevant to real-world problems. We are too often preoccupied with our particular research interests and not the problems confronted by the practitioner. We must direct our attention to the goals of treatment, the goals of intervention. We must turn away from the less-than-profitable pursuit of knowledge about the etiology of the disorders we treat and turn full attention to what we are trying to accomplish.

An epidemiological model of treatment evaluation focuses on the relationships between/among specified outcome variables (as defined in our treatment plans) and those client, therapist, treatment, and environmental variables that serve as determinants (whether obviously causal or descriptively conditional) of whom will benefit from our interventions and whom will not. The epidemiologic model of the search for the incidence and prevalence of outcomes associated with disease processes has an important analogy with treatment.

The risk factors we identify in our research on treatment outcome have the same logical status as those risk factors associated with disease processes. Our patients may be conceptualized in terms of susceptibility to a failure to benefit from treatment (as the average person is susceptible to a particular disease process). It is equally important to identify clinical populations who may be characterized as resistant to the influence of extratreatment factors that are not under our control, but that may influence to a greater degree whether the treatment gains will be permanent. Just as some individuals are resistant to disease, some patients will be made preventively resistant by our intervention. (cf, Mienttinen 1985 for a mathematical treatment of the definition of susceptibility and resistance).

It is time to turn away from our focus on risk factors of disease and disorder, which make prospective patients eligible for preventive activities, and turn our spotlight on the risk factors of our treatment. Agreement that the individual, as measured by our outcome variable set, has benefited from our intervention requires only that the initial pretreatment set be correlated with outcome sets measured during the course of treatment and followup. The primary goal of *preintervention* research then is to identify those sets of factors that are correlated with positive and negative outcomes. This is essentially an epidemiological approach to the study of the distribution of outcomes in [clinical] populations as a function of determinants.

Once these determinants have been identified as key indicators of risk, the clinician can develop interventions designed to exploit these relationships (cf, Krantz & Moos 1988; Marlatt 1988). It is at this stage that confirmatory research comes into play. Since the clinician's solution has not been tested in any fashion, there is no ethical justification for not employing the power of the experimental method. This includes the random assignment of patients to new and old treatments. In fact, we may argue that it is ethically incumbent upon the clinician to evaluate the intervention scientifically. This argument follows from two assumptions. First, since the intervention has not been tested it has only doubtful face validity—not the best criteria upon which to make a clinical choice, although often it is the only one available. Second, since the outcome is unknown, the logic of risk assessment must be observed. Each treatment has a specific risk of failure associated with it. It is essential to learn or estimate the relative risk associated with the contrast of old and new treatments. While we may know how many of our patients fail under the old system, we have no such knowledge about the new treatment designed to remedy the situation. We do not want to run the risk of the cure being worse than the disease. Finally, let us note that under these circumstances the oft-cited weakness of evaluation research, the lack of proper comparison groups, is no longer tenable.

Marlatt (Marlatt & Gordon 1985; Marlatt 1988) and like-minded researchers and clinicians have paved the way in the search for risk factors associated with relapse. This search has forced a confrontation with the realities of the clinical situation. In our choice of treatment strategies, such as controlled gambling versus abstinence, there is always risk to our patients. It is time we quantified the risks as well as the costs-benefits. This situation is no different than the use of epidemiological procedures to quantify the risk of surgery versus no surgery for a life-threatening condition.

While we now know that treatment can be effective, we typically are unable to tell the clinician why it works. Consequently we cannot advise the clinician to do things any differently than before. We need to be concerned with the development of a theory of practice consistent with the way in which practice operates at present. We need to adopt an epidemiological frame of reference in which recognition of the long and insidious induction period of chronic disorders such as compulsive gambling, or those we treat in substance abuse, may not permit us to establish any neat causal relationships relevant to treatment. Attention to causes is of use only when we can intervene to break the cause-effect relationship. We must place greater initial emphasis on a correlational or descriptive approach that allows us to base our interventions on such epidemiological concepts as relative risk and attributable risk for specific treatment outcomes. Our concern with cause-effect relationships should be limited to those that occur in close proximity to our interventions. These are relationships that the practicing clinician can note and understand. That is one of the values of frequent measurement before, during, and long after formal treatment has ended.

The collection of data on multiple variables under conditions that do not take up a great deal of the clinicians task is thus clearly fundamental at this stage of the development of "risk" and "benefit" assessment procedures that will lead eventually to the discovery of risk and benefit determinants.

The reasons our models have not been useful for practice, although some have stimulated exciting and important research, are complex. We believe the answer resides in the failure of researchers and clinicians to recognize that historically what has been lacking are not models of addiction or compulsive gambling (see Taber, 1987) but models of treatment practice. For example, practitioners and theorists alike fail to distinguish between models of addiction and models of treatment such as abstinence and controlled gambling. Each of these is an intervention based upon assumptions about the etiology of the addiction. What is required is not evaluation of treatment outcome between rival interventions, but evaluation of the interaction of treatment with patient variables that predict who is at risk. Risk must be defined in terms of outcome. Abstinence and controlled gambling (or controlled drinking) are treatments, not outcomes. Controlled gambling is a behavior (means) designed to accomplish goals (ends). Abstinence is also a behavior (the absence or withholding of a response) to be used to achieve goals. Neither is an outcome that defines the success of our treatment.

Our models of practice require a basis in practice procedure if we are to gain the confidence of the clinician. The clinician needs to know whose behavior to change, not what caused it in the first place (Gambino & Shaffer 1979). While knowledge of the cause of a disorder may at times be useful, in most cases it is not.

The field of the treatment of the pathological/compulsive gambler should take heed of the history of its sister addictions, drug and alcohol abuse and dependence. We cannot afford the luxury of maintaining a separation of practice from research and the researcher from the practitioner. The lessons to be learned from the large-scale studies (Simpson 1984; Hubbard, Rachal, Craddock & Cavanaugh 1984) conducted under the aegis of the National Institute of Drug Abuse (Tims & Ludford 1984) is that research into the evaluation of treatment process and outcome must be considered a priority and not an afterthought (Jaffe 1984). We now have the methodology to apply to our practices in such a way that our clients will benefit greatly. Any other course of action should be considered unethical and irresponsible. We may not know why treatment works, but we can learn for whom it works and for whom it does not. As clinicians we can then apply this knowledge to design more efficient interventions and evaluate the outcome of these. Treatment "as usual" can no longer be considered acceptable.

"Einstein said, 'To raise new questions, new possibilities, to regard old problems from a new angle, requires creative imagination and marks real advance in science' " (cited in Graham 1988). We hope we have succeeded in some measure to advance our efforts at treatment research. That at least has been our goal.

References

Abt, V. 1987. Advancing research on problem gambling. Paper presented to the Seventh International Conference on Gambling and Risk Taking, Reno, Nevada.

Brown, R. I. F. 1987. Pathological gambling and associated patterns of crime: Comparisons with alcohol and other drug addictions. *Journal of Gambling Behavior*, 3, 98–114.

Cooke, D. J. 1987. The significance of life events as a cause of psychological and physical disorder. In B. Cooper (ed.) *The epidemiology of psychiatric disorders*. 67–80. Baltimore: John Hopkins University Press.

Cooke, D. J., & Hole, D. J. 1983. The aetiological importance of stressful life events. *British Journal of Psychiatry*, 143, 397–400.

Cooper, B. (ed.) 1987. *The epidemiology of psychiatric disorders*. Baltimore: Johns Hopkins University Press.

Cooper, B., & Morgan, H. G. 1973. *Epidemiological Psychiatry*, Springfield, Illinois: C.C. Thomas.

Cornfield, J. 1951. A method for estimating comparative rates from clinical data: Applications to cancer of the lung, breast, and cervix. *Journal of the National Cancer Institute*, 11, 1269–1275.

Custer, R. L., & Custer, L. F. 1978. Characteristics of the recovering gambler: A survey of 150 members of gamblers anonymous. Paper presented at the Fourth National Conference on Gambling, Reno, Nevada.

Dohrenwend, B. P., Link, B. G., Kern, R., Shrout, P. E., & Markowitz, J. 1987. Measuring life events: The problem of variability within event categories. In Cooper, B. (ed.) *The epidemiology of psychiatric disorders*, 103–119, Baltimore: Johns Hopkins University Press.

Donovan, D. M. 1988. Assessment of addictive behaviors: Implications of an emerging biopsychosocial model. In Donovan, D. M., & Marlatt, G.A. (eds.) *Assessment of Addictive Behaviors*, 3–48. New York: Guilford Press.

Franklin, J., & Richardson, R. 1988. A treatment outcome study with pathological gamblers: Preliminary findings and strategies. In Eadington, W. R. (ed.) Proceedings of the Seventh International Conference on Gambling and Risk Taking. 5, 392–407. Reno, Nevada: University of Nevada.

Gambino, B., & Shaffer, H. 1979. The concept of paradigm and the treatment of addiction. *Professional Psychology*, 10, 207–223.

Graham, S. 1988. Enhancing creativity in epidemiology. *American Journal of Epidemiology*, 128, 249–253.

Harris, T. 1987. Recent developments in the study of life events in relation to psychiatric and physical disorders. In Cooper, B. (ed.) *The epidemiology of psychiatric disorders*, 81–102. Baltimore: Johns Hopkins University Press.

Hubbard, R. L., Rachal, J. V., Craddock, S. G., & Cavanaugh, E. R. 1984. Treatment outcome prospective study (TOPS): Client characteristics and behaviors before, during, and after treatment. *Drug abuse treatment evaluation: strategies, progress, and prospects*. Washington, D.C.: DHHS, GPO.

Jacobs, D. F. 1988. A common theoretical approach for understanding and treating addictive behaviors. Paper presented at First Annual Symposium on Compulsive Gambling, Center for Addiction Studies, Harvard Medical School, Cambridge, Massachusetts (June).

Jaffe, J. H. 1984. Evaluating drug abuse treatment: A comment on the state of the art. *Drug abuse treatment evaluation: strategies, progress, and prospects*. 13–28. Washington, D.C.: DHHS, GPO.

Journal of Abnormal Psychology. 1988. 97(2).

Kahn, H. A. 1983. *An introduction to epidemiological methods*. New York: Oxford University Press.

Kleinbaum, D. G., Kupper L. L., and Morgenstern, H. 1982. *Epidemiological Research: Principles and Quantitative Methods*. New York: Van Nostrand.

Krantz, S. E., & Moos, R. H. 1988. Risk factors at intake predict nonremission among depressed patients. *Journal of Consulting and Clinical Psychology*, 56, 863–869.

Lilienfeld, A. M., & Lilienfeld, D. E. 1980. *Foundations of Epidemiology*. New York: Oxford University Press.

Maisto, S. A., & Connors, G. J. 1988 Assessment of treatment outcome. In Donovan, D. M., & Marlatt, G. A. *Assessment of Addictive Behaviors*, 421–453, New York: Guilford Press.

Marlatt, G. A. 1988. Matching clients to treatment: Treatment models and stages of change. In Donovan, D. M. & Marlatt, G. A. (eds.) *Assessment of Addictive Behaviors*. New York: Guilford Press.

Marlatt, G. A., & Gordon, J. R. (eds.) 1985. *Relapse prevention: Maintenance strategies in the treatment of addictive behaviors*. New York: Guilford Press.

Miettinen, O. S. 1985. *Theoretical epidemiology: Principles of occurrence research in medicine*. New York: Wiley & Sons.

Paykel, E. S. 1978. Contribution of life events to causation of psychiatric illness. *Psychological Medicine*, 8, 245–253.

Robins, L. N. 1978. Psychiatric epidemiology, *Archives of General Psychiatry*. 35, 697–702.

Rothman, K. J. 1986. *Modern Epidemiology*. Boston: Little, Brown, & Co.

Sadoun, R. 1987. Place and role of the clinical psychiatrist in epidemiological research. In Cooper, B. *The epidemiology of psychiatric disorders*, 227–233, Baltimore: Johns Hopkins University Press.

Sainsbury, P., & Kreitman, N. 1975. *Methods of psychiatric research: An introduction for clinical psychiatrists*. Second Edition, London: Oxford University Press.

Shaffer, H. J. 1986. Conceptual crises and the addictions: A philosophy of science perspective. *Journal of Substance Abuse Treatment*, 3, 285–296.

Shaffer, H., & Gambino, B. 1979. Addiction paradigms II: Theory, research, and practice. *Journal of Psychadelic Drugs*, 11, 299–303.

———. 1984. Addiction paradigms III: From theory-research to practice and back. *Advances in Alcohol and Substance Abuse*, 3, 135–152.

Shaffer, H., & Neuhaus, C. 1985. Testing hypotheses: An approach for the assessment of addictive behaviors. In Milkman, H. & Shaffer H. (eds.) *The addictions: Multidisciplinary perspectives and treatments*. Lexington, Massachusetts, Lexington Books.

Shepherd, M. 1978. Epidemiology and clinical psychiatry. *British Journal of Psychiatry*, 133, 289–298.

Simpson, D. D. 1984. National treatment system evaluation based on the drug abuse reporting program (DARP) followup research. *Drug abuse treatment evaluation: strategies, progress, and prospects*, 29–41. Washington, D.C.: DHHS, GPO.

Taber, J. I. 1987. Compulsive gambling: An examination of relevant models. [Special Issue] *Journal of Gambling Behavior*, 3, 219–223.

Taber, J. I., McCormick, R. A., & Ramirez, L. F. 1987 The prevalence and impact of major life stressors among pathological gamblers. *The International Journal of the Addictions*, 22, 71–79.

Tims, F. M., & Ludford, J. P. 1984. *Drug abuse treatment evaluation: Strategies, progress, and prospects*. Washington, D.C.: DHHS, U.S. GPO.

Weissman M., & Klerman, G. 1978. Epidemiology of mental disorders: Emerging trends in the United States. *Archives of General Psychiatry*, 35, 705–712.

16
Treatment for Compulsive Gambling: Where Are We Now?

Blase Gambino, Ph.D.
Thomas Cummings

I t is considered somewhat of an axiom that self-examination is a valuable process. It is in this spirit that we present this self-evaluation of the formal treatment of compulsive gambling by those who direct the programs. The information contained in this report was obtained from a national survey of directors of existing programs engaged in the treatment of compulsive gambling. This type of assessment is valuable in several respects. First, given the limited number of formal programs currently in existence, the sample may be considered highly representative of the present state of the field. Second, the information is relevant to the future development of the field. Third, the report serves to describe a number of relationships that reflect the structural and dynamic aspects of past and present efforts to treat the compulsive gambler. Fourth, the report provides a comparison that highlights some of the differences between extant gambling treatment programs. Finally, we present some recommendations on the establishment of appropriate evaluation methodology.

Method

A survey document was developed for use by the Massachusetts Council on Compulsive Gambling by Jacqueline S. Vilmas of the University of

Thanks are extended to Howard Shaffer and Sharon Stein for their helpful input and comments on earlier drafts of this chapter.

Preparation of this chapter was supported, in part, by a contract (#2322905893) from the Massachusetts Department of Public Health.

Requests for reprints should be sent to Thomas Cummings, executive director, Massachusetts Council on Compulsive Gambling, 190 High Street, Boston, Mass. 02110.

Massachusetts at Boston. The survey instrument was mailed to the twenty-two programs in operation at the time of the survey. The list was prepared by the council. Of these, fifteen programs (68 percent) returned completed questionnaires. A sixteenth was completed by a private practitioner who sees compulsive/pathological gamblers on a regular basis.

All analyses were conducted using the Statistical Package for the Social Sciences (SPSS). The cluster analysis reported in figure 16–1 employed the method of average linkage between groups with cosine of vectors of variables as the measure. The cosine measures similarity of patterns.

Results and Discussion

The respondents are clinicians active in the treatment of compulsive gambling. The primary disciplinary training of the respondents was as follows: psychologist (six), social worker (five), psychiatrist (two), counselor (two), and other (one). Our report will begin with a look at a program-by-program breakdown of services offered and type of clinical population treated. This analysis is presented in table 16–1.

Individual Programs and Services Offered

For convenience, we order the programs in terms of whether they offer hospital-based rehabilitation. The first eight programs (A–H) provide such inpatient services. Of these, the first five (A–E) are VA medical centers. The last program (P) is the private practitioner who has been included for comparative reasons. It may be seen in the upper part of table 16–1 that there are only four current programs devoted solely to the treatment of the compulsive gambler. The remaining programs treat additional clinical populations. These include psychiatric (two), alcohol (three), and drug abuse (seven) in various combinations with the treatment of compulsive gambling.

It is also shown in table 16–1 that six programs offer some form of detoxification process, and all programs treat patients on an outpatient basis. This is a significant finding because it suggests that patients can expect treatment to extend beyond the hospital setting and into the community. Unfortunately, we did not ask whether hospital-based programs selected patients on an either/or basis—that is, do some programs screen patients to determine outpatient versus inpatient status while others maintain a single track? This is important because it may reflect a basic distinction in treatment philosophy. Early programs used an inpatient format. In part, however, this was a function of the historical medical context of the hospital setting in which treatment for pathological gambling was introduced.

If we exclude the private practitioner (P), we find that, of the remaining fifteen programs, thirteen (87 percent) conduct assessment and referral, nine (60 percent) carry out prevention activities, and twelve (80 percent) present education and training programs. It is also of interest to note that only two programs offer day-care services for children, and these are both hospital-based. This lack of day-care services, while not unique to the treatment of compulsive gambling, should not be ignored. If we are to make headway in our efforts to attract female compulsive gamblers into treatment, as well as provide assistance to the spouse of the married (Thoms & Franklin, this volume), such services should become more

Table 16–1
Services Offered by Individual Program

Services	Hospital Rehabilitation A B C D E F G H								Other Programs I J K L M N O P								Total
Treatment Populations:																	
Compulsive Gambling (CG)	N	N	N	N	N	Y	N	N	N	Y	Y	N	N	Y	N	N	4
CG & Psychiat. Dis. (P)	N	N	N	N	N	N	N	N	Y	N	N	N	N	N	Y	N	2
CG-P & Alchol. Abuse (A)	N	Y	N	N	N	N	N	N	N	N	N	Y	N	N	N	Y	3
CG-A & Drug Abuse (D)	Y	N	Y	N	N	N	N	N	N	N	N	N	Y	N	N	N	3
CG-P-A-D	N	N	N	Y	Y	N	Y	Y	N	N	N	N	N	N	N	N	4
Twenty-four-Hour Services:																	
Hospital Rehabilitation	Y	Y	Y	Y	Y	Y	Y	Y	N	N	N	N	N	N	N	N	8
Medical Detox	N	N	N	N	Y	N	Y	Y	N	N	N	N	N	N	N	N	3
Non-medical Detox	Y	N	N	Y	Y	N	Y	N	N	N	N	N	Y	N	N	N	5
Other 24-hour services	Y	N	N	N	Y	N	N	N	N	Y	N	N	Y	N	N	Y	5
Less Than Twenty-four-Hour Services:																	
Daycare	N	N	N	Y	Y	N	N	N	N	N	N	N	N	N	N	N	2
Outpatient	Y	Y	Y	Y	Y	Y	Y	Y	Y	Y	Y	Y	Y	Y	Y	Y	16
Assessment & Referral	Y	Y	Y	Y	Y	Y	Y	Y	Y	Y	N	Y	N	Y	Y	N	13
Prevention	N	Y	N	Y	Y	Y	Y	N	Y	Y	N	Y	N	Y	N	N	9
Education & Training	Y	Y	Y	Y	Y	Y	Y	Y	Y	Y	N	Y	N	Y	N	N	12
Other	Y	N	N	N	N	N	N	N	N	N	N	Y	N	N	N	N	2
Total:	7	5	4	7	9	5	7	5	4	5	1	5	2	4	2	1	

readily available. While many female gamblers are single, many have children who require care (Lesieur, this volume). There is also the need to care for children in those cases where spouse involvement is essential.

Structural and Dynamic Characteristics

Tables 16–2a, 16–2b, and 16–2c present a description of hospital versus outpatient-only programs in terms of a number of structural attributes. Since hospital programs for compulsive gamblers are partly the result of historical factors, such as the extension of the treatment of alcoholic veterans to veterans with gambling problems, we also provide a breakdown according to whether the programs also treat drug abusers (drugs included), or whether they also treat both drug and alcohol abuse (mixed). We arbitrarily selected staff size and treatment experience as the major structural defining characteristics.

If we look first at the last three columns in table 16–2a, we find there has been a major shift from hospital-based to outpatient programs. Only one of the six programs established in the last five years offers hospital rehabilitation. Further examination shows that program to be involved in the treatment of drug abuse. Table 16–2b shows that the modal number of patients treated is between fifty and 250. Five of these programs are inpatient. All treat drug-abusing clients as well as the compulsive gambler. Table 16–2c reveals the current advantage that outpatient programs hold in terms of numbers treated. Five of the seven programs that treated fifty or more patients in 1987 provided outpatient treatment only. We would add that our use of the term advantage does not refer to the quality of treatment. Closer examination indicates that of the two inpatient programs, one treated alcohol-dependent patients, and the second included drug abuse as well.

Table 16–2a
Treatment Experience: Years of Operation

	Drugs Excluded v. Drugs Included		Single v. Mixed Populations		Hospital v. Outpatient		Total
	no drugs	drugs	single	mixed	yes	no	
Years Treating							
LT 2 years		1		1		1	1
2–5 years	4	1	4	1	1	4	5
5–10 years	4	5	2	7	6	3	9
GT 10 years	1			1	1		1
Total	9	7	6	10	8	8	16
%total	56.3%	43.8%	37.5%	62.5%	50.0%	50.0%	100.0%

Table 16–2b
Treatment Experience: Total Number of Patients Treated

	Drugs Excluded v. Drugs Included		Single v. Mixed Populations		Hospital v. Outpatient		Total
	no drugs	drugs	single	mixed	yes	no	
Total Treated							
LT 50	2	1	1	2	1	2	3
50–250	2	6	2	6	5	3	8
250–500	4		3	1	1	3	4
GT 1000	1			1	1		1
Total	9	7	6	10	8	8	16
%total	56.3%	43.8%	37.5%	62.5%	50.0%	50.0%	100.0%

Forecast for the '90s? If we use the midpoint of each range as an estimate, it would appear that these sixteen programs have treated approximately 3,775 patients in more than ten years of service. This averages out to about 235 per program. If we eliminate the oldest program, the total is 2,775 patients within the last ten years; an average of 185. By comparison, on the basis of the numbers reported treated last year, we get estimates of 770 or ninety-six patients per program. Extrapolating ten years, we find an expected total of 7,700, or an expected increase of about 177 percent, over the last decade. For those who find this rough estimate discouraging, it should be kept in mind that it does not reflect the actual growth rate for the treatment of compulsive gambling. That requires figures not requested in this survey. For example, if we use the lower bounds of each interval rather than the midpoint, the estimated

Table 16–2c
Treatment Experience: Number of Patients Treated Last Year

	Drugs Excluded v. Drugs Included		Single v. Mixed Populations		Hospital v. Outpatient		Total
	no drugs	drugs	single	mixed	yes	no	
Treated 1987							
LT 10	2	1	1	2	1	2	3
10–50	1	5	1	5	5	1	6
50–100	4	1	3	2	2	3	5
GT 100	2		1	1		2	2
Total	9	7	6	10	8	8	16
%total	56%	44%	38%	63%	50%	50%	100%

change would be 538 percent, whereas use of the upper bound provides an estimate of only an 85 percent increase.

Staffing patterns (table 16–3) do not appear to discriminate between the hospital and non-hospital–based rehabilitation programs. The programs are divided equally in terms of having fewer than or more than twenty-five counselors on staff (75 percent have fewer than twenty-five). A similar situation holds for the total number of compulsive gambling counselors. We find from table 16–3 that 56 percent of the programs have fewer than ten compulsive gambling counselors on staff. Since this survey did not ask programs to indicate whether counselors were *only* assigned to compulsive gambling, we cannot relate size of staff to numbers treated. When we consider the staffing size as a function of whether chemically dependent patients were also treated by the program, the results indicate that such programs tend to have greater numbers of staff counselors.

Dynamic Attributes

Eleven (73 percent) of the programs shown in table 16–4 indicated that they have separate programs for compulsive gambling and substance abuse populations. In part, this reflects recent trends toward outpatient programs devoted solely to compulsive gambling. As we will see, however, the data suggest it also may be because of staff perceptions of the compar-

Table 16–3
Total Number of Staff and Compulsive Gambling Counselors

	Drugs Excluded v. Drugs Included		Single v. Mixed Populations		Hospital v. Outpatient		Total
	no drugs	drugs	single	mixed	yes	no	
Total Counselors							
LT 25	7	5	5	7	6	6	12
25–50	1	2		3	2	1	3
50–100	1		1			1	1
Total	9	7	6	10	8	8	16
%total	56.3%	43.8%	37.5%	62.5%	50.0%	50.0%	100.0%
Gambling Therapists							
LT 10	5	4	4	5	5	4	9
10–25	3	3	1	5	3	3	6
25–50	1		1			1	1
Total	9	7	6	10	8	8	16
%total	56.3%	43.8%	37.5%	62.5%	50.0%	50.0%	100.0%

Table 16–4
Separate Programs for Gamblers and Chemically Dependent

	Drugs Excluded v. Drugs Included		Single v. Mixed Populations		Hospital v. Outpatient		Total
	no drugs	*drugs*	*single*	*mixed*	*yes*	*no*	
Separate Program							
yes	9	2	6	5	4	7	11
no		4		4	4	0	4
Total	9	6	6	9	8	7	15
%total	56%	44%	38%	63%	50%	50%	100%

ability of substance-abusing and compulsive-gambling populations. We turn next to a consideration of these attributions as shown in table 16–5.

Respondents were asked to rate the similarity of chemically dependent and compulsive-gambling population; the actual question read: In comparison with treatment for chemical dependency, the treatment of compulsive gambling is in your opinion: Identical. 80 percent to 90 percent the same. And so on. The results are presented in table 16–5. While none of the respondents perceives these populations as identical, six (38 percent) view them as 80 to 90 percent similar, and five (31.3 percent) as 50 to 80 percent alike. To see how this relates to the existence of separate programs, we combined the identical and 80-90 percent ratings (similar) and the 50-80 percent and 20-50 percent (different) to get the results shown in table 16–6 (these data exclude the private practitioner). From this perspective, it appears that if the program views these populations as differ-

Table 16–5
Perception of Similarity between Addictive Populations

	Drugs Excluded v. Drugs Included		Single v. Mixed Populations		Hospital v. Outpatient		Total
	no drugs	*drugs*	*single*	*mixed*	*yes*	*no*	
Population Similarity							
80%–90%	1	5	1	5	4	2	6
50%–80%	3	2	2	3	4	1	5
20%–50%	5		3	2		5	5
Total	9	7	6	10	8	8	16
%total	56.3%	43.8%	37.5%	62.5%	50.0%	50.0%	100.0%

Table 16–6
Separate Programs and Perceptions
of Similarity

| | Similarity of Populations | | |
Separate	Similar	Different	Total
Yes	3	8	11
No	3	1	4
Total	6	9	15

ent, the odds are about eight to one that it will have a separate program rather than treat compulsive gamblers with those who are chemically dependent.

A closer examination of table 16–5 indicates that the existence of a separate program for the treatment of the compulsive gambler is actually a function of whether a drug abuse population is treated by the program. All the programs that treat gamblers alongside chemically dependent clients are those involved in the treatment of drug abuse. Each program in which alcohol is the drug of abuse treats the compulsive gambler in a separate program. This may be a significant finding. Our outreach efforts to educate programs that treat the drug abuser and/or the alcoholic, may have to take into account the likelihood of a philosophy that fails to discriminate between addictions. As Shaffer & Gambino (in press) have noted, drug treatment programs typically provide uniform treatment regimens, rather than tailor plans to the individual. This approach is in keeping with the "one true light" assumption held by many, if not most, treatment providers, that all clients will respond to the same style of treatment (Shaffer & Gambino 1984).

Treatment Success and Followup Measures

Treatment Success. Table 16–7 reveals that of those who responded to the question, "What percent of patients successfully complete treatment?" five of the programs report that more than 75 percent successfully complete treatment. An additional seven programs claim a success rate between 50 and 75 percent. The remaining programs reported in at 30 to 50 percent. It is difficult to judge these success rates given the recentness of the treatment of compulsive gambling, and the small number of programs. On the whole, the ranges reported are comparable, if not better, than those reported for substance abuse treatment. If we accept these numbers at face value, it is clear there is much room for improvement. We make the obvious caveat that an accurate assessment of performance requires a

Table 16–7
Reported Rates for Successful Completion of Treatment

	Drugs Excluded v. Drugs Included		Single v. Mixed Populations		Hospital v. Outpatient		Total
	no drugs	drugs	single	mixed	yes	no	
Success Rates							
30%–50%	2	2	1	3	2	2	4
50%–75%	5	2	4	3	2	5	7
Over 75%	2	3	1	4	4	1	5
Total	9	7	6	10	8	8	16
%total	56.3%	43.8%	37.5%	62.5%	50.0%	50.0%	100.0%

more precise definition of success than the question employed in this survey. All the respondents stated that success was defined in terms of abstinence and "improved life functioning." In future surveys, it will be important to learn more precisely how each program defines life functioning; for example, the use of the Addiction Severity Index (McLellan, Luborsky, Woody & O'Brien 1980) as modified by some programs for discharge evaluation in compulsive gambling (Franklin & Richardson 1988).

However life functioning is defined, it is clear from the survey that abstinence is a primary and perhaps predominant outcome measure in all programs. This view is a direct outgrowth of the disease model perspective (Blume 1987), which has guided the evaluation of the treatment of alcoholism and more recently, drug abuse (cf, Shaffer 1985). Reliance on abstinence as the sole outcome measure hindered our efforts in the evaluation of treatment alternatives and programs in substance abuse (Lewis, Dana & Blevin 1988). A major problem in the choice of abstinence is the failure to distinguish between abstinence as outcome and abstinence as treatment. Since this is typically confounded, to rely solely on abstinence as the major defining criteria is misleading and methodologically faulty.

Followup. Although much recommended in theory (Lewis, et al. 1988), programs in the addictions have been slow to adopt followup protocols in practice (Caddy 1980). The need for followup is particularly vital if we are to document our failures as well as our successes. While it may not be self-evident, it should be understood that each success only reinforces what we know. Each failure thus provides substantially more information (this is the essential logic that underlies theory testing and the use of statistical null hypothesis tests). With this in mind, we note from Table 16–8a that four (27 percent) programs do not conduct followup activities.

Table 16–8a
Programs Conducting Followup Activities

	Drugs Excluded v. Drugs Included		Single v. Mixed Populations		Hospital v. Outpatient		Total
	no drugs	drugs	single	mixed	yes	no	
Conduct Followup?							
yes	6	5	4	7	7	4	11
no	2	2	1	3	0	4	4
Total	8	7	5	10	7	8	15

The programs that treat the chemically dependent are about half as likely to followup patients as those who treat only the compulsive gambler. Of those who do, a slight majority (60 percent) followup patients after a one-year interval. Of these, three also conduct assessments at three- and six-month intervals. Three of the other programs begin followup after six months and then again at one year. The remaining three programs con-

Table 16–8b
Reported Rates of Success at Followup

	Drugs Excluded v. Drugs Included		Single v. Mixed Populations		Hospital v. Outpatient		Total
	no drugs	drugs	single	mixed	yes	no	
3 Mo. Success (%)							
N/A	7	5	4	8	5	7	12
20%–50%		1		1	1		1
50%–75%		1		1	1		1
Over 75%	1		1			1	1
6 Mo. Success (%)							
N/A	3	5	3	5	5	3	8
20%–50%	1	2		3	2	1	3
50%–75%	3		1	2	1	2	3
Over 75%	1		1			1	1
12 Mo. Success (%)							
N/A	3	3	3	3	2	4	6
20%–50%	2	2		4	2	2	4
50%–75%	2	1	1	2	3		3
Over 75%	1	1	1	1	1	1	2
Total	8	7	5	10	8	7	15

Table 16–9
Programs Which Conduct Prevention Activities

	Drugs Excluded v. Drugs Included		Single v. Mixed Populations		Hospital v. Outpatient		Total
	no drugs	drugs	single	mixed	yes	no	
Conduct Prevention							
yes	6	3	4	5	5	4	9
no	3	4	2	5	3	4	7
Total	9	7	6	10	8	8	16
%total	56%	44%	38%	63%	50%	50%	100%

duct a single assessment at the end of one year following completion of treatment.

The programs that conducted followup assessment were asked to measure their rate of success as revealed through these studies. The results are reported in table 16–8b. The table reveals the expected pattern that with time more patients will be classified as failures. The modal success rate is 20 to 50 percent as compared with 50 to 75 percent reported for treatment completion.

We close this section by noting briefly the results on prevention activities reported in table 16–9. Prevention refers to activities that reduce or stabilize the incidence (occurrence of new cases) of compulsive gambling, thus reducing or stabilizing its prevalence (the total number of cases). Nine programs report they engage in activities related to prevention. These programs are almost evenly divided between hospital and outpatient-only programs. On further examination, we find that the majority are programs that either treat only compulsive gamblers or also treat the alcohol-dependent patient.

Followup and Prevention

The importance of followup and prevention is much discussed in the literature of all the helping professions. The former is critical in obtaining valuable information about long-term effects of treatment and environmental/community variables that mitigate relapse or support gains acquired by treatment. Prevention is much talked about in the literature on health promotion and disease prevention. It is particularly important for chronic diseases (Mason, Koplan & Layde 1987) and for such chronic disorders as mental illness and the addictive disorders.

Because of the central importance of these two activities, we decided to take a closer look at their relationship to some of the study variables. Table 16–10 summarizes this information; for convenience of presentation we have collapsed the categorical information to create a series of 2 × 2 tables.

While overall experience, as indicated by years and total treated, are favorable toward the likelihood of conducting followup studies, the numbers treated last year indicate that all programs are almost equally likely to conduct followup of discharged patients. Alternatively, while a larger number of staff counselors favors a followup procedure by three to one, this relationship is reversed when we consider the number of compulsive gambling counselors. The odds jump to about eleven to one in favor of followup for programs with fewer than ten counselors as opposed to having more than ten compulsive gambling counselors. This may very well be caused by counselors in the larger programs splitting their time between compulsive gambling and substance abuse.

In like fashion, experience is related to whether a program will engage in prevention activities. The greater the years of treatment, total number treated, and total treated last year, the more likely the program is involved with prevention. On the other hand, the total number of staff counselors only slightly favors prevention. Again, we find that programs with fewer than ten compulsive gambling counselors are more likely to engage in

Table 16–10
Follow-up and Prevention Activities

	Follow-up		Prevention	
	Yes	No	Yes	No
Years in Treatment				
5 or more	8	1	6	3
less than 5	3	3	3	3
Total Treated				
Over 250	5	0	4	1
Under 250	6	5	5	6
Treated Last Year				
50 or more	5	2	5	2
Less than 50	6	3	4	5
Number of Staff Counselors				
More than 25	9	3	7	5
Less than 25	2	2	2	2
Compulsive Gambling Counselors				
10 or more	3	4	3	4
less than 10	8	1	6	3
Separate Programs				
Yes	8	3	8	3
No	3	2	1	4

prevention than those with more than ten; the difference is not nearly as great, however, as it was with the likelihood of followup studies.

Similarity of Treatment Programs

It is reasonable to ask whether programs that treat the compulsive gambler are very similar or very diverse. We have noted there are three basic types of programs that can be distinguished depending on whether they treat alcohol and/or drug abuse in addition to the compulsive gambler. Several techniques may be used to answer this question. For a number of reasons related to the data and the number of cases, we chose to employ a technique known as cluster analysis. Cluster analysis is similar to factor analysis in that it reduces a large number of dimensions to a smaller set. The result of this analysis is to determine a measure of similarity (or dissimilarity) by which cases can be grouped into like (or unlike) clusters. The results are shown in figure 16–1. The programs are labeled as OP, outpatient, IP, inpatient, and inpatient VA. Some clarification of figure 16–1 is in order, especially for those unfamilar with cluster analysis. The analysis begins by considering each program as a separate cluster. At the outset of analysis, therefore, there are fourteen separate clusters. The program computes a measure of similarity for each program and then matches the two programs with the closest values. The process continues at each stage of analysis by comparing the value of any clusters formed with the values of all remaining programs and clusters until one complete cluster has been formed. For example, the top half of Figure 16–1 indicates that in the first stage programs 9 (IP2) and 12 (VA5) were judged most similar and should form the first cluster. In stage 2, programs 5 (VA2) and 8 (IP1) are clustered together. At this stage of the analysis there are eleven clusters. Nine of these represent single programs, and two represent the formation of single clusters made from the combination of matched pairs of programs: One cluster formed by programs 9 and 12 and the second from programs 5 and 8. The upper half of figure 16–1 indicates the stages at which each cluster is formed. Thus at stage 4 ten clusters have been formed. Seven individual programs and three clusters formed by the union of 9 and 12 (stage 1), 5 and 8 (stage 2), and 1, 2, and 7 (stages 3 and 4). These formations are shown pictorially in the bottom half of figure 16–1 in a dendogram.

The cluster analysis suggests that programs are not very similar with the exception of IP2 and VA5 and between VA2 and IP1. These programs are all hospital-based and all engage in followup and prevention activities. They differ primarily in that the former two provide detoxification, view the treatment of the two populations as more similar, and treat fewer numbers of patients than the latter. Examination of the number of clusters that appear between the values of fifteen and twenty in the dendogram of revealed essentially two separate clusters. These programs are distinguishable on the basis of treating the chemically dependent (upper half) or not (lower half). Those clusters formed during the middle stages of the analytic process reflect differences in treatment experience and perceptions of the similarities between the compulsive gambler and the chemically dependent. The programs that make up the clusters in the upper half perceive

Agglomeration Schedule Using Average Linkage (between Groups)

Stage	Clusters Cluster 1	Combined Cluster 2	Coefficient	Stage Cluster Cluster 1	1st Appears Cluster 2	Next Stage
1	9	12	1.000000	0	0	6
2	5	8	.985666	0	0	5
3	2	7	.971797	0	0	4
4	1	2	.968316	0	3	5
5	1	5	.963540	4	2	8
6	6	9	.957024	0	1	7
7	6	11	.939149	6	0	11
8	1	14	.938440	5	0	12
9	4	13	.938343	0	0	11
10	3	10	.929320	0	0	12
11	4	6	.928667	9	7	13
12	1	3	.902803	8	10	13
13	1	4	.900580	12	11	0

Dendrogram Using Average Linkage (between Groups)

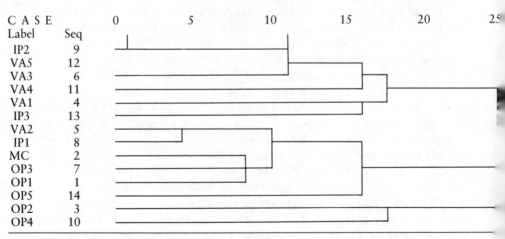

Figure 16–1 Cluster Stage Formation and Dendrogram Using Rescaled Distance

the compulsive gambler as more similar to the chemically dependent than do those in the clusters in the bottom half. They also have been in operation for longer periods of time. There is thus a wide diversity among treatment programs, although this is less so for the inpatient programs. Such diversity is probably developmentally healthy at this stage of the expansion of treatment for the compulsive gambler.

Treatment Strategies

In this final section, we examine the types of treatment interventions favored by our respondents. Each program was asked to indicate for the treatment techniques listed in the first column of table 16–11 whether the staff of his or her program felt intervention to be of no use, little use, moderate use, very useful, or critically useful. We decided the most valuable approach to analyzing these results was to compare the likelihood that a program that treated drug abusers as well as the compulsive gambler would find a particular intervention to be critically useful. This was

Table 16–11
Program Perception of Critical Strategies

Treatment Technique	No Drugs	Drugs
Information on compulsive gambling	14.8*	
Individual psychotherapy	6.0	
Family involvement	4.4	
Use recovered gamblers	3.5	
Couples therapy	3.2	
Insight-oriented therapy	2.6	
Assertiveness training	1.5	
Environmental reconstruction	1.5	
Cognitive restructuring	1.4	
Anxiety reduction methods	1.4	
Gestalt techniques	1.3	
Supportive counseling	1.3	
Group psychotherapy		5.0**
Directive counseling		4.8
Legal advocacy		4.7
Paradoxical intention		4.6
Vocational rehabilitation		3.1
Behavioral techniques		3.1
Team counseling		3.1
Restitution planning		2.0
Values clarification		1.7
Financial counseling		1.7
Information on dual addictions		1.3

*Each value gives the odds that a program that does not treat drug abuse client will perceive the listed technique as a critical treatment strategy.

**Same as above but applies to perceptions of programs that also treat drug abuse clients.

contrasted with those programs that treat only the compulsive gambler or that also treat alcohol abusers. Each comparison represents the odds that those programs defined by the column head (No Drugs, Drugs) are likely to view a treatment procedure as critical. For example, the odds ratio of 1.3 for supportive counseling in the column headed No Drugs is interpreted as reflecting the odds that a program that treats the compulsive gambler but not drug abusers will view this technique as critical relative to a program that treats the drug abuser in addition to the compulsive gambler.

With only sixteen respondents, we did not compute any significance levels for the odds ratios we report. We thus consider only those interventions for which the odds are at least two to one as clinically meaningful for distinguishing a programs treatment emphasis. The greatest separation occurs with perception of the need to provide information on compulsive gambling. Programs that do not treat drug abusers along with compulsive gamlers are almost fifteen times more likely to view this as a critical element of treatment. This may well reflect the lack of emphasis by the drug abuse programs on compulsive gambling as a priority addiction. It may be seen that information on dual addictions is favored only slightly more by drug abuse programs. In other words, compulsive gambling is one more addiction rather than a separate informational entity.

The most striking difference to be found in table 16–11 is the distinction between which type of program emphasizes individual or group psychotherapy. Programs that do not treat the drug-abusing individual are six times more likely than those that do to view individual as critical. Conversely, the latter programs are five times more likely than the former to perceive group psychotherapy as critical. Another important distinction is the relative emphasis on insight versus behavioral therapies. The behavioral approach is three times more likely to be viewed by drug abuse programs to be critical, while insight therapy is favored by those programs that do not treat the drug abuse client. Additional distinctions are found between the perception of criticalness by drug abuse programs for directive counseling, legal advocacy, paradoxical intention, vocational rehabilitation, and team counseling. These all tend to reflect a behavioral orientation. The programs that do not include the drug abuser among their clients tend to favor family involvement, the use of recovered gamblers as counselors, and couples therapy as critical elements compared to programs that do treat the drug abuser. These are essentially oriented to a verbal therapy perspective.

Perhaps more important for our purposes than distinctions are the similarities between these types of programs. These would appear to be considered equally important to the treatment of the compulsive gambler by both types of programs. These include values clarification, financial counseling, information on dual addictions, cognitive restructuring, environmental reconstruction, and supportive counseling. Restitution planning, considered by many as essential to the treatment of the compulsive gambler, is found to be favored by the drug abuse programs on a 2:1 basis. Perhaps more significantly, only six of the sixteen respondents (38 percent) view restitution as critical to treatment. Four of these treat the drug abuser as well as the compulsive gambler.

Average Actual and Expected Length of Treatment

Finally, we asked respondents to indicate the length of treatment as designed by the program and to compare this with the estimated actual length of treatment in practice. Because of the difficulty in coding these responses, we have chosen to reproduce them for the reader. These are presented in table 16–12 without comment.

Closing Comments

We noted the trend toward establishing outpatient treatment for compulsive gambling. While the question has been debated, and in some minds

Table 16–12
Reported Designed and Actual Treatment Length

Designed Length:	Actual Estimated Length:
Varies with individual	14 daily intensive sessions 15 outpatient sessions
18 months	12 months
7–35 days inpatient 6 months optional followup	21 days inpatient
21 days inpatient	21 days inpatient
30 days inpatient	30 days inpatient
1–2 years	18 months average
6 months	unknown
21 days inpatient 1–4 years outpatient	21 days inpatient 1–4 years outpatient
30 days inpatient 14 days intensive outpatient 1–2 years outpatient	not reported
21 days inpatient	29 days
? weeks inpatient	4 weeks
21 days inpatient	21 days
21 days inpatient	21 days
varies	4–6 weeks inpatient 6 months outpatient
not designed	10 months outpatient

resolved in favor of an outpatient philosophy, the decision has not been based on hard evidence obtained from methodologically sound program evaluation studies (cf, Franklin & Richardson 1988). The current trend of newer programs appears to be away from inpatient to a focus on outpatient-only treatment. The reasons for this, however, appear to be associated with cost considerations and patient numbers rather than the efficacy of the treatment models engendered by these settings. It is also in keeping with current concepts of treatment in the least restrictive environment.

The lack of followup at early and regular intervals for up to two to five years, or longer, is unfortunate. We are only now learning much from studies in alcohol and drug abuse about the value of long-term followup studies, especially as these relate to effective outcome evaluation (Marlatt 1988). These studies have much to reveal about the variables associated with the potency of treatment, as well as helping to identify important risk factors associated with relapse (Marlatt & Gordon 1985). While it is true that the treatment of compulsive gambling is in its relative infancy compared to the substance abuse addictions, the focus on the first year provides a narrow view that limits our ability to understand treatment failure and relapse, and to develop evidence on prognostic indicators of success.

For example, while many individuals treated for substance abuse may relapse during the first year (estimated as high as 90 percent, [Polich, Armor & Braiker 1981]), a significant number of these will recover on their own without additional formal treatment (Shaffer & Jones 1989). Correct classification of these cases requires two things: extended and frequent followup and a criterion measure of success that avoids the inherent weaknesses associated with the more common dichotomous view of outcome—abstinent or relapsed. Such a dichotomy precludes consideration of changes over time and the direction of change, such as whether gambling is increasing, decreasing, or stable. It also prevents a definition of gambling (or drinking or drug-taking) as a continuous variable and thus mitigates against the concept of controlled gambling (Dickerson 1987), a treatment strategy whose time many believe has come (Rosecrance, this volume). Furthermore, if the induction period (Rothman 1986) for relapse after treatment is longer than one year, and is preceded by one or more lapses, then this important aspect of the process will be missed. The failure to correctly classify lapse and relapse through continued long-term followup is a significant omission. We would add that it also contributes to a reduction in success rates since we may incorrectly classify lapse as relapse (Marlatt & Gordon 1985). It also ignores the finding that many individuals spontaneously recover (Shaffer & Jones 1989), and precludes our determining whether the spontaneous rate is increased following treatment, an important consideration.

Any definition of treatment outcome must be multivariate in nature, as is the nature of the underlying causes (Shaffer 1986). This requires a reliance on followup data and multiple measures, rather than the use of a "dipstick" approach (Marlatt 1983 p. 1102) in which the client comes up dry (abstinent) or wet (gambling). It should measure changes across time that indicate how the patient adjusts to life events. At present, life events as psychosocial stressors is viewed by DSM-III-R (APA 1987) as possibly providing supplemental information to official diagnoses. It is suggested that such information may be useful for planning treatment and predicting outcome. The position adopted by APA is essentially an exploratory one that places such information in the category of important, but not essential, research. This reflects the fact that only recently has epidemiological evidence been obtained that documents the significant relationship between life events and physical and psychological disorders (cf, Cooper 1987). In the field of compulsive gambling, Taber (Taber, McCormick & Ramirez 1987) has provided the first evidence that life events may be critical to the development of compulsive gambling. Taber (unpublished manuscript) has now provided an explanatory theory based on his creative insight into this relationship gained from years of working with the compulsive gambler. We would recommend that such information be routinely collected at intake and during followup. In Massachusetts, the first compulsive gambling treatment center has opened at Mount Auburn Hospital in Cambridge. Such data have been incorporated into the intake system of the program and it is our expectation that these data will be revealing. Preliminary analyses have revealed a significant number of such events in the year before entry into treatment reported by almost all patients (see Gambino, this volume for a description of the positive effects of one such event). The role of such psychosocial stressors (positive as well as negative) must also be explored for effects associated with relapse.

We noted the lack of consistency in followup evaluation among the programs sampled. We would like to close by stressing the need for frequent and long-term followup assessment. Everyone is aware of the difficulty in evaluating treatment because such factors as subject selection and attrition typically operate to threaten the validity of our conclusions. We need to employ procedures that will minimize the loss of clients to followup and insure that comparable measurements are obtained before, during, and after treatment. This requires considerable attention to the concept of continuity of care. Evaluation must begin with the initial intake and patients need to be encouraged to participate. It must be made clear to patients that continuous evaluation and frequent followup is valuable and will help to enhance the likelihood of a long-term successful outcome. Frequent followup is particularly crucial if patients are highly mobile. It has an even more important function: "It offers an extremely low cost continuity of care after formal treatment has ended. Such care may influence the course of recidivism and/or help to consolidate the gains made during the course of treatment" (Caddy 1980, 161).

Evaluation of treatment outcome (and treatment process) requires that we be receptive to information that is not always positive with respect to our efforts. Our responsibility as providers of treatment is to optimize the quality of treatment. This requires a willingness to make changes in our procedures and revisions in our theories of clinical practice whenever the data indicate that improvement will follow such change. Theories of practice historically arise from practice and are then confirmed through research. Once confirmed, such theory returns to guide practice. Our clinical practice is always guided by theory, whether articulated or not (Gambino & Shaffer 1979). If practice is to lead to theory refinement, evaluation of treatment must occur on a continuing basis. Theory and practice can thus interact through the evaluation process. Once confirmed by research, improved theory betters practice and better practice leads to refinements for the next stage of theory development.

References

American Psychiatric Association (1987). *Diagnostic and Statistical Manual,* third edition, revised. Washington, D.C.: Author.

Blume, S. B. 1987. Compulsive gambling and the medical model. *Journal of Gambling Behavior, 3,* 237–247.

Caddy, G. R. 1980. A review of problems in conducting alcohol treatment outcome studies. In L. C. Sobell, M. B. Sobell, & E. Ward (eds.) *Evaluating alcohol and drug abuse treatment effectiveness: Recent advances.* 151–176. New York: Pergamon Press.

Cooper, B. (ed.). 1987. *The epidemiology of psychiatric disorders.* Baltimore: Johns Hopkins University Press.

Dickerson, M. 1987. The future of gambling research: Learning from the lessons of alcholism. *Journal of Gambling Behavior, 3,* 248–256.

Franklin, J., & Richardson, R. 1988. A treatment outcome study with pathological gamblers: Preliminary findings and strategies. In W.R. Eadington (ed.) *Proceedings of the Seventh International Conference on Gambling and Risk Taking, 5,* 392–407. Reno, Nevada: University of Nevada.

Gambino, B., & Shaffer, H. 1979. The concept of paradigm and the treatment of addiction. *Professional Psychology, 10,* 207–223.

Lewis, J. A., Dana, R. Q., & Blevins, G. A. 1988. *Substance abuse counseling: An individualized approach.* Pacific Grove, Calif: Brooks, Cole, Publishing.

Marlatt G. A. 1988. Matching clients to treatment: Treatment models and stages of change. In D. M. Gordon & G. A. Marlatt *Assessment of addictive behaviors* (474–484). New York: Guilford Press.

———. 1983. The controlled drinking controversy: A commentary. *American Psychologist, 38,* 1097–1109.

Marlatt, G. A., & Gordon, J. R. (eds.). 1985. *Relapse prevention: Maintenance strategies in the treatment of addictive behaviors.* New York: Guilford Press.

Mason, J. O., Koplan, J. P., & Laydee, P. M. 1987. The prevention and control of chronic diseases: Reducing unnecessary deaths and disability—a conference report. *Public Health Reports, 102,* 17–20.

McLellan, A. T., Luborsky, L., Woody, G. E., & O'Brien, C. P. 1980. An improved diagnostic instrument for substance abuse patients: The addiction severity index. *Journal of Nervous and Mental Disorders, 168,* 26–33.

Polich, J. M., Armor, D. J., & Braiker, H. B. 1981. *The course of alcoholism: Four years after treatment.* New York: Wiley.

Rothman, K. J. 1986. *Modern Epidemiology.* Boston: Little, Brown & Co.

Shaffer, H. J. 1986. Conceptual crises and the addictions: A philosophy of science perspective. *Journal of Substance Abuse Treatment, 3,* 285–296.

Shaffer, H., & Gambino, B. 1984. Addiction paradigms III: From theory-research to practice and back. *Advances in Alcohol Abuse and Substance Abuse, 3,* 135–152.

Shaffer, H. J., & Jones, S. B. 1989. *Quitting cocaine.* Lexington, Massachusetts: Lexington Books.

Shaffer, H. J. 1985 The disease controversy: Of metaphors, maps, and menus. *Journal of Psychoactive Drugs, 17,* 65–76.

Taber, J. I., McCormick, R. A., & Ramirez, L. F. (1987). The prevalence and impact of major life stressors among pathological gamblers. *International Journal of the Addictions, 22,* 71–79.

Index

About the Contributors

Milton Earl Burglass, M.D., M.P.H., M.Div., M.S., F.A.A.F.P., Faculty, Center for Addiction Studies at Harvard Medical School, Cambridge, Massachusetts.

William Eadington, Ph.D., is a professor of economics, University of Nevada, Reno, Nevada.

Joanna Franklin, M.S., C.A.C., is director of training, Gambling Treatment Program at Taylor Manor Hospital, Baltimore, Maryland.

Durand F. Jacobs, Ph.D., is chief of Psychology Service at Jerry L. Pettis Memorial Veterans Hospital, Loma Linda, California, and professor, Department of Psychiatry at Loma Linda University Medical School, Loma Linda, California.

H. Roy Kaplan, Ph.D., is Professor, Florida Institute of Technology School of Management, Melbourne, Florida.

Henry R. Lesieur, Ph.D., Department of Sociology and Anthropology at St. John's University, Jamaica, New York and editor, Journal of Gambling Behavior, National Council on Compulsive Gambling, New York, New York.

Rena Nora, M.D., is chief of psychiatry at Veterans Administration Medical Center, Lyons, New Jersey, and clinical professor of psychiatry at Robert Wood Johnson Medical School of the University of Medicine and Dentistry of New Jersey.

John Rosecrance, Ph.D., is associate professor, Criminal Justice Department, University of Nevada, Reno, Nevada.

Richard J. Rosenthal, M.D., is assistant clinical professor of psychiatry, University of California Los Angeles, and president of the California Council on Compulsive Gambling, Inc., Los Angeles, California.

Henry Steadman, Ph.D., is president of Policy Research Associates, Inc., Delmar, New York.

Donald Thoms, M.S., is director at St. Vincent's North Richmond Gamblers Treatment Center, New York City, New York.

Rachel Volberg, Ph.D., is a research associate at Policy Research Associates, Inc., Delmar, New York.

Norman E. Zinberg, M.D., is a clinical professor of psychiatry, Department of Psychiatry at Harvard Medical School and The Cambridge Hospital, Cambridge, Massachusetts.

About the Editors

Dr. Shaffer is an assistant professor of psychology in the department of psychiatry at Harvard Medical School. In addition, he is director of the Center for Addiction Studies at Harvard Medical School and the Department of Psychiatry at the Cambridge Hospital, as well as chief psychologist at the North Charles Institute for the Addictions.

Dr. Shaffer is a licensed clinical psychologist in Massachusetts and New Hampshire. He is a certified health care provider in psychology by the Council for the National Register of Health Care Providers in Psychology.

Currently, Dr. Shaffer serves as an associate editor of *The Psychology of Addictive Behaviors* and *The Journal of Substance Abuse Treatment*. He is also an editorial board member of the *Journal of Psychoactive Drugs* and *Advances in Alcohol and Substance Abuse*.

Dr. Shaffer contributes extensively to the professional literature. His research influences the way addictive behaviors are conceptualized, assessed, and treated. In addition to research, his interests include teaching, conducting psychotherapy, and consulting.

Dr. Shaffer's areas of special interest include consultation to organizations on mental health and human relations issues, substance use and abuse treatment and prevention, linking research and clinical practice, the addictive behaviors, and maintaining an active private practice.

Sharon A. Stein, Ed.M., M.A., is a lecturer on psychology in the Department of Psychiatry at the Cambridge Hospital and Harvard Medical School. In addition, she is projects coordinator and a faculty member of the Center for Addiction Studies, Harvard Medical School and the Department of Psychiatry, Cambridge Hospital.

Ms. Stein is studying in the Human Development and Psychology program at Harvard University Graduate School of Education. Ms. Stein's research concerns the relationship between human development and recovery from addictive behavior, as well as developing and testing methods for preventing addiction problems.

Blase Gambino, Ph.D., is director of the Compulsive Gambling Research and Education program at the Center for Addiction Studies, Harvard Medical School, Department of Psychiatry at the Cambridge Hospital. Dr. Gambino's current research interests are in the development of a clinical epidemiology of addictions. He is also involved in the development of an epidemiological data base, the function of which will be to provide the necessary knowledge and information required by treatment providers, researchers, and educators.

Thomas N. Cummings is executive director of the Massachusetts Council on Compulsive Gambling, Inc., and president of the National Foundation on Problem Gambling, Inc.

He is also treasurer and a member of the Board of Trustees of the American Academy of Health Care Providers in the Addictive Disorders.

Mr. Cummings is a former educator and lives in Braintree, Massachusetts, with his wife, Nancy. He is founder of the Massachusetts Council on Compulsive Gambling, Inc., and is primarily responsible for Massachusetts legislation authorizing a program for compulsive gambling.